COMPARATIVE GU[illegible] TO NUTRITIONAL SUPPLEMENTS

A Compendium of Products Available in the United States and Canada

by

Lyle MacWilliam, BSc, MSc, FP

3rd Edition

Copy Editing
Arlene MacWilliam

Research, Editing and Layout
Gregg Gies

Cover Design
Ian Black, MGDC

Comparative Guide to Nutritional Supplements

A Compendium of Products Available in the United States and Canada

Published by Northern Dimensions Publishing
a division of MacWilliam Communications Inc.
Vernon, British Columbia, CANADA

This comparative guide is produced for educational and comparative purposes only. No person should use the information herein for self-diagnosis, treatment or justification in accepting or declining any medical treatment for any health-related problems. Some medical therapies, including the use of medicines, may be affected by the use of certain nutritional supplements. Therefore, any individual with a specific health problem should seek advice by a qualified medical practitioner before starting a supplementation program. The decision whether to consume any nutritional supplement rests with the individual, in consultation with his or her medical advisor. Furthermore, nothing in this manual should be misinterpreted as medical advice.

This comparative guide is intended to assist in sorting through the maze of nutritional supplements available in the marketplace today. It is not a product endorsement and does not make any health claim, other than to document recent findings in the scientific literature. This comparative guide was not commissioned by any public sector or private sector interest, or by any company whose products may be represented in this document. The research, development and findings are the sole creative effort of MacWilliam Communications Inc.

Neither the publisher nor the author may be held responsible for the accuracy of information provided by or obtained from third parties, including but not limited to information gathered from nutritional supplement companies, medical and scientific journals, newspapers, magazines and/or Internet web sites.

National Library of Canada Cataloguing in Publication Data

MacWilliam, Lyle Dean
Comparative guide to nutritional supplements : a compendium of products available in the United States and Canada / by Lyle MacWilliam ; copy editing, Arlene MacWilliam ; research, editing and layout, Gregg Gies. -- 3rd ed.

Includes bibliographical references.
ISBN 0-9732538-0-0

1. Dietary supplements. I. MacWilliam, Arlene. II. Gies, Gregg.
III. Title.
RM258.5.M33 2003 613.2 C2003-910601-2

Dedication

In memory of my mother and father,
who taught me that the greatest legacy
one can leave is to have made
a difference in the lives of others

With Thanks

This book is the culmination of years of effort in developing the scientific rationale, and in refining and enhancing the analytical models used to conduct our comparative analysis. With each edition, we have built on our previous work, in order to provide consumers with a comprehensive, up-to-date and reliable source of information on the science of nutritional supplementation and the products available. To do so, we have, admittedly, stood on the shoulders of others; the insights, knowledge and guidance gleaned from the scientific authorities we have referenced in developing our analytical models have been invaluable resources.

I am deeply indebted to my wife, Arlene, who has patiently endured my emotional highs and lows, as I have struggled to pull together a seemingly endless volume of scientific and product research. Without her sharp editorial eye, her unwavering demand for balance and rigour, and her innate ability to bring me back to centre, the quality of this final work would have been severely compromised.

I am also indebted to my associate, Gregg Gies, a true Master in the science of Information Technology and a tireless researcher, whose ability to ferret out information knows no bounds. As the technical and creative director, Gregg's hand is written large throughout this publication.

To Ian Black of Ian Black Concepts, I owe a heartfelt "thank you." Ian's kind offer to provide his extensive talents in the cover design and the creative aspects of the publication has provided immeasurable value to the finished work.

I would also like to recognize a special individual whose mentorship, unbeknownst to him, has influenced me greatly. Dr. Denis Waitley has the precious gift of perspective and the ability to inspire those around him to "push the envelope" and reach beyond themselves. Like so many others whose lives he has touched, I have benefited greatly from his counsel.

Last, but certainly not least, my thanks to you, the purchaser of this guide, for your support. In particular, I am grateful to those of my readership who have provided feedback on previous editions of this guide; the encouragement, support and constructive criticism received from so many of you continue to inspire me, in what has truly become a labour of love. Thank you.

May health be your constant companion,

Lyle MacWilliam
April, 2003

Table of Contents

PREFACE

WHAT'S IN THIS GUIDE

Where Do I Find Information On...?

This guide seeks to educate consumers about the science and value of nutritional supplementation, and to provide them with a simple, reliable tool with which to compare nutritional products.

Section I: Aging, Oxidative Stress and Degenerative Disease

Section I of this guide discusses the theories of aging and the intricate links between aging, oxidative stress and degenerative disease. The remarkable protective powers of the endogenous and dietary antioxidants and their role in mitigating the aging process are examined. Five degenerative disease processes are highlighted, including recent scientific evidence supporting the use of nutritional supplementation as a preventive measure.

Section II: Criteria for Advanced Supplementation

Section II reviews the substantial scientific evidence employed in developing the fourteen analytical criteria imbedded in the product-rating methodology used in this comparative guide.

Creation of the *Final Product Score*, based on these fourteen criteria, has been an evolutionary process. With each edition of this comparative guide, we have built on previous research as newly published scientific findings have become available. The result has been the creation of a robust analytical model, based on the scientific literature and the independent recommendations of our seven cited authorities.

In each of the chapters of Section II, the reader is introduced to one of the fourteen criteria and the scientific evidence supporting its use. For those who find the reading a little technical, we refer you to the highlighted text. For those who wish to explore the science of advanced nutrition, we invite you to "dive in."

Section III: How the Comparisons were Made

Section III provides further explanation of the *Final Product Score* and introduces the *Blended Standard*, a nutritional benchmark we have created based on the independent recommendations of seven scientific authorities. A brief biographical background of each of the seven authorities and their specific recommendations for optimal daily nutritional intake is also provided.

The use of the *Blended Standard*, as a benchmark for optimal nutrition and the foundation for the *Final Product Score*, is featured. The *Final Product Score* is described in detail in Chapter 17. This fourteen-point score is the heart of our comparative analysis; it provides a rigorous quantitative evaluation and relative ranking of all products, based on the *Blended Standard* benchmark.

Section III also provides a summary of the 25 top-rated products, listed according to *Final Product Score*. From this list, the top six products are profiled. These are products of exceptional standing and merit your serious attention as a consumer. Included is a brief profile of each company, with contact information, company history and general information. Points of interest on product formulations, including a breakout of the individual product criteria ratings and information on manufacturing processes (if available), is also provided.

Section IV: Graphical Comparisons

In Section IV, selected products from companies throughout the United States and Canada are graphically compared to the *Blended Standard* benchmark. With each graph, we have provided the *Final Product Score* for that product, illustrated as both a percentage ranking and a five-star rating. This allows easy comparison of relative product ratings.

In writing this comparative guide, over 1,000 American and Canadian nutritional products were initially examined. Over five hundred qualifying products, representing the best in the line-up of more than 210 companies, were further evaluated, and their respective nutrient contents were compared to the selected nutritional standards. Two hundred and thirty-two (232) finalists, representing the top-rated product(s) from each manufacturer, were then selected and compared graphically. (Some companies have more than one product represented, if they market in both Canada and the United States.) The graphical illustrations allow the reader to visually compare the nutritional contents of leading brand-name supplements, in relation to the *Blended Standard.*

Section V: Appendices

The appendices provide a listing of all 500-plus products reviewed in this *Comparative Guide.* Appendix A provides an alphabetical listing by company and product name. Appendix B provides a listing according to *Final Product Score.* Information on the country of origin and dosage considerations are also provided in each appendix.

Practice Due-Diligence

If you are using this guide to select a nutritional product, you may also wish to contact the company you have chosen and request that they furnish answers to the *Product Quality Checklist* provided in Chapter Four.

Above all, practice due-diligence. Make certain you are providing your body with the very best nutritional supplements that science can offer — your health is too precious to compromise.

Section I

Aging, Oxidative Stress & Degenerative Disease

This section provides the reader with an in-depth look at:

- theories of aging
- free radicals and oxidative stress
- cellular antioxidants: how they function
- aging, oxidative stress and degenerative disease

Theories of aging and the links between aging and oxidative stress are investigated. The remarkable protective powers of endogenous and dietary antioxidants are discussed. Five degenerative disease processes are presented, and recent scientific evidence supporting the use of nutritional supplementation as a preventive measure is highlighted.

Life is just one damned thing after another.
— *Elbert Hubbard (1856-1915)*
from The Philistine

CHAPTER ONE

AGING

Avoidable or Inevitable?

Why do we age?

Why do some of us age more gracefully than others? Why will one person succumb to cancer, heart disease or diabetes early in life, while another will live disease-free and healthy for more than a century? Is there a limit to how old we can grow, or is our allotted time merely blind chance, a fatalistic roll of the dice, or the fixed rhythm of a slow dance etched into our existence? What role do diet and lifestyle play? Can we make a difference to our own futures?

Each of us ponders these questions as we examine our own mortality. Our bodies, although marvellous in their complexity, are nonetheless mere biological machines. Like any machine, our parts wear out, break down and fall off until, like the Skin Horse in Margery Williams' children's classic *The Velveteen Rabbit*, we become very shabby and our seams begin showing in all the wrong places — we *become real.* It is all a part of aging.

To understand how the machinery of the cell operates, how it wears out, and how the eventual breakdown of cells, tissues and organs impacts the health of the entire organism, is to begin to understand the aging process itself — the long and winding road from birth to death.

Theories of Aging

Over the years, scientific researchers have put forth several theories of aging that reveal a common thread. These modern aging theories generally fall into two camps: structural damage theories and programmed obsolescence theories.

Structural damage theories are concerned with the molecular damage that accumulates inside cells over time. Programmed obsolescence theories engage the concept that aging and death are the inevitable consequences of the workings of an internal biological clock, programmed at conception, which decides when cells can no longer operate and reproduce at a rate sufficient to maintain health.

Structural Damage Theories

Structural damage theories of aging, while varied, propose that the molecular components of cells, over time, begin to malfunction and break down, leading to a gradual loss of cellular function. There have been several such theories put forth over the years, some of which are described below.[1]

Wear and Tear

The Wear and Tear Theory postulates that the daily grind of life — abuse or overuse in particular — literally wears the body out, leading to disease states. The theory implies that there is no inherent limit to aging, just a statistical one. Over time, disruption, wear and damage eventually erode a cell's ability to function properly. The degeneration of cartilage and eventual grinding of bone on bone is an example of the aging process on body joints, as the rate of wear and tear begins to exceed the body's ability to repair.

Waste Accumulation

This theory proposes that, as we age, our cells accumulate waste products, a consequence of the normal metabolic processes within the cells. The build-up of this toxic sludge may eventually compromise normal cell functions. Lipofuscin pigments, or liver spots, common in the elderly, are an example of this waste material, which accumulates in the skin and internal organs as we age.

Faulty Reconstruction

Throughout life, the body is constantly rebuilding and repairing itself. Some researchers believe that, as we age, the repair process begins to produce faulty reconstruction materials, which compromise the repair job and weaken the cell — much like renovating a house with poor quality building materials, which diminish the integrity of its final structure. The manufacture of faulty proteins, caused by alterations in the chromosomes of the somatic (body) cells, may be the means through which this process operates.

Immuno-suppression

The thymus gland, or gland of youth, located at the base of the throat, declines in size from infancy (when it weighs about 250 gm) to late adulthood (when it weighs about 3 gm). The thymus plays a role in the autoimmune system, the body's primary defence against disease. Age-related reduction in the size of the thymus appears to correspond to a reduction in activity of the immune system, suggesting that the thymus may play a significant role in the aging process.[2]

Errors and Repair

Similar to the Faulty Reconstruction Theory, the Errors and Repair Theory proposes that the aging process results, in part, from damage to the molecular structure of DNA (the genetic blueprint of our cells). According to geneticist Bruce Ames of the University of California at Berkeley, the cell can repair over 99 percent of these point mutations. However, thousands of errors go unrepaired each day, leading to a lifelong accumulation of molecular rubbish that creates errors in the manufacture of related proteins, thereby accelerating the aging process.

Caloric Restriction

Proposed by Dr. Roy Walford of the UCLA Medical School, the Calorie Restriction Theory, based on years of research on longevity, attempts to answer observations gleaned from animals fed a high nutrient/low-calorie diet, Walford demonstrated that calorie restriction, along with optimal nutrition, dramatically retards the aging process. According to Walford's theory, an individual following a calorie restriction regime will lose weight gradually until reaching a point of metabolic efficiency, which provides for maximum health and lifespan. Results to date, however, have not shown calorie restriction in humans to be particularly effective in slowing the aging process (perhaps because it is so hard to follow a rigorous lifelong regime of self-denial).

Molecular Cross-linkage

Postulated in 1942 by Johan Bjorksten, the theory advances the concept that molecular cross-linking between protein molecules (such as the collagen found in our skin, tendons and ligaments) and the complexing (glycation) of structural proteins and fats with excess glucose disrupts the activities of these molecules, impairing cellular function. Advanced glycation end products (AGEs), which cause the yellowing of teeth, are a good example of this type of activity. Glycation may also be one of the reasons that diabetics, who have chronically high levels of blood sugar (glucose), exhibit accelerated aging.

Mitochondrial Damage

Mitochondria are minute organelles that are the respiratory centres within our cells. Think of them as the "powerhouses of the cell," miniature blast furnaces, where the fuel of the cell is converted into useable energy to drive its metabolic machinery. There is strong evidence that free radicals, molecular fragments constantly generated from the oxidative processes within the mitochondrial membrane, damage and eventually destroy the organelle. Once mitochondria are lost, the cell cannot replace them; this leads to an inexorable loss of energy and imperils cellular function.

Despite significant progress in aging research, none of the theories previously mentioned explains the full story; most address only *part* of the aging puzzle. The aging process is multi-dimensional, so it may involve all of the proposed mechanisms; or, perhaps, the answer lies within the common thread that *unifies* them all — the Free Radical Theory.

Free Radical Theory of Aging

Biochemist and professor emeritus of medicine, Dr. Denham Harman, proposed the Free Radical Theory in 1954. Like many bold scientific advances, investigators largely ignored and even derided Dr. Harman's proposal — until several studies in the late 1960s overwhelmingly validated his brilliant insight.

According to Harman, aging occurs when cells sustain injury from the lifelong and unrelenting attack of molecular fragments known as free radicals. The carnage inflicted by their uncontrolled assault damages the integrity of important cellular molecules — the proteins, fats, carbohydrates and nucleic acids of the cell.

Over time, the cumulative damage destroys molecular fidelity and cellular function. It then spreads outward, to involve the tissues and organs, accelerating the aging process and ultimately manifesting as some form of degenerative disease.

Investigators have now linked over 80 degenerative diseases to free radical-induced oxidative stress. Harman believes that such diseases are not separate entities, but rather different forms of expression of the aging process, influenced by genetic endowment and environmental factors. Today, it is estimated that 80 to 90 percent of all degenerative diseases involve free radical activity. Which disease strikes you depends as much on the roll of the genetic dice, cast at your conception, as on your individual lifestyle and lifelong dietary choices.

We will go deeper into the concept of free radicals and how they inflict their damage to the cell in Chapter Two. Suffice it to say, aging is now understood to be a culmination of this oxidative damage, which inevitably causes the machinery of the cell to fail. Managing the aging process, therefore, becomes a matter of reducing the rate of oxidative assault. This, in turn, is a reflection of lifestyle, diet and genetic endowment.

Genetic Endowment Theories

Evidence suggesting a genetic role to aging first arose from the work of Leonard Hayflick, back in 1962 — just around the time other scientists discovered that free radicals really did exist in biological systems (as well as within political systems!).

In his studies on human tissue cultures, Hayflick observed that human cells possess an upper limit to their ability to divide. Approaching 50 cell divisions, the cells divide less frequently and take on increasingly irregular forms, assuming a granular appearance with distorted size and shape. This altered appearance ushers in a twilight state of senescence (cell cycle arrest), followed by apoptosis[3] (programmed death of the cell) — a process that, until recently, was thought to be irreversible.

From his observations, Hayflick concluded that the lifespan of organisms appears to be regulated by some sort of "biological clock," programmed at conception and pre-set for a precise number of ticks — in the case of humans, about 50, corresponding to a potential lifespan of approximately 120 years.

Even if Hayflick took cells and froze them after 20 cell divisions, the results bore no difference. Once thawed, the cells "remembered" that they had only 30 doublings left and proceeded accordingly.

From his observations, Hayflick concluded that the lifespan of organisms appears to be regulated by some sort of "biological clock," programmed at conception and pre-set for a precise number of ticks — in the case of humans, about 50, corresponding to a potential lifespan of approximately 120 years.

Hayflick Limit

This upper limit to cell division is known as the Hayflick limit, and it differs according to species. The potential lifespan of dogs, for example, runs about 20 years; the average lifespan of butterflies is only a few weeks; and the common fruit fly has a lifespan of a mere 35 days — all are species-specific variations on the internal workings of Hayflick's biological clock. Surprisingly, Hayflick's conclusions appear to be in agreement with historical data on human mortality rates.

About 200 years ago, the *average* human lifespan was roughly 25 years of age: high childhood mortality, gruelling lifestyles and infectious disease took an early toll. Just over 100 years ago, the average lifespan increased to approximately 50 years of age. Today, the average lifespan is around 70 to 75 years of age, and it's predicted it will increase to 80 to 85 years within a few decades. Yet, despite the steady increase in our average lifespan, our *maximum* lifespan has remained constant at about 120 years.

Improved medical care, in particular the discovery of antibiotics, has offered more of us the prospect of exploring the outer limits of our lifespan. Yet, the maximum human lifespan, corresponding to Hayflick's limit for cell division, has not changed. We appear to have come up against a glass ceiling, beyond which we cannot move. The oldest person officially documented, Jeanne Louise Calment (who credited her longevity to port wine, a diet rich in olive oil, and her sense of humour), lived to 122 years — according to modern secular records, no one has lived longer. Why is this?

The answer may lie on the ends of our chromosomes.

Telomere Theory

Based on Hayflick's pioneering work, scientists theorized that his proposed biological clock may be located on the ends of the chromosomes, the tiny threads of genetic material that lie coiled within the nuclei of our cells. Each of the 23 pairs of chromosomes contain molecular "caps," called telomeres, that act much like the protective plastic caps on shoelaces. They also play an important role in cell division.

Each time a cell replicates, the telomeres get a bit shorter until, after about 50 cell divisions, the caps are but a fraction of their original length. Scientists now believe that the *length* of the telomeres may be the timing mechanism that limits further cell division and signals the end of the cell's lifespan.[4,5]

In the early '70s, Russian scientist Alexaie Olovnikov and Nobel Laureate James Watson (co-discoverer of the molecular structure of DNA) individually proposed that the shortening of the telomeres might lead to cellular aging.[6] As the cell repeatedly divides, the telomeres get shorter and, as they get shorter, they are increasingly able to influence and alter the way the cell expresses its genetic code. The consequence, each concluded, is cellular aging.

Investigators believe that, by their continued shortening, telomeres increase their control over gene expression and determine not only the ultimate age of the cell, but also the risk for the development of degenerative processes (expressed, eventually, as disease at the level of the organism).[7]

However, there is some exciting news on the horizon! Researchers have discovered that cancer cells and reproductive cells are exceptions to the Hayflick limit. These cells manufacture telomerase, an enzyme that causes the telomeres to lengthen, allowing the cells to continue to divide well past the lifespan of ordinary cells. In recent experiments, somatic (body) cells exposed to this enzyme continue to divide well past their normal lifespan.[8]

Researchers now believe that engineering of the gene sequence that controls the manufacture of telomerase enzyme may make it possible to defy the aging process and allow us to increase our lifespan well past our allotted 120 years.

The Telomere Theory may explain why we have an upper limit to our allotted lifespan; however, it does not answer the question of why so few of us are actually able to *attain* it.

For that, we need to look elsewhere.

Longevity-gene Theory

Dr. Thomas Perls, assistant professor of geriatrics at Harvard School of Medicine, has blazed a very wide trail into the scientific question of longevity. Dr. Perls studies centenarians, people who have lived for over one hundred years. He became fascinated with the extremely old while working at a rehabilitation centre in Boston. Like other physicians at the time, he assumed that his centenarian patients would be the sickest; however, to his astonishment, Perls discovered that they were far healthier than

Breaking Research: L-Carnosine

Recent research has shown that l-carnosine, a multifunctional dipeptide made up of the amino acids beta-alanine and l-histidine, has the remarkable ability to rejuvenate cells approaching senescence.

In a groundbreaking series of experiments, Australian researchers found that human fibroblasts (connective tissue cells) grown in a medium containing carnosine lived significantly longer than fibroblasts grown in the same medium without carnosine. Unlike the carnosine-deprived cells, the carnosine-rich cells retained their youthful appearance and growth patterns. Carnosine also increased the lifespan of old cells, allowing them to surpass their natural Hayflick limit and continue living up to 70 cell divisions.[9,10]

Other researchers have confirmed that carnosine's rejuvenating effects also extend to the entire organism. In a recent Russian study, senescence-accelerated mice given carnosine-treated water demonstrated a 20 percent increase in their lifespan. While the carnosine did not appear to alter the maximum lifespan, it did significantly increase the number of mice surviving into old age.[11,12]

Further work on the anti-aging potential of carnosine, particularly with respect to its reported ability to prevent formation of senile plaque (tangled fibrils of protein) found in the brain tissue of suffers from Alzheimer's disease, is continuing and initial results are encouraging.[13]

Researchers at the Life Extension Foundation (LEF), a worldwide organization dedicated to the investigation of scientific methods of treating disease, aging and death, suggest that carnosine's anti-aging action appears to be "pluripotent," working in a multitude of ways and along the many pathways of the aging process. According to LEF, this simple dipeptide stands alone as one of the most promising life extension discoveries yet made.

anyone would imagine. Most were able to avoid devastating diseases until the last few years of their life.

Nine years of further study, with over 1500 centenarians, led Perls to some fascinating insights about the very old:[14] attaining an extremely old age was not a process of declining health, but of avoiding disease. Rather than *the older you are the sicker you get*, the study revealed that *the older you are, the healthier you have been* — becoming old and becoming ill are not inseparable.

Perls concluded that living to 100 or beyond did not necessarily mean living with disease and disability; living to 100 meant a life lived in exceptionally good health, with a short period of decline at the end. The evidence teased from Perls' work points to an inescapable conclusion: the ability to live to an extremely old age is a blend of both genetic endowment and lifestyle.

Lifestyle Factors Influential

With few exceptions, most centenarians in Perls' study never smoked, few drank to excess and none was, or had been, obese. Of particular note was the fact that all were exceptionally adept at managing stress and at getting along with others. Full of humour, Perls' centenarians, as a group, were gregarious and optimistic people, involved with life to the fullest — clearly, lifestyle choices and behavioural factors played an important role in influencing their longevity. Longevity also appeared to possess a distinct gender bias: amongst this elite fellowship, there were five times as many women as men, suggesting a strong genetic link.

Genetic Basis Uncovered

In fact, Perls' data showed that the most important difference, by far, in a person's ability to reach extreme old age, was genetic. A handful of genes — perhaps as few as five or ten — appears to confer longevity, and has such a marked effect that the pattern of inheritance can be traced back through multiple generations.

According to Perls, the genes controlling longevity may operate by limiting the activity of free radicals in the body, suggesting an important antioxidant role in the aging process. Antioxidants are chemical agents or enzymes that quench free radical formation by donating electrons and converting the free radical into a harmless molecule, such as water. (We'll talk more about these important cellular agents later.)

A recent finding that centenarians have substantially higher levels of antioxidants and lower levels of free radicals in their blood than people 20 to 30 years younger provides further support for the antioxidant argument. Longevity genes, in fact, may be involved in the formation or regulation of specific cellular antioxidants or antioxidant enzyme systems (such as catalase, glutathione peroxidase and superoxide dismutase), providing critical internal support for the cell in its lifelong battle against free radical toxins.

While Perls' work sheds considerable light on the genetic basis of longevity, his investigations also highlight the important contributions of lifestyle and behavioural factors. Genetic endowment, indeed, plays a central role in determining one's longevity; however, good genes alone will not necessarily keep you alive to celebrate your hundredth birthday — the rest is up to you.

The Confluence of Theories

Perls' findings of a possible antioxidant role played by the body's longevity genes brings us back, full circle, to the structural damage theories of aging — in particular, Harman's Free Radical Theory. Recall that Harman proposed that cellular aging is a consequence of the cumulative oxidative damage to the cell's biochemical machinery, caused by the proliferation of free radical toxins. Perls' work, in addition to exposing a genetic link to aging, uncovers an important antioxidant role that supports Harman's thesis.

Two apparently divergent scientific views about how the body ages (the structural damage theories on the one hand and genetic endowment theories on the other) eventually expose the same

Clones: Frozen in Time

If Hayflick's theory is correct, it may explain why most attempts at cloning have had disappointing results — the animals have already lived part of their lives prior to birth.

Optimistic estimates show the number of successful somatic cell transfers (the process used to create Dolly, the first animal cloned from an adult cell) is only about one in 50 attempts.* Even then, most cloned domestic and laboratory animals have died young or suffered serious biological abnormalities.

Even success story and cloning 'poster sheep' Dolly developed age-related disorders early in life and died recently from a type of lung disease most common in older sheep. While normal sheep live 11 to 12 years, Dolly, cloned from a six-year-old animal, was only six when she died. She died what seemed to be a premature death. Researchers confirmed that her telomeres were significantly shorter than for other sheep of her chronological age.

But do the math...the cell Dolly was cloned from had already lived six years, and she lived another six. That's a total of 12 years, about average.

Of course, there are many complex factors involved in cloning, but it is interesting to note that many of the conditions befalling cloned animals are age-related disorders in their natural-born cousins.

* Touchette N. "A Superstar Exits the Stage." *Genome News Network*, Feb. 21, 2003, http://gnn.tigr.org/articles/02_03/dolly.shtml

culprit. Free radical-induced oxidative damage, indeed, appears to be the biochemical trigger that lies at the very heart of growing old.

Beginning at the molecular level, within the cells of our body, and moving outward — like ripples in a pond — to involve tissues, organs, and eventually the organism itself, the interplay between oxidative damage and degenerative disease *defines* the course of aging.

Implications

If certain genes control the aging process by limiting free radical damage, for those not blessed with this genetic advantage, supplementation with natural dietary antioxidants may provide an alternative means of achieving longevity.

In his book *Living to 100: Lessons in Living to Your Maximum Potential at any Age*, Thomas Perls concludes:

> *Because they act in a preventive capacity, antioxidants should be used in appropriate amounts from early in life, to keep free radical damage at bay as long as possible.*
>
> *Most centenarians studied did not have a history of antioxidant use; however, their genes that allow them to age slowly appear to have potent antioxidant effects.*
>
> *The rest of us have no choice but to fight back with antioxidants and other sensible lifestyle choices to make up for our relative genetic disadvantage.*

The fact is, there is nothing we can do to roll the genetic dice in our favour; they were cast at the time of our conception. What a select few are able to enjoy through the good fortune of genetic endowment, the rest of us will simply have to do by hand — through sensible lifestyle choices, proper diet and daily supplementation with natural antioxidants.

Attaining extremely old age was not a process of declining health, but of avoiding disease. Rather than the older you are the sicker you get, the study showed the older you are, the healthier you have been — becoming old and becoming ill are not inseparable.

Moreover, the earlier you begin, the better. Science is now discovering that damage from oxidative stress begins early in life, sowing the seeds for degenerative disease and accelerated aging. With healthy lifestyle choices, a little common sense, and an ounce or two of prevention, we may not only add years to our lives, we may add a lot of *good* years to those that we are given.

Like Margery William's Velveteen Rabbit, we can all *become real* — and remain healthy too!

1 White PA and McLeod DM. *Doctor's Secrets: The Road to Longevity.* Source Graphics and Print, Kelowna, BC, 2001, 28-36.

2 Mader S. *Inquiry into Life, 4th Edition.* Wm C Brown, Dubuque IA, 1985, p258.

3 White PA and McLeod DM. *Doctor's Secrets: The Road to Longevity.* Source Graphics and Print, Kelowna, BC, 2001, 38-39.

4 Ibid

5 Murray MT and Pizzorno J. *Encyclopedia of Natural Medicine.* Prima Health, Rocklin CA, 1998, pp 166-167.

6 Cutler RG. "Peroxide Producing Potential of Tissues: Inverse Correlation with Longevity of Mammalian Species." *Proc Nat Acad Sci* 1985, **82**: 4798-802.

7 Ibid.

8 Starr C and Taggart R. *Biology: The Unity and Diversity of Life (9th ed).* Brooks/Cole, Pacific Grove CA, 2001, p778.

9 McFarland GA and Holliday R. "Retardation of the senescence of cultured human diploid fibroblasts by carnosine." *Exp Cell Res* 1994, **212(2)**: 167-75.

10 McFarland GA and Holliday R. "Further evidence for the rejuvenating effects of the dipeptide L-carnosine on cultured human diploid fibroblasts." *Exp Gerentol* 1999, **34(1)**: 35-45.

11 Yuneva MO et al. "Effect of carnosine in age-induced changes in senescence-accelerated mice." J *Anti-Aging Med* 1999, **2(4)**: 337-42.

12 Bodyrev A et al. "Carnosine protects against excitotoxic cell death independently of effects on reactive oxygen species." *Neuroscience* 1999, **94(2)**: 571-7.

13 Munch G et al. "Influence of advanced glycation end-products and AGE-inhibitors on nucleation-dependent polymerization of beta-amyloid peptide." *Biochim Biophys Acta* 1997, **1360(1)**: 17-29.

14 Perls, TT and Silver, MH. *Living to 100: Lessons in Living to your Maximum Potential at Any Age.* Basic Books, New York NY, 1999.

Cells let us walk, talk, think, make love and realize the bathwater is cold.

— Lorraine Cudmore

CHAPTER TWO

THE MIRACLE OF THE CELL

Respiration — an Electron Cascade

Human beings — the paragon of animals — are biological machines so evolved that our complexity invokes awe in even the most brilliant of scientific minds. Our cells are the building blocks of life, miraculous biochemical factories far more intricate than we can ever hope to imagine. It is here that the dance of life bursts forth on a scale of complexity simply inconceivable. Every second, countless chemical reactions take place in each of our body's trillions of cells, intricately choreographed in a wondrous biochemical symphony.

Life is a constant flow of energy, and it moves in our cells through a transfer of electrons from one molecule to the next. When a molecule gives up electrons it is *oxidized*; when it accepts electrons it is *reduced*. Oxidation and reduction, the chemical "yin" and "yang," power the machinery of the cell to let flow the river of life. Scientists call this process *respiration*.

The most important medical discovery of the last half-century concerns 'free radicals' and 'antioxidants.' Free radicals have been linked to (at last count) about 60 diseases. And we now have evidence that antioxidants can stop and (in some instances) even reverse the damage done by free radicals...

— Dr. Robert D. Willix Jr.

It begins with a molecule of glucose, the energy source of the cell. Through a complex series of oxidation-reduction reactions, glucose is broken down to its component parts and energy is captured. Throughout this process, electrons move between molecules to the terminal step, where they combine with oxygen and hydrogen to form water.

In simple terms, respiration is nothing more than controlled oxidation or combustion, much like the burning of wood or the rusting of iron. In our cells, however, biological catalysts — specialized proteins called enzymes — control each step. Enzymes allow the "oxidative fires" of the cell to burn at a much lower temperature, releasing energy in small packets that the cell can capture and store. The result of this biologically-controlled oxidation is essentially the same as simple combustion: complex molecules are broken down to water and carbon dioxide, releasing energy.

Along the way, some of the exchanged electrons invariably escape and leak out of the respiratory centres of the cell to react with ambient oxygen, generating toxic oxygen free radicals. It's estimated that two to five percent of the electrons that pass through the cell's respiratory processes convert molecular oxygen into superoxide molecules and other oxygen free radical species.[1] This continuous flux of free radicals generates considerable oxidative stress in human tissues and threatens the integrity of essential biomolecules.

Life's quintessential paradox is that oxygen — the giver of life — is also our mortal enemy. While absolutely essential for cellular respiration, oxygen's involvement in life's processes lies at the heart of growing old.

What are Free Radicals?

Chemically speaking, free radicals are molecules or molecular fragments that have an unpaired electron. Highly unstable and extremely short-lived, these chemical intermediates have a lifespan measured in trillionths of a second or less. Their presence in biological systems was first reported in the early 1960s,[2,3] when scientists observed exceedingly short-lived events in enzyme-controlled oxidation-reduction reactions (like those that take place inside our cells). Because of their unpaired electrons, free radicals are extremely volatile, reacting aggressively with other molecules at the instant of their creation.

Oxidation-reduction, free radicals, unpaired electrons — this might sound like pretty tedious stuff; but it's not. In fact, life's quintessential paradox is that oxygen — the giver of life — is also our mortal enemy. While absolutely essential for cellular respiration, oxygen's involvement in life's processes lies at the very heart of growing old.

Oxygen is not the only molecule to form free radicals. During the process of respiration, the transfer of electrons from one molecule to the next generates other highly reactive free radical species. We now know that excessive free radical formation in cells can be induced through exposure to such things as environmental pollutants, industrial chemicals, agricultural pesticides, cigarette smoke and radiation. Even vigorous exercise will release a damaging flood of free radicals that can injure your cells if they're not protected.

During their fleeting existence, these highly unstable particles can inflict considerable harm. Like sparks from a spitting fire that burn holes in your living room carpet, these supercharged particles leap around the cell, damaging its internal machinery. Free radicals leave a virtual killing field of destruction in their wake, punching tiny holes in cell membranes, altering the cell's molecular blueprint, and tearing apart protein and lipid molecules — nasty stuff, with nasty consequences for the cell.

Nature's Fire Wardens

According to Dr. Edward West,[4] "It is essential that in biological oxidation-reduction the transfer [of energy] takes place in a manner that controls the potentially destructive effects of free radical formation and conserves biological function [within the cell]." The fundamental control mechanisms, referred to by West, lie in the function of the enzyme systems needed for the reactions to proceed, as well as in the cell's natural defence mechanisms — antioxidants.

> ***People are missing the point when they debate which antioxidant is the "magic bullet." Just like firefighters on the front line, who replenish and reinforce one another, antioxidants work best when they work together — a process called synergy.***

Antioxidants are nature's fire wardens — complex molecules that police the chemical processes of the cell and snuff out the firestorm of free radicals that continuously erupts. As long as we have sufficient antioxidant stores in our cells, the damage is minimized. However, if we lack sufficient antioxidant reinforcements, the cumulative damage of these free radical "sparks" will injure the delicate fabric of life. Such oxidative damage is now believed to be the dark force behind the onset of degenerative disease. In fact, a multitude of degenerative disease processes have now been linked to oxidative stress.[5] Dr. Ray Strand, in his book, *Bionutrition*, adroitly calls the battle against oxidative stress "the war within." [6]

Until the development of Harman's Free Radical Theory, free radicals were thought to exist only outside the body. In 1968, further work by Harman showed that a small amount of vitamin E added to the diet increased lifespans in mice by about five percent.[7] Until then, not much was known about the relevance of vitamin E or other biological antioxidants; science simply did not understand the importance of such molecules in the protection of the cell against oxidative assault.

My own research on free radicals and dietary supplementation with vitamin E, conducted in the 1970s, showed that ionizing radiation (gamma rays) caused severe damage to cell membranes, punching tiny holes in their surfaces and causing them to become leaky.[8] The work also shed some light on the ability of vitamin E to quench the peroxidation of membrane lipids (a process whereby the oxidization of a fat molecule creates a chain reaction of further oxidation).[9]

In 1971, Dr. Richard Passwater became the first scientist to publicly describe the nutritional role of antioxidants. Since that time, research on these important nutrients has grown prodigiously. Today, vitamin A, vitamin C, vitamin E, beta-carotene, coenzyme Q_{10}, selenium, zinc, l-glutathione, alpha-lipoic acid, n-acetyl-cysteine, proanthocyanidins, bioflavonoids and many other tongue-twisting names, have stepped into the limelight — free radical fighters against the millions of oxidative hits that each cell of your body sustains every day. Over a 70-year lifespan, that adds up to some 17 *tons* of free radicals![10]

Symphony and Synergy

Antioxidants quench the highly reactive free radicals, stopping them dead in their tracks *before* they can cause structural damage to the cell. They do this by scavenging the unpaired electron from the free radical, rendering the molecule harmless. In the process, the antioxidant itself is altered chemically.

Some antioxidants are regenerated by the presence of other antioxidants (a principal reason why you should always supplement with a wide spectrum of antioxidants, rather than just one). Other antioxidants are converted to entirely different compounds or are excreted from the body. Your body produces some antioxidants, while others must be obtained through the diet.

The endogenous antioxidants (those manufactured by the cell) include many of the body's natural enzymes, coenzymes and sulfur-containing molecules, such as glutathione. The dietary antioxidants include vitamin A (and the related carotenoids, including beta-carotene), vitamins E and C, and the myriad of bioflavonoids and sulfur-containing compounds derived from fruits and vegetables. While not themselves antioxidants, many minerals also form vital parts of the different antioxidant systems in the body. These include selenium, iron, manganese, copper and zinc.[11]

Teamwork — the Operative Phrase

People are missing the point when they debate which antioxidant is the "magic bullet." Just like firefighters on the front line, who replenish and reinforce one another, antioxidants work best when they work together. This is known as *synergy*, an idiom coined by Dr. Richard Passwater, which denotes the fact that antioxidants work as a team; synergy implies that the effect of the whole is *greater* than the sum of its parts.

Antioxidants also work in different areas of the cell. Vitamin E is the premier antioxidant of the cellular membrane, quenching free radical-induced lipid peroxidation within the membrane itself. Vitamin C is king in the extracellular fluids and works alongside glutathione in the cytoplasm (fluid) of the cell. Both vitamin C and vitamin E, along with selenium, enhance the effect of beta-carotene. Coenzyme Q_{10} (CoQ_{10}) works deep within the mitochondrion (the powerhouse of the cell), assisting in the energy transfer reactions and rejuvenating vitamin E. Together with vitamin E, CoQ_{10} protects the mitochondrial membranes from the oxidative "fires" of respiration. Alpha-lipoic acid, along with a family of powerful antioxidants called proanthocyanidins (found in grape seed and pine bark extracts), regenerates vitamin C, which in turn rejuvenates vitamin E.

Together, these free radical fighters toil in their daily battle, protecting the cell in a *symphony of synergy*. It's a masterpiece written by Mother Nature.

Antioxidant Enzyme Systems

The first line of defence against free radicals employed by the cells of our bodies consists of three protective enzyme systems: superoxide dismutase (SOD), catalase and glutathione peroxidase. These three antioxidant systems work together to rid our cells of the toxic oxygen free radicals generated through respiration.

There are several other detoxification processes at work within

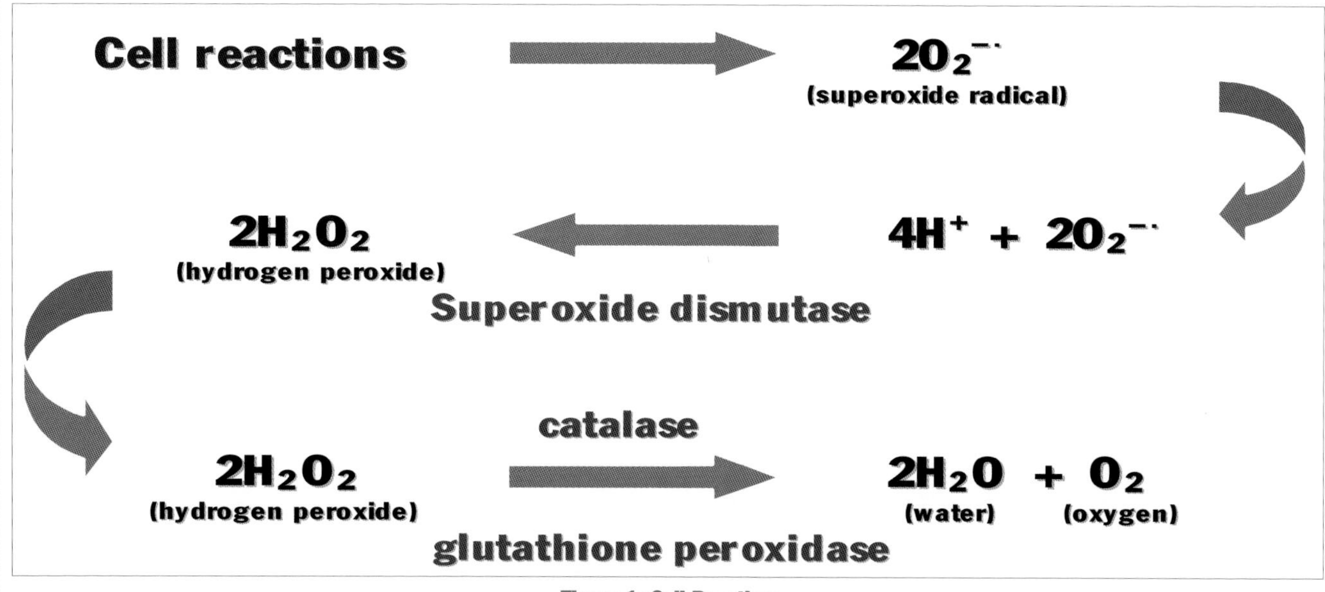

Figure 1: Cell Reactions

Toxic oxygen free radicals are continously created by our cells' many metabolic activities. Fortunately, nature has provided us with three antioxidant enzymes that work together to eliminate the threat. Under the prodding of superoxide dismutase (an antioxidant enzyme), free radicals combine with hydrogen ions to form hydrogen peroxide. To remove hydrogen peroxide, itself a potent free radical agent, the cell next enlists the talents of two more antioxidant enzyme systems, catalase and glutathione peroxidase. Working together, catalase and glutathione peroxidase cleave the hydrogen peroxide molecules to produce harmless water and molecular oxygen.

our cells, but the simplified reaction model shown in Figure 1 is a good example of how the cell's principal detoxification mechanisms team up to rid the body of damaging superoxide radicals, generated by the cell's own metabolic processes.

As we age, we gradually lose our ability to make these important antioxidant enzymes. This may be related to the shortening of chromosomal telomeres and their increasing control over genetic expression, or to the accumulation of errors in the genes regulating the manufacture of particular antioxidant enzymes (to read about these mechanisms, please refer to the previous chapter). Whatever the cause, once cells can no longer make sufficient amounts of the critical antioxidant enzymes — or produce faulty copies that don't work very well — free radicals begin to accumulate and oxidative damage, the genesis of the aging process, ensues.

In simplistic terms, our bodies slowly begin "rusting away" from within.

Implications

The scientific evidence points increasingly to oxidative distress as the causative factor for biological aging; it appears that damage caused by relentless oxidative assault to the cell causes its metabolic machinery to malfunction and eventually fail. We have much to learn about the precise mechanisms through which antioxidants counteract free radical assaults. The challenge now is to clarify the process through which the initial oxidative damage propagates outward to affect the organs and the body itself. Answers to these questions will further enlighten the intricate relationship between aging and degenerative disease.

1 Forman HJ and Boveris A. "Superoxide radical and hydrogen peroxide in mitochondria." in: *Free Radicals in Biology (vol 5),* Pryor WA (ed), Academic Press, New York NY, 1982, 65-89.

2 Caldin EF. *Fast Reactions in Solution.* John Wiley & Sons, New York NY, 1964.

3 Roughton FJW, and Chance B. *Techniques of Organic Chemistry (2nd edition).* Friess SL, Lewis ES and Weissberger A. (eds) Interscience 1963, **VIII (II)**: 704.

4 West ES, Todd W, Mason HS and Van Bruggen JT. *Textbook of Biochemistry 4th edition.* The Macmillan Co., Toronto ON, 1970, 899-903.

5 Davies K. "Oxidative stress, the paradox of aerobic life." *Biochemical Society Symposia* 1995, **61**: 1-31.

6 Strand R. *Bionutrition: Winning the War Within.* Comprehensive Wellness Publishing, Rapid City SD, 1998.

7 Harman D. "Free radical theory of aging: effect of free radical reaction inhibitors on the mortality rate of male LAF mice." *J Gerontol* 1968, **23(4)**: 476-482.

8 MacWilliam LD and Bhakthan NMG. "Radiation-induced enzyme efflux from rat heart: sedentary animals." *Recent Advances in Studies on Cardiac Structure and Metabolism.* 1976, Vol **9:(The Sarcolema)** 447-460.

9 MacWilliam LD. *Radiation-Induced Changes in the Profiles of Certain Key Enzymes in Rat Myocardium and Serum: Effects of Exercise and Dietary Supplementation with Vitamin E.* MSc Thesis, Simon Fraser University, Burnaby BC, 1974.

10 Passwater RA. *All About Antioxidants.* Avery Publishing, New York NY, 1998, pp 22-23.

11 Passwater RA. *All About Antioxidants.* Avery Publishing, New York NY, 1998, pp 9-10.

A wise man should consider that health is the greatest of all blessings.

— Hippocrates (470 – 410 BC)

CHAPTER THREE

Degenerative Disease

The Heart of the Matter

The press release headline announces the grim findings: "Sudden cardiac deaths are increasing in young people, especially among women." The report, from the U.S. Centers for Disease Control and Prevention, released March 1, 2001, documents a decade-long rise in ischemic heart disease and cardiomyopathy in young adults between the ages of 15 and 34, with an alarming 30 percent increase in women.

Presented during the American Heart Association's Annual Conference on Cardiovascular Disease Epidemiology and Prevention, the study fingers lifestyle factors, including smoking, poor dietary habits, lack of physical activity, and adolescent obesity, as the likely causes.[1]

Not long ago, common wisdom held that heart disease was a malady of the elderly. Today we can see that it is just not so. Heart disease starts in childhood: the patterns of diet and exercise that develop during our early years cast the mold for lifelong habits. Research shows that children, during their early development, possess sensitive windows for nutritional programming. Dietary patterns established during their early years will imprint long-term consequences.[2] Today, birth weight and weight at one year are recognized as predictive markers for cardiovascular disease in adulthood.[3]

In 1912, cardiovascular disease was so rare it took years to find. Yet, in less than 100 years, the changes wrought to our lifestyle, environment, and to the food we eat have made cardiovascular disease the number one killer in North America.

Even more worrisome is recent evidence of atherosclerosis (hardening of the arteries) in infants and children two to fifteen years of age. A 1998 study, reported in the *New England Journal of Medicine*, found that the prevalence of atherosclerosis begins in childhood and increases with age. The findings show that the disease affects about 30 percent of adolescents between the ages of 16 and 20 years, 50 percent of young adults between 21 and 25, and 75 percent of adults 26 to 39.[4,5]

That is correct — read those numbers again. By the time we reach the ripe young age of 39, three-quarters of us have the beginnings of cardiovascular disease, most without any knowledge of the fact. For many, our first warning barely precedes our last breath. Does it have to be like this? Not on your life.

It is hard to believe, but cardiovascular disease, the nation's Public Enemy #1, is a problem cultivated by modern society. In 1912, the *Journal of the American Medical Association* published the first clinical report on cardiovascular disease in America. The disease was so rare it took years to find.[6] Yet, in less than 100 years, the changes wrought to our lifestyle, environment, and to the food we eat have made cardiovascular disease the number one killer in North America.

Homocysteine — the Heart Breaker

Elevated blood levels of a simple, sulfur-containing amino acid may be the dark force behind heart disease and many other degenerative diseases of the modern world. It is estimated that 10 to 15 percent of heart attacks and strokes may be caused by elevated homocysteine levels alone.[7]

Recent studies show that high levels of homocysteine are responsible for the development of the fatty cholesterol plaques that lead to atherosclerosis or hardening of the arteries. High levels of homocysteine irritate the inner walls of the arteries, creating small oxidative lesions. The body, in its attempt to repair the damage, patches the tears with cholesterol, which acts as a sealing compound.[8] Problems arise if the LDL cholesterol has been oxidized by the homocysteine. Oxidized LDL cholesterol (also known as the "really bad stuff") stimulates specialized immune system cells, called macrophages, to swing into action. The macrophages stuff themselves with oxidized cholesterol and turn into pathologic foam cells. These foam cells then stick to the arterial wall, leading to the development of fatty atherosclerotic streaks.[9,10] In diabetics, oxidized LDL cholesterol becomes glycosylated (cross-linked with sugar), making it even more adept at hardening the arteries.[11,12] This is one of the reasons that diabetics often exhibit advanced cardiovascular deterioration.

The 1992 Physician's Health Study, conducted by Meir Stampfer[13] of the Harvard School of Public Health, looked at blood homocysteine levels in 15,000 physicians. The authors concluded that even mildly elevated levels of homocysteine are directly related to heart disease. Subsequent studies confirm that high levels of homocysteine place people at increased cardiovascular risk.[14] It is estimated that for every ten percent increase in blood homocysteine levels there is a similar increase in the risk of heart disease.[15,16] Other studies indicate that people with elevated blood homocysteine face four times the risk of peripheral vascular disease (damage to the blood vessels of the body, outside the heart) than do people with normal levels.[17]

The massive Framingham Heart Study,[18] which followed twins over a 26-year period, showed a significant increase in carotid artery stenosis (narrowing of the main arteries of the neck) consistent with elevated homocysteine levels. Other studies confirm a positive link between blood homocysteine levels and the risks of arteriosclerosis (hardening of the arteries without plaque formation)[19] and myocardial infarction (sudden heart attack).[20] High homocysteine levels are implicated, as well, in the development of peripheral vascular disease,[21] diabetes,[22] arthritis, kidney disease, cancer and neural tube birth defects.[23]

The Homocysteine Equation

To make matters worse, homocysteine is a potent neurotoxin. It destroys the myelin sheath protecting nerve cells and causes them to "short-circuit," much like a frayed electrical wire. Many neurological diseases, such as depression, schizophrenia, multiple sclerosis, Parkinson's disease, Alzheimer's dementia and age-related cognitive decline, are associated with high levels of homocysteine and low levels of the B-complex vitamins.[24] In fact, recent studies confirm that deficiencies in vitamin B_{12} and folate are dangerously common in older people, who often suffer from many of the above-mentioned degenerative diseases.[25]

High homocysteine levels are implicated in the development of many disease conditions, including peripheral vascular disease, diabetes, arthritis, kidney disease, cancer and neural tube birth defects.

Vitamin B_6 helps the body convert homocysteine into two other amino acids, cysteine and taurine. Vitamin B_{12} and folate each change homocysteine back to its precursor, methionine. In the absence of these three important vitamins, blood homocysteine builds to harmful levels and the damage begins; but supplement with any of the three and homocysteine levels begin to fall. One study found that supplementing with all three vitamins reduced homocysteine levels by 50 percent.[26]

The scientific evidence rests its case. Homocysteine is, indeed, a "heart breaker." High blood levels of this simple amino acid have cut short many dreams — and all for the want of three inexpensive vitamins.

Major Cancer Finding

The headline in the *Los Angeles Times* says it all: "Study Ties Most Cancer to Lifestyles, not Genetics."[31] Citing 88 years of data on tens of thousands of twins, the report, published July 13, 2000 in the *New England Journal of Medicine*,[32] underscores the conclusions from a host of other studies. Simple lifestyle choices and the avoidance of environmental risk factors can prevent many cancers. While not negating the influence of genes, which appears to account for approximately 30 percent of total cancer risk, the report places the burden of guilt on poor dietary habits, smoking, alcohol consumption, lack of exercise, and exposure to environmental toxins.

A 1997 report released by the American Institute for Cancer Research and the World Cancer Fund highlights the importance of diet in cancer prevention. The report claims that dietary change could prevent three to four million cases of cancer, worldwide, every year.[33] Its key recommendation is to choose a diet that is predominantly plant-based and includes a wide variety of vegetables, fruits and grains. An estimated 30 to 35 percent of all cancers are related to diet.

A comprehensive review of 172 epidemiological studies from around the world drew similar and almost universal findings. Researchers from the University of California at Berkeley found overwhelming evidence that fruits and vegetables in the diet provide a huge protective effect against almost every type of cancer.[34]

There is also increasing evidence that dietary patterns in childhood play a significant role in the development of cancer as an adult.[35,36] Similar findings emphasize the importance of lifelong physical activity and the maintenance of a healthy body weight in cancer prevention.[37]

Despite what we know about the importance of lifestyle and nutrition, cancer continues to be the second leading cause of disease in North America. Without major advances in prevention, one out of three U.S. and Canadian citizens living today will succumb to cancer. The American Institute for Cancer Research estimates that cancer will strike 1.2 million Americans each year (1997 estimates) and exceed $110 billion in total health and related costs. The lifetime risk for developing some form of cancer is now one out of three for women and one out of two for men. According to figures released by the *Journal of the American Medical Association*, adult males now entering their '40s and '50s have more than twice the cancer rates of their grandfathers. Women who smoke have five to six times the cancer rates of their grandmothers.[38]

The World Health Organization estimates that, in 1996, ten million cases of cancer occurred around the world. It expects the number to grow to 14.7 million within the next fifteen years.

A Medical Vietnam

If you don't protect yourself, your chance of avoiding cancer is about as good as the flip of a coin. Unfortunately, once you have contracted the disease, your overall chance of survival is considerably

Good News!

The good news is that heart disease can easily be prevented and even reversed. Controlling homocysteine-induced oxidative damage with vitamins B_6, B_{12} and folic acid and supplementing with natural antioxidants are key factors in preventing and reversing heart disease. Vitamin E, vitamin C, beta-carotene and the intracellular antioxidants glutathione, n-acetyl-cysteine and coenzyme Q_{10} are all important in the ongoing battle against oxidative stress. Three antioxidants in particular, vitamin E, beta-carotene and coenzyme Q_{10}, provide specific protection against oxidation of human LDL cholesterol.[27,28,29]

The strongest association with heart disease appears to be a deficiency in vitamin E. Studies show that supplementation with 400 to 800 International Units (IU) of this inexpensive vitamin can reduce the incidence of heart attacks by 77 percent. As well, dietary supplementation of the various forms of vitamin E (alpha- and beta-tocopherol and the tocotrienols) helps reverse the development of cholesterol plaque.[30]

All said, optimal nutrition, combined with lifestyle changes, including smoking cessation and daily physical exercise, are essential components in a holistic approach to sound cardiac health.

lower. The problem is, having been developing silently for 10 to 20 years, cancer is already well advanced by the time it shows up on the radar screen. Doctors immediately roll out their heavy artillery — surgery, chemotherapy, radiation — but in reality, there is not a lot that they can do at this point. "Cut, burn and poison" have become the indispensable tools of the trade.

Over the last thirty years, survival rates for cancer have not improved. Since former U.S. President Richard Nixon's 1971 declaration of war on cancer, well over 30 billion dollars have been poured into a campaign some critics have labelled a "medical Vietnam."[39] According to Nobel Laureate, Dr. Linus Pauling, "Everyone should know that the war on cancer is largely a fraud." We have been desperately searching for the magic bullet, while ignoring the underlying cause.

> ***Do not fear cancer; the human body is incredibly tough ... given the right nutrition, exercise and lifestyle, it will resist cancer for a lifetime.***
> **— Lewis Thomas, President Sloan Kettering Cancer Hospital**

Cancer is not a single disease, but a group of over 100 diseases with a generally similar etiology (cause). The key to fighting cancer, therefore, lies in *prevention.* There is growing medical evidence that cancer may initially develop through oxidative damage to the cell's molecular blueprint or DNA. The proliferation of toxic free radicals, created by external environmental influences, as well as the cell's own metabolic processes, can overwhelm a cell whose antioxidant stores are low.

Whether caused by poor diet, environmental toxins or genetic predisposition, it is now believed that free radical damage is the "biochemical trigger" that sets the destructive process of cancer in motion. Research shows that, once developed, cancerous tumors generate their own free radicals and promote further mutations and abnormal cell growth. Like a fire feeding on itself, unchecked cancer growth is invasive and deadly.

However, given the chance, Mother Nature can summon some powerful allies to the battlefront.

Antioxidants Form Front-Line Defence

Antioxidants, biological molecules that scavenge free radicals, form an army of potent free radical fighters. Together, they are the cell's biological shield against many forms of cancer and other degenerative diseases whose primary cause is oxidative stress. Antioxidants protect the cell in three ways: by seeking out and destroying damaging free radicals, by enhancing the body's natural immune responses, and by reducing the cancer cell's ability to adhere to surrounding tissues.

> ***There is also increasing evidence that dietary patterns in childhood play a significant role in the development of cancer as an adult.***

Have a look at what antioxidants can accomplish in the battle against cancer:

Vitamin A

In an authoritative review of vitamin A, Kummet and Meyskins (1983)[40] concluded that retinol (vitamin A) conferred a protective effect for almost all sites of cancer. Other research suggests that beta-carotene (pro-vitamin A) has an even stronger effect against cancer than does vitamin A.[41,42] A study of pre-menopausal women with a positive history of breast cancer showed strong evidence of the synergy of multiple antioxidants. Those who consumed high levels of alpha and beta-carotene, lutein, zeaxanthin, vitamin C and vitamin A were three times less likely to contract the disease than those who did not.[43]

Vitamin C

Ascorbic acid (vitamin C) is also a powerful cancer antagonist and demonstrates a protective effect against a wide variety of cancers.[44] In one study, a diet supplemented with vitamin C, vitamin E and beta-carotene significantly reduced the risk of cancer in both smokers and non-smokers.[45] In another investigation, men with high levels of vitamin C showed a significantly lower incidence of cancer of the stomach, colon and rectum.[46]

Population-based studies provide strong evidence of a protective effect of vitamin C for non-hormone-dependent cancers. A review of 46 such studies found that high levels of vitamin C intake provided an approximate two-fold protective effect, compared with low intake. As well, several lung cancer studies describe a marked reduction in the risk of disease that correlates with increased levels of vitamin C intake.[47]

Vitamin E

Alpha-tocopherol (vitamin E) is another potent cancer fighter. A fat-soluble vitamin, it is predominant in the cell membrane, where it combats lipid peroxidation. In a double-blind, placebo-controlled study, Finnish men supplementing with just 50 IU of vitamin E reduced their risk of prostate cancer by one-third.[48] In a recent study, Pastori and co-workers found that a combination of alpha-tocopherol and lycopene (a carotenoid found in tomatoes) inhibited prostate cell proliferation by 90 percent.[49] As well, a ten-year study of 21,000 men revealed that those with high dietary intakes of vitamin E reduced their risk of all types of cancer by 30 percent.[50]

The studies also reveal that, in order to provide their protective benefits, vitamin E and vitamin C are required in amounts far greater than those prescribed in the current Canadian and U.S. dietary recommendations. These recommendations indicate the amounts of nutrients needed to avoid nutritional deficiencies; many experts now believe that the regulations do not reflect the greater daily requirements needed for optimal nutrition and protection against degenerative disease.

Selenium

Selenium is a mineral that kicks butt. An extensive review of its antioxidant properties shows that selenium can inhibit the development of induced cancers of the liver, breast, skin and colon.[51] A 1998 Arizona study showed that mortality from prostate cancer dropped 63 percent in subjects taking as little as 200 micrograms (µg) per day of selenomethionine (an easily absorbed form of selenium).[52] The same study found that men with normal PSA (prostate-specific antigen) levels who supplemented with selenium reduced their risk of prostate cancer by 74 percent. Similar studies demonstrate that daily supplementation with as little as

200 μg of selenium can decrease the risk of colon cancer by 60 percent and lung cancer by 30 percent.[53]

Coenzyme Q_{10}

Coenzyme Q_{10}, or ubiquinone, is an important component of the cell's metabolic furnaces. Located in the mitochondria, CoQ_{10} behaves like a vitamin by acting as a cofactor to three important enzyme systems in the cell's central metabolic pathway. As well as being important in the proper functioning of the heart muscle, this coenzyme has powerful antioxidant properties. It has been used successfully to treat breast cancer in humans and has prevented experimentally-induced cancers in mice.[54] High doses of CoQ_{10}, at 390 milligrams (mg) per day, have proven effective in producing regression of tumors in breast cancer patients, some of whom exhibited metastasis (spreading) to other organs.[55]

L-Glutathione

Glutathione is an endogenous antioxidant used by the cell to help eliminate toxic metabolic waste products, such as hydrogen peroxide. A potent detoxicant in the liver, it is on the front line of defence against environmental carcinogens.[56] One recent study showed that supplementing with a combination of glutathione, vitamin E, vitamin C and mixed carotenoids was effective in protecting against UV-induced skin damage, which is known to cause premature aging and skin cancer.[57]

In order to provide their protective benefits, vitamin E and vitamin C are required in amounts far greater than those prescribed in the current Canadian and U.S. dietary recommendations. These recommendations indicate the amounts of nutrients needed to avoid nutritional deficiencies; they do not reflect the greater daily requirements needed for optimal nutrition and protection against degenerative disease.

Enough said: contrary to the myth that vitamins just make for expensive urine, that is not what the science shows. Understanding how to prevent oxidative damage through lifestyle and dietary change — and through supplementation with natural antioxidants — offers a host of new possibilities in cancer prevention and treatment.

Type II Diabetes

While medical science has been vigilant in its fight against infectious disease, it has been dilatory in its response to new enemies at our gates: the diseases of affluence, brought on by the convergence of longevity and lifestyle. One such enemy, and a leading cause of death in the developed world, is diabetes mellitus — the epidemic of the new millennium. More than 15 million Americans and two million Canadians have contracted the disease, and over 70 million Americans exhibit pre-clinical symptoms, most without any knowledge of the fact.

People often underestimate diabetes as a simple sugar imbalance, readily corrected with medication. In fact, it is a complex medical disorder with serious long-term implications for cardiovascular and nerve health, kidney function and eyesight. Because its expression is largely dependent on lifestyle issues, including diet, weight control and exercise, disease management is complex and challenging.

There are two types of diabetes. About one in ten diabetics have insulin-dependent diabetes (IDDM), also known as Type I or juvenile-onset diabetes. Type I diabetics lack the ability to produce sufficient insulin to control their blood sugar levels. Ninety percent of diabetics, however, have Type II diabetes, also known as non-insulin-dependent (NIDDM) or adult-onset diabetes. Those predisposed to Type II diabetes generally produce plenty of insulin and often have elevated levels of the hormone in their blood. The problem, instead, lies in their body's *resistance* to insulin.

Insulin Resistance Syndrome

Insulin Resistance Syndrome[58] — the silent stalker — is the dark force behind Type II diabetes. The syndrome is a clinical precursor of full-blown Type II diabetes and affects up to 25 percent of the adult population in North America.

A host of related symptoms mark the onset of the disease, including: high blood pressure (hypertension), elevated blood triglycerides (fats), altered cholesterol ratios, accelerated hardening of the arteries, proliferation of cells in the arterial walls, development of abdominal obesity, and adverse changes in blood lipids (glycosylation).

The symptoms often lie unnoticed until irreversible damage occurs. Left unchecked, the cycle of steadily increasing hyperinsulinemia (high insulin levels in the blood) will eventually announce itself as full-blown Type II diabetes. Not everyone who exhibits insulin resistance will develop diabetes; however, virtually everyone who develops Type II diabetes started with insulin resistance — and the prognosis is chilling: people with insulin resistance have triple the risk of heart disease, and of those who develop frank diabetes, 80 percent will die from cardiovascular complications. Clearly, early detection of the disease — before it reaches its end stage — is paramount.

Lifestyle and Diet

The development of insulin resistance is determined much more from diet and lifestyle than genetic predisposition. Chronic exposure to high levels of insulin (in part, a consequence of diets high in refined sugars) appears to cause the cells of the body to "decommission" their insulin recognition systems. As a result, the hormone can no longer perform its task of moving glucose into the cells for storage. The consequence is the onset of a vicious cycle of hyperglycemia (abnormally high levels of blood sugar) that results in even higher levels of insulin (hyperinsulinemia) as the pancreas struggles to correct the problem.

Also related to insulin resistance are excess abdominal fat and lifestyle factors that contribute to obesity. A 1995 study in the *New England Journal of Medicine* showed that a predisposition toward visceral obesity (deposition of abdominal fat) was associated with increased insulin resistance, the metabolic precursor of full-blown Type II diabetes.[59] In fact, one of the best predictive markers for insulin resistance is excess body weight, in particular weight over the belt-line.

The central issue of whether obesity causes insulin resistance, or whether insulin resistance causes obesity, remains unclear. According to Slagle,[60] excess insulin production leads to the deposition of excess body fat, with consequent weight gain, especially around the waist. While others support this view,[61] it is not universally accepted. However, one thing *is* clear: four out of five diabetics are obese.

Chronic stress is also a predictive marker for the onset of insulin resistance. Stress induces a hormone cascade, as the body responds physiologically to a perceived threat. This, in turn, leads to elevated blood sugar levels, followed by an elevation of blood insulin levels.[62] Other risk indicators to watch out for include a lack of regular exercise, high blood cholesterol, constant thirst and frequent urination, a craving for sugar, and elevated blood pressure in excess of 140/90.

Research shows that regular vigorous exercise, combined with a low-glycemic diet, is the best and quickest way to overcome insulin resistance.[63] Exercise improves cardiovascular function, enhances the body's ability to metabolize glucose and reduces stress. Loss of weight, through exercise and diet, correlates with a return to normal levels of insulin resistance. In fact, weight loss is the single most effective approach to the treatment of insulin resistance and reduction in risk of developing Type II diabetes.[64]

Shedding pounds appears to re-sensitize the cells of the body to the insulin hormone. Exercise-induced weight loss stimulates the production of additional insulin receptor sites on the cell membranes of muscle tissue and reactivates those sites already present. This enhances the body's ability to utilize the insulin present and reduce chronic hyperglycemia, thereby normalizing both blood sugar and insulin levels.

Herbal Supplements — A Natural Approach to Diabetes Treatment

Before the advent of modern drug therapy, successful diabetes treatment consisted of plant-based remedies indigenous to many native cultures. According to naturopathic physician Dr. Michael Murray, "The last 20 years of scientific investigation have, in fact, confirmed the efficacy of many herbal remedies, many of which are remarkably effective and have few or no side effects." Murray argues that the proper treatment of the diabetic patient requires the integration of diet and lifestyle changes, along with the use of nutritional and herbal therapies.[67]

The following are some of these natural remedies, used for centuries by Ayurvedic, Oriental and Native American healers, recommended by Murray:[67]

- ✔ *Gymnema sylvestre*, used for centuries by East Indian Ayurvedic healers, is effective in treating both Type I and Type II diabetes. Studies indicate that extracts from the plant stimulate regeneration of the hormone-producing beta-cells within the pancreas.[68,69]
- ✔ *Pterocarpus marsupium*, another plant with a long history of use in Eastern cultures, also works to prevent and reverse damage to pancreatic beta-cells in diabetic patients.
- ✔ *Momordica charantia*, or bitter melon, is a powerful hypoglycemic agent. Charantin, an extract of the plant, is reportedly more potent than the prescription drug Tolbutamide.[70] One peer-reviewed study showed that two ounces of *charantia* extract improved glucose tolerance in 73 percent of diabetic subjects.[71]
- ✔ *Vaccinium myrtillus* (bilberry) and *Vitris vinifera* (grape seed) extracts appear to regenerate vitamin C and inhibit microvascular hemorrhaging, common in diabetic retinopathy.
- ✔ *Gingko biloba*, used as a diabetic remedy in traditional Chinese medicine (TCM) for centuries, has been shown to reduce peripheral vascular damage and nerve dysfunction, common in the diabetic patient.[72]

Type II diabetes and its precursor insulin resistance are serious disorders that threaten to challenge healthcare systems throughout the world. Yet, they are entirely preventable. Sensible diet, daily exercise and good nutritional supplementation, including the use of herbal remedies, are the key ingredients in a cost effective, holistic approach to prevention.

The End Game

Left unchecked, the chronic intake of high glycemic foods, combined with a sedentary lifestyle, will result in a gradual rise in blood insulin levels. As the body struggles to compensate, the pancreas increases insulin production to meet the demand; at this point, blood sugar levels — while high — can still be controlled. Eventually, the burden placed on the pancreas can become too great, leading to the development of abnormal pancreatic beta-cells and the consequent loss of insulin production.

Once this balance is tipped, insulin production rapidly falls, blood sugar levels soar, and chronic hyperglycemia gives way to full adult-onset diabetes. Unfortunately, most diagnoses and treatments occur far too late in the game. Medical intervention usually occurs only after the beta-cells have sustained damage, often to the point of becoming totally dysfunctional.

Lifestyle and Nutrition are Key

A recent review article, published by the prestigious Mayo Clinic, confirms that the traditional treatment of adult-onset diabetes has focused primarily on normalizing blood sugar levels[65] rather than tackling the causative factors. Dr. Ray Strand, a practicing physician and a strong advocate of nutritional intervention, argues that many pharmaceutical remedies used to control Type II diabetes can actually *increase* blood insulin levels. This, in turn, increases the risk of cardiovascular disease in the diabetic patient. Says Strand,[66] "It really comes down to a common thread and that is we're treating the wrong thing ... focusing on treating blood sugar levels instead of insulin resistance, which is really the underlying problem."

Controlling insulin resistance — not the high blood sugar levels caused by it — is the key to disease management. However, tackling the causative factors for insulin resistance involves changes to both diet and lifestyle and stresses the need for a more natural and holistic model of disease management.

Nutritional Intervention

What most people don't realize is that a proper balance of micronutrients, the vitamins, minerals, trace elements and plant-based nutrients required for proper cellular function, is a critical part of reducing insulin resistance.

Magnesium deficiency is one of the most under-diagnosed electrolyte deficiencies in modern medicine. In fact, 90 percent of Type II diabetics are deficient in this inexpensive mineral. Since 1976, we have known that magnesium deficiency correlates to the onset of Type II diabetes, yet few physicians prescribe magnesium to their diabetic patients. Daily supplementation in the range of 400 milligrams significantly improves insulin sensitivity.

Individuals predisposed to adult-onset diabetes may also be deficient in several other important micronutrients, including chromium, vanadium, zinc and a host of important antioxidants. As well, they frequently exhibit a deficiency in dietary protein and a general imbalance in their protein-to-carbohydrate ratio. This is likely due to dietary patterns that favor excessive intake of dietary fats and high-glycemic foods that break down quickly into simple sugars, causing a rapid spike in blood sugar levels.

Other nutritional factors effective in mitigating symptoms of insulin resistance and adult-onset diabetes include vitamin E, vitamin C, vitamin K, beta-carotene, alpha-lipoic acid, flaxseed oil, vitamin B_3, vitamin B_6, vitamin B_{12}, biotin, manganese, copper, vanadium and zinc. Chromium is a particularly potent insulin sensitizer and a key component in the body's ability to regulate blood sugars. Interestingly, 90 percent of the U.S. population does not consume even the *minimum* recommended daily dose of this important mineral.

Loss of weight, through exercise and diet, correlates with a return to normal levels of insulin resistance. In fact, weight loss is the single most effective approach to the treatment of insulin resistance and reduction in the risk of developing Type II diabetes.

Prevention of the disease is first and foremost. We now know that much of the initial damage from high blood sugar levels occurs through the oxidation of fats to form toxic lipid peroxides. Numerous recent studies show that vitamin E, a fat-soluble antioxidant, provides significant protection against this damage. Clinical trials show that supplementation with vitamin E, alone, causes a marked improvement of insulin action and a reduction in blood sugar levels and oxidative stress.

Reduction of blood sugars and prevention of lipid peroxidation provide added protection against the onset of heart disease, common in the diabetic patient. Fats and sugars are powerful free radical protagonists, so it is important to reduce these in the diet and in the body. The key to prevention of Type II diabetes is a combination of factors, including a low-glycemic diet fortified with essential fatty acids, nutritional supplementation targeted to enhance insulin sensitivity, enhanced antioxidant protection and regular aerobic exercise. It is a sensible strategy, which works wonders as it sheds pounds.

Osteoporosis — Are You at Risk?

Not long ago, conventional medical wisdom held that osteoporosis was an age-related disease — an irreversible process caused by the sudden reduction of estrogen in postmenopausal women and consequent loss of calcium from the bone.

Times have changed. Today, we know that osteoporosis is a chronic degenerative disease that is pediatric in origin and one that will strike without consideration of gender. It is also a disease largely of our own making; we have brought it about through poor diet, a lack of regular exercise and exposure to pharmaceutical drugs used in the treatment of other disease processes.[73]

Osteoporosis occurs when resorption of calcium from our bones into the blood proceeds too quickly or deposition of calcium occurs too slowly. Quietly, but incessantly, this silent thief robs us of bone mass, gradually leaching calcium and other minerals from the bone matrix, until a fracture suddenly heralds its presence.[74]

Preventable but *not* curable, osteoporosis strikes with crippling force, frequently rendering its victims incapable of even the simplest of tasks. Of those patients who suffer an osteoporotic fracture of the hip, 20 to 24 percent will die within a year, and up to 75 percent of survivors will have some level of permanent disability.[75] Like diabetes, osteoporosis is an epidemic of global dimensions.

Conventional Approaches

For many years, we believed that we could conquer osteoporosis with conventional hormone replacement therapy and other pharmaceutical interventions. This mistaken notion has proven costly. Hormone (estrogen) Replacement Therapy (HRT) in postmenopausal women *can* temporarily slow bone loss and decrease the risk of fracture; however, the effect is transient at best. After a few years, calcium loss recurs at normal rates.[76] Estrogen is one of the most potent drugs in the entire pharmacopoeia and the use of estrogen replacement as a prophylactic measure ignores the very real dangers of exposing women to the documented risks of endometrial and breast cancer, heart disease and stroke. [77]

There are a number of other pharmaceutical interventions currently used, including sodium fluoride, raloxifene, calcitonin and the bisphosphonate drugs.[79,79,80]. Few of these designer drugs work particularly well, none will cure osteoporosis and some come with rather nasty side effects.[81] In fact, none of the pharmaceutical treatments for osteoporosis can compare to simple calcium and vitamin D supplementation, which lowers the risk of fracture by up to 70 percent.[82]

Epidemiological Findings

Osteoporosis is currently responsible for 1.5 million fractures each year and carries an economic burden to the U.S. healthcare system of $17 billion annually.[83] In Canada, osteoporosis may be as common in men as it is in women. Initial results of a recently completed five-year study reveal spinal fracture rates in men and women that were virtually identical.[84] In Australia, current direct costs for treating osteoporotic factures now exceed AU$1.9 billion,[85] and the disease now causes 15,000 debilitating hip factures each year. With an aging population similar to Canada and the U.S., the incidence of osteoporotic fractures in Australia and New Zealand is also rising rapidly.

Unfortunately, there is no cure for osteoporosis, and while contemporary medical science continues in its quest for the magic bullet, millions more succumb to the disease. The good news is that, finally, there is a growing awareness in the medical and scientific communities that what we have done in the past has not served us well. We must turn, instead, toward measures that are more natural. *Prevention* — not cure — should be our vision.

Like most other degenerative diseases, osteoporosis is almost entirely preventable. In fact, simple lifestyle choices could have prevented up to 90 percent of current cases of osteoporosis. That's correct — fresh air, exercise and optimal nutrition could have saved millions of people the agony of osteoporosis and billions of dollars for our beleaguered healthcare systems.

The Bare Bones about Bones

While we tend to think of our skeleton as inert, like the brick walls of a house, our bones are in constant dynamic balance with our bodies. At any given moment, in millions of sites within our skeletal structure, small segments of old bone are dissolved and new bone matrix is laid down to replace it — a process known as bone remodelling. Through bone remodelling, we replace the mineral content of our bones every few years.[86] This means that Mother Nature has gifted us the opportunity to create better bones for our bodies. It also means that, if the dynamics of mineral balance go awry, we can rapidly deplete our calcium stores and our bones will become progressively weaker — just like acid rain on cement.

For that reason, proactive programs to maximize bone health are critical to prevention. Most people are aware of the need for lots of calcium; however, many other minerals, and the balance between them, are also important. Magnesium increases calcium retention in the bone. Phosphorus, vitamin D, vitamin K, manganese, boron, zinc and copper also enhance calcium deposition and build strong bones. Vitamin C stimulates formation of the collagen matrix in bone tissue, and Vitamins B_6, B_{12} and folic acid reduce the loss of bone minerals by modulating blood homocysteine levels.

Because bone growth occurs during our youth, the peak bone mass attained early in life becomes the single most important determinant of lifelong skeletal health. After 30 to 35 years of age, bone destruction begins to overtake bone growth, with a net loss of about 0.3 percent per year. For women, this annual loss accelerates up to ten-fold at menopause, continuing for a period of about five to seven years.[87]

It's important to note that osteoporosis is *not* always the result of excessive bone loss. The truth is, an individual who does not reach optimal bone mass during childhood and adolescence may develop osteoporosis *without* the occurrence of accelerated calcium loss. That is why — particularly for young girls — developing the highest bone mass possible during adolescence will provide the best natural means of prevention against osteoporosis later in life.

An individual who does not reach optimal bone mass during childhood and adolescence may develop osteoporosis without the occurrence of accelerated calcium loss. That is why - particularly for young girls - developing the highest bone mass possible during adolescence will provide the best natural means of prevention against osteoporosis later in life.

Am I at Risk?

Unless you have a bone scan, you won't know whether you have osteoporosis until you suffer a fracture. However, here are some things to watch out for. You are a prime candidate for osteoporosis if you have the following risk indicators:

- ✔ female and of Caucasian or Asian descent;
- ✔ in mid-to-late adulthood (peri-menopause) or experienced early menopause;
- ✔ a low body mass index (BMI) or a small frame;
- ✔ a family history of osteoporosis;
- ✔ a smoker or a history of excessive use of alcohol;
- ✔ live a sedentary lifestyle.

What should you do if you think you're at risk for osteoporosis or have noticed a gradual loss of height or posture? Firstly, get a bone scan and, if it reveals low mineral density, ask your doctor what he or she recommends to reduce the resorption of minerals that is the cause of the disease. If the response is to intervene with hormone replacement or a drug therapy program, seek a second opinion — fast. Secondly, start making some serious lifestyle changes.

Key Prevention Strategies

Current research suggests that building strong bones in our youth is the most effective preventive measure we can take; however, much can also be done by those who find themselves in a situation of ostoepenia, or low bone density — a precursor to full-blown osteoporosis.

Proper diet is everything

Right from the get-go, we need to emphasize the importance of a plant-based diet, with whole grains, legumes and sea vegetables providing a natural balance of the required minerals and nutrients. Leafy green vegetables and legumes are a richer and more balanced source of calcium and minerals than milk and dairy products. In fact, recent evidence suggests that a high consumption of dairy products during adulthood may lead to an increase in the prevalence of osteoporosis.

We now know that poor diet and lifestyle choices can destroy bones.[88] High-sugar, high-fat diets create acidity and leach bone calcium, while diets high in dairy products and protein appear to disrupt the calcium/phosphorus balance and accelerate calcium loss. Salt and caffeine also negatively affect calcium status, and excessive alcohol and smoking turn your bones into noodles.

In a nutshell:

- ✔ reduce your intake of refined and processed foods, especially white bread and white flour products;
- ✔ increase your intake of complex carbohydrates, found in fresh fruits and whole grains;
- ✔ increase your consumption of essential fatty acids, found in flaxseed and fish oils;
- ✔ whenever possible, substitute soy or fish for red meat; and,
- ✔ eat more highly colored fruits, particularly the dark berries, filled with antioxidants.

Exercise is essential

Couch potatoes take note: the lack of weight-bearing exercise *markedly* accelerates bone loss. Every doctor is familiar with the rapid wasting of muscle and loss of bone density that comes with prolonged inactivity, such as bed rest. Patients confined to bed for a prolonged period can lose up to 30 percent of their bone mass.

Vigorous weight-bearing exercise stresses bone and muscle tissue, stimulates bone formation, and increases bone density. No bones about it, regular weight-bearing exercise is an absolute *must* to build and maintain peak bone density — and the sooner in life you begin, the better.

Both the U.S. National Academy of Science and Health Canada now recognize calcium supplementation as an effective means of restoring bone mineral status and believe it should form a fundamental part of a lifelong program of prevention and maintenance.

Estrogen alternatives

For those postmenopausal women confused about the recent estrogen replacement controversy, consider talking to a medical professional knowledgeable about the use of natural progesterone. Recent studies have shown that natural progesterone, combined with proper diet and exercise, steadily increases bone density, regardless of age. One study revealed a 29 percent increase in bone mass and density within three years of beginning therapy.[89]

Vitamin D is vital

Vitamin D, obtained through sunlight, diet and supplementation, is vital to calcium absorption. Sunlight stimulates the formation of vitamin D, without which the body cannot absorb calcium. Vitamin D supplementation is particularly important for the elderly, those confined indoors, and those who live in northern climates. A recent U.S. study of hospital in-patients found that vitamin D deficiency was common, despite the fact that many met or exceeded the recommended daily nutritional intake.[90]

Supplementation a must

Currently, adolescent girls throughout America receive less than 60 percent of the Recommended Daily Allowance (RDA) for calcium. In fact, we now recognize poor calcium nutrition as a leading risk factor in osteoporosis. That is why it is important to supplement our diets with calcium, magnesium and vitamin D. Both the U.S. National Academy of Science and Health Canada now recognize calcium supplementation as an effective means of restoring bone mineral status and believe it should form a fundamental part of a lifelong program of prevention and maintenance. Numerous studies show that calcium supplementation at 500 to 1,200 mg/day, with vitamin D at 500 to 800 IU/day, significantly reduces bone loss and decreases the risk of osteoporotic fracture.[91,92,93,94]

Calcium supplementation also increases bone mineral content in children and adolescents.[95,96,97] That's good news, because as little as a five percent increase in adolescent bone density can reduce the risk of adult-onset osteoporosis by a whopping 40 percent.[98] In fact, good calcium nutrition and attainment of high bone density during adolescence leads to improved bone health and reduced osteoporotic risk later in life.[99,100,101]

The correlation between obesity and diabetes is strong and the prognosis is disturbing. Overweight couch potatoes, young and old alike, are showing up in diabetes clinics with increasing frequency.

Supplementing with multiple minerals and vitamins, including calcium, appears to provide even greater protection against bone loss than supplementing with calcium alone.[102] In particular, addition of vitamin D and magnesium complement calcium's bone-building talents.

Several other vitamins and minerals, including vitamins C, B_6, B_{12}, folic acid, vitamin K, copper, manganese and zinc, all support the efficacy of a broad-spectrum approach to the enhancement of bone mineral status.[103,104] Fortunately, all of these nutrients can be found in their proper balance in some of the higher quality nutritional supplements available on the market today.

Obesity — A Worldwide Epidemic

Epidemic is a strong word, particularly when used by the ultra-conservative *Journal of the American Medical Association*; however, that is how several articles in the October 27, 1999 Special Edition describe the prevalence of overweight and obesity in the U.S. According to the journal, excess body fat is among the most pressing medical problems in North America today.

The articles paint a sobering landscape of a nation on the precipice of a healthcare catastrophe. The percentage of adult Americans who are obese has literally exploded in the last two decades. From 1991 to 1998 alone, the prevalence of obesity in the U.S. adult population increased from 12 percent to 18 percent — a 50 percent hike in seven short years. During the same period, the number of overweight children doubled.[105]

Obesity is generally accepted as a Body Mass Index (BMI) greater than the 85th percentile for a given age and gender, or approximately 14 kg (30 lb) of excess weight for the average male adult. By that definition, 22 percent of the U.S. population is now obese.[106]

Using data from the Third National Health and Nutrition Examination Survey (NHANES III), conducted between 1988 and 1994, Must[107] and co-workers concluded that more than half of the U.S. adult population was, at the time, either overweight or obese. Accordingly, the authors called for a concerted national effort to prevent and treat obesity rather than its consequences.

Chubby Chickens

Is a little "happy fat" really all that bad? According to nutrition and fitness expert, Dr. Michael Colgan, the answer is an unequivocal *yes*. In his book, *The New Nutrition: Medicine for the Millennium*, [108] Colgan cites the Framingham study, a 26-year, gold-standard study conducted throughout the United States. The results provide indisputable proof that weight gain in adulthood causes a marked increase in the risk of all types of cardiovascular disease.[109] According to the findings, a marginal increase in body mass causes a significant elevation in blood pressure; conversely, reducing excess weight provides an immediate drop, correlating with the amount of weight lost.[110]

Excess weight is associated with an increase in cardiovascular disease, Type II diabetes, hypertension, stroke, cancer and osteoarthritis.[111] In a major study conducted by the American

Cancer Society, men who were 40 percent overweight showed higher levels of prostate, colon and rectal cancer. Women who were obese revealed increased breast, ovarian, uterine, gall bladder, cervical and endometrial cancer.[112]

Using data compiled from the massive NHANES III survey, researchers found that the prevalence of obesity among six- to seventeen-year-olds more than doubled between 1988 and 1991. The study, reported in the *Archives of Pediatrics and Adolescent Medicine*, found that 22 percent of U.S. children and adolescents fit the criteria for overweight — up significantly from a survey conducted three years prior.[113]

So, what is going on here? Why are so many people, young and old alike, becoming "chubby chickens"?

The Couch Potato Kid

The fact is, many of today's kids are chronic couch potatoes. Some 20 to 40 percent of American and Canadian youngsters are physically unfit and only one-third of high school students are active on a regular basis. A 1988 Neilson Report reveals that, by the end of the 1980s, children were watching 25-1/2 hours of television each week. With the explosion in the use of video games and the Internet over the last decade, the number of hours spent in sedentary activity has almost certainly increased.

A recent World Health Organization (WHO) report confirms the trend, finding that one-quarter of adolescent Canadian girls are active only one-half hour or less per week outside of school.[114] Kids with "couch potato" lifestyles are packing on the pounds, and overweight kids grow up to be overweight adults. It's as simple as that.

> ***If you have no time for exercise, you'd better reserve a lot of time for disease.***
> **- Dr. Michael Colgan**

In a recent study on diabetes in children, the American Diabetes Association reported that 85 percent of young people contracting the disease are obese. Furthermore, where less than four percent of childhood diabetes in 1990 was Type II (normally associated with middle age), the frequency now averages 20 percent, and varies from eight percent to 45 percent, depending on the age group. The correlation between obesity and diabetes is strong and the prognosis is disturbing. Overweight couch potatoes, young and old alike, are showing up in diabetes clinics with increasing frequency.

That is why, when it comes to your health, even a slight overweight problem is serious. A study conducted by the Harvard School of Public Health (1993)[115] tracked mortality rates of almost 20,000 male Harvard graduates, excluding those who smoked. The results showed that the less an individual weighed throughout life, compared to others of the same body size, the lower was the risk of death at any given age. Men who were 20 percent below average weight for their size had the best chance of living a long and healthy life.

Love Handles and Lifestyles

With a death toll that comes second only to smoking, obesity as a contributing factor to death now claims nearly 300,000 lives each year in the U.S.[116] The alarming increase in obesity is not limited to North America. In Japan, the prevalence of obesity in men has doubled since 1982. The most dramatic increase, however, is in the United Kingdom, where the incidence has *more* than doubled since 1980.[117]

The trend is strong, accelerating and not limited to the developed world. Obesity is also increasing rapidly in Third World nations, as they adopt the lifestyles and dietary patterns common to the West. There is no doubt about it — obesity is "wide spread."

Can the problem be resolved?

Absolutely! Obesity is, for the most part, a simple problem of biochemical economics. Just like a bank account, deposit more money than you take out and, over time, your savings will grow. Similarly, if your body takes in more energy than it puts out, over time *you* will grow. Most people can reduce their "fat-bank" accounts through basic dietary and lifestyle change. A low-glycemic and low-fat diet, combined with a daily program of aerobic and weight-bearing exercise, will do wonders to maintain the proper balance in your metabolic bank account — and your heart will dearly thank you for it.

Just one last thing: keep in mind that obesity and hyperlipidemia (high blood fats) lie at the root of many other degenerative diseases linked to oxidative stress. Those pesky little free radicals just love to make mayhem in fat — and when you're obese it's a free radical's finest fantasy!

1 Centers for Disease Control and Prevention (Press Release). "Sudden cardiac deaths are increasing in young people, especially among young women." Paper presented at the *41st Annual Conference on Cardiovascular Disease Epidemiology and Prevention,* San Antonio TX, March 1, 2001.

2 Lucas A. "Programming by Early Nutrition: An Experimental Approach." *J Nutr* 1998, **128(2)**: 401S-406S.

3 Barker DJ. "Fetal nutrition and cardiovascular disease in later life." *Br Med Bull* 1997, **53(1)**: 96-108.

4 Berenson GS, Srinivasan SR, Bao W et al. "Association between multiple cardiovascular risk factors and atherosclerosis in children and young adults. The Bogalusa Heart Study." *N Engl J Med* 1998, **338(23)**: 1650-1656.

5 Wood T. "The prevention of chronic degenerative disease is a lifelong challenge." *Lifelong Nutrition Magazine*, Nov 1999.

6 Colgan M. *The New Nutrition: Medicine for the Millennium.* Apple Publishing, Vancouver BC, 1995, pp 48-51.

7 Boushey CJ, Beresford SA, Omenn GS et al. "A quantitative assessment of plasma homocysteine as a risk factor for vascular disease. Probable benefits of increasing folic acid intakes." *JAMA* 1995, **274(13)**: 1049-1057.

8 Ross R, and Glomset JA. "The Pathogenesis of atherosclerosis." *New Engl J Med* 1976, **295(7)**: 369-377.

9 Strand R. *Bionutrition: Winning the War Within.* Comprehensive Wellness Publishing, Rapid City SD, 1998, pp 18-26.

10 Steinberg D, Parthasarathy S, Carew TE et al. "Beyond Cholesterol. Modifications of low-density lipoprotein that increases its atherogenicity." *New Engl J Med* 1989, **320(14)**: 915-924.

11 Strand R. *Bionutrition: Winning the War Within.* Comprehensive Wellness Publishing, Rapid City SD, 1998, pp 78-83.

12 Diaz MN, Frei B, Vita JA et al. "Antioxidants and atherosclerotic heart disease." *New Engl J Med* 1997, **337(6)**: 408-416.

13 Stampfer MJ, Malinow MR, Willett WC et al. "A prospective study of plasma homocyst(e)ine and risk of myocardial infarction in US physicians." *JAMA* 1992, **268(7)**: 877-881.

14 Glueck CJ, Shaw P, Lang JE et al. "Evidence that homocysteine is an independent risk factor for atherosclerosis in hyperlipidemic patients." *Am J Cardiol* 1995, **75(2)**: 132-136.

15 Loehrer F, Angst CP, Haefeli WE et al. "Low whole-blood S-adenosylmethionine and correlation between 5-methyltetrahydrofolate and homocysteine in coronary artery disease." *Arterioscler Thromb Vasc Biol* 1996, **16(6)**: 227-233.

16 Franken DG, Boers GH, Blom HJ et al. "Treatment of mild hyperhomocysteinemia in vascular disease patients." *Arterioscler Thromb* 1994, **14(3)**: 465-470.

17 Firshein R. *The Nutraceutical Revolution*. Riverhead Books, New York NY, 1998, pp 144-160.

18 Selhub J, Jacques PF, Bostom AG et al. "Association between plasma homocysteine concentrations and extracranial carotid-artery stenosis." *New Engl J Med* 1995, **332(5)**: 286-291.

19 McCully KS. "Vascular pathology of homocysteinemia: Implications for the pathogenesis of arteriosclerosis." *Am J Pathol* 1996, **56**: 111-128.

20 Arnesen E, Refsum H, Bonaa KH et al. "Serum total homocysteine and coronary artery disease." *Intl J Epidemiol* 1995, **24(4)**: 704-709.

21 Boushey CJ, Beresford SA, Omenn GS et al. "A quantitative assessment of plasma homocysteine as a risk factor for vascular disease. Probable benefits of increasing folic acid intakes." *JAMA* 1995, **274(13)**: 1049-1057.

22 Munshi MN, Stone A, Fink L et al. "Hyperhomocysteinemia following a methionine load in patients with non-insulin-dependent diabetes mellitus and macrovascular disease." *Metabolism* 1996, **45(1)**: 133-135.

23 Firshein R. *The Nutraceutical Revolution*. Riverhead Books, New York NY, 1998, pp 144-160.

24 Ibid

25 Bottiglieri T. "Folate, vitamin B_{12} and neuropsychiatric disorders." *Nutr Rev* 1996, **54(12)**: 382-390.

26 Firshein R. *The Nutraceutical Revolution*. Riverside Books, New York NY, 1998, pp 144-160.

27 Esterbauer H, Dieber-Rotheneder M, Striegl G et al. "Role of vitamin E in preventing the oxidation of low-density lipoprotein." *Am J Clin Nutr* 1991, **53(1 Suppl)**: 314S-321S.

28 Jialal I, Norkus EP, Cristol L et al. "beta-Carotene inhibits the oxidative modification of low-density lipoprotein." *Biochim Biophys Acta*. 1991, **1086(1)**: 134-138.

29 Stocker R, Bowry VW and Frei B. "Ubiquinol-10 protects human low density lipoprotein more efficiently against lipid peroxidation than does alpha-tocopherol." *Proc Natl Acad Sci* 1991, 88(5): 1646-1650.

30 Passwater RA. *All About Antioxidants*. Avery Publishing, New York NY, 1998, pp 31-42.

31 Mestel R. "Study Ties Most Cancer to Lifestyles, Not Genetics." *Los Angeles Times*, Los Angeles, CA, July 13, 2000.

32 Lichtenstein P, Holm NV, Verkasalo PK, et al. "Environmental and heritable factors in the causation of cancer-analyses of cohorts of twins from Sweden, Denmark, and Finland." *N Engl J Med* 2000, **343(2)**: 78-85.

33 Potter JD, Chavez A, Chen J et al. "Food, Nutrition and the Prevention of Cancer: A Global Perspective." *American Institute for Cancer Research and the World Cancer Research Fund*, report published Sept, 1997.

34 Strand R. *Bionutrition: Winning the War Within*. Comprehensive Wellness Publishing, Rapid City SD, 1998.

35 Dietz WH. "Childhood Weight Affects Adult Morbidity and Mortality." *J Nutr* 1998, **128(2)**: 411S-414S.

36 Must A and Lipman RD. "Childhood energy intake and cancer mortality in adulthood." *Nutr Rev* 1999, **57(1)**: 21-24.

37 Food Insight. "Experts Agree on Key Advice to Reduce Cancer Risk." *Food Insight*. Nov/Dec, 1997.

38 Davis DL, Dinse GE and Hoel DG. "Decreasing cardiovascular disease and increasing cancer among whites in the United States from 1973 through 1987. Good news and bad news." *JAMA* 1994, **271(6)**: 431-437.

39 Cooper KH. *Advanced Nutritional Therapies*. Thomas Nelson Inc, Vancouver BC, 1996, pp 37-56.

40 Kummet T and Meyskins F. "Vitamin A: a potential inhibitor of human cancer." *Semin Oncol* 1983, **10(3)**: 281-289.

41 Menkes MS, Comstock GW, Vuilleumier JP et al. "Serum beta-carotene, vitamins A and E, selenium, and the risk of lung cancer." *N Engl J Med* 1986, **315(20)**: 1250-1254.

42 Colditz GA, Branch LG, Lipnick RJ et al. "Increased green and yellow vegetable intake and lowered cancer deaths in an elderly population." *Am J Clin Nutr* 1985, **41(1)**: 32-36.

43 Zhang S, Hunter DJ, Forman MR et al. "Dietary carotenoids and vitamins A, C and E and risk of breast cancer." *J Natl Cancer* Inst 1999, **91(6)**: 547-556.

44 Ames BN. "Dietary carcinogens and anticarcinogens. Oxygen radicals and degenerative diseases." *Science* 1983, **221(4617)**: 1256-1264.

45 Duthie SJ, Ma A, Ross MA et al. "Antioxidant supplementation decreases oxidative DNA damage in human lymphocytes." *Cancer Res* 1996, **56(6)**: 1291-1295.

46 Bjelke E. "Epidemiologic studies of cancer of the stomach, colon, and rectum; with special emphasis on the role of diet." *Scan J Gastroenterol Suppl* 1974, **31**: 1-235.

47 Block G. "Vitamin C and cancer prevention: the epidemiologic evidence." *Am J Clin Nutr* 1991, **53(1 Suppl)**: 270-282.

48 Smigel K. "Vitamin E reduces prostate cancer rates in Finnish trial: U.S. considers follow-up." *J Natl Cancer Inst* 1998, **90(6)**: 416-417.

49 Pastori M, Pfander H, Boscoboinik D et al. "Lycopene in association with alpha-tocopherol inhibits at physiological concentrations proliferation of prostate carcinoma cells." *Biochem Biophys Res Commun* 1998, **250(3)**: 582-585.

50 Knekt, P, Aromaa A, Maatela J et al. "Serum vitamin E and risk of cancer among Finnish men during a 10-year follow-up." *Am J Epidemiol* 1988, **127(1)**: 28-41.

51 Ames BN. "Dietary carcinogens and anticarcinogens. Oxygen radicals and degenerative diseases." *Science* 1983, **221(4617)**: 1256-1264.

52 Clark LC, Dalkin B, Drongrad A et al. "Decreased incidence of prostate cancer with selenium supplementation: results of a double-blind cancer prevention trial." *Br J Urol* 1998, **81(5)**: 730-734.

53 Strand R. *Bionutrition: Winning the War Within*. Comprehensive Wellness Publishing, Rapid City SD, 1998, pp 43-57.

54 Proceedings of the International Symposia. *Biomedical and Clinical Aspects of Coenzyme Q*. Vol 1-4, New York, NY, 1977-1984.

55 Lockwood K, Moesgaard S, Yamamoto T et al. "Progress on therapy of breast cancer with vitamin Q 10 and the regression of metastases." *Biochem Biophys Res Commun* 1995, **212(1)**: 172-177.

56 Warholm M, Guthenberg C, Mannervik B et al. "Purification of a new glutathione S-transferase (transferase mu) from human liver having high activity with benzo(alpha) pyrene-4,5-oxide." *Biochem Biophys Res Comm* 1981, **98(2)**: 512-519.

57 Steenvoorden DP and van Henegouwen GM. "The use of endogenous antioxidants to improve photoprotection." *J Photochem Photobiol* 1997, **41(1-2)**: 1-10.

58 American Heart Association. Syndrome X. *www.americanheart.org/* Nov, 2000.

59 Widen E et al. "Association of a Polymorphism in the (beta) - Adrenergic -Receptor Gene with Features of the Insulin Resistance Syndrome in Finns." *N Eng J Med* 1995, **333(6)**: 348 - 51.

60 Slagle P. "What is Syndrome X?" *http://www.rehabmall.com/healthyliving/slagle/vol15.htm*, Nov, 2000.

61 Strand R. "Syndrome X." *Notes from the Physician's plenary* USANA Health Sciences International Convention, Salt Lake City, July 2000.

62 Slagle P. "What is Syndrome X"? *http://www.rehabmall.com/healthyliving/slagle/vol15.htm*, Nov, 2000.

63 "Syndrome X Solution: Exercise and Diet." AP article, *http://www.kcbsz.com/sh/health/dietandnutrition/* Nov, 2000.

64 Greiger L. "Syndrome X." Heart Information Network *http://www.heartinfo.com/nutrition/syndx*, Jan, 2001.

65 Editorial Article, "Improving the Adverse Cardiovascular Prognosis for Type II Diabetes." *Mayo Clinic Proc* 1999, **74 (2)**: 171-180.

66 Strand, R. "Important Information on Type II Diabetes by Dr. Ray Strand." e-mail communications, Nov, 2000.

67 Murray MT. *The Healing Power of Herbs (2nd edition)*, Prima Health, Rocklin CA, 1995, pp 357-361.

68 Baskaran K et al. "Antidiabetic effect of a leaf extract from *Gymnema sylvestre* in non-insulin dependent diabetes mellitus patients." *J Ethnopharmacol* 1990, **30**: 281-294.

69 Shanmugasundaram ERB et al "Use of *Gymnema sylvestre* extract in the control of blood glucose in insulin-dependent diabetes mellitus." *J Ethnopharmacol* 1990, **30**: 295-305.

70 Murray MT and Pizzorno J. *Encyclopedia of Natural Medicine (2nd editon)*. Prima Publishing, Roseville CA, 1998, p 425.

71 Welihinda J et al. "Effects of *Momordica charantia* on the glucose tolerance factor in maturity-onset diabetes." *J Ethnopharmacol* **17**: 277 - 282, 1986.

72 Murray MT. *The Healing Power of Herbs, 2nd edition*, Prima Health, Rocklin CA, 1995, pp 357-361

73 Sellman, S. "Osteoporosis - the Bones of Contention." *Nexus Magazine* **5(6)**: Nov 1998.
74 Merck Manual of Diagnosis and Therapy, "Osteoporosis" *www.merck.com/*, 2002.
75 Society of Obstetricians and Gynaecologists of Canada, "What is Osteoporosis?" *www.sogc.org/*, 2002.
76 Lee, JD et al. "The Truth about Osteoporosis." *www.johnleemd.com/*, 2002.
77 Maté G. Opinion Editorial. Globe and Mail, Toronto, July 16, 2002.
78 Merck Manual of Diagnosis and Therapy, "Osteoporosis" *www.merck.com/*, 2002.
79 Ullom-Minnich P. "Prevention of osteoporosis and fractures." *Am Fam Phys* 1999, **60:** 194-202.
80 Ibid
81 Ettinger B et al. "Multiple Outcomes of Raloxifene Evaluation." *JAMA* 1999, 282: 637-645.
82 Cumming RG and Nevitt MC. "Calcium for the prevention of osteoporitic fractures in postmenopausal women." *J Bone Miner Res* 1997, **12:** 1321-1329.
83 National Osteoporosis Foundation, "Disease Statistics: Fast Facts." *www.nof.org/*, 2002
84 Adashi R. "The Canadian Multi-centre Osteoporosis Study." In: Canadian Press article, Nov, 2001.
85 Sambrook P. "Health Professionals Information: Osteoporosis Australia Medical and Scientific Committee." *www.osteoporosis.org.au/*, 2002.
86 Lee JD et al. "The Truth about Osteoporosis." *www.johnleemd.com/*, 2002.
87 Merck Manual of Diagnosis and Therapy, "Osteoporosis" *www.merck.com/*, 2002.
88 Colgan M. *The New Nutrition: Medicine for the Millennium.* Apple Publishing, Vancouver BC, 1995.
89 Lee JD et al. "The Truth about Osteoporosis." *www.johnleemd.com/*, 2002.
90 Thomas MK et al. "Hypovitaminosis D in medical inpatients." *New Engl J Med* 1998, **338(12)**: 777-783.
91 Dawson-Hughes B, Dallal GE, Krall EA et al. "A controlled trial of the effect of calcium supplementation on bone density in postmenopausal women." *N Engl J Med* 1990, **323(13):** 878-83.
92 Johnston CC, Miller JZ, Slemenda CW et al. "Calcium supplementation and increases in bone mineral density in children." *N Engl J Med* 1992, **327(2)**: 82-7.
93 Chapuy MC, Arlot ME, Dubouef F et al. "Vitamin D3 and calcium to prevent hip fractures in elderly women." *N Engl J Med* 1992, **327(23)**: 1637-42.
94 Dawson-Hughs B, Harris SS, Krall EA et al. "Rates of bone loss in postmenopausal women randomly assigned to one of two dosages of vitamin D." *Am J Clin Nutr* 1995, **61(5)**: 1140-5.
95 Lloyd T, Andon MB, Rollings N et al. "Calcium supplementation and bone mineral density in adolescent girls." *JAMA* 1993, **270(7)**: 841-4.
96 Nowson CA, Green RM, Hopper JL et al. "A co-twin study of the effect of calcium supplementation on bone density during adolescence." *Osteoporosis Intl* 1997, 7(**3**): 219-25.
97 Wood T. and McKinnon T. "Calcium-Magnesium-Vitamin D Supplementation Improves Bone Mineralization in Preadolescent Girls." *Clinical Research Bulletin.* USANA Health Sciences, 2001.
98 Bacharach, B. Stanford University.
99 Sandler RB, Slemenda CW, LaPorte RE et al. "Postmenopausal done density and milk consumption in childhood and adolescence." *Am J Clin Nutr* 1985, **42(2)**: 270-4.
100 Halioua L and Anderson JJ. "Lifetime calcium intake and physical activity habits: independent and combined effects on the radial bone of healthy premenopausal Caucasian women." *Am J Clin Nutr* 1989, **49(3)**: 534-41.
101 Nieves JW, Golden AL, Siris E et al. "Teenage and current calcium intake are related to bone mineral density of the hip and forearm in women aged 30-39 years." *Am J Epidemiol* 1995, **141(4)**: 342-51.
102 Strause L et al. "Spinal bone loss in postmenopausal women supplemented with calcium and trace minerals." *J Nutr* 1994, **124:** 1060-4.
103 Saltman PD and Strauss LG. "The role of trace minerals in osteoporosis." *J Am Coll Nutr* 1993, **12(4)**: 389-9.
104 Abraham GE and Grewal H. "A total dietary program emphasizing magnesium instead of calcium: Effect on the mineral density of calcaneous bone in postmenopausal women on hormonal therapy." *J Reprod Med* 1990, **35(5)**: 503-7.
105 Wood T. "Nutrition in the News: JAMA special issue on weight management." *www.usana.com/research/magazine/00jan/2xshtml*, March, 2001.
106 Mokdad AH, Serdula MK, Dietz WH et al. "The Spread of the obesity epidemic in the United States, 1991-1998." *JAMA* 1999, **282(16)**: 1519-1522.
107 Must A, Spadano J, Coakley EH et al. "The disease burden associated with overweight and obesity." *JAMA* 1999, **282(16)**: 1523-1529.
108 Colgan M. *The New Nutrition: Medicine for the Millennium.* Apple Publishing, Vancouver, BC, 1995.
109 Hubert HB, Feinleib M, McNamara PM et al. "Obesity as an independent risk factor for cardiovascular disease: a 26-year follow-up of participants in the Framingham Heart Study." *Circulation* 1983, **67**(5): 968-977.
110 Garrison RS et al. "The Framingham Study." *Cardiovascular Disease Newsletter* March, 1985.
111 Must A, Spadano J, Coakley EH et al. "The disease burden associated with overweight and obesity." *JAMA* 1999, **282(16)**: 1523-1529.
112 American Cancer Society. "Cancer Prevention Study: 1959 to 1979." *American Cancer Society*, New York NY, 1980.
113 International Food Information Council. "Growing Kids: A Weighty Issue." *Food Insight*. http://ificinfo.health.org. Nov/Dec, 1995.
114 National Institute of Nutrition. "Healthy Eating Healthy Living for Children." *Rapport* (newsletter), Nov, 1995.
115 Lee IM, Manson JE, Hennekens CH et al. "Body weight and mortality. A 27-year follow-up of middle-aged men." *JAMA* 1993, **270(23)**: 2823-2828.
116 Allison DB, Fontaine KR, Manson JE et al. "Annual deaths attributable to obesity in the United States." *JAMA* 1999, **282(16)**: 1530-1538.
117 Brown DB. "About Obesity." *A summary report of the International Obesity Task Force (IOTF).* www.obesity.chair.ulaval,ca/IDTF.htmLAVALuniversity, March, 2001.

Section II

Criteria for Advanced Supplementation

This section provides the reader with an in-depth look at:

- **the need for supplementation**
- **the concept of advanced nutrition**
- **choosing a quality nutritional supplement**
- **fourteen critical quality-selection criteria**

The need for nutritional supplementation is presented and the concept of optimal nutrition — beyond the RDA — is explored. Fourteen quality-selection criteria, developed for the comparison of nutritional products, and the scientific evidence supporting each are discussed in detail.

Optimal nutrition is the Medicine of the Future.

— Dr. Linus Pauling (1901-1994)
Nobel Laureate in Chemistry and Peace

CHAPTER FOUR

NUTRITIONAL OPTIMIZERS

It Pays to Take Your Vitamins

After 20 years, the American Medical Association (AMA) has completely reversed its anti-vitamin stance and now encourages all adults to supplement daily with a multiple vitamin.

A landmark review of 38 years of scientific evidence by Harvard researchers, Dr. Robert Fletcher and Dr. Kathleen Fairfield, convinced the conservative *Journal of the American Medical Association (JAMA)* to rewrite its policy guidelines regarding the use of vitamin supplements.

In two reports, published in the June 19, 2002 edition of *JAMA*, the authors conclude that the current North American diet, while sufficient to prevent vitamin deficiency diseases (such as scurvy and pellagra), is inadequate to support the need for optimal health. [1,2]

> *Insufficient vitamin intake is apparently a cause of chronic diseases. Recent evidence has shown that sub-optimal levels of vitamins (below standard), even well above those causing deficiency syndromes, are risk factors for chronic diseases such as cardiovascular disease, cancer and osteoporosis. A large portion of the general population is apparently at increased risk for this reason.*
>
> — Dr. Robert Fletcher and Dr. Kathleen Fairfield

In the study, the authors examine several nutrients, including vitamins A, B_6, B_{12}, C, D, E, K, folic acid and several of the carotenoids (alpha- and beta-carotene, cryptoxanthin, zeaxanthin, lycopene and lutein). Among their conclusions, they note:

- ✔ folic acid, vitamin B_6 and B_{12} are required for proper homocysteine metabolism, and low levels of the vitamins are associated with increased risk of heart disease;
- ✔ inadequate folic acid status increases the risk of neural tube defects and some cancers;
- ✔ vitamin E and lycopene appear to decrease the risk of prostate cancer;
- ✔ vitamin D is associated with a decreased risk of osteoporosis and fracture, when taken with calcium;
- ✔ inadequate vitamin B_{12} is associated with anemia and neurological disorders;
- ✔ low levels of the carotenoids appear to increase the risk of breast, prostate and lung cancer;
- ✔ inadequate vitamin C is associated with increased cancer risk; and,
- ✔ low vitamin A status is associated with vision disorders and impaired immune functions.

In a striking departure from *JAMA's* anti-vitamin stance of the last twenty years, the authors conclude that, given today's diet, daily supplementation with a multiple vitamin is a prudent preventive measure against chronic disease. The researchers base their guidance on the fact that more than 80 percent of the American population does not consume anywhere near the five-per-day servings of fruits and vegetables required for optimal health.

> *All of us grew up believing that if we ate a reasonable diet, that would take care of our vitamin needs. But, the new evidence, much of it in the last couple of years, is that vitamins also prevent the usual diseases we deal with everyday — heart disease, cancer, osteoporosis and birth defects.*
>
> — Dr. Robert Fletcher

JAMA's last comprehensive review of vitamins, conducted in the 1980s, concluded that people of normal health do not need to take a multivitamin and can meet all their nutritional needs through diet. The sudden "about-face," along with *JAMA's* public declaration that supplementation is now deemed important to your health, underscores the strength of the scientific evidence that now prevails.

The *JAMA* declaration also underscores a growing concern among nutrition experts that the current recommended daily allowances (RDAs) for vitamins and minerals are too low. The RDAs were originally established to prevent acute vitamin deficiency disorders; however, a growing volume of evidence supports the argument that higher levels of many vitamins and minerals are necessary to achieve optimal health.

Epidemiological Evidence

Much of the evidence supporting the need for daily supplementation as a preventive measure comes from large population-based (epidemiological) studies. Among them is a study conducted some years ago by three eminent scientists, Nobel Laureate Dr. Linus Pauling, Dr. Richard Passwater and Dr. Jim Enstrom. They examined mortality rates in elderly Californians, and what they found was remarkable: the death rate for supplement users was significantly lower than for non-users. Male supplement users had a 22 percent lower risk of death and female users a 46 percent lower risk, over a given time period.[3]

Later, Enstrom and co-workers found that supplementation with vitamin C, in excess of 250 mg per day (much above the RDA standard), reduced the risk of male mortality from cardiovascular disease by 42 percent and lowered the risk of death by all causes by 35 percent, providing an estimated six-year increase in life expectancy.[4]

In two large studies of self-supplementation, vitamin E was associated with reduced coronary risk. The studies, conducted among 39,910 male health care professionals and 87,245 female nurses, found that men and women who took vitamin E supplements for more than two years showed a 37 percent and 41 percent reduction, respectively, in the risk of heart disease. [5,6] These results support a recent large-scale study conducted at Laval University, Quebec, which found a 69 percent reduction in ischemic heart disease and a 47 percent reduction in cardiac-related deaths among long-term consumers of nutritional supplements.[7] As well, a study reported in the *Journal of the American Geriatrics Society* found that centenarians had substantially higher levels of antioxidants and lower levels of free radicals in their blood than people 20 to 30 years younger.[8]

Centenarians had substantially higher levels of antioxidants and lower levels of free radicals in their blood than people 20 to 30 years younger.

It is true that epidemiological and observational studies, such as the above, cannot establish cause and effect. This is because the results noted may not be due entirely to nutritional supplementation; there may be other factors at work behind the scenes. The only way to test cause-effect relationships conclusively is through randomized, double-blind, placebo-controlled trials — the "gold standard" for scientific inquiry.

The Clinical 'Disconnect'

Unfortunately, many such trials have yielded disappointing results that are at variance to those reported in observational studies. On the one hand, dozens of observational studies show beneficial associations between eating fruits and vegetables high in antioxidants and reductions in the risks of cardiovascular disease and several cancers; on the other hand, many clinically controlled studies, in which volunteers have taken specific antioxidants, have failed to demonstrate the same level of efficacy in mitigating risk.[9]

For example, despite great promise shown by the phytonutrient, beta-carotene, three out of four recent clinical trials, including a twelve-year study of U.S. physicians, found no significant cardio-protective effect. Only one, which used a cocktail of different antioxidants, including beta-carotene, showed a significant benefit. Likewise, several randomized trials of vitamin E have yielded mixed results. *The Cambridge Heart Antioxidant Study* (CHAOS) did reveal that supplementation with 400-800 IU of alpha-tocopherol reduced the risk of heart attack and death from cardiovascular disease; however, a multi-centre Italian study (GISSI Prevention Trial), conducted on heart attack survivors, suggested that vitamin E had no effect on the rate of heart attack or stroke.

Well-designed, multi-year clinical studies in healthy subjects are essential to evaluate further the preventive merits of nutritional supplementation.

This apparent "disconnect" between the evidence reported in observational studies and that reported in clinical studies has thrown confusion into the debate on the merits of nutritional supplementation.

While puzzling, this apparent incongruity has several possible explanations.

✔ Firstly, in order to isolate the experimental variable, many controlled clinical studies — by design — evaluate the effect of a *single* antioxidant; conversely, the protective effects of antioxidants may be due precisely to their demonstrated *synergies* when working in concert, such as can be found in whole fruits and vegetables or broad-spectrum nutritional supplements.

✔ Secondly, negative clinical results may simply indicate that researchers have been looking at the wrong antioxidant or at dosages insufficient to provide significant benefit.

✔ Thirdly, many of the studies (such as the Italian GISSI study) were conducted on people who had already been gravely ill and were on several other medications, which may have obscured or negated the effect of the nutrient evaluated; in this respect, any clinically significant results would be more curative than preventive in nature.

✔ Fourthly, the limited time frames of many of these trials ignore the potential benefits of *long-term* supplementation; this argues the case for the implementation of longitudinal (multi-year) supplementation studies, specifically designed to assess the benefits and the mitigation of risks.

For these reasons, well-designed, multi-year clinical studies in healthy subjects are essential to evaluate further the preventive merits of nutritional supplementation. Such studies must be encouraged in order to augment the growing body of scientific evidence that supports the rationale for advanced nutritional supplementation — evidence so compelling that it is now recognized by the American Medical Association and a legion of scientific investigators.

A Confusing Landscape

The world of nutritional supplements is a confusing landscape for most people. Arcane terminologies, metric measures and comparisons of individual nutrient formulations leave most people scratching their heads in bewilderment. How does a milligram compare to a microgram? What is an International Unit? Why do some products use mineral salts, while others use chelated minerals? What is a chelated mineral anyhow? How can a consumer make an *informed* choice?

The next time you are in a pharmacy or health-food store, stop and watch how shoppers make their purchase decisions. Often, they will pick up a product, glance at the label and then pick up another to compare. Next, they may go to the individual nutrient supplements and investigate this avenue of choice. Often they end up simply walking away. Confused? You bet.

People often approach nutritional supplementation in a piecemeal fashion. Some take vitamin E to promote cardiovascular health. Others use vitamin C or zinc to support healthy immune function. Many simply skip from one product to another, month after month, chasing the latest buzzword or "magic bullet" that has been flaunted in the media. This approach to choosing a nutritional supplement is just plain wrong. It runs counter to the most basic principles of optimal nutrition — *balance and completeness.*

Symphony and Synergy

The human body is a complex organism that requires a full complement of essential vitamins, minerals and antioxidants for optimal performance. When taken together in balanced amounts, these nutrients provide the bricks and mortar to build a strong foundation for long-term health. Leave any nutrient out or provide it in insufficient quantity and it will weaken the strength of that foundation.

A quality nutritional product should contain a complete range of vitamins, minerals, cofactors and trace elements, as well as a diverse group of potent antioxidants. It must also supply these nutrients in the correct balance and at potencies shown to promote lifelong health. Avoid nutritional fads — insist on *balance, completeness* and *quality*. Your health depends on it.

Are Nutritional Supplements Safe?

Consumers have a right to expect the highest quality and safety from their nutritional products, just as they have come to expect this from their pharmaceutical products. What many people do not know is just how *risky* some of those pharmaceutical products are, even when properly used.

A supplement must supply nutrients in the correct balance and at potencies shown to promote lifelong health. Avoid nutritional fads — insist on balance, completeness and quality. Your health depends on it.

A 1998 study, reported in the *Journal of the American Medical Association*, showed that in one year (1994) over 2.2 million patients experienced serious drug reactions. That same year, an estimated 106,000 patients died from the "appropriate" use of pharmaceuticals.[10] More recently, the new wonder drug Viagra® has been linked to more than 500 deaths and 1,500 heart attacks, strokes and other vascular events.[11] According to Cohen,[12] many of these deaths were reported in men with no major medical problems, and *before* they even had sex.

Death by adverse reaction to pharmaceutical drugs is, in fact, one of the leading causes of mortality in the U.S.[13] Conversely, data on mortality from nutritional supplements, compiled from 1987 to 1994 by the U.S. Poison Control Centers, recorded only *five* deaths. These data clearly validate the sentiment proffered by sports nutritionist, Dr. Michael Colgan, that "Used in any sensible amounts, vitamins and minerals are about as toxic as apple pie."

The problem is, some people assert that the *Recommended Dietary Allowances* (RDAs) are yardsticks for safety that should not be exceeded. This is false. In fact, the RDAs (*Recommended Nutritional Intakes* or RNIs, in Canada) were originally developed to help people avoid acute nutritional deficiencies, such as scurvy, rickets and beriberi, now rarely seen in our modern world. In other words, they established the *minimal*, not the *optimal*, values for nutritional intake.

There are several nutrients, particularly the antioxidants, where the safe level of intake is magnitudes higher than the RDA or the new U.S./Canada *Dietary Reference Intake* (DRI) standard. The safe tolerable level of intake for vitamin E (1,000 mg), for example, is almost 70 times that of its DRI (15 mg). For vitamin C, the safe tolerable level (2,000 mg) is 22 times that of its DRI (90 mg). For a number of vitamins — including thiamin, riboflavin, biotin, pantothenic acid and vitamin B_{12} — there are *no* intake levels that have been found to cause any significant adverse effects. Limits set for these nutrients are simply precautionary.

There are two nutrients commonly found in multivitamin formulations that *do* warrant a note of caution because of their potential for cumulative toxicity. Long-term intakes of high levels of vitamin A and iron have been associated with toxicity implications.

- ✔ Ingestion of too much vitamin A can be toxic, particularly if there are defects in liver function.[14, 15] In pregancy, dosages greater than 10,000 IU of vitamin A have been shown to cause birth defects, particularly during the first seven weeks after conception. Women who may become pregnant should limit their supplemental vitamin A intake to below 5,000 IU or, preferably, supplement with beta-carotene.[16]
- ✔ Iron at high dosages becomes a potent oxidant and free radical generator that can accelerate oxidative damage of cholesterol, with the consequent onset of atherosclerosis. Iron overload also increases the risk of infection, cancer[17] and myocardial infarction (heart attack).[18] Caution is warranted, particularly with chewable children's tablets, if using nutritional supplements containing iron.

The Food and Nutrition Board of the Institute of Medicine (United States) has recently published a list of *Upper Limits* (UL) for a number of common nutrients. The UL of a nutrient is the upper level of intake of that nutrient deemed to be *safe* for use by adults. The table on page 66 shows that these *Upper Limits* are, in most cases, significantly higher than the advanced levels of nutritional supplementation recommended by numerous scientific authorities. In short, with the exception of those few nutrients that demonstrate potential cumulative toxicity, there exists a wide margin of safety. So, go ahead and enjoy your "apple pie."

Choosing a Quality Supplement

Safety and *balance* are two reasons that people should choose a professionally formulated, broad-spectrum nutritional supplement, rather than ordering à la carte. While the chance of accidental overdose is small, some combinations of nutrients can inhibit or heighten the actions of others. Too much zinc, for example, taken as a stand-alone supplement, can upset the metabolism of other minerals in the body. High levels of ascorbic acid (vitamin C) and citric acid can dramatically increase the uptake of iron, a mineral well known for its cumulative toxicity. Taking a high-dose iron supplement in combination with high levels of vitamin C could pose a significant health risk for the unsuspecting consumer.

To be frank about it, the average consumer has limited ability to select the individual nutrients in their most bioavailable forms and dispense them in appropriate and balanced amounts. It is far better to purchase a professionally designed broad-spectrum nutritional supplement in which the questions of completeness, potency, balance and synergy have been factored into the formulation.

Besides, trying to swallow a bucket of pills three times a day is enough to cause anyone to falter on their good intentions!

Are All Supplements Created Equal?

Another legitimate concern for the consumer is the question of safety in the manufacturing process. Purity is paramount. Consumer assurance that a particular product has surpassed the highest standards for quality, purity and guaranteed potency can only be met through compliance with U.S. and Canadian *Good Manufacturing Practices* (GMPs) for pharmaceuticals. These stringent criteria, used as a quality benchmark by the pharmaceutical industry, ensure the highest level of quality control and purity, right from the raw material to the finished product.

The United States Regulatory Landscape

In the United States, the 1994 *Dietary Supplement Health and Education Act* (DSHEA) places dietary supplements in a special category under the general umbrella of *foods*. Consequently, compliance with pharmaceutical (USP) GMPs and pre-market approval are not required in their manufacture. In addition, under the Act, the *manufacturer* is responsible for determining that the supplements it manufactures or distributes are safe and that any representations or claims made about the products are substantiated. Hence, manufacturers *do not* require pre-market approval from the U.S. Food and Drug Administration (FDA) to sell their products.

Somewhere between 20 to 40 percent of U.S. dietary supplement products fail to meet analyses for label claim. With quality control like that, people should be asking if what is on the label is really in the bottle.

Currently, there are no FDA regulations that establish minimum standards of practice for the manufacturing of dietary supplements. While the authority intends to issue regulations on good manufacturing practices (focusing on identity, purity, strength, quality and composition), current reference standards are entirely *voluntary*. At present, the manufacturer is solely responsible for establishing its own manufacturing practices and quality control measures. What's more, the burden of proof for unsafe or adulterated products and false or misleading labelling lies solely with the FDA, rather than with the manufacturer. It's a regulatory loophole that is laughable — and some manufacturers are doing just that!

In its 2001 *Overview of Dietary Supplements,*[19] the FDA admits, "Because it is often difficult to know what information is reliable and what is questionable, consumers may want first to contact the manufacturer about the product they intend to purchase." In other words, *Buyer Beware!*

The issue here is not that the ingredients in a product are necessarily unsafe; the problem is that unhygienic manufacturing processes or lack of stringent quality control standards can allow serious *contamination* or *adulteration* of a product. Dr. John Cardellina, of the U.S.-based Council for Responsible Nutrition, emphasizes that, "Somewhere between 20 to 40 percent of [U.S.] dietary supplement products fail to meet analyses for label claim." With quality control like that, people *should* be asking if what is on the label is *really* in the bottle.

For a number of vitamins — including thiamin, riboflavin, biotin, pantothenic acid and vitamin B_{12} — there are no intake levels that have been found to cause any significant adverse effects. Limits set for these nutrients are simply precautionary.

The FDA concedes that it has encountered products on the U.S. market that are not accurately labelled. It recently discovered several products that contained potentially harmful contaminants. In a press release dated March 7, 2003, the agency cites the following examples of safety violations:

- ✔ One firm recalled its dietary supplements because of contamination with excessive amounts of lead;
- ✔ Another firm recalled its product after it found that the supplement contained only 35 percent of the amount of folic acid claimed on the label;
- ✔ Another firm recalled a niacin product after it received reports of nausea, vomiting, liver damage and heart attack associated with the use of its product (a supply firm mislabelled a bulk ingredient container that subsequently was used by another firm in making a product, which contained almost ten times more niacin than the allowable safe limit).

In the same press release, the U.S. Food and Drug Administration announced it is taking action to help consumers obtain accurately labelled and unadulterated dietary supplements. The agency is proposing a new regulation to require that all manufacturers of nutritional products adopt current good manufacturing practices (CGMPs) in the manufacturing, packing and storage of such products.

According to the press release, the proposed regulation would, for the first time, establish standards to ensure that dietary supplements and dietary ingredients are not adulterated with contaminants or impurities, and are labelled to accurately to reflect the active ingredients and other ingredients in the product.

The Canadian Scene

In Canada, unlike the U.S., nutritional supplements are regulated as drugs. Consequently, all manufacturers of nutritional supplements must apply for a Drug Identity Number (DIN). The application process involves a thorough pre-market product evaluation for compliance with pharmaceutical-quality manufacturing and labelling standards. No nutritional supplement can be sold in Canada without prior regulatory approval, and all such products must prominently display their DIN identity on the label. While this process assures that the product, upon licensing, has met established quality and safety standards, post-market compliance is another matter.

While vitamin and mineral supplements sold in Canada must travel through the DIN approval process, herbal products are currently treated as foods. Standards of manufacturing and quality control of these products are more lenient than the pharmaceutical standards used for vitamins and minerals. Consequently, safety in the cultivation and processing of herbal products and their extracts has become an issue of growing concern.

All Canadian nutritional supplements, including vitamins, minerals and herbal supplements sold in dosage form, will soon fall under the purview of Health Canada's newly created Directorate of Natural Health Products. This agency, at the time of writing (March 2003), is in the final stages of developing a new regulatory structure with the mandate to assure quality, safety and access for a wide variety of natural health products. Approval is now underway for new regulations that — if not compromised during the lengthy (and contentious) endorsement process — will make Canada a leader in the international community within the area of natural health products.

Product Quality Checklist

Here's a quick do-it-yourself ten-point test to help you evaluate whether a particular product is worthy of your consideration. Ask yourself these questions:

✔ Is the product delivered in a single dose? (A once-a-day tablet simply cannot provide the levels of potency needed for optimal nutrition without being too large to swallow.)

✔ Are the potency levels of the ingredients high enough to provide optimal daily nutritional intake *without* compromising safety?

✔ Are the ingredients provided in their most bioavailable form? (Mineral salts are not as well absorbed as chelated minerals or minerals bound to an organic carrier.)

✔ Is the safety profile of each ingredient thoroughly researched and evaluated?

✔ Does the company meet United States and Canadian *pharmaceutical* guidelines — *not* food-grade guidelines — for Good Manufacturing Processes (GMPs)?

✔ Is the product formulated to meet pharmaceutical standards for full disintegration and dissolution?

✔ Is the product potency guaranteed for a specified shelf life?

✔ Is the product independently tested and guaranteed for potency and safety?

✔ Is the product manufactured in-house? (or is it contracted out to the lowest bidder?)

✔ Is the product free of ingredients that may have cumulative toxicities (pre-formed vitamin A and iron)?

If the product meets all of these criteria, you know that you have a nutritional supplement of exceptional quality. If it doesn't, keep looking.

In reality, it is just not feasible for the consumer to consider all these points about a product simply by scanning the label. Many nutritional manufacturers don't make such detailed information easily available — and that's precisely the reason for this comparative guide.

1 Fairfield KM and Fletcher RH. "Vitamins for chronic disease prevention in adults: scientific review." *JAMA* 2002, **287(23)**: 3116-26.
2 Fletcher RH and Fairfield KM. "Vitamins for chronic disease prevention in adults: clinical applications." *JAMA* 2002, **287(23)**: 3117-29.
3 Enstrom JE and Pauling L. "Mortality among health-conscious elderly Californians." *Proc Natl Acad Sci* 1982, **79(19)**: 6023-6027.
4 Enstrom JE, Kanim LE and Klein MA. "Vitamin C intake and mortality among a sample of the United States population." *Epidemiology* 1992, **3(3)**: 194-202.
5 Stampfer MJ, Hennekens CH, Manson JE et al. "Vitamin E consumption and the risk of coronary disease in women." *N Engl J Med* 1993, **328(20)**: 1444-1449.
6 Rimm EB, Stampfer MJ, Ascherio A et al. "Vitamin E consumption and the risk of coronary disease in men." *N Engl J Med* 1993, **328(20)**: 1450-1456.
7 Meyer F, Bairati I and Dagenais GR. "Lower ischemic heart disease incidence and mortality among vitamin supplement users." *Can J Cardiol* 1996, **12(10)**: 930-934.
8 Passwater RA. *All About Antioxidants.* Avery Publishing, New York NY, 1998, pp 51-61.
9 Willett WC. *Eat, Drink and Be Healthy: The Harvard Medical School Guide to Healthy Eating.* Simon & Schuster, New York NY, 2001, pp 160-163.
10 Lazarou J, Pomeranz BH and Corey PN. "Incidence of adverse drug reactions in hospitalized patients: a meta-analysis of prospective studies." *JAMA* 1998, **279(15)**: 1200-1205.
11 Azarbal B. et al."Adverse Cardiovascular Events Associated with the Use of Viagra." *J Am Coll Cardiol* 2000, **35(SupplA)**: 553A-554A.
12 Cohen J. "Medications' Side Effects: Why They Occur And How You Can Prevent Them." *Life Extension Magazine* 2003, **9(3)**: 47-68
13 Moore CB and Moore JL. "Eating Right May not Be Enough." *Lifelong Nutrition* June/July, 2000.
14 Murray MT. *Encyclopedia of Nutritional Supplements.* Prima Publishing, Rocklin CA, 1996, pp 37-38.
15 Hatoff DE, Gertler SL, Miyai K et al. "Hypervitaminosis A unmasked by acute viral hepatitis." *Gastroenterology* 1982, **82(1)**: 124-128.
16 Rothman KJ, Moore LL, Singer MR et al. "Teratogenecity of high vitamin A intake." *N Eng J Med* 1995, **333(21)**: 1369-1373.
17 Gordeuk VR, Bacon BR and Brittenham GM. "Iron overload: causes and consequences." *Annual Rev Nutr* 1987 **7**: 485-508.
18 Salonen JT, Nyyssonen K, Korpela H et al. "High stored iron levels are associated with excess risk of myocardial infarction in eastern Finnish men." *Circulation* 1992, **86(3)**: 803-811.
19 Center for Food Safety and Applied Nutrition. "Over view of Dietary Supplements" U.S Food and Drug Administration, http://www.cfsan.fda.gov/~dms/ds-oview.html#regulate, 2001

The facts of the present won't sit still for a portrait.
They are constantly vibrating, full of clutter and confusion.

— *Macneile Dixon*

CHAPTER FIVE

Advanced Nutrition

Completeness

While it is theoretically possible to obtain all your nutritional needs from the foods you eat, research shows that North Americans don't even come close to meeting their daily nutritional intake of essential nutrients. Data compiled by the U.S. Department of Agriculture reveal that at least 40 percent of Americans routinely consume less than 60 percent of the recommended daily intake for essential nutrients.[1] Other comprehensive studies (NHANES I and II, the Ten State Nutrition Survey and the USDA nationwide food consumption studies) reveal widespread sub-clinical deficiencies for many nutrients. For selected nutrients, over 80 percent of participants in specific age groups consume less than the recommended dietary allowance (RDA).[2,3]

There is a big difference between caloric intake and nutritional value. Most North Americans consume far too many calories, derived from the fats, proteins and carbohydrates (macronutrients) in our foods. However, we fall woefully short in the intake of micronutrients — the vitamins, minerals and trace elements needed in minute amounts. For this reason, it makes sense to turn to a broad-spectrum nutritional supplement in order to enhance the nutritional value of our daily diet. Consuming a high quality supplement that provides all the known vitamins, minerals and antioxidants in balanced amounts is like taking out an insurance policy against possible nutritional insufficiency.

> ***Most North Americans consume far too many calories from the fats, proteins and carbohydrates (macronutrients) in our foods. However, we fall woefully short in the intake of micronutrients — the vitamins, minerals and trace elements needed in minute amounts.***

Published Recommendations

Over the years, scientific research has documented numerous micronutrients required for optimal health. We now know that the body requires approximately 17 vitamins and vitamin-like substances, a diverse group of plant-based antioxidants, at least 14 trace elements and minerals, and several compounds important in glutathione and lipid metabolism. The body cannot manufacture many of these substances; they must be obtained through the diet. Newly discovered plant-derived compounds are added to the list as science uncovers further evidence of the substantial health benefits of many of these phytonutrients.

To derive the universe of the 39 essential nutrients and nutrient groups referenced in this comparative guide, we have enlisted the recommendations of seven published scientific authorities. Each of these authorities has independently prescribed their recommendations for optimal nutrition, based on available scientific evidence. Their individual recommendations are incorporated into our *Blended Standard* benchmark and our *Final Product Score*, both of which, in turn, are integrated into the analytical model used in this guide. Details of the *Blended Standard* and the *Final Product Score* are presented in Section III.

Potency

Since their inception in the 1940s, the U.S. Recommended Dietary Allowances (RDAs) and the Canadian Recommended Nutrient Intakes (RNIs) have been updated on a number of occasions. Unfortunately, while originally created to establish nutritional baselines, they have become de facto guidelines for optimal nutritional intakes. It is important to understand that these nutritional allowances represent the minimum criteria necessary to prevent deficiencies. The recommendations do not — and were never intended to — represent the nutrient intakes required for long-term optimal health.

Recent advances in nutritional research now recognize the need to determine optimum levels of nutrient intake as a means of preventing degenerative disease. In response, the United States and Canada have embarked on a joint review and update of the scientific data in order to develop a new harmonized nutritional standard. Through Health Canada and the National Academy of Sciences in the United States, Canadian and U.S. nutritional experts are working together to create the new Dietary Reference Intake (DRI) standards. These harmonized reference standards represent a shift away from avoiding nutritional deficiencies and toward optimizing health.

Dietary Reference Intakes Fall Short

Although still a work in progress, DRI standards have been determined for a number of vitamins and minerals. For others, the revision process continues. Ultimately, the Dietary Reference Intakes will replace the RDA standards in the United States and RNI standards in Canada. While a step in the right direction, it is the opinion of many nutritional experts that the new DRI standards still come up short, when considering the nutritional needs for prevention and optimal health.

Prevention of degenerative disease appears to require levels of nutrients that exceed these new standards. For example, the newly revised DRI for vitamin E is 22-23 IU per day. Yet, several clinical and epidemiological studies show that much higher doses (100-800 IU/day) are needed to reduce the risk of heart disease. The 1995 Cambridge Heart Antioxidant Study (CHAOS) showed that patients with angina who consumed 400-800 IU per day of vitamin E suffered 47 percent fewer non-fatal heart attacks than did patients who did not receive supplementation.[4] Other studies involving vitamin E also show that advanced intakes of this inexpensive vitamin can reduce the risk of major cardiovascular events by 33-50 percent or more.[5,6,7,8] To do so, however, requires daily supplementation at levels significantly higher than the current Canada/U.S. guidelines.

While a step in the right direction, the new DRI standards still come up short when considering the nutritional needs for prevention and optimal health.

Advanced levels of other vitamins, minerals and antioxidants have also demonstrated protective effects against several degenerative disease processes:

- ✔ Selenium, at 200 µg per day, rather than the 55 µg per day recommended in the DRI, was found to reduce the incidence of total cancer mortality, including prostate, colon and lung cancer.[9]
- ✔ Administration of 500-1,000 µg per day of folic acid, somewhat higher than the DRI of 400 µg per day, was required to reduce homocysteine levels, a known risk factor in heart disease.[10]
- ✔ Long-term supplementation with high levels of vitamin C, well above the DRI standard of 75-90 mg per day, reduced the risk of cataracts by 83 percent.[11]
- ✔ Advanced intakes of calcium and vitamin D have been shown to reduce the risk and slow the progress of osteoporosis.[12,13] Concerns about osteoporosis and indications of a positive association between calcium intake and bone mass have recently led an international scientific panel to recommend daily supplementation of calcium at levels that greatly exceed the current recommended intakes.[14]

Interestingly, many of above studies also highlight the requirement for long-term supplementation before reductions in risk become evident. Short-term use of nutritional supplements does not appear to exhibit such profound protective effects.

Implications

Current research reveals that optimization of the preventive powers of many nutrients requires supplementation at levels significantly greater than those recommended in the RDA and the even the new DRI standard.

Accordingly, the presence of 39 essential nutrients and their respective potencies, as recommended by our cited nutritional authorities, form the first two criteria in the 14-point product score used in this comparative guide.

1 Balch PA. *Prescription for Nutritional Healing*. Avery Books, New York NY, 2002, pp9-15.

2 National Research Council. *Diet and Health: Implications for Reducing Chronic Disease Risk*. National Academy Press, Washington DC, 1989.

3 National Research Council. *Recommended Dietary Allowances (10th ed)* National Academy Press, Washington DC, 1989.

4 Stephens NG, Parsons A, Schofield PM et al. "Randomized controlled trial of vitamin E in patients with coronary disease: Cambridge Heart Antioxidant Study (CHAOS)." *Lancet* 1996, **347(9004)**: 781-786.

5 Stampfer MJ, Hennekens CH, Manson JE et al. "Vitamin E consumption and the risk of coronary disease in women." *N Engl J Med* 1993, **328(20)**: 1444-1449.

6 Rimm EB, Stampfer MJ, Ascherio A et al. "Vitamin E consumption and the risk of coronary heart disease in men." *N Engl J Med* 1993, **328(20)**: 1450-1456.

7 Losonczy KG, Harris TB and Havlik RJ. "Vitamin E and vitamin C supplement use and risk of all-cause and coronary heart disease mortality in older persons: the Established Populations for Epidemiologic Studies of the Elderly." *Am J Clin Nutr* 1996, **64(2)**: 190-196.

8 Meyer F, Bairati I and Dagenais GR. "Lower ischemic heart disease incidence and mortality among vitamin supplement users." *Can J Cardiol* 1996, **12(10)**: 930-934.

9 Clark LC, Combs GF Jr, Turnbull BW et al. "Effects of selenium supplementation for cancer prevention in patients with carcinoma of the skin. A randomized controlled trial. Nutritional Prevention of Cancer Study Group." *JAMA* 1996, **276(24)**: 1957-1963.

10 Wood T. "Conventional Wisdom vs. Advanced Nutrition." *Lifelong Nutrition* June/July, 2000.

11 Jacques PF, Taylor A, Hankinson SE et al. "Long-term vitamin C supplement use and prevalence of early age-related lens opacities." *Am J Clin Nutr* 1997, **66(4)**: 911-916.

12 Reid IR, Ames RW, Evans MC et al. "Long-term effects of calcium supplementation on bone loss and fractions in postmenopausal women: a randomized controlled trial." *Am J Med* 1995, **98(4)**: 331 -335.

13 Dawson-Hughes B, Harris SS, Krall EA et al. "Effect of calcium and vitamin D supplementation on bone density in men and women 65 years of age or older." *N Engl J Med* 1997, **337(10)**: 670-676.

14 NIH Consensus Development Panel on Optimal Calcium Intake. "Optimal Calcium Intake." *JAMA* 1994, **272(24)**: 1942-1948.

Facts are the air of scientists. Without them you can never fly.

— Linus Pauling (1901-1994)
Nobel Laureate in Chemistry and Peace

CHAPTER SIX

BIOAVAILABILITY

A Matter of Form

Minerals are essential components of our cells and serve as cofactors in the thousands of enzyme-controlled reactions that power the machinery of the cell. Throughout the body, minerals form critical structural elements, regulate the action of nerves and muscles, help maintain the cell's osmotic (water) balance, and modulate the pH (acidity) of the cell and extracellular fluids. While minerals comprise only four to five percent of our total body weight, life would not be possible without them.

Digestion in a Nutshell

To understand how the body absorbs minerals we need to look at the digestive process: the breakdown of nutrients into their basic parts and their preparation for absorption.

Digestion begins when food mixes in the mouth with starch-digesting enzymes, secreted by the salivary glands. Next, the masticated nutrients enter the stomach, where they mix with hydrochloric acid and protein-cleaving enzymes. The partially digested food mass then enters the small intestine to mix with several digestive enzymes and bile salts. Here, fats are emulsified and broken down into fatty acids, carbohydrates are reduced to simple sugars, and the partially digested protein fragments are cleaved into smaller fragments (peptides) and individual amino acids.

Throughout this process, minerals separate from the food and dissociate into ions (electrically charged atoms in solution). Ionized minerals can then pass freely through the intestinal wall and into the blood. They also attach themselves to amino acids, or other organic acids, and "hitch a ride" with these carriers, which are preferentially absorbed by the cells lining the small intestine. From here, the carriers and their attached minerals enter the blood and then travel to the liver, to be readied for use by the cells of the body.

According to Balch,[1] when nutritional supplements are taken with a meal, the minerals are automatically chelated with amino acids during the digestive process — one of the reasons it is best to consume your supplements with a meal. This implies that there are no differences in mineral bioavailability (the ability to be absorbed and used by the body) between supplements that use chelated- and organic-mineral complexes and those that use less expensive inorganic mineral salts. However, such is not the case.

For one thing, as people age they lose their ability to produce sufficient stomach acid, making it increasingly difficult to dissolve and ionize common mineral salts. For another, complex mineral interactions can inhibit absorption and influence mineral bioavailability.

An ionized mineral is one that is broken down into its component parts and dissolved into solution. For example, the mineral salt calcium carbonate ($CaCO_3$) dissociates in water into the calcium ion (Ca^{+2}) and the carbonate ion (CO_3^{-2}). The reaction sequence is:

$$CaCO_{3\,(s)} \longrightarrow Ca^{+2}_{(aq)} + CO^{-2}_{3\,(aq)}$$

Absorption Interference

Whether released from foods through digestion or the dissolution of supplements, ionized minerals are prone to a variety of absorptive interferences. Many components of our daily diet, including other minerals, can interfere with, and sometimes block, the absorption of certain minerals, making them unavailable to the body.[2]

Natural fibre, such as that found in fruits and cereals, has a depressing effect on the absorption of minerals supplied as inorganic mineral salts. Surprisingly, recent evidence shows that a fibre-rich diet can even deplete the body's mineral status when minerals are provided as inexpensive mineral salts, resulting in a negative mineral balance.[3,4]

Once minerals are ionized, they migrate to specialized receptor sites on the cells that line the inner surface of the small intestine. Here, the minerals attach to carrier proteins to be transported into the cells and, from there, into the bloodstream. These minerals actively compete with one another for attachment sites and, consequently, may inhibit the absorption of one another. According to Couzy,[5] such interactions between minerals can be profound and have significant implications for health.

Considering the ready availability of dietary supplements that use inexpensive mineral salts, these mineral-mineral and mineral-substrate interferences take on considerable importance. Imagine taking a mineral supplement in good faith and going into a negative mineral balance — actually *losing* ground for the very minerals you consumed!

The short of it is this: avoid the use of supplements that provide minerals in the form of inorganic mineral salts (such as oxides, carbonates, sulfates and phosphates). While less expensive to manufacture, supplements using mineral salts do not appear to provide optimal nutritional value.

The Value of Chelated Minerals

To increase the bioavailability of minerals, many manufacturers chemically bond the mineral to an amino acid or organic acid carrier.

These chelated minerals are believed to mimic the natural mineral chelates that form during the digestion process. Beyond their reported superior bioavailability, chelated minerals appear to have lower absorptive interference and better tolerance in the gut than the less expensive mineral salts.[6]

A true mineral-amino acid chelate is a product resulting from the reaction of a mineral ion with amino acids, the natural building blocks of proteins. This reaction produces an organic complex, where special chemical bonds, called ligands, hold the mineral firmly in place. These bonds protect the mineral from the fierce competition for the cellular receptor sites that the ionized mineral forms must endure. Instead, the amino acid chelate is preferentially absorbed, intact, into the cells lining the intestinal wall. This takes place through a separate "peptide route" — a special molecular doorway, designed specifically for the uptake of amino acids.[7, 8]

Many components of our daily diet, including other minerals, can interfere with, and sometimes block, the absorption of certain minerals, making them unavailable to the body.

While not chelates in the true sense of the word, minerals joined to organic acids, such as citrate, malate, succinate, alpha-ketoglutarate and aspartate (known, collectively, as Krebs cycle intermediates), are also believed to be preferentially absorbed. These organic acids are essential to the central metabolic pathway of the cell. Consequently, they are selectively absorbed through the gut, along with the attached mineral (which piggybacks along for the ride).

Both Krebs cycle intermediates and amino acid chelates fulfill all the requirements for an optimal carrier molecule.[9] They are easily metabolized, non-toxic, helpful in increasing the absorption of the mineral carried, and are almost completely degraded and employed in other areas of the cell's metabolism.

Although nutritionists agree that it is the biological effect of the mineral we are after, it is well known that the other half of the compound can have a significant impact on the effectiveness of the mineral supplement. This other half, known as the carrier, can affect bioavailability, tissue retention, safety and chemical interactions with other minerals. The value of amino acids and organic acids, as mineral sources, lies in their ability to increase the absorption of the mineral to which they are bound, and in their ability to be utilized fully by the cell as a nutrient source. Every bit of the compound — mineral as well as carrier — is nutritionally functional.

Thus, minerals delivered in chelated form avoid the competitive inhibitions to absorption and the mineral-mineral interactions experienced by ionized minerals. Organic acid complexes also provide needed acidity to promote absorption in the gut. Finally, both the mineral-amino acid chelates and the mineral-organic acid complexes appear to be better tolerated by the human gut than simple mineral salts.[10]

Beware the Great Pretenders

A word of caution about chelated minerals: many companies promote the use of hydrolized proteins, or "proteinates," as their chelated mineral form. Proteinates are nothing more than minerals joined to large protein fragments. Because these proteinates are incompletely digested proteins, the protein fragment remains to be broken down into its constituent amino acids — and it will be, once digested. The minerals bound to the protein fragments are released during this process. Once released, they become subject to the same competition for absorption as the less expensive mineral salts. Because of the certain breakdown of the protein fragment in the gut, it is likely that these mineral protienates are of little, if any, nutritional value in enhancing bioavailability.[11]

What's more, mineral complexes formed from randomly sized protein fragments are of varying molecular weights. Consequently, it is not possible to accurately quantify the amount of the mineral that is being complexed. This leads to significant quality control issues, with respect to stated mineral potencies.[12]

So, What's the Bottom Line?

The question of mineral form versus bioavailability has been an issue of contention within the scientific community for some time. This is largely because of the complexities of the human digestive process and the multitude of interactions between minerals and other digestive products.

Some studies appear to refute the claims of superior bioavailability of chelates.[13,14, 15] On the other hand, several studies provide convincing evidence that chelated minerals are preferentially absorbed.[16,17,18,19,20,21,22,23] One must also keep in mind that many of these studies have been conducted on animals, rather than humans, and often under rather artificial circumstances. This brings to question what is truly happening in the human gut, with respect to the complexities of mineral absorption.

While recognizing that controversy continues to surround this issue, this comparative guide acknowledges the consensus of our selected nutritional authorities. This consensus supports the use of mineral-amino acid chelates and mineral-organic acid (Krebs cycle) complexes as superior mineral forms, with respect to maximum absorption and bioavailability.[24,25,26,27,28]

1 Balch PA. *Prescription For Nutritional Healing.* Avery Publishers, New York NY, 2002, p54.

2 Albion Laboratories. "A Healthy Start." *Albion Research Notes Newsletter.* June 1997, **6(2)**: 1-5.

3 Knudsen E et al. "Zinc, Copper and Magnesium Absorption from a fibre-rich diet." *J Trace Elem Med Biol.* 1996, **2(10)**: 68-76.

4 Schardt FZ. "Effects of doses of certain cereal foods and zinc on different blood parameters in performing athletes." *Ernahrungswuiss.* 1994, **3(33)**: 207-216.

5 Couzy F et al. "Nutritional implications of the interactions between minerals." *Prog Food Nutr Sci.* 1993, **17(1)**: 65-87.

6 Greger JL and Krashoc CL. "Effects of a variety of calcium sources on mineral metabolism in anemic rats." *Drug Nutr Interact* 1988, **5(4)**: 387-94.

7 Kratzer F et al. "Chelates in Nutrition." CRC Press, Florida, 1986, p9.

8 Ashmead, HD et al. *Intestinal Absorption of Metal Ions and Chelates.* Charles C Thomas Pub., Springfiled Ill, 1985, p215.

9 Murray MT. *Encyclopedia of Nutritional Supplements.* Prima Health, Rocklin CA, 1996, p162.

10 Reavley M. *New Encyclopedia of Vitamins, Minerals, Supplements and Herbs.* M Evans & Co. New York, NY, 1998, p4.

11 Albion Laboratories. "Is it a Real Chelate?" *Albion Research Notes Newsletter.* Aug 2000, **9(2)**: 1-4.

12 Ibid.

13 Henry RP et al. "Absorbability and cost effectiveness in calcium supplementation." *J Am Coll Nutr* 2001, **20(3)**: 239-46.
14 Rojas LX et al. "Relative bioavailability of zinc methionine and two inorganic zinc sources fed to cattle." *J Trace Elem Med Biol* 1996, **10**(4): 205-9.
15 Greger JL and Krashoc CL. "Effects of a variety of calcium sources on mineral metabolism in anemic rats." *Drug Nutr Interact* 1988, **5**(4): 387-94.
16 Sakhee K et al. "Meta-analysis of calcium bioavailability: a comparison of calcium citrate with calcium carbonate." *Am J Ther* 1999, **6**(6): 313-21.
17 Wapnir A. "Copper absorption and bioavailability." *Am J Clin Nutr* 1998, **67**(**5 suppl**): 1054s-1060s.
18 Johnson MA et al. "Copper, iron, zinc, and manganese in dietary supplements, infant formulas and ready-to-eat breakfast cereals." *Am J Clin Nutr* 1998, **67**(**5 suppl**): 1035s-1040a.
19 Kincaid RL et al. "Zinc oxide and amino acids as sources of dietary zinc for calves: effects on uptake and immunity." *J Dairy Sci* 1997, **80**(7): 1381-88
20 Rojas LX et al. "Relative bioavailability of two organic and two inorganic zinc sources fed to sheep." *J Anim Sci* 1995, **73**(4): 1202-07.
21 Fairweather-Tait SJ et al. "A preliminary study of the bioavailability of iron- and zinc-glycine chelates." *Food Addit Contam* 1992, **9**(1): 97-101.
22 Smith AM and Picciano MF, "Relative bioavailability of seleno compounds in the lactating rat." *J Nutr* 1987, **117**(4): 725-31.
23 Nicar MJ and Pak CY. "Calcium bioavailability from calcium carbonate and calcium citrate." *J Clin Endocrinol Metab* 1985, **61**(2): 391-3.
24 Balch PA. *Prescription for Nutritional Healing.* Avery Publishers, New York, NY, 2002, p54.
25 Strand R. *Bionutrition: Winning the War Within.* Comprehensive Wellness Publishing, Rapid City SD, 1998, p135.
26 Colgan M. *The New Nutrition: Medicine for the Millennium*, Apple Publishing, Vancouver BC, 1995, pp 91-97.
27 Murray MT and Pizzorno J. *Encyclopedia of Natural Medicine.* Prima Health, Rocklin CA, 1998, p718.
28 Murray MT. *Encyclopedia of Nutritional Supplements.* Prima Health, Rocklin CA, 1996, p162.

There is a single light of science,
and to brighten it anywhere is to brighten it everywhere.
— *Isaac Asimov (1920-1992)*

CHAPTER SEVEN

BIOACTIVITY OF VITAMIN E

Natural vs. Synthetic

Vitamin E (alpha-tocopherol) functions as a chain-breaking antioxidant that prevents the propagation of lipid peroxidation. Found in leafy green vegetables, vegetable oils and nuts, intakes of small quantities of this fat-soluble vitamin (as little as 100 IU per day), have been associated with a significantly reduced risk of heart disease in both men and women.[1] Epidemiological studies show that dietary intakes of this important nutrient are alarmingly low throughout the United States. The National Health and Nutrition Examination Survey (NHANES III, 1988-91) and the Continuing Survey of Food Intakes of Individuals (CSFII, 1994) indicate that the dietary intake of vitamin E for most Americans does not even meet the recommended daily allowance of 22 IU/day.[2] This recommended allowance is based only on the alpha-tocopherol form of the vitamin.

A Matter of Form

The generic term, vitamin E, includes all of the various structural forms of tocopherol that exhibit biological activity. Because of its chemical nature, vitamin E has eight possible structural variants, or isomers, seven of which are found only in synthetic vitamin E preparations. For this reason, vitamin E is the exception to the paradigm that natural and synthetic vitamins are equal.

Natural vitamin E, extracted from vegetable oilseeds, such as soybeans, is also called *d*-alpha-tocopherol. Synthetic vitamin E, also known as *dl*-alpha-tocopherol, or *all-rac* tocopherol, is produced commercially, in a process that yields a mixture of eight different compounds. Only 12.5 percent of synthetic vitamin E is the biologically active *d*-alpha-tocopherol. The other seven isomers have the same chemical formula, but possess a different structural formula, based on the position and spatial orientation of methyl (-CH_3) groups attached to the main carbon skeleton. Think of it this way: you have a right hand and a left hand, both with the same basic structure. However, your right hand is the mirror image of your left hand (in chemical terms, they are geometric isomers).

In the case of vitamin E, there are eight different geometric combinations, with biological activities ranging from 21 to 90 percent of the activity of *d*-alpha-tocopherol. According to Traber (1998), synthetic vitamin E (*all-rac*-alpha-tocopherol), known incorrectly as *dl*-vitamin E, has a biological activity about two-thirds that of natural vitamin E. However, this figure has recently been revised downward. New evidence regarding the biological

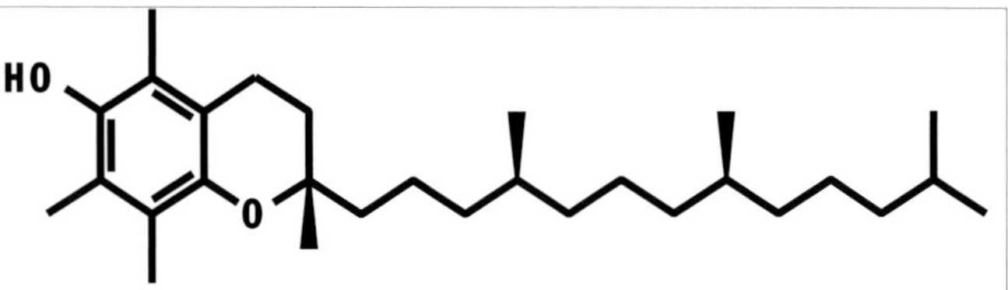

HO … O

d-alpha tocopherol

activity of synthetic vitamin E has prompted the National Academies of Science to recognize synthetic vitamin E as possessing only one-half the biological activity of (natural) *d*-alpha-tocopherol.[3]

By law, vitamin supplements must possess the biological potency printed on the label.[4] The International Unit (IU), a standard of measurement, was developed to compensate for the differences between natural and synthetic forms of vitamin E. Supplements containing 400 IU of vitamin E should, therefore, have the same measurable potency, whether they contain natural or synthetic vitamin E (more synthetic vitamin E is put into the formulation to bring it up to potency). But do they?

Natural is Better *(naturally)*

As well as showing the highest level of biological activity, natural vitamin E appears to be quickly absorbed into human cells. In contrast, the synthetic forms are metabolized (broken down) and excreted in the urine. The assimilation of natural vitamin E appears to be a result of the action of specific binding proteins produced in the liver. These proteins preferentially bind and transport (natural) *d*-alpha-tocopherol, to the exclusion of other (synthetic) forms of the vitamin.[5]

As well as showing the highest level of biological activity, natural vitamin E appears to be quickly absorbed into human cells. In contrast, the synthetic forms are metabolized (broken down) and excreted in the urine.

> *Because some of the [forms] of alpha-tocopherol present in [synthetic] alpha-tocopherol are not useable by the body, synthetic alpha-tocopherol is less bioavailable and only about half as potent [as natural vitamin E].*
>
> — **Linus Pauling Institute**

Japanese researchers compared the assimilation of natural versus synthetic vitamin E and found it required 300 mg of synthetic E to equal the blood levels of 100 mg of natural E.[6] In another study, researchers at Tennessee State University discovered that subjects provided with equal doses of chemically-labelled natural and synthetic vitamin E preferentially absorbed the natural form. The U.S. study also found that natural vitamin E levels in the blood increased twice as much as synthetic vitamin E levels. Curiously, the umbilical cords of pregnant women showed levels of natural vitamin E that were triple the synthetic levels.[7] These findings strongly suggest that natural vitamin E should be the supplemental form of choice in prenatal nutritional formulations.

Finally, long-term assimilation studies, conducted recently at Oregon State University, confirm that the body excretes synthetic vitamin E three times faster than the natural form,[8] making it less available for metabolic use.

Implications

The evidence demonstrating the greater biovailability, preferential absorption, preferential assimilation and lower rates of excretion of natural *d*-alpha-tocopherol over the synthetic form of the vitamin is conclusive. Despite the use of the IU measure to account for differences in biological activity of natural versus synthetic vitamin E, it is clear that natural *d*-alpha-tocopherol should be the standard by which to judge nutritional quality.

Accordingly, discrimination between these isomeric forms of vitamin E is incorporated, where applicable, throughout the product score criteria used in this comparative guide.

1 Traber MG. *The Biological Activity of Vitamin E*, Linus Pauling Institute, Oregon State University, http://lpi.orst.edu/sp-su98/, 1998.

2 National Institutes of Health. *Facts about Dietary Supplements.* www.cc.nih.gov/ccc/supplements/, 2002.

3 National Academies Press, *Dietary Reference Intakes for Vitamin C, Vitamin E, Selenium and Carotenoids, Food and Nutrition Board*, Institute of Medicine, Washington D.C., 2000.

4 Gerber JM. *Therapeutic Update on Vitamin E.* http://www.chiroweb.com/.

5 Challum J. "Natural vs Synthetic Vitamin E." *Nutrition Science News*, New Hope. com, 2002.

6 Kiyose C et al. "Biodiscrimination of alpha-tocopherol stereoisomers in humans after oral administration." *Am J Clin Nutr* 1997; **65**:785-9.

7 Burton GW et al. "Human plasma and tissue alpha-tocopherol concentrations in response to supplementation with deuterated natural and synthetic vitamin E." *Am J Clin Nutr* 1998, **67**: 669-84.

8 Traber MG et al. "Synthetic as compared with natural vitamin E is preferentially excreted as a-CEHC in human urine: studies using deuterated alpha-tocopherol acetate." *FEBS Letters*, 1998, **437**: 145-8.

**Vitamins, if properly understood and applied,
will help us to reduce human suffering to an extent
which the most fantastic human mind would fail to imagine.**

*— Albert Szent-Györgyi (1893-1986)
Nobel Laureate in Physiology and Medicine*

CHAPTER EIGHT

Cardiac Health Support

The Heart of the Matter

Epidemiological research has consistently revealed that individuals with a high dietary intake of antioxidant vitamins have a lower than average risk of cardiovascular disease.[1] This evidence is particularly consistent for vitamin E and beta-carotene.[2] As well, many clinical studies show magnesium supplementation to be of significant benefit in the treatment of cardiac arrhythmias (irregular heart beat) and the depletion of potassium that accompanies a magnesium deficit. Many cardiovascular events, such as angina pectoris (chest pain), congestive heart failure (failure to pump blood efficiently) and cardiomyopathy (weakening or damaging of the heart muscle), are related to magnesium status.[3] Likewise, coenzyme Q_{10} (CoQ_{10}), an essential component in cellular energy production, is prevalent in the heart muscle. Low tissue levels of CoQ_{10} have been associated with several cardiovascular complications, including angina, congestive heart failure, cardiomyopathy, hypertension (high blood pressure) and mitral valve prolapse (failure of the valve to close properly).[4] Research suggests that this triad of nutrients — coenzyme Q_{10}, vitamin E and magnesium — plays a central role in the maintenance of cardiac health and the prevention of disease states.

Magnesium

A cofactor for over 300 enzyme systems and one of several nutrients responsible for carbohydrate metabolism, magnesium is a mineral essential for many fundamental processes in the body.[5] All enzymatic reactions involving the cell's principal energy storage molecule, ATP (adenosine triphosphate), require magnesium. The metallic mineral is also required for protein synthesis, the manufacture of DNA and fatty acids, the breakdown of glucose, and the elimination of toxic wastes.[6] Magnesium is also essential for the formation of healthy bones, and it interacts with calcium in the regulation of blood vessels, the contraction of skeletal and cardiac muscle, and the conduction of nerve impulses.

Many individuals with congestive heart failure (CHF) have a magnesium deficiency. The level of the mineral in the blood is associated with the ability of the heart muscle to beat properly. Survival rates of CHF patients correlate directly to magnesium status.[7] Supplementation with magnesium is also of benefit in the treatment of cardiac arrhythmias and the prevention of potassium depletion (both minerals play an important role in the proper functioning of the heart).[8,9,10,11] Deficiency in magnesium has been observed in cardiomyopathy and mitral valve prolapse. In fact, over 85 percent of patients with mitral valve prolapse exhibit a chronic magnesium deficiency, which is relieved through supplementation.[12,13] Several other studies confirm improvement in heart function in patients with cardiomyopathies when supplemented with magnesium.[14,15,16,17]

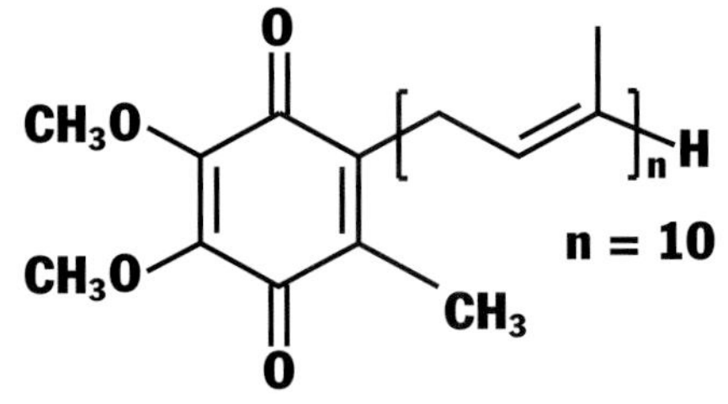

CH_3O, CH_3O, O, O, CH_3, H, n = 10

Coenzyme Q_{10}

Because the mineral acts in so many ways to enhance cardiac function and optimize cellular metabolism, magnesium is widely recognized as a critical nutrient for general cardiac support.

Coenzyme Q_{10}

Coenzyme Q_{10} is an energy coenzyme that plays a central role the respiratory pathway within the mitochondria (energy centres) of the cell. As such, the coenzyme is fundamental for energy production. Not surprisingly, the heart muscle, liver, kidneys and pancreas contain the highest levels of CoQ_{10}. Synthesized by all cells of the body, particularly the liver, the coenzyme is also a powerful antioxidant. Its ability to quench free radical damage helps maintain the structural integrity of cellular and mitochondrial membranes, where it serves to reduce oxidation of low-density lipoprotein (LDL) cholesterol.[18] However, as aging proceeds, the body's ability to synthesize this get-up-and-go nutrient diminishes, which may partially explain our loss of vitality as we age.

CoQ_{10} supplementation confers therapeutic benefits in several disease states, including heart failure, ischemic heart disease (reduced blood supply), hypertension and certain muscular dystrophies (progressive weakening of the skeletal muscles).[19] Deficiency of CoQ_{10} results from impaired synthesis of the coenzyme, a consequence of more general nutritional deficiencies; it is common among individuals with heart disease and many other cardiovascular dysfunctions, including angina pectoris, hypertension, mitral valve prolapse and congestive heart failure. Such individuals respond well to increased tissue levels of CoQ_{10}. In one study, CoQ_{10} proved effective in reversing mitral valve prolapse, with relapse rarely occurring in patients who had taken CoQ_{10} supplementation for over three months.[20]

Several double-blind studies in patients with various cardiomyopathies also show the benefits of CoQ_{10} supplementation. Langsjoen and co-workers reported an 89 percent improvement rate in 80 cardiomyopathy patients treated with CoQ_{10}.[21] The coenzyme also appears to moderate blood pressure through an unusual mechanism of action: by lowering cholesterol levels and stabilizing the vascular system through its antioxidant properties, thereby reducing vascular resistance. Several studies confirm a lowering of both systolic (pumping) and diastolic (resting) pressures in the range of 10 percent through CoQ_{10} supplementation.[22,23,24]

One of the most metabolically active tissues of the body, the heart muscle is particularly susceptible to the effects of CoQ_{10} deficiency. In one study, patients with stable angina treated with 150 mg/day of CoQ_{10} reduced their frequency of attacks by 53 percent and markedly increased their treadmill exercise performance.[25] Other clinical studies have shown that supplementation with 100 mg/day of CoQ_{10} in patients with congestive heart failure can provide results more positive than those obtained from conventional drug therapy.[26]

The evidence speaks for itself: coenzyme Q_{10} is an antioxidant powerhouse with clinically-demonstrated efficacy in restoring and enhancing cardiac function and in protecting against oxidative damage to the energy centres in the heart muscle and other tissues.

Vitamin E

The therapeutic benefits of supplementation with vitamin E are clear (see Chapter Seven). Alpha-tocopherol, above all of the antioxidants, may offer the greatest protection against heart disease. Vitamin E's cardio-protective effect appears to stem from its ability to bind to LDL cholesterol, protecting it from free radical-induced oxidative damage and the consequent build-up of atherogenic plaque. Low levels of vitamin E in the blood are predictive of a heart attack almost 70 percent of the time.[27]

Results from the Iowa Women's Health Study, which investigated 35,000 postmenopausal women, showed that vitamin E consumption significantly reduced the risk of death from coronary heart disease.[28] Another large study, conducted by the Harvard School of Public Health, showed that men who consumed at least 67 mg (100 IU) of vitamin E per day for at least two years had a 37 percent lower risk of heart disease than those who did not take supplements.[29]

Vitamin E's proven efficacy in protecting against atherosclerosis and in reducing risks from coronary heart disease place it high on the list of cardio-protective nutrients.

Implications

The scientific evidence demonstrating the importance of the *Cardiac Health Triad* of vitamin E, coenzyme Q_{10} and magnesium is compelling. Supplementation with these three nutrients may provide significant long-term benefits in the maintenance of cardiovascular health and the prevention of heart disease.

Accordingly, the *Cardiac Health Triad* — at dosages recommended by our cited nutritional authorities — is included as an important component in our product score criteria.

1 Mancini M et al. "Antioxidants in the Mediterranean Diet." *Can J Cardio* 1995, **11 (Supp G)**: 105G-109G.
2 Steinberg D et al. "Antioxidants in the prevention of human atherosclerosis." *Circulation* 1992, **85**: 2337-44.
3 Gottlieb SS et al. "Prognostic Importance of Serum Magnesium Concentration in Patients with Congestive Heart Failure." *J Am Coll Cardiol* 1990, **16**: 827-31.
4 Murray MT and Pizzorno J. *Encyclopedia of Natural Medicine*. Prima Health, Rocklin CA, 1998, pp 504 - 505.
5 Colgan M. *Optimum Sports Nutrition*. Advanced Research Press, New York NY, 1993, pp 193-194.
6 Reavley N. *The New Encyclopedia of Vitamins, Minerals, Supplements and Herbs*. M. Evans & Co., New York NY, 1998, pp 263-277.
7 Gottlieb SS et al. "Prognostic Importance of Serum Magnesium Concentration in Patients with Congestive Heart Failure." *J Am Coll Cardio* 1990, **16**: 827-31.
8 McLean RM. "Magnesium and its Therapeutic Uses: A Review." *Am J Med* 1984, **96**: 63-76.
9 Altura BM. "Basic Biochemistry and Physiology of Magnesium: A Brief Review." *Magnes Trace Elem* 1991, **10**: 167-71.
10 Purvis JR and Movaked A. "Magnesium Disorders and Cardiovascular Disease." *Clin Cardiol* 1992, **19**: 556-68.
11 Altura BM. "Ischemic Heart Disease and Magnesium." *Magnesium* 1988, **7**: 57-67.
12 Galland LD et al. "Magnesium Deficiency in the Pathogenisis of Mitral Valve Prolapse." *Magnesium* 1986 **5**: 165-174.
13 Fernandez JS et al. "Therapeutic Effect of a Magnesium Salt in Patients Suffering from Mitral Valve Prolapse and Latent Tetony." *Magnesium* 1985 **4**: 283-9.
14 McLean RM. "Magnesium and its Therapeutic Uses: A Review." *Am J Med* 1994, **96**: 63-76.
15 Altura BM. "Basic Boichemistry and Physiology of Magnesium: A Brief Review." *Magnes Trace Elem* 1991, **10**: 167-71.
16 Purvis JR and Movahed A. "Magnesium Disorders and Cardiovascular Disease." *Clin Cardiol* 1992 **15**: 556-68.
17 Brodsky MA et al. "Magnesium Therapy in New-onset Atrial Fibrillation." *Am J Cardiol* 1994, **73**: 1227-29.
18 Kagan VE et al. "Coenzyme Q_{10}: Its role in scavenging and generation of radicals in membranes." *Handbook of Antioxidants*. Cadenas E and Pacher L (eds), Marcel Dekker Inc., New York NY, 1996.
19 Litaree GP et al. "Clinical aspects of coenzyme Q: Improvement of cellular bioenergetics or antioxidant protection?" *Handbook of Antioxidants*. Cadenas E and Pacher L (eds), Marcel Dekker Inc., New York NY, 1996, pp 203-39.
20 Oda T and Homomoto K. "Effect of Coenzyme Q_{10} on the Stress-Induced Decrease of Cardiac Performance in Pediatric Patients with Mitral Valve Prolapse." *Japan Circ J* 1984, **48**: 1387.
21 Langsjoen PH et al. "Response of Patients in Classes III and IV of Cardiomyopathy to Therapy in a Blind and Cross-over Trial with Coenzyme Q_{10}." *Proc Nat Acad Sci* 1995 **82**: 4240.
22 Digiese V et al. "Mechanisms of action of Coenzyme Q_{10} in Essential Hypertension." *Curr Ther Res* 1992, **51**: 668-672.
23 Langsjoen P et al. "Treatment of Essential Hypertension with Coenzyme Q_{10}." *Mol Aspects Med* 1994, **15 (Suppl)**: S265-72.
24 Digiesi V et al. "Coenzyme Q_{10} in Essential Hypertension." *Mol Aspects Med* 1994, **15(Suppl)**: S257-63.
25 Kamidawa T et al. "Effects of Coenzyme Q_{10} on Exercise Tolerance in Chronic Stable Angina Pectoris." *Am J Cardiol* 1985, **56**: 247.
26 Hofman-Bang C et al. "Coenzyme Q_{10} as an Adjunctive Treatment of Congestive Heart Failure." *J Am Coll Cardiol* 1992, **19**: 216A.
27 Bellizi MC et al. "Vitamin E and Coronary Hearth Disease: The European Paradox." *Eur J Clin Nutr* 1994, **48**: 822-31.
28 Kushi LH et al. "Intake of Vitamins A, C and E and postmenopausal breast cancer." *Am J. Epidemiol* 1996, **144(2)**: 165-74.
29 Rimm EB. "Vitamin E consumption and the risk of coronary heart disease in men." *New Eng J Med* 1993, **328(20)**: 1450-56.

Nothing in life is to be feared, it is only to be understood.
— Marie Curie (1867-1934)
Nobel Laureate in Physics

CHAPTER NINE

HOMOCYSTEINE REDUCTION SUPPORT

Cardiovascular System Protection

The homocysteine theory, developed in 1969 by Kilmer McCully, proposes that elevated levels of homocysteine, a sulfur-containing amino acid, may be involved in the process of atherosclerosis (hardening of the arteries). The theory was actively criticized and almost forgotten[1] until work by Meir Stampfer[2] revived scientific interest. Stampfer reviewed blood homocysteine levels of 15,000 participants in the Physician's Health Study and concluded that even mildly elevated levels were causally related to heart disease. Those with the highest levels of homocysteine had three times the risk of developing a heart attack than those with the lowest levels. Forty major clinical studies now confirm that homocysteine levels are a predictive marker for heart disease, stroke and peripheral artery disease.

Forty major clinical studies now confirm that homocysteine levels are a predictive marker for heart disease, stroke and peripheral artery disease.

A powerful oxidizing agent, homocysteine is now believed to be responsible for the initial damage to the inner walls of the arteries and the subsequent initiation of plaque formation. Twenty to forty percent of patients with heart disease have elevated levels of homocysteine.[3,4] Deficiencies in vitamin B_6, vitamin B_{12} and folic acid can increase circulating levels of homocysteine; together, these nutrients reduce circulating homocysteine levels by helping to convert it to methionine, a harmless amino acid used by the cell for other functions.

Vitamin B_6

Vitamin B_6 (pyridoxine) is one of the essential, water-soluble B-complex vitamins. It functions as a coenzyme, working with over one hundred other enzyme systems in the cell. With a central role in amino acid metabolism, B_6 is vital in regulating blood homocysteine levels.[5] In one study, a six-week supplementation program with vitamin B_6 and folic acid showed that treatment with both vitamins normalized blood homocysteine levels in 92 percent of participants, significantly reducing the risk of adverse cardiovascular events.[6]

Human nutritional requirements for vitamin B_{12} are small; however, it is estimated that a significant percentage of individuals — particularly vegetarians — may be deficient.

A more recent study, reported in 1998 in the American Heart Association journal, *Circulation*, provides further evidence of the importance of vitamin B_6 in preventing heart disease. Researchers measured blood levels of homocysteine, folic acid, vitamin B_{12} and vitamin B_6 and showed conclusively that those with high levels of homocysteine or with low levels of folate and B_6 had an appreciably greater risk of heart disease.[7]

A large-scale study of 80,082 women taking part in the Nurses' Health Study supports these findings. The results of this investigation showed that those with the highest intake of vitamin B_6 had 30 percent less risk of heart attack than those in the low intake group. Combining vitamin B_6 and folate dropped the level of risk by over 50 percent.[8]

Folic Acid

One of the water-soluble B-complex vitamins, folic acid (folate) plays a central role in regulating cellular metabolism and cell division. Folic acid deficiencies are related to a number of disease states, most of which can be avoided or reversed through proper diet or supplementation.

Epidemiological studies show a strong association between folic acid status, cancer risk[9] and neural tube defects in infants.[10] There is also convincing evidence that folic acid plays a major role in determining the level of risk for cardiovascular disease and stroke.[11,12] But, there is a caveat: Ubbink and co-workers (1993)[13] found that supplementation with folic acid will lower homocysteine levels *only* if adequate blood levels of vitamins B_6 and B_{12} are also present. This apparent synergy between the vitamins B_6, B_{12} and folic acid, in reducing cardiovascular risk, has been reported in several recent studies.[14,15,16]

Vitamin B_{12}

Vitamin B_{12} (cobalamin) is another of the water-soluble B-complex vitamins and one of the few essential substances in the human body that contains the trace element cobalt. As a coenzyme, vitamin B_{12} activates an enzyme responsible for the cyclic metabolism of folic acid. Consequently, a dietary deficiency of B_{12} will result in an interruption of folic acid production. For this reason, a deficiency of vitamin B_{12} can mimic a folic acid deficiency. Dietary supplementation with both vitamin B_{12} and folic acid results in markedly lower levels of homocysteine. One study found that supplementing with both B_{12} and folate lowered homocysteine levels even in individuals with normal blood levels of these nutrients.[17]

Human nutritional requirements for vitamin B_{12} are small; however, it is estimated that a significant percentage of individuals — particularly vegetarians — may be deficient.

Vitamin B_{12} deficiency is also common in the elderly and can result in impaired nerve function, depressed mental acuity and the development of symptoms mimicking Alzheimer's disease. In fact, it is estimated that up to 42 percent of the elderly may be deficient in this important nutrient, which may also explain the prevalence of age-related depression in seniors.[18] The likelihood of widespread sub-clinical deficiencies of vitamin B_{12}, particularly in the elderly, provides a strong argument for daily supplementation.

Implications

The scientific evidence highlighting the synergistic role of vitamins B_6, B_{12} and folic acid in reducing blood homocysteine levels and cardiovascular risk is substantive. Because high circulating homocysteine levels are a primary risk factor for cardiovascular disease, supplementation with all three B-complex vitamins is warranted as a preventive measure. This is particularly so for the elderly, with respect to the noted age-related decline of vitamin B_{12}. We have termed this triad of B-complex vitamins the *Homocycteine Reduction Triad.*

Accordingly, supplementation with the *Homocysteine Reduction Triad*, at levels deemed suitable for optimal nutritional health by our cited nutritional authorities, is included as an important component in our product score criteria.

1 Stacey, M. "The Fall and Rise of Kilmer McCully." *New York Times Magazine*, 1997, **Aug:** 26-29.

2 Stampfer MJ et al. "A perspective study of plasma homocycsteine and risk of myocardial infarction." *U.S. Phys J Am Med Assoc* 1992, **268:** 877-881.

3 Glueck CJ et al. "Evidence that Homocysteine is an Independent Risk Factor for Atherosclerosis in Hyperlipidemic Patients." *Am J Cardiol* 1995, **75:** 132-36.

4 Landren F et al. "Plasma Homocysteine in Acute Myocardial Infarction: Homocysteine-Lowering Effect of Folic Acid." *J Int Med* 1995, **237:** 381-88.

5 Ellis JM and McKully KS. "Prevention of myocardial infarction by vitamin B_6." *Res Commun Mol Pathol Pharmacol* 1995, **89:** 208-20.

6 Van den Berg M et al. "Combined Vitamin B_6 plus Folic Acid Therapy in Young Patients with Arteriosclerosis and Hypohomocysteinemia." *J Vasc Surg* 1994, **20(6):** 933-940.

7 Robinson K. "Low circulating folate and vitamin B_6 concentrations: risk factors for stroke, peripheral vascular disease, and coronary artery disease. European COMAL Group." *Circulation* 1998, **279(5):** 359-64.

8 Rimm EB et al. "Folate and vitamin B_6 from diet and supplements in relation to risk of coronary heart disease among women." *JAMA* 1998, **279(5):** 359-64.

9 Mason JB. "Folate Status: Effects on Carcinogenesis." *Folate in Health and Disease.* Bailey LB (ed.) Marcel Dekker Inc., New York NY, 1995, pp 361-378.

10 Scott JM et al. "Folate and Neural Tube Defects." *Folate in Health and Disease* Bailey. LB (ed.) Marcel Dekker Inc., New York NY, 1995, pp 329-360.

11 Selhub J et al. "Vitamin status and intake as primary determinants of homocysteinemia in an elderly population." *JAMA* 1993, **270:** 2693-8.

12 Selhub J et al. "Association between plasma homocysteine and extracranial carotid artery stenosis." *N Eng J Med* 1995, **332:** 286-91.

13 Ubbink JB et al. "Hyperhomocysteinemia and the response to vitamin supplementation." *Clin Invest* 1993, **71:** 993-8.

14 Landgren F et al. "Plasma Homocysteine in Acute Myocardial Infarction: Homocysteine-lowering Effect of Folic Acid." *J Int Med* 1995, **237(4):** 381-88.

15 Van den Berg M et al. "Combined Vitamin B_6, Folic Acid Therapy in Young Patients with Arteriosclerosis and Hyperhomocysteinemia." *J Vasc Surg* 1994, **20(6):** 933-40.

16 Morrison HI et al. "Serum Folate and Risk of Fatal Coronary Heart Disease." *JAMA* 1996, **275(24):** 1893-6.

17 Glueck CJ et al. "Evidence that Homocysteine is an Independent Risk Factor for Atherosclerosis in Hyperlipidemic Patients." *Am J Cardiol* 1995, **75:** 132-36.

18 Murray MT. *Encyclopedia of Nutritional Supplements.* Prima Health, Rocklin CA, 1996, pp 127-29.

Reality is merely an illusion, albeit a very persistent one.
— Albert Einstein (1897-1955)
Nobel Laureate in Physics

CHAPTER TEN

Bone Health Complex

No Bones About It

As living tissue, bones require 24 bone-building materials, including trace elements and protein. The most important minerals include calcium, magnesium, phosphorus and potassium; equally important is the balance between these minerals.

Strong bones need lots of calcium, but calcium supplementation also requires the presence of magnesium, which increases calcium retention in the bone. Phosphorus, another important component in bone formation, must be in proper balance with calcium. Too much of it, from soft drink consumption or high protein intake, will suck the calcium right back out of the bone and weaken its integrity. Vitamins D and K are also vital for enhanced calcium deposition, while manganese, silicon, boron, zinc and copper are required to strengthen the bone's mineral matrix.

One study, conducted in 1995, showed that supplementation with 700 IU of vitamin D reduced the rate of hip fractures by nearly sixty percent.

Vitamin C stimulates formation of the collagen matrix, an important protein component that creates a framework for calcium crystallization. Last but not least, vitamins B_6, B_{12} and folic acid reduce mineral loss by modulating blood homocysteine levels.[1]

Vitamin D

Vitamin D stimulates the absorption of calcium. As a steroid hormone synthesized in the skin, vitamin D regulates calcium absorption from the gut, the deposition of calcium in the bone, and the re-absorption of calcium from the urine. In the skin, sunlight changes 7-dehydrocholesterol, the precursor of vitamin D, into active vitamin D_3, or cholecalciferol. Sunlight's central role in the manufacture of vitamin D is one of the reasons that people living in northern climates or confined indoors often have a deficiency of this important nutrient.

Several studies show that vitamin D, used in combination with calcium, reduces the rate of osteoporotic hip fractures and improves bone mineral status.[1] One study, conducted in 1995, showed that supplementation with 700 IU of vitamin D reduced the rate of hip fractures by nearly sixty percent.[2]

Recent evidence has challenged the current recommended daily intakes for vitamin D established by Canada and the United States. Gallagher[3] argues that the current recommended levels of vitamin D intake might be too low in the elderly, noting that doses of 800 IU per day can lower the incidence of osteoporotic fractures. In a 1999 study, Vieth[4] suggests that the recommended dietary allowance for adults of 5 µg (200 IU) of vitamin D is insufficient to prevent osteoporosis and consequent damage to the parathyroid glands, responsible for regulating blood calcium levels. Recent disclosure of a high prevalence of hypovitaminosis D (low levels of vitamin D) in medical in-patients, including those with vitamin D intakes greater than the recommended daily allowances, has led other researchers to conclude that maintaining recommended intakes at current levels may be insufficient to ensure adequate nutrient stores.[5]

There is merit in these arguments. The original scientific basis for the limited-dose recommendation of vitamin D was arbitrary and based largely on anecdotal reports. While it is reasonable that the daily vitamin D intake could be up to 800 IU per day, Murray[6] recommends a daily intake of 400 IU because the level of active vitamin D does not differ substantially between 400 IU and 800 IU. According to Murray, dosages exceeding 800 IU/day may adversely affect magnesium levels. Other researchers suggest that, except for those with vitamin D hypersensitivity, there is no evidence of adverse effects in doses up to 10,000 IU per day.[7]

Calcium

Through bone remodelling, an ongoing process of bone deposition and resorption, our bones replace much of their mineral content every few years.[8] However, if this dynamic balance is disturbed, through dietary and lifestyle choices or through the side effects of pharmaceutical drugs used to treat other disorders, we can rapidly deplete our calcium stores and our bones will become progressively weaker.

In fact, poor calcium nutrition is now recognized as a leading risk factor in osteoporosis, a disease that is becoming epidemic in our aging society. Numerous studies confirm that calcium supplementation at 500 to1200 mg per day can significantly reduce bone loss and the risk of accidental fracture.[9,10,11] Calcium supplementation has also been found to increase the bone mineral content of children and adolescents.[12,13,14] Several studies confirm that good calcium nutrition during our adolescent years leads to improved bone health and reduced risk of osteoporosis later in life.[15,16,17]

Based on cost-effectiveness and clinical efficacy, calcium and vitamin D should be the first-line therapy in patients at risk for osteoporotic fractures.

— Paul Ullom-Minnich, MD
University of Kansas School of Medicine

Vitamin K

A deficiency in vitamin K leads to impaired bone mineralization due to inadequate osteocalcin levels (osteocalcin is the major, non-collagen protein in the bone). In a 1988 study, Bittensky and co-workers[18] found a strong association between the severity of osteoporotic fracture and reduction in the level of vitamin K in the blood.

A 1997 study of Japanese post-menopausal women found that those women with reduced bone mineral density had significantly lower levels of vitamin K than those with normal bone density.[19] Low levels of the vitamin have also been found in osteoporotic men.[20] Research suggests that intakes much higher than the current recommended levels improve bone formation and bone mineral density.[21] Other studies have shown a high correlation between the levels of vitamin K in the blood and the level of bone density.[22]

In the blood, vitamin K is also involved in the manufacture and conversion of prothrombin to the active enzyme, thrombin, which initiates clot formation.

Because of its propensity to increase the clotting ability of blood and its potential for interference with pharmaceutical anticoagulants, such as warfarin, vitamin K is not included in nutritional supplements sold in Canada. Health Canada requires a prescription for any products containing vitamin K.

Boron

Boron is a trace mineral that has recently gained attention as a protective factor against osteoporosis because of its ability to activate estrogen and vitamin D. In one study, dietary supplementation with as little as 3 mg per day reduced urinary excretion of calcium by 44 percent and dramatically increased blood levels of estrogen.[23]

Boron deficiency appears to affect calcium and magnesium metabolism, leading to alterations in the structure and strength of bone.[24] When combined with magnesium deficiency, boron deficiency appears to be particularly damaging to bone mineral density.[25] While the daily requirement for boron is small, the standard North American diet is severely deficient in boron-rich food sources (such as almonds, grapes, legumes and dried fruits and nuts). Supplementation at 3-5 mg/day will provide an adequate intake.[26]

Because of its novel status, current U.S. and Canadian dietary standards do not yet recognize boron as an essential micronutrient. While allowed in U.S. dietary products, Health Canada does not allow boron to be included in nutritional supplements sold in Canada.

Magnesium

There is growing evidence that magnesium supplementation is just as important as calcium supplementation in the prevention and treatment of osteoporosis. Several studies confirm that women with osteoporosis exhibit a marked depletion in their bone magnesium content[27,28] and reveal other clinical indicators of magnesium deficiency. Magnesium is essential for the normal function of the parathyroid glands. Deficiency of this mineral modifies the action of parathyroid hormone, consequently affecting calcium balance and bone formation. In a study of elderly women, Tucker[29] showed that those women with low dietary intakes of magnesium had significantly lower bone mineral density than those with higher intakes.

Magnesium deficiency impairs vitamin D metabolism, which, in turn, adversely affects bone health.[30] Supplementation with magnesium improves bone mineral status. A two-year placebo-controlled trial, using a relatively low maintenance dose of magnesium, at 250 mg/day, revealed improved bone density of adult post-menopausal women. In contrast, the placebo group demonstrated a slight decrease in bone density.[31]

There is growing evidence that magnesium supplementation is just as important as calcium supplementation in the prevention and treatment of osteoporosis. Several studies confirm that women with osteoporosis exhibit a marked depletion in bone magnesium content and other indicators of magnesium deficiency.

B-Complex Vitamins

Low levels of vitamins B_6, B_{12} and folic acid, common in the elderly, are risk markers for cardiovascular disease and appear to contribute to osteoporosis.[32] As discussed previously, these nutrients are essential to the modulation of blood homocysteine levels. High levels of homocysteine interfere with the cross-linking of collagen proteins, necessary to build a strong bone matrix, and thereby contribute to the onset of osteoporosis. Supplementation with folic acid appears to reduce blood homocysteine levels in post-menopausal women, regardless of their B-complex vitamin status before treatment.[33] Supplementation with all three vitamins provides even better results than with any single nutrient[34] — further evidence of the synergy provided by the "teamwork" approach to supplementation.

Silicon

Studies show that silicon increases bone mineral density and appears to have a role in the prevention and treatment of osteoporosis. Silicon deposition is found in areas of active bone growth, suggesting that it may be involved in the growth of bone crystals and the process of bone mineralization. The mineral is responsible for cross-linking of the collagen strands in the organic matrix and contributes greatly to the final strength and integrity of the bone matrix.[35] Recalcification in bone remodelling may be dependent on adequate dietary levels of silicon, suggesting a preventive role for supplementation with this mineral.

Zinc

A component in over 200 enzymes, zinc is involved in more metabolic reactions than any other mineral. Zinc also modulates the action of several hormones and is necessary for the proper functioning of the immune system. Because the mineral is essential for the proper action of vitamin D, its status plays a central role in bone health. Increased zinc excretion, common in osteoporosis sufferers, is a likely consequence of accelerated depletion of bone mineral content. Diets low in zinc have been shown to slow adolescent bone growth,[36] suggesting that supplementation with zinc during the growth years may help optimize peak bone mineral density.

Implications

Good bone health requires adequate dietary levels of several vitamins, minerals and trace elements. The scientific evidence supports the need for long-term supplementation with several key nutrients in the maintenance of bone health, particularly for women in their peri- and post-menopause years. These nutrients, which we have termed the *Bone Health Complex*, include vitamins D, K, B_6, B_{12}, folic acid, and the minerals boron, calcium, magnesium, silicon and zinc.

Supplementation with those nutrients comprising the *Bone Health Complex*, at levels deemed suitable for optimal nutritional health by our cited nutritional authorities, is included as a component of our product score criteria. This scoring criterion is designed to avoid undo bias against Canadian nutritional products, which by regulation cannot include vitamin K and boron.

1 Murray M and Pizzorno J. *Encyclopedia of Natural Medicine.* Prima Health, Rocklin CA, 1998, pp 718-19.

2 Dawson-Hughes B et al. "Rates of bone loss in post-menopausal women randomly assigned to one of two doses of vitamin D." *Am J Clin Nutr* 1995, **61**: 1140-45.

3 Gallagher JC. "Vitamin D Metabolism and Therapy in Elderly Subjects." *South Med J* 1992, **85(8)**: 2S43-2S47.

4 Vieth R. "Vitamin D supplementation, 25-hydroxyvitamin D concentrations, and safety." *Am J Clin Nutr* 1999, **69**: 842-856.

5 Thomas MK, Lloyd-Jones DM, Thadhani RI et al. "Hypovitaminosis D in medical inpatients." *N Eng J Med* 1998, **338(12)**: 777 -783.

6 Murray MT and Pizzorno J. *Encyclopedia of Natural Medicine.* Prima Health, Rocklin CA, 1998, p 719.

7 Thomas MK, Lloyd-Jones DM, Thadhani RI et al. "Hypovitaminosis D in medical inpatients." *N Eng J Med* 1998, **338(12)**: 777 -783.

8 Lee JD et al. "The Truth about Osteoporosis." www.johnleemd.com/ 2002.

9 Dawson-Hughes B et al. "A controlled trial of the effect of calcium supplementation on bone density in postmenopausal women." *N Eng J Med* 1990, **323**: 878-83.

10 Chapuy MC et al. "Vitamin D3 and calcium to prevent hip fractures in elderly women." *N Eng J Med* 1992, 327: 1637-42.

11 Dawson-Hughes B et al. "Rates of bone loss in postmenopausal women randomly assigned to one of two dosages of vitamin D." *Am J Clin Nutr* 1995, **61(5)**: 1140-5.

12 Lloyd T et al. "Calcium supplementation and bone mineral density in adolescent girls." *JAMA* 1993, 270: 841-4.

13 Nowson CA et al. "A co-twin study of the effect of calcium supplementation on bone density during adolescence." *Osteoporosis Int* 1997, **7(3)**: 219-25.

14 Wood T and McKinnon T. "Calcium-Magnesium-Vitamin D Supplementation Improves Bone Mineralization in Preadolescent Girls." *Clinical Research Bulletin*, USANA Health Sciences, 2001.

15 Sandler RB et al. "Postmenopausal bone density and milk consumption in childhood and adolescence." *Am J Clin Nutr* 1985, **42(2)**: 270-4.

16 Halioua L and Anderson JJ. "Lifetime calcium intake and physical activity habits: independent and combined effects on the radial bone of healthy premenopausal Causcasian women." *Am J Clin Nutr* 1989, **49(3)**: 534-41.

17 Nieves JW et al. "Teenage and current calcium intake are related to bone mineral density of the hip and forearm in women aged 30-39 years." *Am J Epidemiol* 1995, **141(4)**: 342-51.

18 Bittensky L et al. "Circulating Vitamin K Levels in Patients with Fractures." *J Bone Joint Surg* 1988 **70(B)**: 663-4.

19 Kanai T et al. "Serum vitamin K and bone mineral density in postmenopausal women." *Int J Gynaecol Obstet* 1997, **56(1)**: 25-30.

20 Tamatani M. "Decreased circulating levels of vitamin K and 25-hydroxyvitamin D in osteopenic elderly men." *Metabolism* 1998, **47(2)**: 195-9.

21 Reavley N. *The New Encyclopedia of Vitamins, Minerals, Supplements, and Herbs.* M. Evans & Co. New York NY, 1998, pp 177-8.

22 Kanai T et al. "Serum vitamin K and bone mineral density in postmenopausal women." *Int J Gynaecol Obstet* 1997, **56(1)**: 25-30.

23 Neilsen FH et al. "Effect of Dietary Boron in Mineral, Estrogen and Testosterone Metabolism in Postmenopausal Women." *FASEB J* 1987, **1**: 394-97.

24 Nielsen FH. "Biochemical and physiologic consequences of boron deprivation in humans." *Environ Health Perspect* 1994, **102(Suppl.7)**: 59-63.

25 Nielsen FH. "Studies on the relationship between boron and magnesium which possibly affects the formation and maintenance of bones." *Magnes Trace Elem* 1990, **9(2)**: 61-9.

26 Whitaker J. *Dr. Whitaker's Guide to Natural Healing* Prima Publishing, Rocklin CA, 1995, pp 319-20.

27 Cohen L and Kitzes R. "Infrared Spectroscopy and Magnesium Content of Bone Mineral in Osteoporotic Women." *Int J Med Sci* 1981, **17**: 1123-25.

28 Stendig-Lindberg G. "Trabecular Bone Density in a Two Year Controlled Trial of Peroral Magnesium in Osteoporosis." *Magnes Res* 1993, **6**: 155-63.

29 Tucker K et al. "Magnesium intake is associated with bone mineral density (BMD) in elderly women." *J Bone Min Res* 1995, **10(S)**: 466.

30 Rudi RK et al. "Low serum concentrations of 1,25 dihydroxyvitamin D in human magnesium deficiency." *J Clin Endocrinol Metab* 1985, **61(5)**: 933-40.

32 Stendig-Lindberg G. "Trabecular Bone Density in a Two Year Controlled Trial of Peroral Magnesium in Osteoporosis." *Magnes Res* 1993, **6**: 155-63.

32 Brattstrom LE et al. "Folic acid responsive postmenopausal homocysteinemia." *Metab* 1985, **34**: 1073-7.

33 Ibid.

34 Ubbink JB et al. "Hyperhomocysteinemia and the Response to Vitamin Supplementation." *Clin Invest* 1993, **71**: 993-98.

35 Fessenden RJ and Fessenden JS. "The Biological Properties of Silicon Compounds." *Adv Drug Res* 1987, **4**: 95.

36 Ibid.

Nothing has such power to broaden the mind as the ability to investigate systematically and truly all that comes under thy observation in life.
— *Marcus Aurelius (121-180 AD)*

CHAPTER ELEVEN

ANTIOXIDANT SUPPORT

Reinforcements of the Internal War

The scientific evidence supporting the health benefits of supplementing with vitamin C, vitamin E and beta-carotene (pro-vitamin A) is impressive. Consequently, many health practitioners have begun to recommend higher dietary intakes of these important antioxidants as a prudent preventive measure. As was anticipated almost two decades ago by leading researchers,[1] high dose supplementation with antioxidants is gaining a significant role in the prevention and treatment of many of today's common ailments.

Vitamin C

Vitamin C, or ascorbic acid, is the body's most important antioxidant and forms the front line of defence against free radical-induced oxidative damage. An aqueous-phase antioxidant, vitamin C is the sentry against oxidative attack in the extra-cellular fluid and the cytoplasm of the cell. While other animals can manufacture vitamin C, the human species cannot. For us, ascorbate must be obtained through the diet. Because the vitamin is water soluble, any excess is excreted rather than stored; therefore, it must be replenished daily.

Vitamin C, or ascorbic acid, is the body's most important antioxidant and forms the front line of defence against free radical-induced oxidative damage.

Vitamin C is a cofactor or substrate for eight separate enzyme systems involved in various cellular functions, including collagen synthesis, ATP synthesis in the mitochondria and hormone biosynthesis. A potent free radical scavenger, vitamin C works alongside the principal antioxidant enzyme systems in the cell, glutathione peroxidase, catalase and superoxide dismutase. Its primary antioxidant partners include vitamin E and the carotenoids. In fact, ascorbic acid is responsible for regenerating vitamin E oxidized in the process of fighting free radicals.

A recent review highlights the multiple roles played by vitamin C in the prevention and treatment of cancer.[2] Epidemiological data suggest that a strong association exists between a fruit- and vegetable-rich diet high in ascorbate and reduced risks of several cancers, especially cancers of the oral cavity, esophagus, stomach, colon and lung.[3] As well, the clinical evidence provides compelling support for the preventive value of vitamin C supplementation.

Vitamin E

Of all the antioxidants, vitamin E (alpha-tocopherol) may offer the greatest protection against heart disease because of its ability to imbed itself into the LDL-cholesterol molecule and protect it from oxidative damage. Its solubility in lipids (fats) makes the vitamin an important component of the cell membrane, where it works to protect against oxidative damage.

The antioxidant activity of vitamin E is extensive and involves the inhibition of lipid peroxidation in the gut, bloodstream, tissues and cells. These actions result in protection against several important degenerative disorders, including Alzheimer's dementia,[4] some cancers,[5] and, most notably, heart disease. One important study, involving, 2,000 patients with heart disease, found that supplementation with alpha-tocopherol (vitamin E) reduced heart attacks by 75 percent.[6] Two studies, conducted at Harvard and involving 135,000 health care professionals, revealed that those who took daily supplements of vitamin E — even at daily intakes as low as 30 IU — had one-fourth to one-third less coronary risk than those who did not take supplements.[7,8]

Murray and Pizzorno[9] cite several epidemiological studies that demonstrate that vitamin E levels may be more predictive than cholesterol levels in assessing the risk of heart attack or stroke; remarkably, low levels of vitamin E in the blood have been shown to be predictive of a heart attack 70 percent of the time.[10] Vitamin E also boosts immune function, particularly in the elderly,[11] and assists in the recovery from stroke and peripheral artery disease.[12]

The clinical and epidemiological evidence provides conclusive support for the value of vitamin E supplementation. It is important to remember that, with vitamin E, the dosage correlates with the level of protection afforded. While doses as small as 25 mg of alpha-tocopherol offer some protection, according to Murray and Pizzorno,[13] doses greater than 400 IU are required to produce clinically significant results.

Beta-carotene (Pro-vitamin A)

Beta-carotene is the best-known member of the carotenoids, a group of accessory photosynthetic plant pigments that absorb blue-violet and blue-green light. In human nutrition, beta-carotene plays a dual role. As an antioxidant, beta-carotene's extensive conjugated double-bond structure reacts effectively with singlet oxygen radicals, absorbing and diffusing their destructive energy.[14] As pro-vitamin A, beta-carotene contributes in an entirely different way, supplying a portion of the body's requirement for retinol (vitamin A).

Through its conversion to the active forms of retinol (retinal and retinoic acid), beta-carotene plays a central role in the chemistry of vision, the activation of gene expression and the control of cell differentiation (task specialization). Beta-carotene also affects immune function, taste, hearing, appetite, skin renewal, bone development and growth, and embryonic development. Inadequate beta-carotene levels in the blood have been associated with impairment of immune function.[15,16] Supplementation produces regression of leukoplakia (precancerous lesions in the mouth) and demonstrates a strong inverse association with the risk of cervical cancer and dysplasia.[17,18]

Vitamin E levels may be more predictive than cholesterol levels in assessing the risk of heart attack or stroke; remarkably, low levels of vitamin E in the blood have been shown to be predictive of a heart attack 70 percent of the time.

Beta-carotene acts as a natural biological solar filter, protecting against light-induced UV damage to the eye.[19] Many epidemiological and clinical studies support the long-term benefits of beta-carotene intake. Similar findings pertain to its protective actions in heart disease and immune health.[20]

Protective Actions of the Triad

Cancer

While vitamins C, E and beta-carotene each carry out important antioxidant functions on their own, their synergistic activities provide some startling evidence regarding their efficacy. Several epidemiological studies have shown that the combination of vitamins C, E and beta-carotene is capable of significantly reducing the risk of dying from a heart attack or stroke.[21] Conversely, low levels of these nutrients have been associated with an increased risk of mortality from numerous cancers.[22] As well, several studies confirm that alpha tocopherol and beta-carotene play a central role in preventing cancers in the oral cavity.[23,24,25] Other investigators report that vitamins C, E and beta-carotene are important in the regulation of cancer cell differentiation. These three vitamins exhibit powerful cytotoxic (cell killing) effects on cancerous cells and may even revert cancer cells back to normal cell types.[26]

Research shows that supplementation with this antioxidant triad can inhibit liver carcinogenesis,[27] reduce the incidence of reappearance of precancerous polyps found in the colon,[28] and provide a significant reduction in cancer mortality.[29] Numerous studies also confirm a strong inverse relationship between circulating levels of vitamin A, beta-carotene, vitamin E and vitamin C and the risk of cancer mortality. Several studies confirm that low levels of antioxidants in the blood are associated with a high risk for cancer mortality.[30,31,32,33,34,35] All three nutrients appear to exert their anticancer effects through their individual and collective ability to quench free radical species[36] and prevent lipid peroxidation.[37]

Heart Disease

The triad of vitamins C, E and beta-carotene has also proven effective in the reduction and prevention of heart disease. In one large study of over 5,000 Finnish adults, the relationship between dietary intake of vitamin C, vitamin E, beta-carotene and the reduction in risk of coronary mortality was significant for both sexes.[38] Another large population study, relating antioxidant intake to the prevalence of coronary artery disease, found that blood levels of vitamins C, E and beta-carotene were significantly lower and oxidized lipids significantly higher in coronary disease patients, compared to the normal population.[39]

Research indicates that the protective action of this triad of antioxidants may be exerted through the quenching of the oxidation of low density (LDL) lipoproteins. This protective mechanism has been noted in several studies,[40,41,42] providing evidence of a preventive role in reducing the fatty plaque buildup characteristic of atherosclerosis.

Other studies provide more evidence of the preventive role of vitamins C, E and beta-carotene in the reduction of the risk of ischemic heart disease[43] and myocardial infarction (heart attack).[44] The evidence for the mitigation of risk is so strong that some investigators conclude that a major determinant for heart attack may, in fact, be vitamin deficiency. Accordingly, they have recommended nutritional supplementation for the prevention of cardiovascular disease.

The evidence for the mitigation of risk is so strong that some investigators conclude that a major determinant for heart attack may, in fact, be vitamin deficiency. Accordingly, they recommend nutritional supplementation for the prevention of cardiovascular disease.

General Considerations

Low circulating levels of vitamins C, E and beta-carotene are implicated in the development of cataracts in the eye. Low serum levels of beta-carotene and vitamin E appear to increase the risk of cataract formation;[45] conversely, high serum levels have been shown to reduce the prevalence of cataract formation.[46,47] High doses of these antioxidant nutrients also exhibit general immunostimulatory, anti-inflammatory and anti-thrombotic (anti-clotting) effects.[48] These actions appear to be related to the abilities of the triad to quench oxidative assault.[49]

Finally, there is evidence that, when used in combination, the actions of these antioxidant partners are synergistic in nature, providing a level of protection that strikingly exceeds the sum of their individual contributions.[50]

Implications

Optimal levels of vitamins C, E and beta-carotene, which we have termed the *Antioxidant Triad,* play a central role in the general health of the cell. The role of this triad in the mitigation of several chronic disease processes and the demonstrated synergy of its component nutrients in reducing oxidative stress are of considerable nutritional merit.

Accordingly, supplementation with the *Antioxidant Triad* of vitamins A, C and beta-carotene, at levels deemed suitable for optimal nutritional health by our cited nutritional authorities, is included as a component of our product score criteria.

1 Crary EJ and McCarty MF. "Potential Clinical Implications for High Dose Nutritional Antioxidants." *Med Hyp* 1984, **13(1)**: 77-98.

2 Segala M. (ed). Life Extension Foundation. *Disease Prevention and Treatment (3rd edition).* Life Extension Media, Hollywood Fl, 2000, p 691.

3 Fontham ETH. "Vitamin C, vitamin C-rich foods and cancer: epidemiological studies." *Natural Antioxidants in Human Health and Disease, Frie B (ed),* Academic Press, New York NY, 1994, pp 157-190.

4 Sano M et al." A controlled trial of selegiline, alpha-tocopherol, or both as treatment for Alzheimer's disease." *N Eng J Med* 1997, **336**: 1216-22.

5 Machlin LJ. "Critical assessment of the epidemiological data concerning the impact of antioxidant nutrients on cancer and cardiovascular disease." *Critical Rev Food Sci and Nutr* 1995, **35**: 41-50.

6 Stephens NG et al. "Randomised controlled trial of viamin E in patients with coronary disease: Cambridge Heart Antioxidant Study (CHAOS)." *Lancet*, 1996, **347**: 781-6

7 Stampfer MJ et al. "A prospective study of vitamin E consumption and risk of coronary disease in women." *N Eng J Med* 1993, **328**: 1444-49.

8 Rimm EB et al. "Vitamin E consumption and risk of coronary heart disease among men." *N Eng J Med.* 1993, **328**: 1450-56.

9 Murray MT and Pizzorno J. *Encyclopedia of Natural Medicine.* Prima Health, Rocklin CA, 1998, p92.

10 Bellizi MC et al. "Vitamin E and Coronary Heart Disease: The European Paradox." *Eur J Clin Nutr* 1994, **48**: 822-31.

11 Meydani SN et al. "Vitamin E supplementation and in vivo immune response in healthy elderly subjects." *J Am Med Assoc* 1997, **277**: 1380-86.

12 Murray MT and Pizzorno J. *Encyclopedia of Natural Medicine.* Prima Health, Rocklin CA, 1998, p 93.

13 Ibid

14 Handelman GJ. "Carotenoids as scavengers of active oxygen species." *Handbook of Antioxidants.* Cadenas E and Parker L, (eds), Marcel Dekker Inc. New York NY, 1996, pp 259-314.

15 Ulrich R et al. "Serum Carotene Deficiency in HIV-infected Patients." *AIDS* 1994, **8**: 661-65.

16 Omene JA et al. "Serum Beta-Carotene Deficiency in HIV-infected Children." *J Natl Med Assoc* 1996, **88**: 789-93.

17 La Vecchia C et al. "Dietary Vitamin A and the Risk of Invasive Cervical Cancer." *Int J Cancer* 1984, **34**: 319-22.

18 Romney S et al. "Retinoids and the Prevention of Cervical Dysplasia." *Am J Ob Gyn* 1982, **141**: 890-94.

19 Burton G and Ingold K. "Beta-Carotene: An Unusual Type of Lipid Antioxidant." *Science* 1984, **24**: 569-73.

20 Swanson JE and Parker RS. "Biological Effects of Carotenoids in Humans." *Handbook of Antioxidants.* Cadenas E and Parker L, (eds), Marcel Dekker Inc. New York NY, 1996, pp 337-70.

21 Whitaker J. *Dr. Whitaker's Guide to Natural Healing.* Prima Health, Rocklin CA, 1995, p16.

22 Stahelin HB et al. "Plasma Antioxidant Vitamins and Subsequent Cancer Mortality in the 12 year Follow-up on the Prospective Basel Study." *Am J Epidemiol* 1991, **133(8)**: 766-775.

23 Garewal H et al. "Beta-Carotene and other Antioxidant Nutritional Agents in Oral Leukoplakia." *CCPC-93: Second International Cancer Chemo Prevention Conference*, April 28-30, 1993, Berlin Germany, 1993.

24 Kaugers G et al. "The Role of Antioxidants in the Treatment of Oral Leukoplakia." *CCPC-93: Second International Cancer Chemo Prevention Conference*, April 28-30, 1993, Berlin Germany, 1993.

25 Kaugers G et al. "Serum and Tissue Antioxidant Levels in Supplemented Patients with Premalignant Oral Lesions." *FASEB J* 1993, **7(4)**: A519.

26 Lupulescu A. "The Role of Vitamins A, Beta Carotene, E and C in Cancer Cell Biology." *Int J Vitam Nutr Res* 1994, **64(1)**: 3-14.

27 Nakae D et al. "Inhibitory Effects of Vitamin C and E Derivatives on Rat Liver Carcinogenesis Induced by a Choline-deficient L-Amino Acid (CDAA)-Defined Diet." *Proc Ann Meet Am Assoc Canc Res* 1993, **34**: A729.

28 Ponz de Leon M et al. "Antioxidant Vitamins (A, E and C) and Lactulose in the Prevention of the Recurrence of Adenomatous Polyps: Preliminary Results of a Controlled Study." *Brit J Canc* 1990, **62(3)**: 496.

29 Taylor PR et al. "Prevention of Esophageal Cancer: The Nutrition Intervention Trials in Linxian, China: Linxian Nutrition Intervention Trials Study Group." *Canc Res* 1994, **54 (Suppl)**: 2029s-2031s.

30 Le Gardeur BY et al. "A Case-control Study of Serum Vitamins A, E and C in Lung Cancer Patients." *Nutr Cancer* 1990, **14(2)**: 133-40.

31 Nakae D et al. "Inhibitory Effects of Vitamin C and E Derivatives on Rat Liver Carcinogenesis Induced by a Choline-deficient L-Amino Acid (CDAA)-Defined Diet." *Proc Ann Meet Am Assoc Canc Res* 1993, **34**: A729.

32 De Vries H and Snow GB. "Relationships of Vitamins A and E and Beta-carotene Serum Levels to Head and Neck Cancer Patients with and without Second Primary Tumors." *Eur Arch Otorhindaryngol* 1990, **247(6)**: 368-370.

33 Potischman NA. "The Associations Between Breast Cancer and Biochemical and Dietary Indicators of Nutrient Status." *Dissertation Abstracts Int* 1989, **50(3)**: 909.

34 Salonen JT et al. "Risk of Cancer in Relation to Serum Concentrations of Selenium and Vitamins A and E: Matched Case-control Analysis of Prospective Data." *Brit Med J* 1985, **290(6466)**: 417-20.

35 Wei Q et al. "Vitamin Supplementation has a Protective Effect on Basal Cell Carcinoma." *Am Soc Prev Oncol (17th Annual Meeting: March, 1993),* Tuscon Arizona, 1993.

36 Pontaire E et al. "Increase in Singlet Oxygen Protection of Erythrocytes by Vitamin E, Vitamin C and Beta Carotene Intakes." *Biochem Mol Biol Int* 1995, **35(2)**: 371-74.

37 Courtiere A et al. "Lipid Peroxidation in Aged Patients. Influence of an Antioxidant Combination." *Therapie* 1989, **44(1)**: 13-17.

38 Knekt P et al. "Antioxidant Vitamin Intake and Coronary Mortality in a Longitudinal Population Study." *Am J Epidemiol* 1994, **139(12)**: 1180-89.

39 Singh RB et al. "Diet, Antioxidant Vitamins, Oxidative Stress and the Risk of Coronary Artery Disease: The Peerzada Perspective Study." *Acta Cardiol* 1994, **49(5)**: 453-467.

40 Jialal I and Grundy SM. "Effect of Combined Supplementation with Alpha-tocopherol, Ascorbate and Beta-carotene on Low Density Lipoprotein Oxidation." *Circulation* 1993, **88(6)**: 2780-86.

41 Harris WS. "The Prevention of Atherosclerosis with Antioxidants." *Clin Cardiol* 1992, **15(9)**: 636-40.

42 Jendryczko A. "Prevention of Atherosclerosis with the Help of Antioxidants." *Pol Tyg Lek* 1994, **49(20-22)**: 456-458.

43 Gey KF and Puska P. "Plasma Vitamins E and A Inversely Correlated to Mortality from Ischemic Heart Disease in Cross-Cultural Epidemiology." *Ann NY Acad Sci* 1989, **570**: 268-282.

44 Singh RB et al. "Plasma Levels of Antioxidant Vitamins and Oxidative Stress in Patients with Acute Myocardial Infarction." *Acta Cardiol* 1994, **49(5)**: 441-452.

45 Knekt P et al. "Serum Antioxidant Vitamins and Risk of Cataract." *Br Med J* 1992, **305(6866)**: 1392-94.

46 Jacques PF et al. "Antioxidant Status in Persons with and without Senile Cataract." *Arch Opthalmol* 1988, **106(3)**: 337-340.

47 Robertson JM et al. "Vitamin E Intake and the Risk of Cataracts in Humans." *Ann NY Acad Sci* 1989, **570**: 372-82.

48 Crary EJ and McCarty MF. "Potential Clinical Applications for High-dose Nutritional Antioxidants." *Med Hyp* 1984, **13(1)**: 77-98.

49 Nicol M. "Vitamins and Immunity." *Allerg Immunol* 1993, **25(2)**: 70-73.

50 Palozza P and Krinsky NI. "Beta-Carotene and alpha-Tocopherol are Synergsitic Antioxidants." *Arch Biochem Biophys* 1992, **297(1)**: 184-187.

Science is wonderfully equipped to answer the question "How?" but it gets terribly confused when you ask the question "Why?"

— Albert Einstein (1879-1955)
Nobel Laureate in Physics

CHAPTER TWELVE

GLUTATHIONE

Systemic Protector

Glutathione (GSH) is a simple tripeptide, a small protein that consists of three amino acids: glutamic acid, cysteine and glycine. Because of the chemical nature of sulfur-containing cysteine, glutathione effortlessly donates electrons, accounting for its powerful antioxidant properties. (The ease by which an antioxidant donates electrons to quench free radicals is its defining prowess.) Intracellular glutathione status is a sensitive indicator of cellular health and of the cell's ability to resist toxic challenge. Severe glutathione depletion quickly leads to cell death; experimental glutathione depletion has been found to induce cellular apoptosis (suicide).[1,2]

An important water-phase antioxidant, glutathione is an essential component in the Glutathione Peroxidase System, one of three pre-eminent free radical scavenging mechanisms in the cell. Glutathione peroxidase enzymes serve to detoxify peroxides, including hydrogen peroxide (H_2O_2), generated within cellular membranes and lipid-dense areas of the cell — in particular the mitochondrial membrane.

The cumulative damage wrought by oxygen and other free radical species is now recognized as a principal contributor to the degenerative disease process and the progressive loss of organ function, commonly recognized as aging.

Guarding the Mitochondria

Glutathione depletion at the cellular level invokes extensive damage to the mitochondria, the energy centres of the cell. Depletion of mitochondrial glutathione, in fact, may be the ultimate factor determining a cell's vulnerability to oxidative attack.[3] Nowhere is glutathione's presence more vital than in these cellular "furnaces," where a cascade of oxidation-reduction reactions complete the final steps in respiration — a process known as *oxidative phosphorylation*.

Throughout this process, electrons invariably escape and react with ambient oxygen to generate toxic free radicals.[4] It is estimated that two to five percent of the electrons that enter the mitochondrial "furnaces" are converted to oxygen free radicals,[5] generating considerable oxidative stress for the cell.[6,7] These free radicals, like sparks from a fire, pose an immediate threat to other cellular components, such as the DNA, enzymes, structural proteins and lipids.

The cumulative damage wrought by oxygen and other free radical species is now recognized as a principal contributor to the degenerative disease process and the progressive loss of organ function, commonly recognized as aging.[8] Consequently, the cell is constantly challenged to seek out and destroy these free radical "sparks" before they can inflict lasting damage. Minimizing such oxidative assaults may prove to be the ultimate challenge of being alive. For this reason, the formidable reducing power of glutathione is of profound importance to the cell.

Regenerator and Synergist

Several other applications call on glutathione's talents, including protection against exogenous (external) oxidative assaults and as an agent in the various detoxification pathways of the body.

Glutathione helps regenerate other antioxidants, themselves depleted from their task of fending off free radical challenges. Glutathione-induced regeneration, in fact, may be the mechanism used by the cell to conserve the lipid-phase antioxidants, vitamin A, vitamin E and the carotenoids.[9] Recent investigations confirm that dietary vitamin C can protect against tissue damage resulting from glutathione depletion; likewise, supplementation with glutathione or its precursors can quickly replenish vitamin C deficiencies.[10,11]

Thus, glutathione and ascorbic acid — two of the pre-eminent cellular antioxidants — are tightly linked: glutathione can conserve vitamin C and vitamin C can conserve glutathione. Together, these two antioxidant powerhouses protect the entire spectrum of biomolecules within the cell and facilitate the cell's optimal performance.[12]

Detoxicant Supreme

We live in an increasingly dangerous world, as documented daily in the media. Still, our most immediate threats are the thousands of toxic substances that we breathe, consume in our foods and absorb through our skin every day. From a single puff of cigarette smoke, with its trillions of free radicals, to the ubiquitous halocarbons found in plastics, pesticides, herbicides and dry-cleaning solvents, we are chronically exposed. From the toxic effects of heavy metals, industrial solvents and pharmaceutical products[13] — even the amalgams in our teeth — we are increasingly vulnerable. From birth to death, our bodies must prevail against an unrelenting assault from these exogenous toxic agents.

Fortunately, nature, in her wisdom, has evolved mechanisms through which the cells of our bodies can rid themselves of this toxic debris. Unfortunately, modern humankind, in its ignorance, has created such a flood of xenobiotics (materials foreign to the cell) that these protective systems are very frequently overwhelmed.

The liver is the organ most involved with the detoxification of xenobiotics, and it is the main repository for glutathione. In the specialized hepatocyte cells of the liver, glutathione is conjugated (joined) to many of the toxic chemicals, including heavy metals, solvents and fat-soluble pesticides. Conjugation of a toxin with glutathione renders the toxin water-soluble and prepares it for excretion from the body via the kidneys and the bile. The power of glutathione in the conjugation and elimination of toxins is prodigious, accounting for up to 60% of all liver metabolites in the bile. While our cells use six different detoxification pathways, conjugation with glutathione appears to be the *primary* route employed.

Glutathione Depletion

Because of its twin roles as a lipid-phase antioxidant and as a primary agent for detoxification, the demands on the cellular glutathione pool can be overwhelming, frequently leading to depletion.

Many pharmaceutical products are known to diminish glutathione from the liver, kidneys, heart and other tissues.[14] For example, overuse of acetaminophen, a common over-the-counter painkiller, can deplete liver glutathione, rendering the organ vulnerable to acute damage from other exogenous toxins, such as alcohol.[15] (The combination of acetaminophen and alcohol can have serious consequences beyond a simple hangover.)

Many other exogenous factors have been shown to deplete glutathione stores, including a dietary deficiency of methionine (a glutathione precursor),[16] ionizing radiation,[17] acute tissue injury,[18,19] iron overload from hemochromatosis [20] and excessive alcohol intake.[21] Even strenuous aerobic exercise can rapidly deplete glutathione and other antioxidant stores from muscle tissue. For habitual exercisers and elite athletes, supplementation with glutathione precursors appears to be a prudent preventive measure. [22]

Probably more than for any single nutrient, lifestyle choices and their effects on glutathione status can prove fateful. A combination of negative lifestyle factors, including smoking, alcohol and drug abuse, prolonged emotional and physical stress, and unhealthy dietary choices, can summon a sustained oxidative assault to the body, depleting glutathione reserves to the point of distress. Beyond this, the body's defences are quickly overwhelmed and free radical damage compounds, with grim consequences for the cell.

Here is how it appears to unfold: as tissue levels of glutathione and other antioxidants diminish, cells (usually those enduring the highest level of oxidative attack) begin to die. Zones of damaged tissue appear and begin to spread as free radical damage propagates outward, eventually encompassing other tissues and organs. This propagating wave of destruction is the manifestation of degenerative disease.

Glutathione Deficiency and Disease

According to several studies, glutathione depletion is a major contributory factor in diseases of the liver.[23,24] Shigesawa and coworkers[25] documented marked decreases in plasma and liver glutathione levels in individuals with viral hepatitis and both alcoholic and non-alcoholic liver disease. Studies of a number of pulmonary diseases, including obstructive pulmonary disease and pulmonary fibrosis, also note glutathione deficiencies.[26]

Other studies document a reduced capacity to detoxify free radicals in individuals with multiple sclerosis; the key factor appears to be a reduced level of the glutathione peroxidase enzyme system.[27,28,29] Many of these studies note that supplementation with selenium significantly enhances glutathione peroxidase activity. One study, conducted on AIDS patients, found that supplementation with selenium provided a dramatic elevation of glutathione peroxidase activity in HIV-positive subjects.[30] The likely mechanism involves selenium-induced activation of the glutathione peroxidase enzyme. Correlations also exist between depleted levels of glutathione, low glutathione peroxidase activity and the onset of atherosclerosis.

Glutathione depletion also dramatically inhibits immune functions[31,32] and increases vulnerability to infection. As well, chronic viral infections deplete glutathione stores. Patients diagnosed with hepatitis C and early HIV infection have been found to be deficient in blood glutathione.[33,34]

Depletion of glutathione stores is also implicated in the development of several neurological disorders. Because the brain is highly oxygenated and rich in polyunsaturated lipids, it is a fertile area for nutrient deficiency-induced free radical assault. Correlations between the level of lipid peroxidation in Parkinson's disease[35] and glutathione status point toward glutathione depletion as a causative factor.[36] Alzheimer's patients show similar patterns of abnormally low glutathione.

> ***The glutathione status of a cell ... will perhaps turn out to be the most accurate single indicator of the health of the cell. That is, as glutathione levels go, so will go the fortunes of the cell.***
> ***— Parris Kidd, Ph.D.***

Supplementation

While dietary glutathione is efficiently absorbed in the gut, the same may not be the case for nutritional supplementation. Oral dosing appears to raise glutathione levels, albeit with great variability between subjects. In one study, oral supplementation raised glutathione levels from two to five-fold.[37] In another study, absorption of a single dose of 3,000 mg was negligible.[38] Such variations raise concern about the efficacy of supplementing with glutathione itself. As a tripeptide (protein fragment), glutathione would tend to be hydrolyzed (broken down) during the digestive process. This leads some researchers to conclude that oral supplementation with glutathione does not appear to be cost effective in light of other methods available.[39]

Vitamin C Replenishes Glutathione

In contrast, daily supplementation with vitamin C appears sufficient to enhance and maintain good tissue glutathione levels, provided the necessary metabolic precursors for glutathione synthesis are also available. One double-blind study found that red blood cell glutathione levels increased nearly 50 percent when subjects were given 500 mg per day of ascorbic acid (vitamin C).[40] In patients with hereditary glutathione insufficiency, Jain and coworkers found vitamin C to be more effective and less costly in raising glutathione levels than n-acetyl cysteine, another well-known and effective glutathione booster.[41] Vitamin C appears to boost glutathione levels by helping the body manufacture it.

When given orally, S-adenosyl methionine (SAM-e) is also effective in raising red blood cell and liver glutathione.[42] Unfortunately, while sold in the United States, SAM-e is not yet commercially available in Canada.

Cysteine, the metabolic precursor that most severely limits the synthesis of glutathione, is another nutrient that has proven very effective in boosting glutathione levels.[43] Unfortunately, at high doses cysteine has been found to auto-oxidize, raising questions about its safety as an oral supplement.[44] N-acetyl cysteine (NAC), however, is another story.

Few experts in the field continue to doubt that free radical propagation, antioxidant depletion and the accumulation of endogenous toxins are involved in the degenerative disease process. Glutathione is the one nutrient that is active on all these fronts. For this reason, optimal tissue levels of glutathione are an absolute prerequisite for cellular health and longevity.

N-Acetyl Cysteine

N-acetyl cysteine (NAC) is a cysteine precursor that appears to avoid the problems of auto-oxidation attributed to cysteine. In the cell, NAC converts easily to cysteine, which, in turn, converts to glutathione. NAC is well absorbed in the intestinal tract and has been found to significantly boost glutathione levels in deficient subjects. As well, NAC demonstrates strong antioxidant, anti-mutagenic and anti-carcinogenic properties. Doses of up to 600 mg per day have proven to be an effective and safe means of optimizing tissue glutathione levels.[45] Interestingly, while both NAC and vitamin C are effective in boosting tissue glutathione insufficiency, one study demonstrated that vitamin C was both *more* effective and *less* expensive than NAC.[46]

A Word of Caution

The use of NAC products has become increasingly popular as a means of optimizing tissue glutathione; however, caution against too much of a good thing is advised.[47] There is evidence that, at high doses (exceeding 1-2 g/day), NAC can also act as a pro-oxidant and begin contributing to the level of oxidative stress.[48]

Other Nutritional Factors

Several other nutrients play a vital role in glutathione metabolism through their participation in the glutathione peroxidase pathway. Selenium, essential for the activation of glutathione peroxidase, acts as a cofactor for the enzyme; its supplementation markedly boosts enzyme activity.

Selenium dosing significantly enhances the activity of glutathione peroxidase in HIV-positive individuals who exhibit abnormally low enzyme activity.[49] As well, a study of patients with multiple sclerosis found that supplementation with high doses of selenium, vitamin C and vitamin E raised glutathione peroxidase activity five-fold, conferring a marked enhancement of cellular antioxidant status.[50]

Other nutrients required for the optimal functioning of the glutathione peroxidase system are riboflavin (vitamin B_2) and niacin (vitamin B_3). Both nutrients are important for their role in the energy transfer reactions that are a part of this vital antioxidant enzyme system.

Implications

The scientific evidence supporting the importance of glutathione as an antioxidant and detoxicant is cogent. Few experts in the field continue to doubt that free radical propagation, antioxidant depletion and the accumulation of endogenous toxins are involved in the degenerative disease process. Glutathione is the *one* nutrient that is active on all these fronts. For this reason, optimal tissue levels of glutathione are an absolute prerequisite for cellular health and longevity.

Accordingly, supplementation with glutathione precursors and with those nutrients involved in the glutathione peroxidase pathway, at levels deemed suitable for optimal nutritional health by our cited nutritional authorities, is included as a component of our product score criteria.

1 Duke RC et al. "Cell suicide in health and disease." *Sc Am* 1996, **12:** 79-87.

2 Slater AFG et al. "Signalling mechanisms and oxidative stress in apoptosis." *Toxicol Letts* 1995, **82/83:** 149-53.

3 Kidd P. "Glutathione: Systemic Protectant Against Oxidative and Free Radical Damage." www.thorne.com/altmedrev/, 2002.

4 Forman HJ and Boveris. "Superoxide radical and hydrogen peroxide in mitochondria." in: *Free Radicals in Biology (Vol 5).* Pryor WA (ed), Academy Press, New York NY, 1982, pp 65-89.

5 Ibid.

6 Kidd PM. "Natural Antioxidants' First Line of Defence." in: *Living with the Aids Virus: A Strategy for Long-term Survival.* PMK Biomedical-Nutritional Consulting, Albany CA, 1991, pp 115-142.

7 Cross CE et al. "Oxygen radicals and human disease (conference proceedings)." *Conn Int* Med 1987, **107:** 526-545.

8 Ibid.

9 Meister A. "Minireview: Glutathione-ascorbic acid antioxidant system in animals." *J Biol Chem* 1994, **269 (13):** 9397-9400.

10 Anderson ME. "Glutathione and glutathione delivery compounds." *Adv Pharmacol* 1997, **38:** 65-78.

11 Meister A. "Mitochondrial changes associated with glutathione deficiency." *Biochim Biophys Acta* 1995, **1271:** 35-42.

12 Kidd P. "Glutathione: Systemic Protectant Against Oxidative and Free Radical Damage." www.thorne.com/altmedrev/, 2002.

13 Hoyumpa AM and Schenker S. "Drugs and the liver." in: *Gastroenterology and Hepatology: The Comprehensive Visual Reference, Current Medicine.* Maddrey C (ed.), Philadelphia PA, 1996, 6.1-6.22.

14 Ibid.

15 Kidd P. "Glutathione: Systemic Protectant Against Oxidative and Free Radical Damage." www.thorne.com/altmedrev/, 2002.

16 Lomaestro BM and Malone M. "Glutathione in health and disease: pharmacotherapeutic issues." *Ann Pharmacother* 1995, **29:** 1263-73.

17 Biaglow JE et al. "Role of glutathione and other thiols in cellular response to radiation and drugs." *Drug Metab Rev* 1989, **20:** 1-12.

18 Yagi K. "Assay for serum lipid peroxide level and its clinical significance." in: *Lipid Peroxides in Biology and Medicine.* Yagi K (ed.), Academic Press, New York NY, 1982, pp 223-242.

19 Spies CD et al. "Influence of N-acetyl cysteine on indirect indicators of tissue oxygenation in septic shock patients: results from a prospective, randomized, double-blind study." *Crit Care Med* 1994, **22:** 1738-1746.

20 Cross CE et al. "Oxygen radicals and human disease (conference proceedings)." *Ann Intern Med* 1987, **107:** 526-545.

21 Lieber CS. "Alcohol-induced liver disease." in: *Gastroenterology and Hepatology: The Comprehensive Visual Reference, Current Medicine.* Maddrey C (ed.), Philadelphia PA, 1996, 9.1-9.21.

22 Ji LL. "Oxidative stress during exercise: implication of antioxidant nutrients." *Free Rad Biol Med* 1995, **18(6):** 1079-1086.

23 Lomaestro BM and Malone M. "Glutathione in health and disease: pharmacotherapeutic issues." *Ann Pharmacother* 1995, 29: 1263-73.

24 Loguercio C et al. "Alteration of glutathione, cysteine and glutathione synthetase in alcoholic and non-alcoholic cirrhosis." *Scand J Clin Lab Invest* 1992, **52:** 207-13.

25 Shigesawa T et al. "Significance of plasma glutathione determination in patients with alcoholic and non-alcoholic liver disease." *J Gastroenterol Hepatol* 1992, 7: 7-11.

26 Lomaestro BM and Malone M. "Glutathione in health and disease: pharmacotherapeutic issues." *Ann Pharmacother* 1995, **29:** 1263-73.

27 Shukla UKS et al. "Erythrocyte Glutathione Deficiency in Multiple Sclerosis." *Acta Neurol Scand* 1977 **56:** 542-50.

28 Jensen GE et al. "Leucocyte Glutathione Peroxidase Activity and Selenium Level in Multiple Sclerosis." *J Neurol Sci* 1980, **48:** 61-7.

29 Mazella GL et al. "Blood Cell Glutathione Peroxidase Activity and Selenium in Multiple Sclerosis." *Eur Neurol* 1983, **22:** 442-6.

30 Delmas-Beauvieux MC et al. "The Enzymatic Antioxidant System in Blood and Glutathione Status in Human Immunodeficiency Virus (HIV)-Infected Patients: Effects of Supplementation with Selenium or Beta-Carotene." *Am J Clin Nutr* 1996, **64:** 101-7.

31 Droge W et al. "Functions of glutathione and glutathione disulfide in immunology and immunopathology," *FASEB J* 1994, **8:**1131-38.

32 Fidelus RK and Tsan MF. "Glutathione and Lymphocyte activation: a function of aging and auto-immune disease." *Immunol* 1987, **61:** 503-08.

33 Anderson ME. "Glutathione and glutathione delivery compounds." *Adv Pharmacol* 1997, **38:** 65-78.

34 Droge W et al. "Role of cysteine and glutathione in HIV infection and cancer cachexia: therapeutic intervention with N-acetyl cysteine." *Adv Pharmacol* 1997, **38:** 581-600.

35 Lohr JB and Browning JA. "Free Radical Involvement in Neuropsychiatric Illnesses." *Psychopharmacol Bull* 1995, **31:** 159-65.

36 Jenner P "Oxidative damage in neurological disease." *Lancet* 1994, **344(8925):** 796-8.

37 Hunjan MK and Evered DF. "Absorption of glutathione from the gastrointestinal tract." *Biochim Biophys Acta* 1985, **815:** 184-8.

38 Witschi A et al. "The Systemic Availability of Oral Glutathione." *Eur J Clin Pharmacol* 1992, **43:** 667-9.

39 Kidd P. "Glutathione: Systemic Protectant Against Oxidative and Free Radical Damage." www.thorne.com/altmedrev/, 2002.

40 Johnston CJ et al. "Vitamin C Elevates Red Blood Cell Glutathione in Healthy Adults." *Am J Clin Nutr* 1993, **58:** 103-5.

41 Jain A et al. "Effect of Ascorbate and N-Acetylcysteine Treatment in a Patient with Hereditary Glutathione Synthetase Deficiency." *J Pediatr* 1994, **124:** 229-33.

42 Lomaestro BM and Malone M. "Glutathione in Health and Disease: pharmacotherapeutic issues." *Ann Pharmacother* 1995, **29:** 1263-73.

43 Tateishi H et al. "Relative contributions of sulfur atoms of dietary cysteine and methionine to rat liver glutathione and proteins." *J Biochem* 1981, **90:** 1603-1610.

44 Kidd P "Glutathione: Systemic Protectant Against Oxidative and Free Radical Damage." www.thorne.com/altmedrev/, 2002.

45 Van Zandwijk N. "N-acetyl cysteine (NAC) and glutathione (GSH): antioxidant and chemopreventive properties, with special reference to lung cancer." *J Cell Biochem Suppl.* 1995, **22:** 24-32.

46 Jain A et al. "Effect of Ascorbate and N-Acetylcysteine Treatment in a Patient with Hereditary Glutathione Synthetase Deficiency." *J Pediatr* 1994, **124:** 229-33.

47 Murray M and Pizzorno J. Encyclopedia of Natural Health. Prima Health, Rocklin CA, 1998, pp 117-8.

48 Kleinveld HA et al. "Failure of N-Acetyl Cysteine to Reduce Low Density Lipoprotein Oxidizability in Healthy Subjects." *Eur J Clin Pharmacol* 1992, **43:** 639-42.

49 Delmas-Beauvieux MC et al. "The Enzymatic Antioxidant System in Blood and Glutathione Status in Human Immunodeficiency Virus (HIV)-Infected Patients: Effects of Supplementation with Selenium or Beta-Carotene." *Am J Clin Nutr* 1996, **64:** 101-7.

50 Horrobin DF. "Multiple Sclerosis: The Rational Basis for Treatment with Colchicine and Evening Primrose Oil." *Med Hypoth* 1979, **5:** 365-78.

Let thy food be thy medicine and thy medicine be thy food.
— Hippocrates (470-410 BC)

CHAPTER THIRTEEN

Metabolic Support

Exposing the Silent Stalker

Diabetes, now the seventh leading cause of death in the United States, is a chronic disorder of carbohydrate, fat and protein metabolism. The disease first appears as a constellation of metabolic changes associated with hyperinsulinemenia (elevated insulin levels) and hyperglycemia (elevated blood sugar levels). This condition, a precursor to full-blown diabetes, is commonly known as *Insulin Resistance Syndrome*. Untreated, insulin resistance will develop into full-blown diabetes; with it comes greatly magnified risks of heart disease, stroke, eye and kidney disease, and loss of nerve function.

Non-Insulin-Dependent (or Type II) Diabetes Mellitus (NIDDM) is a disease strongly associated with a sedentary lifestyle and the modern western diet. Inadequate physical activity, combined with a diet high in refined sugars, saturated fats and proteins, and low in dietary fibre, has resulted in an epidemic in obesity throughout both Canada and the United States. The prevalence of Type II diabetes has correspondingly risen alarmingly. Obesity is, in fact, a hallmark of the disease.[1,2,3] Almost 90 percent of those diagnosed with Type II diabetes are obese at the time of diagnosis.

One possible explanation for the emergence of Type II diabetes in children is the increase in obesity and decreased physical activity of children. Obesity is now reaching epidemic proportions in the U.S. and elsewhere.
— American Diabetes Association

Nutritionally based strategies to optimize metabolic support involve a number of measures; one of these includes broad-spectrum supplementation with vitamins B_3, B_6, B_{12}, biotin, vitamins C and E, chromium, magnesium, manganese and zinc. Together, these nutrients play a central role in regulating insulin levels, enhancing insulin sensitivity, and mitigating other physiological factors associated with Type II diabetes and its metabolic precursor, insulin resistance.

Chromium

Chromium is an essential mineral known to increase the efficiency of insulin, one of the hormones responsible for the control of blood sugar. Chromium enhances cellular sensitivity to the hormone by binding with several amino acids to form a complex known as Glucose Tolerance Factor (GTF).[4,5,6] GTF allows insulin to bind with its receptor sites, resident on the surface of the cell membrane.

Studies show that supplementation with chromium improves insulin action, decreases fasting blood sugar levels and decreases total cholesterol and triglyceride levels.[7]

Reversing chromium deficiency through nutritional supplementation has been found to lower body weight while, at the same time, increase lean muscle mass.

Sub-clinical chromium deficiency is widespread in North America, and it is a likely contributor to the increasing prevalence of Insulin Resistance Syndrome and Type II diabetes. According to Murray,[8] at least 200 micrograms of elemental chromium per day appears necessary for optimal blood sugar regulation.

Vitamin C

High dose vitamin C (2,000 mg per day) has been shown to reduce the accumulation of sorbitol, a metabolic by-product of glucose metabolism, known to cause chronic complications in the diabetic patient.[9] Studies also show that vitamin C supplementation inhibits the glycosylation of proteins (the complexing of protein with sugar), a process that is elevated several-fold in diabetics. Because insulin facilitates the transport of ascorbic acid into cells, many diabetics do not have sufficient vitamin C within their cells *despite* adequate dietary intake. This chronic deficiency of vitamin C in the diabetic is problematic and leads to vascular disorders, elevated blood cholesterol and depression of the immune system.[10]

Accordingly, high dose supplementation with vitamin C is an issue of primary concern for the diabetic or pre-diabetic sufferer. Recent studies reveal that vitamin C supplementation, alone, provides a more effective means of correcting sorbitol accumulation than current pharmaceutical approaches.[11,12]

Vitamin E

Vitamin E is also important in the prevention of diabetes. Studies show that low vitamin E status results in a marked increase in the risk of developing the disease.[13] Supplementation improves insulin sensitivity and helps reduce long-term complications. One study of elderly patients concludes that high-dose supplementation with alpha-tocopherol improves insulin sensitivity and glucose tolerance in healthy patients, with an even more dramatic improvement evident in diabetic patients.[14]

Vitamin B_3

Like chromium, vitamin B_3 (niacin) is an important component of the GTF and is central in enhancing the body's sensitivity to insulin. A cofactor in many energy transfer reactions, niacin assists in energy production, fat and carbohydrate metabolism, and several other metabolic processes.

There is evidence that supplementation with the niacinamide form of B_3 prevents the onset of diabetes in experimental animals.[15] Similar findings are reported in human clinical trials, where some newly diagnosed Type I diabetics experienced a complete reversal of their condition through dietary supplementation with niacinamide.[16] Mitigation of damage to the insulin-producing beta-cells within the pancreas appears to be its "modus operandi."[17]

Europeans have long used *inositol hexaniacinate*, a safe and effective form of niacin that has been found to lower elevated blood lipids associated with both forms of diabetes. This form of B_3 appears to improve blood flow and blood sugar levels better than standard niacin.[18]

Biotin

An essential cofactor for several enzymes, biotin is vital for normal carbohydrate metabolism and the biosynthesis of fatty acids and proteins. Supplementation may help improve blood sugar control in the diabetic and pre-diabetic individual by enhancing insulin sensitivity and increasing the activity of enzymes involved in the breakdown of glucose.[19] As little as 16 mg per day of biotin results in a marked lowering of blood sugar levels in Type I diabetics; similar results are reported at doses as low as 9 mg per day in Type II diabetics.[20]

Minerals

Magnesium: Several minerals are involved in the prevention and treatment of insulin resistance and full-blown Type II diabetes; one of the most important is magnesium. Magnesium deficiency is common in insulin resistance and diabetes. The mineral is intimately involved in several areas of glucose metabolism. Accordingly, the pre-diabetic and diabetic patient may require double the current recommended daily intake for this mineral.[21]

Manganese: Like magnesium, manganese is involved in many of the enzymatic reactions controlling glucose metabolism. Important in the enzyme superoxide dismutase (SOD), manganese enhances SOD activity and, in turn, increases the level of antioxidant protection. Deficiency in manganese, common in Insulin Resistance Syndrome and Type II diabetes, leads to bone and joint abnormalities, impaired pancreatic function, reduced reproductive capacity, and abnormal carbohydrate and lipid metabolism. Studies reveal that diabetics have only half the manganese levels of normal individuals.[22]

Zinc: Zinc is critical for proper insulin action. The mineral protects the beta-cells of the pancreas, where the hormone is manufactured. Diabetics excrete excessive amounts of zinc, and the mineral must be replaced through diet or supplementation.[23] Supplementation with zinc improves insulin levels and accelerates wound healing.[24,25]

Implications

Vitamins B_3, B_6, B_{12}, C, E, biotin, and the trace elements chromium, magnesium, manganese and zinc are essential for proper metabolic support and the regulation of glucose metabolism. Millions of North Americans suffer unknowingly from insulin resistance, the metabolic precursor for Type II diabetes, placing themselves at increased risk of several cardiovascular and neurological disorders. While the development of insulin resistance is multi-factorial, the research shows that complications associated with the disorder may be mitigated through targeted dietary supplementation and lifestyle change.

Accordingly, supplementation with vitamins B_3, C, E, biotin and the trace elements chromium, magnesium, manganese and zinc (collectively termed *Metabolic Support*), at levels deemed suitable for optimal nutritional health by our cited nutritional authorities, is included as an important component in our product score criteria.

1 Hughes T et al. "Effects of caloric restriction and weight loss on glycemic control, insulin release and resistance and atherosclerotic risk in obese patients with Type II diabetes mellitus." *Am J Med* 1984, 77: 7-17.

2 Cambell PJ and Carlon MG. "Impact of obesity in insulin action in NIDDM." *Diabetes* 1993, **42**: 405-10.

3 Smith U. "Insulin Resistance in Obesity, Type II Diabetes and Stress." *Acta Endocrinol Suppl* 1984, **262**: 67-69.

4 Anderson R et al. "Beneficial Effect of Chromium for People with Type II Diabetes." *Diabetes* 1996, **45(suppl 2)**: 124A/454.

5 Offenbacher E and Stunger F. "Beneficial Effect of Chromium-rich Yeast on Glucose Tolerance and Blood Lipids in Elderly Patients." *Diabetes* 1980, **29**: 919-25.

6 Mertz M. "Chromium Occurrence and Function in Biological Systems." *Physiol Rev* 1969, **49**: 163-237.

7 Mooradian AD et al. "Selected Vitamins and Minerals in Diabetes." *Diabetes Care* 1994, **17**: 464-79.

8 Murray MT and Pizzorno J. *Encyclopedia of Natural Medicine*, Prima Health, Rocklin CA, 1998, p 417.

9 Davie SJ at al. "Effect of Vitamin C on Glycosylation of Proteins." *Diabetes* 1992, **41**: 167-73.

10 Ibid.

11 Murray MT and Pizzorno J. *Encyclopedia of Natural Medicine*, Prima Health, Rocklin CA, 1998, p 417.

12 Cunningham J et al. "Vitamin C: An Aldose Reductase Inhibitor that Normalizes Erythrocyte Sorbitol in Insulin-Dependent Diabetes Mellitus." *J Am Coll Nutr* 1994, **4**: 34-50.

13 Salonen JT et al. "Increased Risk of Non-Insulin-Dependent Diabetes Mellitus at Low Plasma Vitamin E Concentrations: A Four Year Follow-up Study in Man." *Br Med J* 1995, **311**: 1124-27.

14 Paolisso G et al. "Chronic Intake of Pharmacological Doses of Vitamin E Might be Useful in the Therapy of Elderly Patients with Coronary Heart Disease." *Am J Clin Nutr* 1995, **61**: 848-52.

15 Murray MT and Pizzorno J. *Encyclopedia of Natural Medicine*, Prima Health, Rocklin CA, 1998, p 418.

16 Cleary JP. "Vitamin B_3 in the Treatment of Diabetes Mellitus: Case Reports and Review of the Literature." *J Nutr Med* 1990, **1**: 217-25.

17 Andersen HU et al. "Nicotinamide prevents Interleukin-I Effects on the Accumulated Insulin Release and Nitric Oxide Production in Rat Islets of Langerhans." *Diabetes* 1994, **43**: 770-77.

18 Murray MT and Pizzorno J. *Encyclopedia of Natural Medicine*, Prima Health, Rocklin CA, 1998, p 419.

19 Koutsikos D et al. "Oral glucose tolerance test after high dose I.V. biotin administration in normoglycemic patients." *Ren Fail* 1996, **18(1)**: 131-7.

20 Maeboski M et al. "Therapeutic Evaluation of the Effect of Biotin on Hyperglycemia in Patients with Non-Insulin-Dependent Diabetes Mellitus." *J Biochem Nutr* 1993, **14**: 211-18.

21 Murray MT and Pizzorno J. *Encyclopedia of Natural Medicine*, Prima Health, Rocklin CA, 1998, p 421.

22 Mooradian AD and Morley JE. "Micronutrient Status in Diabetes Mellitus." *Am J Clin Nutr* 1987, 45: 877-95.

23 Ibid.

24 Hegazi SM et al. "Effect of Zinc Supplementation on Serum Glucose, Insulin, Glucagon, Glucose-6-phosphatase and Mineral Levels in Diabetics." *J Clin Biochem Nutr* 1992, **12**: 209-15.

25 Engel ED et al. "Diabetes Mellitus: Impaired Wound Healing from Zinc Deficiency." *J Am Pod Assoc* 1981, 71: 536-44.

The most exciting phrase to hear in science, the one that heralds new discoveries, is not 'Eureka!' (I found it!) but 'That's funny ...'
— *Isaac Asimov (1920-1992)*

CHAPTER FOURTEEN

Phenols and Flavonoids

Food-based Antioxidant Protection

Biochemical, clinical and epidemiological studies all confirm that a diet rich in animal products and saturated fats, common to western and northern European cultures, raises atherogenic LDL cholesterol levels and increases the prevalence of heart disease.

In contrast, a diet rich in carbohydrates and fibre, where the principal sources of fats are the *monounsaturated fatty acids* (MUFAs) — as found in the olive oil-rich Mediterranean diet common to southern Europe — modulates cholesterol levels and is associated with a low incidence of heart disease.[1,2,3,4] The evidence clearly shows that a diet enriched with MUFAs lowers LDL (bad) cholesterol, enhances HDL (good) cholesterol and provides resistance to oxidative damage.[5,6]

The traditional Mediterranean diet is characterized by an abundance of plant foods, such as bread, pasta, vegetables, salad, legumes, fruits and nuts. Olive oil is the principal source of fat. Meat consumption consists of low to moderate amounts of fish and poultry, with little red meat. Eggs, dairy products and red wine are also consumed in low to moderate amounts.

Epidemiological comparisons reveal the striking health benefits provided by such a diet. In adult Greek men in 1960, premature mortality from coronary heart disease was 90 percent lower than that for men in the United States; the life expectancy for Greek men, at the time, was the highest in the world.[7] Among Greek women, breast cancer rates were less than half those in the United States. The overall prevalence of several other chronic diseases was also markedly lower than for individuals in northern and central European countries.[8] Modern western influence on the traditional Mediterranean diet has since degraded these noted health benefits.

> *The scientific evidence is sufficient to justify a campaign of forced action to influence policy makers ... and the public to accept the benefits of olive oil and the principles of the Mediterranean diet, and make it more a part of the national diet of all nations.*
>
> — International Consensus Panel
> European Commission, Rome, 1997

Apart from the expected cardio-protective effects of a diet low in saturated fats, additional health benefits of the Mediterranean diet are derived from its favourable fatty acid profile[9] and its rich composition of natural antioxidant compounds, known as *polyphenols*. Natural constituents of many fruits and vegetables, polyphenols are particularly prevalent in red wine and olives.

The inverse relationship noted between polyphenol intake and mortality is likely due to the favourable effect of polyphenols on blood lipids, including their oxidizability.[10] The antioxidant actions of polyphenols appear to protect blood lipids from oxidative damage by quenching free radical-induced lipid peroxidation.[11,12] These properties complement and enhance the antioxidant prowess of vitamin C, vitamin E and the carotenoids. Polyphenols possess several other important pharmacological properties. They are anti-bacterial, anti-viral, anti-inflammatory, anti-allergic, anti-hemorrhagic, and vasodilatory.[13,14,15,16,17]

What are Polyphenols?

Polyphenols are a diverse class of compounds found naturally in the leaves, bark, roots, flowers and seeds of plants. Citrus fruits, grapes, olives, tealeaves, bark, vegetables, dark berries, whole grains and nuts are particularly rich sources of these natural antioxidants. Polyphenol pigments are largely responsible for the brightly coloured hues of ripened fruits and vegetables. Within the plant, they guard the cells from disease, filter out harmful ultraviolet light and protect the delicate plant seeds until they germinate. When consumed in the diet, polyphenols become prodigious free radical scavengers, conferring many health benefits. There is evidence that some phenolic compounds also help detoxify the body by chelating with metals and facilitating their removal.[18,19]

When consumed in the diet, polyphenols become prodigious free radical scavengers, conferring many health benefits. There is evidence that some phenolic compounds also help detoxify the body by chelating with metals and facilitating their removal.

There are two major groups of polyphenols, differentiated on the basis of their structural formula: the *flavonoids* and the *phenolic compounds* (derived from phenolic acids). While it is beyond the scope of this guide to delve deeply into the chemical properties of these two groups, explaining their structural differences will provide some clarity for the reader.

The Flavonoids

The flavonoids are known as "nature's biological response modifiers" because of their ability to alter the body's reactions to allergens, viruses and carcinogens, and to protect cellular tissue against oxidative attack. Dr. Albert Szent-Györgi, biochemist and Nobel Laureate credited with discovering vitamin C, uncovered the flavonoids in crude vitamin C preparations extracted from lemon. He initially named the flavonoids vitamin P, because of their noted ability to reduce vascular permeability (leakage).

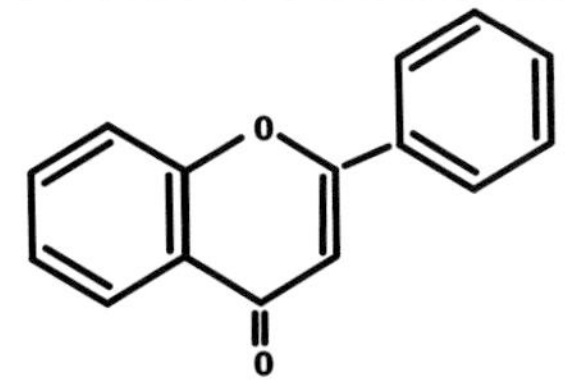

Flavone Ring Skeleton

Flavonoids are found in the edible pulp of many vegetables and fruits, and they impart a bitter taste when isolated. Citrus fruits, such as oranges, lemons, limes, grapefruit and kiwi, are particularly rich sources of the flavonoids. Rose hips, cherries, black currents, grapes, green peppers, broccoli, onions and tomatoes are also high in these compounds, as are many herbs (bilberry, ginkgo, yarrow, hawthorne and milk thistle). Other flavonoid compounds are found in the leaves, bark and seeds of various plant species. The leaves of *Camellia sinensis* (dried to make green and black tea), the bark of the maritime (*Landes*) pine and the seeds of ripened grapes are excellent sources of a variety of flavonoid compounds. As well, soybeans, nuts and whole grains contain a rich source of flavonoids, known as isoflavones.

Flavonoids are important for the health and integrity of blood vessels. Through their ability to decrease permeability, flavonoids can reduce microvascular haemorrhaging and enhance capillary strength. In a large controlled study, Hertog[20] and co-workers demonstrated the remarkable cardio-protective effects of flavonoids and showed a strong association between flavonoid intake and heart disease. The flavonoids confer cardio-protective benefits specifically through their ability to prevent oxidation of cholesterol. This ability is reported to be similar to, and possibly more potent than, the antioxidant powers of vitamins C and E.

Recent scientific literature is replete with studies reporting the beneficial effects of dietary flavonoids in human health. Flavonoids, along with beta-carotene, vitamin C and vitamin E, may be the cell's principal cancer chemopreventive agents. Their abundance in fruits and vegetables underlies the strong correlation between high fruit and vegetable consumption and reduced cancer risk.[21,22,23] Some flavonoids are also known to alter hormonal actions. Isoflavones, derived from soy, flaxseed, nuts and whole grains, have estrogenic properties that can modulate estrogen levels and reduce postmenopausal symptoms.

Today, science has uncovered over 4,000 flavonoid compounds, which are characterized by their chemical structure. The flavonoids are derived from a common molecular skeleton, known as the *flavone ring* (see diagram above). While their diversity is immense, we can categorize the flavonoids into several groups, based on their chemical structure and pharmacolologic effects.

Citrus Flavonoids

Perhaps the largest of the flavonoids groups, the citrus flavonoids are also called the *bioflavonoids*. They are found in the edible pulp of citrus fruits and dark berries. Interest in these compounds stems from their synergistic effects with vitamin C, first observed by Szent Györgi. Studies indicate they can relax smooth muscles in the arteries, reduce permeability and enhance the strength of capillaries, thereby lowering blood pressure and improving circulation. As well as possessing anti-inflammatory properties, citrus flavonoids exhibit powerful antioxidant properties and protect the cardiovascular system from harmful lipid peroxidation.

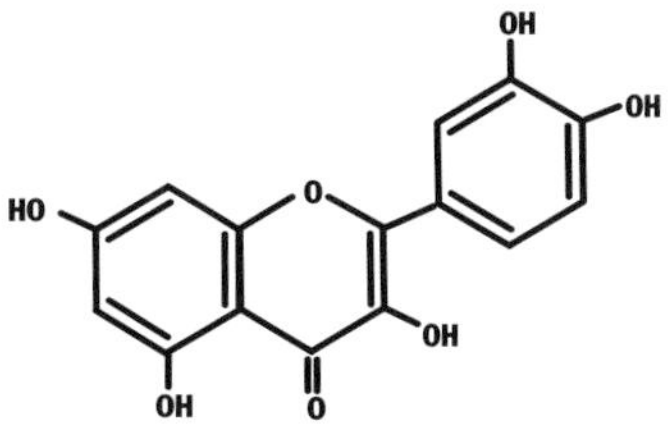

Quercetin

Quercetin (see diagram lower left), one of the most biologically active of the flavonoids, serves as the backbone for many of the citrus flavonoids. Note the similarity in the chemical structure of quercetin to the flavone ring skeleton (see diagram at left). Quercetin is indicated in the prevention of diabetes, due to its ability to enhance insulin production, protect the insulin-producing beta-cells in the pancreas and inhibit platelet aggregation (a principal cause of blood clotting in diabetics).[24] In animal studies, quercetin has proven effective against a wide variety of cancers.[25] Unfortunately, there is little human research available to assess its efficacy.[26]

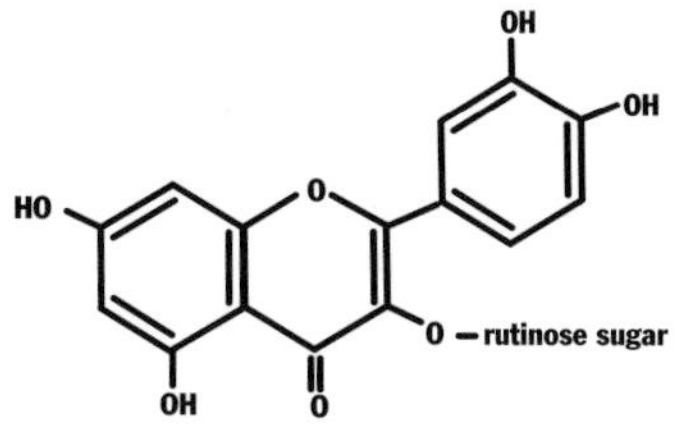

Rutin

Other important citrus flavonoids, including rutin, quercitrin, hesperidin and naringin, are derivatives of quercetin. These compounds differ by having various sugar molecules attached to the quercetin backbone. Note that the only difference between rutin (see diagram above) and quercetin is the addition of the sugar rutinose.

Procyanidolic Oligomers

According to Bagchi,[27] the flavonoids found in grape seed extracts (GSEs) are highly bioavailable and provide significantly greater protection against free radical damage and lipid peroxidation than vitamins C, E and beta-carotene. This finding, however, is controversial; other investigators contend that, on a dosage-equivalent basis, the antioxidant activities of vitamins C, E and beta-carotene are very nearly the same as the GSE flavonoids.[28] While GSEs are certainly very powerful antioxidants, statements about them having 50 times more antioxidant potency than vitamin E appear to be in question.

Proanthocyanidins, the active components of GSEs, are a complex mixture of bioflavonoid compounds, also known as *procyanidolic oligomers* (PCOs). This unique group of flavonoids appears to confer the cardio-protective effects noted in consumers of red wine. PCO compounds also exhibit cytotoxicity (cell-killing ability) against several types of cancer cells, increase intracellular levels of vitamin C, enhance capillary stability and inhibit the destruction of collagen.[29,30] The pigments are concentrated in the seeds of the grape and are incorporated into the finished wine during the fermentation process.[31]

Green Tea Catechins

Green tea, for centuries a staple of the oriental diet, is a rich source of a class of bioflavonoids, called catechins. Note the structural similarities between catechin (see diagram next page) and quercetin (see diagram at left). These antioxidant compounds possess an anti-mutagenic potential, protecting the cellular DNA from oxidative damage.[32] Epidemiological evidence suggests that consumption of green tea may also protect against pancreatic and colorectal cancers.[33] In one population-based controlled study, consumption of green tea appeared to significantly lower the risk of stomach cancer. What's more, the effect was independent of the age at which consumption began.[34] Green tea is a fusion of the leaves from the tea plant, *Camellia sinensis*.

Catechin

Black tea, produced by the fermentation of green tea leaves, does not contain the high levels of catechins found in unfermented green tea and, consequently, may not afford the same benefits. However, recent evidence suggests that the antioxidant activity of black tea preparations is higher than that of most reported dietary agents, based on daily intake; in one study, one cup of black tea was found to provide 262 mg of polyphenols per serving.[35] Therefore, like green tea, black tea is also a rich source of polyphenolic antioxidants.

The Phenolic Compounds

In addition to the flavonoids, there is another major class of polyphenols, known as the *Phenolic Compounds*. These are derivatives of the phenolic acids; hydroxycinnamic acid and hydroxybenzoic acid (see diagrams at right and below). These compounds differ from the flavonoids in that they are composed of a single six-carbon ring, known as an aromatic or cyclic ring, which provides them with a strong electron-donating ability. The many different phenolic compounds found in nature are variations of these basic structures, with a wide variety of different groups attached to this basic hydrocarbon skeleton. The difference in the ring structure in the phenolic compounds, compared to the flavonoids, provides for a slightly different (but just as valuable) chemical nature.

p-Hydroxycinnamic (coumaric) Acid

Turmeric, a rich source of phenolic compounds, is a perennial herb of the ginger family and a major ingredient in curry. The active ingredient of turmeric is curcumin, a yellow-orange pigment long used in Chinese and Ayurvedic (Indian) medicine as an anti-inflammatory. It is also an effective antioxidant, anticarcinogenic, cardiovascular and hepatic agent.

p-Hydroxybenzoic Acid

Another particularly rich source of phenolic compounds is the olive, fruit of the olive tree *Olea europaea*, which grows almost exclusively in countries adjoining the Mediterranean Sea. Hippocrates, the father of modern medicine, used olive oil to treat ulcers, cholera and muscle pains over 2500 yeas ago. A staple in the diet of southern Europe for centuries, the olive has surfaced as the "nouveau cause célèbre" in the world of nutrition and natural health. Rich in monounsaturated fats and phenolic compounds, the cold-pressed oil of olives has long been favoured for cooking and flavouring. Olive oil is now generating serious scientific interest in its broadly confirmed health benefits, a consequence of its rich complement of phenols and its favourable fatty acid profile.

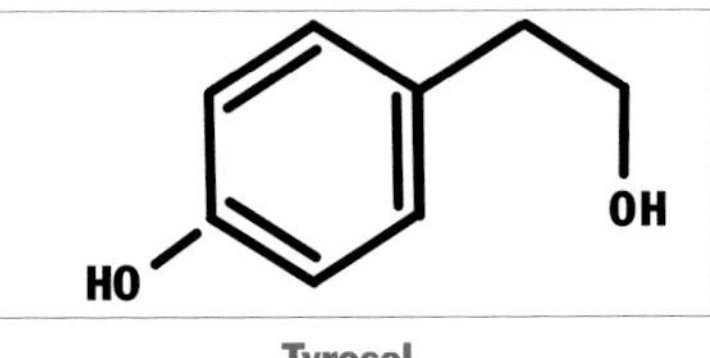

Tyrosol

As the only oil derived from whole fruit, the pungent oil possesses a unique fatty acid composition. Oleic acid, a monounsaturated fatty acid, comprises up to 84 percent of olive oil's fat content and confers the remarkable cardio-protective benefits recently confirmed in the scientific literature.

But the feature that has been creating recent excitement in the scientific community is the high content of phenolic compounds, namely tyrosol, hydroxytyrosol and the oleuropeine glycosides, found in the olive fruit. *Extra Virgin* olive oil, extracted from the first cold press of the olive, derives its unique aroma, pungent taste and high thermal stability from these complex aromatic compounds.[36]

Oleuropein is the source of the extremely powerful disease-resistance properties of olive extracts first noted in the 1960s, when the testing of olive leaf extracts revealed a facile ability to kill a large variety of viruses.[37] The oleuropeine derivatives are isolated from the bark, leaves and fruit of the olive tree.

In spite of the beneficial effects attributed to olive oil, particularly the *Extra Virgin* oil, less than one percent of the phenolic antioxidants in olives actually end up in the finished product. About 99 percent is found in the pulp and wastewater, traditionally discarded after the oil is pressed. Fortunately, researchers now recognize that the olive pulp and the wastewater are valuable sources of these olive-based phenolic compounds, which can be recovered and incorporated into nutritional products.*

Interest in the cardio-protective and antioxidant potential of olive oil arose from the findings of several large European and U.S. studies that compared traditional dietary patterns relating to the incidence of coronary heart disease.[38,39,40] In one study, the death rates of 12,000 middle-aged men from seven countries were evaluated over 15 years. Death from all causes and from coronary heart disease was markedly lower in those individuals who consumed olive oil as their main dietary source of fat.[41] In another study, Hertog and co-workers[42] reported that polyphenol intakes of only a few milligrams per day for prolonged periods resulted in a significantly reduced risk of coronary heart disease in elderly patients.

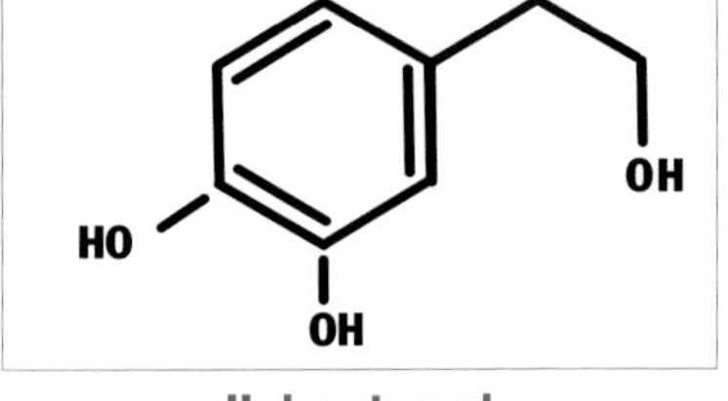

Hydroxytyrosol

Other studies confirm that a diet rich in olive oil prolongs the survival of patients with heart disease. Studies show consumption of the pungent oil reduces the risk of breast and colon cancer[43,44]

* In May 2002, researchers at Usana Health Sciences, Salt Lake City, Utah, announced an exclusive patented process for recovering the phenolic constituents from the olive and by-products formed from the oil extraction process. Usana's Olivol® is now incorporated into their multivitamin/mineral and antioxidant formulation, *Usana Essentials*.

and lowers blood pressure.[45] High bioavailability[46] and the ability to protect LDL cholesterol from oxidative damage[47,48] makes olive oil-based phenolic compounds potent antioxidants,[49] a likely reason for their strong cardio-protective characteristics.

The phenolic compounds of olive oil exhibit a wide range of other protective benefits. They help increase the blood levels of beneficial HDL cholesterol,[50] demonstrate strong anti-inflammatory activity,[51] reduce the risk of blood clotting through reduction of platelet aggregation,[52] improve immune function[53] and exhibit anti-mutagenic properties by preventing oxidative damage to DNA[54] — impressive credentials, indeed, for the humble olive.

According to Visioli,[55] in the areas of highest olive oil consumption the daily dietary intake is approximately 50 grams (g), providing an intake of approximately 25 milligrams (mg) of polyphenols. This amount is in the order of total flavonoid intake that has been associated with a lower incidence of coronary heart disease.[56] There appears, however, to be a wide variance in the level of polyphenols in North American, as opposed to European oils. Owen and co-workers[57] report phenol levels in European oils that are double those found in products assayed by some U.S researchers.[58]

HO HO O O O O C O —CH3 H O O - B - glucopyranose

Oleuropein

Implications

The weight of scientific evidence supporting the health benefits of the dietary consumption of polyphenols is immense. Their power as free radical antagonists, their recognized efficacy in reducing cardiovascular and cancer risks, and their demonstrated pharmacologic properties (as anti-inflammatory, anti-viral, anti-bacterial, anti-allergic, anti-hemorrhagic and immuno-enhancing agents), make an exceptionally strong case for their inclusion in nutritional supplements.

The *International Consensus Statement*, issued recently by the European Commission, promoting the adoption of the Mediterranean diet, echoes the scientific findings: the consumption of olive oil and the phenolic compounds, derived from the fruit of the olive tree, confer profound health benefits.

The biochemistry of polyphenols is an emerging area of nutritional research; because of its novel nature, there is not yet a quantitative consensus among our cited nutritional authorities, with respect to daily intake. While there is definitive recognition that supplementation with polyphenols is highly desired, no *median* recommended daily intake specific to phenolic compounds is yet available. For this reason, we have turned to the emergent scientific literature (Visioli and Galli[59]) in order to establish a recommended daily intake of 25 mg of phenolic compounds as the basis for our *Blended Standard.*

Accordingly, the bioflavonoids (citrus flavonoids, quercetin, quercitrin, hesperidin, rutin, naringin, bilberry extract and the green tea flavonoids) are combined with the procyanidolic oligomers (grape seed and pine bark extracts) to form a component of our product score criteria, listed collectively under the category of *Bioflavonoid Profile.*

The phenolic compounds, including the olive-based phenolic compounds and the phenolic acid derivative, curcumin, form another component of our product score criteria, listed under the category of *Phenolic Compound Profile.*

1 International Consensus Statement. "Olive Oil and the Mediterranean Diet: Implications for Health in Europe." *Brit J Nursing* 1997, **6(12):** 75-677.

2 Keys A et al. "The diet and 15 year death rate in the Seven Countries Study." *Am J Epidemiol* 1986, **124:** 903-15.

3 Willett WC. "Diet and coronary heart disease." *Monogr Epidemiol Biostat* 1990, **15:** 341-79.

4 World Health Organization. "Diet, Nutrition and the Prevention of Chronic Disease." *Report of the WHO Study Group: WHO Technical Report Series,* Geneva, 1990, 797.

5 Reavon P et al. "Feasibility of using an oleate-rich diet to reduce susceptibility of low-density lipoprotein to oxidative modification in humans." *Am J Clinic Nutr* 1991, **54:** 701-706.

6 Parthasarathy S et al. "Low density lipoprotein rich in oleic acid is protected against oxidative modification: implications for dietary prevention of atherosclerosis." *Proc Nat Acad Sci* 1990, **87:** 3984-98.

7 Keys A. *Seven Countries: A Multivariate Analysis of Death and Coronary Heart Disease,* Harvard University Press, Cambridge MA, 1980.

8 World Health Organization. "Food and health indicators: computerized presentation." *WHO Regional Office for Europe, Nutrition Programme,* Copenhagen, 1993.

9 Visioli F and Galli C. "Natural antioxidants and prevention of coronary heart disease: the potential role of olive oil and its minor constituents." *Nutr Metab Cardiovasc Dis* 1995, **5:** 306-314.

10 International Consensus Statement. "Olive Oil and the Mediterranean Diet: Implications for Health in Europe." *Brit J Nursing* 1997, **6(12):** 75-677.

11 Hertog MGL et al. "Flavonoid intake and long-term risk of coronary heart disease and cancer in the Seven Countries Study." *Arch Intern Med* 1995, **155:** 381-386.

12 Hertog MGL et al. "Dietary antioxidant flavonoids and risk of coronary heart disease: the Zutphen Elderly Study." *Lancet* 1993, **342:** 1007-1011.

13 Hanasaki Y, Ogawa S and Fukui S. "The correlation between active oxygen scavenging and antioxidative effects of flavonoids." *Free Radic Biol Med* 1994, **16:** 845-50.

14 Hope WC et al. "In vitro inhibition of the biosynthesis of slow reacting substance of anaphylaxis (SRS-A) and lipoxygenase activity by quercetin." *Biochem Pharmocol* 1983, **32:** 367-71.

15 Duarte J et al. "Vasodilatory effects of flavonoids in rat aortic smooth muscle. Structure-activity relationships." *Gen Pharmocol* 1993, **24:** 857-62.

16 Ratty AK and Das NP. "Effects of flavonoids on non-enzymatic lipid peroxidation: structure-activity relationships." *Biochem Med Metab Biol* 1988, **39:** 69-79.

17 Cavalinni L, Bindoli A and Siliprandi N. "Comparative evaluation of antiperoxidative action of silymarin and other flavonoids." *Pharmacol Res Commun* 1978, **10:** 133-6.

18 Visioli F et al. "Low density lipoprotein oxidation is inhibited in vitro by olive oil constituents." *Atherosclerosis* 1995, **117:** 25-32.

19 Visioli F and Galli C. "Natural antioxidants and prevention of coronary heart disease: the potential role of olive oil and its minor constituents." *Nutr Metab Cardiovasc Dis* 1995, **5:** 306-314.

20 Hertog MG et al. "Dietary antioxidant flavonoids and risk of coronary heart disease: The Zutpher Elderly Study." *Lancet* 1993, **342:** 1007-1011.

21 Hertog MGL et al. "Content of potentially anticarcinogenic flavonoids of 28 vegetables and 9 fruits commonly consumed in the Netherlands." *J Agric Food Chem* 1992, **40:** 2379-83.

22 American Chemical Association. "Food Phytochemical and Cancer Prevention." *ACS Symposium Series,* Ho CT et al (eds.), 547, 1994.

23 Block G. "The data support a role for antioxidants in reducing cancer risk." *Nutr Rev* 1992, **50:** 207-13.

24 Havstein B. "Flavonoids, a class of natural products of high pharmacological potency." *Biochem Pharmocol* 1983, **32:** 1141-48.

25 Muosi I and Pragai BM. "Inhibition of virus multiplication and alteration of cyclic AMP level in cell cultures by flavonoids." *Experimentia* 1985, **41:** 930-31.

26 Murray MT and Pizzorno J. *Encyclopedia of Natural Medicine.* Prima Health, Rocklin CA, 1998, pp 324-25.

27 Bagchi D et al. "Free radicals and grape seed proanthocyanidin extract: importance in human health and disease prevention." *Toxicol* 2000, **148(2-3):** 187-97.

28 Cuomo, J. notes from a personal interview. USANA Health Sciences, Salt Lake City, UT , March 2003.

29 Schwitters B and Masquelier J. "OPC in Practice: Bioflavonols and their Application." *Alpha Omega,* Rome, 1993.

30 Masquelier J. "Procyanidolic Oligomers." *J Parfums Cosm Arom* 1990, **95:** 89-97.

31 Frankel EN et al. "Inhibition of oxidation of low-density lipoprotein by phenolic substances in red wine." *Lancet* 1993, **341:** 454-7.

32 Hasagawa R et al. "Preventive effects of green tea against liver oxidative DNA damage and hepatotoxicity in rats treated with 2-nitropropane." *Food Chem Toxicol* 1995, **33(1):** 961-70.

33 Ji BT et al. "Green tea consumption and the risk of pancreatic and colorectal cancers." *Int J Cancer* 1997, **70(3):** 255-8.

34 Yu GP et al. "Green tea consumption and the risk of stomach cancer: a population-based case-control studying Shanghai, China." *Cancer Causes Control* 1995, **6(6):** 532-8.

35 Rechner AR et al. "Black tea represents a major source of dietary phenolics among regular tea drinkers." *Free Radic Res* 2002, **36(10):** 1127-35.

36 Visioli F et al. "Low density lipoprotein oxidation is inhibited in vitro by olive oil constituents." *Atherosclerosis* 1995, **117(1):** 25-32.

37 Segala M (ed.) *Life Extension Foundation. Disease Prevention and Treatment (3rd edition),* Life Extension Media, 2000, pp 340-341.

38 Keys A et al. "The diet and 15 year death rate in the Seven Countries Study." *Am J Epidemiol* 1986, **124:** 903-15.

39 Willett WC. Diet and coronary heart disease. *Monogr Epidemiol Biostat* 1990, **15:** 341-79.

40 World Health Organization. "Diet, Nutrition and the Prevention of Chronic Disease. Report of the WHO Study Group." *WHO Technical Report Series,* Geneva, 1990, 797.

41 Keys A et al. "The diet and 15 year death rate in the Seven Countries Study." *Am J Epidemiol* 1986, **124:** 903-15.

42 Hertog MGL et al. "Dietary antioxidant flavonoids and risk of coronary heart disease: the Zutphen Elderly Study." *Lancet* 1993, **342:** 1007-1011.

43 Martin-Moreno JM. "Dietary fat, olive oil intake and breast cancer risk." *Int J Cancer* 1994, **58(6):** 774.

44 Bird RP and Lafave LM. "Varying effect of dietary lipids and azoxymethane in early stages of colon carcinogenesis: enumeration of aberrant crypt foci and proliferative indices." *Cancer Detect Prev* 1995, **19(4):** 308-15.

45 Ferrara LA et al. "Olive oil and reduced need for antihypertensive medications." *Arch Intern Med* 2000, **160(6):** 837-42.

46 Vissers MN et al. "Olive oil phenols are absorbed in humans." *J Nutr* 2002, **132(3):** 409-17.

47 Visioli F et al. "Low density lipoprotein oxidation is inhibited in vivo by olive oil constituents." *Atherosclerosis* 1995, **117(1):** 25-32.

48 Vissers MN et al. "Effect of consumption of phenols from olives and extra virgin olive oil on LDL oxidizability in healthy humans." *Free Radical Res* 2001, **35(5):** 619-29.

49 Rabovsky A and Cuomo J. "Olive Oil: Direct Measure of Antioxidant Activity." *Free Radic Biol Med* 1999, **27(Suppl 1):** S42.

50 Mangez-Cruz MA et al. "Effect of minor constituents (non-glyceride compounds) of virgin olive oil on plasma lipid concentrations in male Wistar rats." *Clin Res* 2001, **20(3):** 211-15.

51 Martinez-Dominguez E et al. "Protective effects upon experimental inflammation models of a polyphenol-supplemented virgin olive oil diet." *Inflamm Res* 2001, **50(2):** 102-6.

52 Petroni A et al. "Inhibition of platelet aggregation and eicosanoid production by phenolic components of olive oil." *Thromb Res* 1995, **78(2):** 151-60.

53 Yaqoob P et al. "Effect of olive oil on immune function in middle-aged men." *Am J Clin Nutr* 1998, **67(1):** 129-35.

54 Deiana M et al. "Inhibition of peroxynitrite-dependent DNA base modification and tyrosine nitration by extra virgin olive oil-derived antioxidant hydroxytyrosol." *Free Radic Biol Med* 1999, **26(56):** 762-9.

55Visioli F and Galli C. "Natural antioxidants and prevention of coronary heart disease: the potential role of olive oil and its minor constituents." *Nutr Metab Cardiovasc Dis* 1995, **5:** 306-314.

56 Hertog MGL et al. "Dietary antioxidant flavonoids and risk of coronary heart disease: the Zutphen Elderly Study." *Lancet* 1993, **342:** 1007-1011.

57 Owen RW et al. "Phenolic compounds and squalene in olive oils: the concentration and antioxidant potential of total phenols, simple phenols, secoiridoids, lignans and squalene." *Food Chem Toxicol* 2000, **38(8):** 647-59.

58 Cuomo J. notes from a personal interview. USANA Health Sciences, Salt Lake City, UT, March 2003.

59 Visioli F and Galli C. "Natural antioxidants and prevention of coronary heart disease: the potential role of olive oil and its minor constituents." *Nutr Metab Cardiovasc Dis* 1995, **5:** 306-314.

Touch a scientist and you touch a child.
— *Ray Bradbury*

CHAPTER FIFTEEN

Lipotropic Factors

Preventing Toxic Buildup

In our toxic world, we are exposed to ever-increasing levels of contaminants and harmful chemicals that, once ingested, accumulate in fatty deposits within the body. Because of their relatively high concentration of fatty tissue, the liver and the brain are two primary targets for the bioaccumulation of lipid-soluble toxins, such as heavy metals. Vitamins C, E and beta-carotene, the water-soluble B-complex vitamins, and some of the trace minerals consumed in the diet, play important roles in protecting these tissues from the damage caused by oxidative assault from environmental toxins.[1,2]

However, it is the liver, the body's "purification" unit, which endures the brunt of the action. First in line to deal with the contaminants consumed in our foods or drinking water, the liver is subject to a daily onslaught of noxious challenges. In addition to the external toxic load (a function of lifestyle and environment), the liver must also deal with a range of endogenous (internal) toxins produced by the metabolic processes of our body. Normally, the liver can cope quite handily; however, when things go wrong — a result of chronic nutritional deficiencies, disease or overuse of pharmacological drugs — the workload for the liver can increase dramatically.

The vast majority of all cancers are believed to be due to the effect of environmental carcinogens, combined with deficiencies in dietary micronutrients;[3] therefore, proper functioning of our livers' detoxification systems is critical. High levels of exposure to environmental toxins, coupled with a poorly functioning liver, can profoundly increase our risk of cancer. An investigation of bladder cancer in Italian workers at a chemical plant in Turin, Italy, revealed that those individuals who had defective liver detoxification systems were the unfortunate ones who developed cancer.[4]

> *Up to 90 percent of all cancers are thought to be due to the effects of environmental carcinogens such as those in cigarette smoke, food, water, and air, combined with deficiencies of the nutrients the body needs for proper functioning of the detoxification and immune systems.*
>
> — Dr. Michael Murray
> and Dr. Joseph Pizzorno

Fortunately, proper diet, nutritional supplementation and treatment with herbal remedies can fortify the liver to withstand toxic stress. Within the liver, choline and inositol assist with the task of toxic elimination, helping to mobilize the fatty tissue and remove heavy metals and other noxious compounds.

These agents are known as *lipotropic* (fat-moving) agents because of their ability to mobilize fats and bile (a secretion from the liver that helps emulsify fats during the digestive process). Lipotropic agents have a long history of use within the naturopathic community to help restore and enhance liver function and treat a number of common liver ailments.

Inositol's presence is required for the proper action of several neurotransmitters in the brain, including serotonin and acetylcholine. Several studies confirm inositol's effect on brain disorders, including general panic disorder and obsessive-compulsive disorder.

Dietary lipotropic agents work by increasing the levels of S-adenosylmethionine (SAM-e), the liver's in-house lipotropic agent, and glutathione, the première detoxicant in the body. They have been preferentially used because, until recently, SAM-e has not been commercially available in the United States (it is still restricted in Canada) and dietary glutathione is not well absorbed in the digestive tract.[5]

Choline

Choline acts as a methyl donor, transferring methyl (-CH_3) groups to other molecules essential in the process of lipid mobilization. While it can be manufactured by the conversion of other amino acids, choline has recently been designated an essential nutrient.[6,7] Without choline, fats become trapped in the liver, where they accumulate, along with the fat-soluble toxins they carry, and disrupt proper liver function. Choline also plays an important role in the transmission of signals inside cells and is an essential component of cell membranes.

The vast majority of all cancers are believed to be due to the effect of environmental carcinogens, combined with deficiencies in dietary micronutrients;[3] therefore, proper functioning of our livers' detoxification systems is critical. High levels of exposure to environmental toxins, coupled with a poorly functioning liver, can profoundly increase our risk of cancer.

Studies confirm that choline supplementation, primarily as phosphatidylcholine (*P*-choline), has proven effective in improving mental acuity and as a treatment for asthma[8] and bipolar disorder.[9] Choline also increases levels of acetylcholine, an important neuro-transmitter in the brain. Studies indicate that supplementation with choline counteracts anatomical changes in the brain associated with aging.[10] (Unfortunately, trials with the treatment of Alzheimer's disease have been inconsistent.[11])

During the digestive process, lecithin is converted to choline and fatty acids. Once in the body, however, choline is easily re-converted to *P*-choline. *P*-choline entertains several important physiological functions, including increasing the solubility of cholesterols, lowering blood cholesterol levels, removing cholesterol from tissue deposits, and reducing the tendency of blood platelets to aggregate and clot.[12]

Inositol

Inositol is an unofficial member of the B-complex family and works closely with choline in the task of lipid mobilization and detoxification in the liver. An essential component of cell membranes and the myelin sheath protecting nerve cells, inositol plays an important role in proper nerve action and the regulation of brain and muscle functions.

Inositol's presence is required for the proper action of several neurotransmitters in the brain, including serotonin and acetylcholine. Several studies confirm inositol's anti-depressive actions in the brain,[13,14] including general panic disorder[15] and obsessive-compulsive disorder.[16] Inositol therapy may prove, in fact, to be a useful treatment in the management of clinical depression.[17]

Implications

Our selected nutritional authorities recognize both choline and inositol as essential because of the pivotal role these nutrients play in lipid mobilization and detoxification within the liver. Six out of our seven cited authors recommend daily supplementation with choline at a median level of 59 mg/day and inositol intake at a median level of 125 mg/day. Lecithin, which is converted to choline during the digestive process, is recommended at 350 mg/day.

Accordingly, supplementation with these nutrients, at the levels deemed suitable for optimal nutritional health by our cited nutritional authorities, is included as an important component in our product score criteria.

1 Flora SJS et al. "Prevention of Lead Intoxication by Vitamin B Complex." *Z Ges Hyg* 1984, **30:** 409-11.

2 Shakman RA. "Nutritional Influences on the Toxicology of Environmental Pollutants: A Review." *Arch Env Health* 1974, **28:** 105-33.

3 Murray MT and Pizzorno J. *Encyclopedia of Natural Medicine*, Prima Health, Rocklin CA, 1998, p108.

4 Talska G et al. "Genetically Based N-Acetyltransferase Metabolic Polymorphism and Low-Level Environmental Exposure to Carcinogens." *Nature* 1994, **369:** 154-56.

5 Witschi A et al. "The systemic availability of oral glutathione." *Eur J Clin Pharmacol* 1992, **43:** 667-69.

6 Canty DJ and Zeisel SH. "Lecithin and choline in human health and disease." *Nutr Reviews* 1994, **52:** 327-339.

7 Murray MT. *Encyclopedia of Nutritional Supplements*, Prima Health, Rocklin CA, 1996, p137.

8 Gupta SK and Gaur SH. "A placebo-controlled trial of two dosages of LPC antagonist-choline in the management of bronchial asthma." *Indian J Chest Dis Allied Sci* 1997, **39(3):** 149-56.

9 Stoll AL et al. "Choline in the treatment of rapid-cycling bipolar disorder: clinical and neurochemical findings in lithium-treated patients." *Biol Psychiatry* 1996, **40(5):** 382-88.

10 Ricci A et al. "Oral Choline Alfocerate Counteracts Age-dependent Loss of Mossy Fibres in the Rat Hippocampus." *Mech Aging Dev* 1992, **66(1):** 81-91.

11 Franco-Masidi A et al. "Brain mapping activity and mental performance after chronic treatment with CDP-choline in Alzheimer's disease." *Methods Find Exp Clin Pharmacol* 1994, **16(8):** 597-607.

12 Brook JG et al. "Dietary soya lecithin decreases plasma triglyceride levels and inhibits collagen and ADP-induced platelet aggregation." *Biochem Med Metabol Biol* 1986, **35:** 31-49.

13 Benjamin J et al. "Inositol treatment in psychiatry." *Psychopharmacol Bull* 1995, **31:** 167-175.

14 Levine J et al. "Double-blind, controlled trial of inositol treatment of depression." *Am J Psychiatry* 1995, **152:** 1084-1086.

15 Benjamin J et al. "Double-blind, placebo-controlled, cross-over trial of inositol treatment for panic disorder." *Am J Psychiatry* 1995, **152:** 1084-1086.

16 Levine J. "Controlled trials of inositol in psychiatry." *Eur Neuropsychopharmacol* 1997, **7(2):** 147-155.

17 Murray MT. *Encyclopedia of Nutritional Supplements*, Prima Health, Rocklin CA, 1996, p143.

Organic chemistry is the study of carbon compounds;
biochemistry is the study of carbon compounds that crawl.

— *Michael Adams*

CHAPTER SIXTEEN

POTENTIAL TOXICITIES

Avoiding Too Much of a Good Thing

In order to optimize preventive benefits, the strategy of nutritional supplementation is to encourage long-term use. Consequently, there exists a potential risk for consumers with regard to the cumulative toxicity of particular nutrients. What folly it would be to supplement with high levels of vitamin A and iron, only to find down the road that your investment, instead of promoting wellbeing, had jeopardized your health.

Most nutrients used in nutritional supplements have a high degree of safety; however, some nutrients require a degree of prudence, when it comes to long-term use. Vitamin A (retinol), because of its solubility in fatty tissues, can become toxic when taken in high doses over a long period. As well, chronic iron overload can significantly increase the level of oxidative damage to the cells. Accidental overdose of iron-containing nutritional supplements is a leading cause of fatal poisoning in children.

Supplementation at 5,000-10,000 IU per day of preformed vitamin A — a dose well within the range offered in many popular vitamin supplements — may lead to cumulative toxic overdose.

This is not to say that vitamin A and iron are not important to the health of our cells; both nutrients play crucial roles in cellular metabolism. But it is important to be aware that there exist safe and effective alternatives for meeting the daily requirements for these nutrients *without* compromising one's health through imprudent use.

Because of their importance in cellular health and their cumulative natures within the tissues, both too much and too little vitamin A and iron are problematic. The following discussion will guide you through the merits and the dangers of supplementing with these two nutrients.

Vitamin A

Vitamin A (retinol) is an important component in the maintenance of our eyes, skin, teeth, bones and mucous membranes. The term, retinol, is derived from the fact that the vitamin is an alcohol (*-ol*) and is involved in the functions of the retina of the eye. There are actually two biologically active forms of retinol. Retin*al*, the aldehyde form of retinol, is involved in the chemistry of vision; retin*oic* acid, the acidic form, is important in several other body functions, including cell growth and differentiation (cell specialization).[1]

Retinol also possesses antiviral, anti-carcinogenic and cardioprotective properties.[2] As well, the vitamin assists in the growth and repair of body tissues, and helps bolster immune defences against infection. While retinol exhibits some level of antioxidant activity, its dietary precursor, beta-carotene, is a far more powerful antioxidant and is likely responsible for the vitamin's reported anti-carcinogenic activity.[3]

Deficiency in Vitamin A is one of the most common vitamin deficiencies known and one of the five major nutritional deficiencies common in children under five years of age. It is particularly prevalent in third-world countries, where malnutrition is endemic. While vitamin A-deficient individuals are more susceptible to a number of infectious diseases, including respiratory viral infections and pneumonia, blindness is one of the most serious consequences.[4] Exposure to environmental toxins has been associated with acute retinol deficiency, a likely consequence of enhanced degradation of the vitamin in the liver.[5]

Several epidemiological studies associate low intakes of vitamin A with cancers of the lungs, head and neck.[6] Deficiency may also increase the risk of breast cancer.[7] Other studies report that vitamin A and its derivatives are key components in the prevention and treatment of cancer, including skin malignancies, bronchial cancers, bladder and colorectal tumors.[8,9,10,11]

Vitamin A deficiencies are a causative factor in several other disease processes. Poor vitamin A status is linked to an increased risk of coronary artery disease,[12] myocardial infarction[13,14] and an increased prevalence of diabetic abnormalities.[15] Among children with clinical deficiencies of retinol, supplementation appears to mitigate stress-induced immunological disorders[16] and reduce morbidity and mortality from infectious disease.[17] However, daily intake of the vitamin is a bit of a balancing act, as too much vitamin A can also be quite problematic.

Toxicology of Retinol

Despite the prevalence of vitamin A deficiency, retinol toxicity is a common occurrence. As many as five percent of those who supplement with vitamin A unknowingly suffer from toxicity symptoms.[18] Supplementation at 5,000-10,000 IU per day of preformed vitamin A — a dose well within the range offered in many popular vitamin supplements — may lead to *cumulative* toxic overdose.[19] As well, accidental ingestion of a single, large dose of vitamin A can produce acute toxicity in children.[20] Signs of toxicity include dry damaged skin, brittle nails, irritability, nausea, vomiting and fatigue.

A complicating factor is that individual tolerances for vitamin A vary widely. Retinol toxicity in adults generally requires prolonged supplementation at high doses; however, defects in liver storage and transport, caused by cirrhosis or hepatitis, can induce toxicity in smaller daily doses.

Women who supplement with vitamin A while in early pregnancy should be cautious. Dosages greater than 10,000 IU per day during pregnancy may be responsible for one in 57 cases of birth defects in the United States.[21] Consumption of more than 10,000 IU of vitamin A carries five times the risk of birth defects, compared to pre-natal consumption of less than 5,000 IU per day. Rothman and co-workers[22] found that the prevalence of birth defects appears concentrated in those women who consume high levels of the pre-formed vitamin within the first seven weeks of their pregnancy. The authors conclude that women who *might* become pregnant should limit their retinol intake to below 5,000 IU, or — better yet — supplement with beta-carotene.

Women who supplement with vitamin A while in early pregnancy should be cautious. Dosages greater than 10,000 IU per day may be responsible for one in 57 cases of birth defects in the United States. Consumption of more than 10,000 IU of vitamin A carries five times the risk of birth defects.

Dr. Kenneth Cooper, renowned for his pioneering work in aerobic fitness, recommends avoiding pre-formed vitamin A supplements altogether. Instead, he encourages supplementation with non-toxic beta-carotene (pro-vitamin A). Other nutritional authorities express this general sentiment, some of whom also voice concern regarding the use of retinol supplements when taking vitamin A-derivative skin medications or broad-spectrum antibiotics.[23]

Beta-Carotene — a safe alternative

Beta-carotene, the orange/yellow-colored pigment found in many garden vegetables, is a retinol precursor. The body easily converts beta-carotene by cleaving the molecule into two molecules of retinol, as needed, and thereby avoiding the toxic accumulation of the pre-formed vitamin. Once transformed into active retinol, beta-carotene confers the same beneficial effects as vitamin A.

Other than occasional loose stools or slight discoloration of the skin, even high doses of beta-carotene do not exhibit toxicity. As an added benefit, beta-carotene is a much more potent antioxidant than retinol and provides even greater protection against oxidative challenge. If you overdose on beta-carotene you might turn orange like a carrot — but provided you're not around any large rabbits, you'll be just fine!

One note of caution is warranted: there is some evidence that ingestion of high doses of alcohol with beta-carotene may result in liver damage because of the oxidative conversion of the beta-carotene.[24] Keep in mind, this study was conducted on animals supplemented with a single antioxidant. Other investigations suggest that protection of beta-carotene from alcohol-induced oxidation simply requires other antioxidants to be present[25] — an observation that further supports the importance of broad-spectrum nutritional support.

The body easily converts beta-carotene by cleaving the molecule into two molecules of retinol, as needed, and thereby avoiding the toxic accumulation of the pre-formed vitamin.

Iron

Results from the third National Health and Nutrition Examination Survey (NHANES III) indicate that iron deficiency is common throughout the United States. Those at greatest risk are infants under two years of age, teenage girls, pregnant women and low-income elderly.[26] One study found that some degree of iron deficiency exists in 35 to 58 percent of healthy, young women;[27] the onset of menses (the menstrual cycle) and the proliferation of junk food diets have been cited as probable causes.

A lack of stomach acid (a common consequence of the aging process)[28] and the growing overuse of antacids may contribute to decreased iron absorption. The common misconception that chronic hyperacidity causes gastrointestinal distress has led to an alarming increase in the use of commercial antacids, with a consequent loss of iron status in those who are overly reliant on these products. Iron deficiencies can lead to anemia, learning disabilities, impaired immune functions and extreme fatigue.[29,30] There is evidence that low iron status is a likely cause of all-cause and coronary-related mortality in the elderly.

Iron plays an important role in the physiology of the body. As a central part of the hemoglobin and myoglobin molecules, iron is indispensable to the body's ability to transport gases into and out of the cell. It is also needed in several important enzymes involved in energy production, metabolism and DNA synthesis. Some iron is lost through the breakdown of red blood cells and the excretion of bile. However, due to its importance, the body conserves iron at all costs; the kidneys do not eliminate the metal.

For this reason, iron is a two-edged sword. Consumed as heme-iron (the form found in meats, complexed with the oxygen-carrying pigment hemoglobin), it is easily absorbed and utilized by the body. However, when consumed in excessive amounts as elemental iron (the form generally found in inexpensive mineral supplements), iron can become an aggressive oxidizing agent, adding considerably to the oxidative challenge to the body. (To protect itself against the hostile pro-oxidant nature of iron, the body manufactures a protein, known as transferrin, which binds the metal ion and transfers it to the bone marrow, spleen and liver, to be stored as ferritin.)

Many people, unaware of the dark side of iron, consume iron supplements with abandon, overloading their systems with non-heme iron and actually *increasing* their level of oxidative stress. Others will take iron-containing multivitamins faithfully, believing that they are giving their bodies a lift — and herein lays the problem.

Other nutrients, such as citric acid and vitamin C, common in most multivitamin formulations, are powerful iron-absorption agents and can cause unintentional iron overload. This, in turn, can expose unwary consumers to increased risks of heart disease, cancer, diabetes, osteoporosis and arthritis[31] — not exactly what you want from your nutritional supplement. On the other side of the coin, vitamin E and the minerals zinc, magnesium and copper will *compete* with iron absorption. High calcium intake, in particular, can inhibit iron uptake if present in the same meal or supplement. Separation of calcium intake from iron intake is the *only* effective means of resolving this conflict.[32]

So, some nutrients compete with iron absorption, some enhance it — all in all, quite a dilemma. It is for these reasons that supplemental iron should *not* be taken in combination with other supplements.

The bottom line is this: if you *need* to supplement with iron, do so through your diet. Lean red meat, dark-green leafy vegetables, dried beans and whole grain cereals are your safest sources of iron. Iron consumed through lean meats and other natural food sources will not generally lead to iron overload in normal subjects.[33] Amino acid and Krebs cycle iron chelates are the safest forms, and best tolerated by the gut if supplementation *still* proves necessary.

Some nutrients compete with iron absorption, some enhance it — all in all, quite a dilemma. It is for these reasons that iron should not be taken in combination with other supplements.

Iron Toxicity

The dark side of iron supplementation, relating to its latent toxicity, arises when it is consumed in amounts excessive to the body's needs. While unbound (non-heme) iron is more likely to generate oxidative challenges through free radical generation, excessive iron supplementation in *any* form can create profound problems for the cell. Iron overload can cause deterioration of the gut lining, vomiting and diarrhea, abdominal and joint pain, liver damage, loss of weight and intense fatigue.[34] Acute doses as low as 3 grams can cause death in children.

Approximately one out of every 250 North Americans has *hemochromatosis*, a genetic defect common in those of northern European descent. The disorder causes the body to accumulate and store abnormally high levels of iron. People with hemochromatosis store twice as much iron as others, placing themselves at increased risk for iron overload-related diseases. Symptoms generally occur after 50 years of age and include fatigue, abdominal pain, achy joints, impotence, and symptoms that mimic diabetes.

The bottom line is this: if you need to supplement with iron, do so through your diet. Lean red meat, dark leafy-green vegetables, dried beans and whole-grain cereals are your safest sources of iron.

Evidence from several studies suggests that high levels of iron contribute to a noticeable increase in the risk for cardiovascular disease, likely due to non-heme iron's aggressive pro-oxidant nature. Serum ferretin levels are, in fact, one of the strongest biochemical markers for the progression of atherosclerosis, a consequence of the dramatically increased level of oxidation of LDL cholesterol.[35] A 1995 study, conducted on Finnish men, found that those with high levels of stored iron in the body had a markedly increased risk of heart attack. Men with the highest levels of stored iron showed a level of risk three times that of men with the lowest levels.[36]

Iron accumulation disorders contribute to a variety of other disease states, all of which are degenerative in nature. Studies reveal that chronic iron overload contributes to increased infections, cancer, arthritis, osteoporosis, diabetes and various cognitive dysfunctions.[37,38] Data obtained from the first National Health and Nutrition Examination Survey (NHANES I), linking body-stores of iron and cancer, found that an elevated risk was associated with high iron levels.[39]

Unless you are a woman with regular menses (menstrual periods), the only way to remove excess iron is through bleeding. That is why, for men, iron overload can prove quite problematic to resolve.

Implications

The majority of nutrients used in supplementation have a large measure of safety; however, the use of vitamin A and iron warrants prudence and caution, particularly when consumed by children or pregnant women. As well, supplementation with iron is counter-indicated for those who might carry the genetic trait for hemochromatosis and for those consuming supplements with a high dosage of ascorbate and citrate.

Accordingly, consideration of the levels of vitamin A and iron, in excess of the median *Recommended Daily Intakes* derived from our cited nutritional authorities, forms the final criterion in the 14-point product score used in this comparative guide. This criterion penalizes any product whose score exceeds the established limits for either vitamin A or iron.

1 Reavley N. *The New Encyclopedia of Vitamins, Minerals, Supplements and Herbs.* Bookman Press, New York NY, pp 34-41.

2 Cooper K. *Advanced Nutritional Therapies.* Thomas Nelson Publishers, Nashville TN, 1996, pp 65-72.

3 Murray MT. *Encyclopedia of Nutritional Supplements.* Prima Health, Rocklin CA, 1996, pp 19-38.

4 Raki JS et al. "Childhood Blindness Due to Vitamin A Deficiency in India: Regional Variations." *Arch Dis Child* 1995, 72(4): 330-3.

5 Cullum ME and Zile MH. "Acute polybrominated biphenyl toxicosis alters vitamin A homeostasis and enhances degradation of vitamin A." *Toxicol Appl Pharmacol* 1985, **81**: 177-181.

6 Reavley N. The New Encyclopedia of Vitamins, Minerals, Supplements and Herbs. Bookman Press, New York NY, pp 34-41.

7 Zang S et al. "Measurement of retinoids and carotenoids in breast adipose tissue and a comparison of concentrations in breast cancer cases and control subjects." *Am J Clin Nutr* 1997, **66(3)**: 626-32.

8 Clerice M et al. "[Current Status of the Use of Vitamins (A,E,C,D), Folates and Selenium in the Chemoprevention and Treatment of Malignant Tumors]." *Minerva Med* 1987, **78(6)**: 377-86.

9 Guslandi M. "Vitamin A, Retinol, Carotene and Cancer Prevention." *Br Med J* 1980, **281(6251)**: 1352.

10 Stich HF et al. "Remission of Precancerous Lesions in the Oral Cavity of Tobacco Chewers and Maintenance of the Protective Effect of Beta-Carotene and Vitamin A." *Am J Clin Nutr* 1991, **52(1 Suppl)**: 298S-304S.

11 Paganelli GM et al. "Effect of Vitamin A, C and E Supplementation on Rectal Cell Proliferation in Patients with Colorectal Adenomas." *J Nat Cancer Inst* 1992, **84(1)**: 47-51.

12 Singh RB et al. "Dietary Intake, Plasma Levels of Antioxidant Vitamins and Oxidative Stress in Relation to Coronary Artery Disease in Elderly Subjects." *Am J Cardiol* 1995, **76(17)**: 1233-88.

13 Singh RB et al. "Plasma Levels of Antioxidant Vitamins and Oxidative Stress in Patients with Acute Myocardial Infarction." *Acta Cardiol* 1994, **49(5)**: 441-52.

14 Ruiz RF et al. "Plasma Levels of Vitamins A and E and the Risk of Acute Myocardial Infarct." *Rev Clin Esp* 1997, **197(6)**: 411-16.

15 Kudriashov BA et al. "[Prophylactic Effect of Vitamin A, Neutralizing the Development of Experimental Insulin-dependent Diabetes in Animals]." *Vopr Med Khim* 1993, **39(1)**: 20-22.

16 Pletsityi KD et al. "[Immuno-correcting Activity of Vitamin A in Stress]" *Biull Eksp Biol Med* 1987, **104(11)**: 609-11.

17 Simba RD. "Vitamin A, Immunity and Infection." *Clin Infect Dis* 1994, **19(3)**: 489-99.

18 Reavley N. *The New Encyclopedia of Vitamins, Minerals, Supplements and Herbs.* Bookman Press, New York NY, pp 34-41.

19 Cooper, K. *Advanced Nutritional Therapies.* Thomàs Nelson Publishers, Nashville TN, 1996, pp 65-72.

20 Olsen R (ed). *Nutrition Review's Present Knowledge in Nutrition (6th edition).* Nutrition Foundation, 1987, pp 96-107.

21 Murray MT. *Encyclopedia of Nutritional Supplements.* Prima Health, Rocklin CA, 1996, pp 19-38.

22 Rothman KJ et al. "Teratogenicity of high vitamin A intake." *N Eng J Med* 1995, **333(21)**: 1369-73.

23 Reavley N. *The New Encyclopedia of Vitamins, Minerals, Supplements and Herbs.* Bookman Press, New York NY, pp 34-41.

24 Leo MA et al. "Interaction of ethanol with beta-carotene: delayed blood clearance and enhanced hepatotoxicity." *Hepatology* **15**: 883-89, 1992.

25 Krinsky HI. "Antioxidant Functions of Carotenoids." *Free Rad Biol Med* 1989, 7617-7635.

26 Morley JE. "Nutritional Status of the Elderly." *Am J Med* 1986, **81**: 679-95.

27 Krause MV and Mahan KL. *Food, Nutrition and Diet Therapy, 7th edition.* WB Saunders, Philadelphia PA, 1984, pp128-31.

28 Bezwoda W et al. "The importance of gastric hydrochloric acid in the absorption of non-heme iron." *J Lab Clin Med* 1978, **92**: 108-16.

29 Fairbanks VF and Beutler E. "Iron." in: *Modern Nutrition in Health and Disease (7th edition).* Skils ME and Young VR (eds), Lea and Febiger, Philadelphia PA, 1988, pp 193-226.

30 Cook JD and Lynch SR. "The Liabilities of Iron Deficiency." *Blood* 1986, **68**: 803-9.

31 Crawford RD. "Proposed role for a combination of citric acid and ascorbic acid in the production of dietary iron overload: a fundamental cause of disease." *Biochem Mol Med* 1995, **54(1)**: 1-11.

32 Cooper K. *Advanced Nutritional Therapies.* Thomas Nelson Publishers, Nashville TN, 1996, pp 65-72.

33 Hulten L, Gramatkovski E, Gleerup A et al. "Iron absorption from the whole diet. Relation to meal consumption, iron requirements and iron stores." *Eur J Clin Nutr* 1995, **49(11)**: 794-808.

34 Cooper K. *Advanced Nutritional Therapies.* Thomas Nelson Publishers, Nashville TN, 1996, pp 263-7.

35 Kiechl S et al. "Body iron stores and the risk of carotid atherosclerosis: prospective results from the Brunich Study." *Circulation* 1997, **96(10)**: 3300-07.

36 Tuomainen TP et al. "Association between body iron stores and the risk of acute myocardial infarction in men." *Circulation* 1998, **97(15)**: 1461-6.

37 Gordeuk V et al. "Iron Overload: Causes and Consequences." *Ann Rev Nutr* 1987, **7**: 485-508.

38 Reavley N. *The New Encyclopedia of Vitamins, Minerals, Supplements and Herbs.* Bookman Press, New York, NY, pp 249-62.

39 Stevens R et al. "Moderate elevation of body iron level and increased risk of cancer occurrence and death." *Int J Cancer* **56**: 364-9.

Section III

How the Comparisons were Made

This section provides the reader with an in-depth look at:

- methodology
- limitations of the study
- how to interpret the graphs
- development of the *Blended Standard*
- development of the *Final Product Score*
- the Top Twenty-five nutritional products

The evaluation process is discussed. Specific criteria used for the construction of the Blended Standard scoring methodology and the development of the Final Product Score are presented. An explanation of how to interpret the graphs is provided and the Top Twenty-five nutritional products are presented.

The saddest aspect of life is that science gathers knowledge faster than society gathers wisdom.

— *Isaac Asimov (1920-1992)*

CHAPTER SEVENTEEN

BLENDED STANDARD

How the Comparisons were Made

To provide a quantitative method for rating nutritional products, relative to an established benchmark, we have constructed an analytical model based on the individual recommendations of seven published nutritional authorities. Each authority that we reference is recognized and respected within the scientific, medical or naturopathic communities. Each has also published one or more works, citing specific recommendations for daily nutritional intakes:

✔ **Phyllis Balch, CNC**, is a leading nutritional counselor in America and a recognized advocate of nutritional therapies. She is author of *Prescription for Nutritional Healing: The A-to-Z Guide to Supplements* (2002) and principal author of *Prescription for Nutritional Healing: A Practical A-to-Z Reference to Drug-Free Remedies Using Vitamins, Minerals, Herbs & Food Supplements* (2000). The latter book is co-authored by Dr. James Balch, M.D., a graduate of Indiana University School of Medicine, a member of the American Medical Association, fellow of the American College of Surgeons and a certified urologist. (Note: because of the co-authorship of their 2000 edition of *Prescription for Nutritional Healing*, we recognize the authors as a single reference source.)

✔ **Dr. Michael Colgan, Ph.D.**, is an internationally recognized authority on sports nutrition and author of *The New Nutrition: Medicine for the Millennium* (1995) and *Hormonal Health: Nutritional and Hormonal Strategies for Emotional Well-Being and Intellectual Longevity* (1996). He was a senior member of the Faculty of Science at the University of Auckland and a visiting scholar at Rockefeller University of New York. Dr. Colgan is currently the Director of the Colgan Institute of Nutritional Science, located in San Diego, California and Saltspring Island, British Columbia.

✔ **Dr. Earl Mindell, Ph.D.**, is one of America's leading nutritionists and an internationally recognized authority on nutrition, drugs, vitamins and herbal remedies. He is a registered pharmacist, master herbalist, and a professor of nutrition at Pacific Western University in Los Angeles. Dr. Mindell has authored several books, including *Earl Mindell's Vitamin Bible for the 21st Century* (1999) and *Dr. Earl Mindell's What You Should Know About Creating Your Own Personal Health Plan* (1996).

✔ **Dr. Michael Murray, N.D.**, is one of the world's leading authorities on natural medicine. A meticulously researched author and lecturer, he is a member of the faculty of Bastyr University of Seattle. In addition to his private practice, Dr. Murray has published over 20 books on natural medicine, including the *Encyclopedia of Nutritional Supplements* (1996) and the *Encyclopedia of Natural Medicine* (1998).

✔ **Dr. Richard Passwater, Ph.D.**, is an acknowledged expert in free radical pathology and trace element research. A biochemist renowned for his contributions to the advancement of the science, Dr. Passwater is also the author of best-selling guide, *The New Supernutrition* (1991) and *The Antioxidants* (1997). Acclaimed internationally as a leader in megavitamin therapies, Dr. Passwater is currently Director of the Solgar Nutritional Research Center in Berlin, Maryland.

✔ **Dr. Ray Strand, M.D.**, has been a practicing family physician for 26 years and is a graduate of University of Colorado School of Medicine. An articulate advocate for the integration of optimal nutrition and advanced nutritional therapies in preventive healthcare, Dr. Strand is the author of *Bionutrition: Winning the War Within* (1998) and his most recent publication, *What Your Doctor Doesn't Know About Nutritional Medicine May Be Killing You* (2002).

✔ **Dr. Julian Whitaker, M.D.**, is one of the founders of the California Orthomolecular Medical Society and Director of the Whitaker Wellness Institute, Inc. in Newport Beach, California. Author of the best selling guide, *Dr. Whitaker's Guide to Natural Healing* (1996), he is also the author and publisher of *Health & Healing* — a leading health newsletter in the U.S., with a circulation of nearly 700,000. His numerous health-related articles also appear in such magazines as *Prevention* and *Let's Live.*

The Blended Nutritional Standard

To construct our analytical model, we assessed and pooled the individual recommendations for daily nutritional intake from the seven cited nutritional authorities. While each author's recommendations had a few characteristics not recognized by the others, there was substantial commonality; to create our *Blended Nutritional Standard* (Blended Standard) we exploited those areas of commonality.

For a nutrient to qualify for inclusion in the *Blended Standard,* at least three of the seven authorities must cite a recommended daily intake for the specified nutrient (with one exception).* In all, 39 nutrient categories, consisting of 17 vitamins or vitamin-like factors, 14 minerals, 3 phytonutrient complexes and 5 other nutritional factors, are identified and incorporated into the *Blended Standard.* The dosage for each nutrient is determined by calculating the median value from those authorities that provided a specified dosage recommendation.

With the exception of Passwater's recommendations (which are divided into four fitness categories based on diet, level of health and level of physical activity), the daily levels of intake published by each authority are for the general adult population. Passwater's middle two categories (B and C) are selected to develop the *Blended Standard.* These categories represent individuals who have "average" to "good" diets, "average" health, and who are "somewhat" to "fairly" active. Using the range of values within these two categories, the minimum and maximum recommended intake levels for each nutrient are determined.

> ***In all, 39 nutrient categories, consisting of 17 vitamins or vitamin-like factors, 14 minerals, 3 phytonutrient complexes and 5 other nutritional factors, are incorporated into the Blended Standard.***

Murray,[1] Passwater,[2] Strand,[3,4] Mindell,[5] Whitaker[6] and Balch[7,8] provide a range of recommended intakes for each nutrient, while Colgan[9] cites a specified value. Therefore, for each authority, the *averaged* value for each nutrient is determined. These averaged values are pooled in order to calculate the *median* recommended intake for each nutrient among the seven authorities.

The *Table of Recommended Daily Intakes* on the page 66 shows the specific nutritional recommendations of each authority, along with the median (pooled) value for each nutrient included in the *Blended Standard,* derived from these recommendations.

Limitations of the Study

Individual products might contain ingredients other than those listed in the *Blended Standard*; however, specified ingredients are *not* included in the comparison if those ingredients are not identified in the *Blended Standard.* Additionally, while a manufacturer may list an ingredient identified in the *Blended Standard,* the nutrient is not included in the comparison if the exact amount (µg, mg or IU) of a nutrient is not provided or cannot be determined. For example, if vitamin A is listed as "5,000 IU of vitamin A with beta-carotene" the entire amount is entered as vitamin A because the exact amount of beta-carotene cannot be determined.

Excipients

In determining the relative product scores, no consideration is given to the presence or absence of various fillers, additives, preservatives and coatings; nor are the issues of manufacturing, quality control, raw material sources or purity addressed. Consideration of these factors is, however, crucial to the overall determination of product quality.

Accordingly, we review the top-ranking products (those that have garnered an exceptional *Final Product Score* of 90 percentage points or above), to assess the quality standards employed in their manufacture. This information, along with a breakout of the components of the *Final Product Score,* a description of the product and general information on the company, is available on pages 68 and 69.

Products with Phytonutrients

In constructing the *Blended Standard,* the bioflavonoids, including citrus flavonoids, soy isoflavones, quercetin, quercitrin, hesperidin, rutin, bilberry extract and green tea catechins, are listed under the category of *Bioflavonoid Profile* The phenolic compounds, including the unique olive-based polyphenols and turmeric extracts (curcumin), are listed under the category of *Phenolic Compound Profile.* The procyanidolic oligomers (PCOs), including grape seed and pine bark extracts, form a third component of the bioflavonoid complex. They are combined with the mixed bioflavonoids under the category of *Bioflavonoid Profile* for inclusion in the *Blended Standard.*

Products with Ingredients Not Listed

Some products contain one or more ingredients not included in the *Blended Standard.* These products often include macro-nutritional components, such as amino acids, proteins, and carbohydrate and nucleic acid complexes, which are easily obtained from a balanced diet. Other products contain herbal components that, while recognized for their merit, are not generally acknowledged by the cited nutritional authorities on which we have based our scoring criteria.

Where a product contains ingredients that are not acknowledged in the recommendations from our cited authorities, those ingredients are deemed *non-essential,* for the purposes of this comparison.

Products with Unspecified Dosages

In a few cases, the recommended daily dose of a product is unavailable from the data collected or the information provided by the company. In such cases, the daily dose is "derived" by adjusting the daily intake to provide for up to 400 IU of vitamin D, as indicated in the product formulation. This appears to be the standard daily dosage for vitamin D, as indicated in the vast majority of nutritional supplements, and is just slightly greater than the median daily dosage listed in the *Blended Standard.* For any of these products containing vitamin A, the derived dosage (of up to 400 IU of vitamin D) is restricted by setting an upper allowable daily intake of 10,000 IU of vitamin A, in order to avoid potential cumulative toxicity levels.

Products in Daily Packs

Many manufacturers are now promoting nutritional products sold as packs. Because of the vast number of these products now entering the market, products sold as daily packs are generally excluded from this analysis. They will be compared in a separate publication.

* The biochemistry of polyphenols is an emerging area of nutritional research; because of its novel nature, a quantitative consensus among our cited nutritional authorities is not available. There is definitive recognition that supplementation with polyphenols is highly desired; however, no median recommended daily intake, specific to phenolic compounds, is provided. For this reason, we have turned to the emergent scientific literature (Visioli F and Galli C. Nutr Metab Cardiovasc Dis 1995, 5: 306-314.) in order to establish a recommended daily intake of 25 mg of phenolic compounds as the basis for our Blended Standard.

Health Canada Drug Product Database

In some cases, confirmation of a Canadian product's formulation was only possible through Health Canada's Drug Product Database. While comprehensive, the data format of this database does not list some of the less common phytonutrients as active ingredients in Canadian formulations. The few products whose formulations were obtained solely through this information source are indicated as such in Appendices A and B.

Sources of Information

The formulations of the nutritional products included in this comparative guide come from information provided through:

- ✔ product labels
- ✔ product monographs
- ✔ PDR for Nutritional Supplements (First Edition)[10]
- ✔ Government of Canada's Drug Product Database[11]
- ✔ Compendium of Nonprescription Products[12]
- ✔ as available through corporate web sites and the Internet
- ✔ through direct contact with the company

Interpreting the Graphs

For each product evaluated, the nutrient profile is compared to that of the *Blended Nutritional Standard*, based on the manufacturer's labelling information, including the maximum recommended daily dose. Each comparison rests on the assumption that the labelling is correct with respect to actual composition and dosage. The amount (µg, mg or IU) of each nutrient in the product is compared to the *Blended Nutritional Standard* for that nutrient.

For the purpose of this comparison, the nutrients included in the graphs are *only* those that are contained in the *Blended Nutritional Standard. In other words, if a nutrient is not included in the* Blended Standard *it is not on the graph.* The graphs are based on relative percentage values because this provides the simplest means of comparing different units of measure (µg, mg or IU). The amount of each nutrient in the *Blended Standard*, therefore, represents 100 percent for that nutrient.

Colour of Graphs

Note that each graph changes colour for those nutrients that exceed 100 percent of the recommended daily intake, based on the *Blended Standard*. This makes it easy to depict the nutrients in a product that meet or exceed the recommended daily intakes of the *Blended Standard*. Each bar shown in dark blue represents the amount (up to 100%) of a nutrient in a product, compared to the recommended intake for that nutrient in the *Blended Standard*. Each bar shown in light blue represents the amount that a nutrient in a product exceeds 100 percent of the recommended intake for that nutrient in the *Blended Standard*.

For vitamin A and iron, daily intakes up to 100 percent of the *Blended Standard* are highlighted in yellow. This simply denotes the need for cautionary use of this particular nutrient. Intakes exceeding 100 percent of the values listed in the *Blended Standard* are highlighted in red. (For cautionary information on potential toxicities, please see Chapter Sixteen.)

A numerical nutrient code, related to the specific nutrients in the *Blended Standard*, is provided. To identify the nutrient and its relative potency, its numerical code is simply matched with the numerical code in the legend, available on each even-numbered page in Section IV.

For purposes of visual standardization, any daily intakes exceeding 150 percent of the *Blended Standard* are truncated (capped).

Qualifying the Products

The Upper Limit of daily intake (UL) is a component of the new Dietary Reference Intake (DRI) standards currently under joint development by the United States and Canada. The UL represents the upper level of intake for a specific nutrient deemed to be safe for use by adults.⁺ The ULs for several vitamins, minerals and other nutritional factors have now been determined and are shown in the *Table of Recommended Daily Intakes*, page 66.

All nutritional products considered for inclusion in this comparative guide were assessed initially for excessive potency. Any product containing two or more nutrients with potencies exceeding 150 percent of the Upper Limit was eliminated from further consideration. In the several hundred products evaluated in compiling this comparative guide, only three were screened out for reasons of potency, based on the U.S. Food and Nutrition Board UL criteria.

The Final Product Score

Qualifying products are assessed quantitatively to provide a percentage ranking relative to the *Blended Standard*. Fourteen criteria are employed in determining relative product standings. To receive a full point for any single criterion, the product must meet or exceed the benchmark established for that criterion. Partial points are awarded for the partial fulfillment of each criterion. The fourteenth criterion penalizes the product if the product formulation exceeds defined limits for those nutrients with potential cumulative toxicities.

For those manufacturers having more than one nutritional product, in general, only the top-rated product was chosen, based on Final Product Score. In the case of those companies having products in both the U.S. and Canadian markets, the top-ranked product from each market, if identified, was included.

The development of each criterion is based on scientific evidence available in the literature and presented in Section II. Nutrient potencies are based on the pooled recommendations for daily intake established in the *Blended Standard*. These criteria, detailed below, are an enhancement of those developed for the *Comparative Guide to Nutritional Supplements (2nd edition)*.

1. **Completeness** — *Does the product contain the full spectrum of nutrients listed in the* Blended Standard *and considered essential for optimal health?*

2. **Potency** — *Of those nutrients in the product, what percent are found at potency levels meeting or exceeding 50 percent of the potency for those nutrients in the* Blended Standard*?*

⁺ The Food and Nutrition Board, Institute of Medicine, Washington, DC has recently established the ULs for a number of vitamins and minerals. These values are shown in The Table of Recommended Daily Intakes, page 66

3. Bioavailability — *Does the product contain minerals in their most bioavailable forms as amino acid chelates or organic acid complexes?*

4. Bioactivity of Vitamin E — *Does the product contain only the d-isomer of vitamin E (the natural, biologically active form of alpha tocopherol) or does the product use the d/l isomers of vitamin E (a synthetic form, where the biological activity is about one-half [or less] of the natural vitamin E)?*

5. Cardiac Health Triad — *Does the product contain vitamin E, coenzyme Q_{10} and magnesium, three nutritional components important to cardiac health, at potencies that meet or exceed 50 percent of the* Blended Standard*?*

6. Homocysteine Reduction Triad — *Does the product contain the nutritional triad of vitamin B_6, vitamin B_{12} and folic acid, at levels meeting or exceeding 50 percent of the* Blended Standard*?*

7. Bone Health Complex — *Does the product contain the nutrients shown by clinical studies to be important for optimal bone health (vitamin D, vitamin K, folic acid, vitamin B_6, vitamin B_{12}, boron, calcium, magnesium, silicon and zinc) at potencies equal to or exceeding 50 percent of the potencies listed in the* Blended Standard*?*

8. Antioxidant Triad — *Does the product contain the important antioxidant triad of vitamin E, vitamin C and beta-carotene at potencies equal to or exceeding 50 percent of the potencies listed in the* Blended Standard*?*

9. Glutathione Support — *Does the product contain the nutritional precursors necessary for glutathione synthesis and the proper functioning of the Glutathione Peroxidase Pathway, at potencies equal to or exceeding 50 percent of the potencies listed in the* Blended Standard*?*

10. Metabolic Support — *Does the product contain the nutrients necessary to help regulate glucose metabolism and support the body's ability to generate, store and utilize energy, and are these nutrients available at potencies equal to or exceeding 50 percent of the potencies listed in the* Blended Standard*?*

11. Bioflavonoid Profile — *Does the product contain a mixture of bioflavonoids (citrus flavonoids, soy isoflavones, quercetin, quercitrin, hesperidin, rutin, bilberry extract and green tea catechins,) and proanthocyanidins at potencies that meet or exceed 50 percent of the combined recommended potencies for PCOs and mixed bioflavonoids in the* Blended Standard*?*

12. Phenolic Compound Profile — *Does the product contain phenolic compounds (polyphenolic acids and their derivatives, including curcumin) at a potency level recently established in the literature (25 mg) that has been associated with a reduced incidence of coronary heart disease?*

13. Lipotropic Factors — *Does the product contain the important lipotropic factors, choline (including phosphatidylcholine) and inositol, at levels meeting or exceeding 50 percent of the* Blended Standard*?*

14. Potential Toxicities — *Does the nutritional supplement contain levels of vitamin A and iron that exceed 100% of the* Blended Standard*?*

From these fourteen criteria, a *Final Product Score*, based on a percentage ranking, is calculated. A score approaching 100% represents a product that possesses those characteristics for optimal nutrition, as reflected in the *Blended Standard*; conversely, a low percent score represents a product possessing few, if any, of the characteristics for optimal nutrition, as reflected in the *Blended Standard.* A percentage rating, based on the *Final Product Score* for each product, is translated into a five-star scale and displayed below the appropriate graph. The score is also shown as a percentage ranking for each product, relative to the *Blended Standard.*

Due to the immense number of nutritional products on the market, not all products evaluated are graphically compared. Those products graphically analyzed are selected in order to ensure representation from each company identified. For those manufacturers having more than one nutritional product, in general, only the top-rated product is chosen, based on *Final Product Score.* In the case of those companies having products in both the U.S. and Canadian markets, the top-ranked product from each market, if identified, is included.

All products analyzed, along with their *Final Product Scores*, are listed in Appendices A and B.

1 Murray MT. *Encyclopedia of Nutritional Supplements*, Prima Health, Rocklin CA, 1996, pp 11-12.

2 Passwater RA. *The New Supernutrition*, Simon & Schuster Inc., New York NY, 1998, pp 304-306.

3 Strand RD. *What Your Doctor Doesn't Know About Nutritional Medicine May Be Killing You*, Thomas Nelson Publishers, Nashville TE, 2002, pp 194-195.

4 Strand RT. *Bionutrition: Winning the War Within*, Comprehensive Wellness Publishing, Rapid City SD, 1998, pp 130-133.

5 Mindell E. *Dr. Earl Mindell's What You Should Know About Creating Your Own Health Plan*, Keats Publishing Inc., New Canaan KT, 1996, pp 52-53.

6 Whitaker J. *Dr. Whitaker's Guide to Natural Healing*, Prima Publishing, Roseville CA, 1996, p 37.

7 Balch PA and Balch JF. *Prescription for Nutritional Healing: A Practical A-to-Z Reference to Drug-Free Remedies Using Vitamins, Minerals, Herbs & Food Supplements (3rd edition).* Pengiun Putnam Inc., New York NY, 2000, p 6.

8 Balch PA. *Prescription for Nutritional Healing: The A-to-Z Guide to Supplements (2nd edition).* Pengiun Putnam Inc., New York NY, 2002, pp 9-14.

9 Colgan M. *Hormonal Health: Nutritional and Hormonal Strategies for Emotional Well-Being and Intellectual Longevity (1st ed.),* Apple Publishing, Vancouver BC, 1996, pp 223-226.

10 Hendler SS and Rorvik D. *PDR For Nutritional Supplements: First Edition.* Medical Economics Company, Montvale, NJ, 2001.

11 Therapeutic Products Program. *Drug Product Database.* Health Canada. www.hc-sc.gc.ca/hpb/drug-dpd/.

12 Repchinsky C (ed.) *Compendium of Nonprescription Products*, 7th Edition. Canadian Pharmacist's Association, Ottawa, ON, 2000.

The Blended Standard: Table of Recommended Daily Intakes

Nutritional Components	Units	Balch Average	Colgan Average	Mindell Average	Murray Average	Passwater Average	Strand Average	Whitaker Average	Blended Median	Upper Limits
Vitamins										
Vitamin A	IU	7500	7500		5000	10000		5000	7,500	10,000 IU
Vitamin D	IU	400	400	300	250	350	625	250	350	2000 IU
Vitamin K	ug	300	75		180		75	180	180	ND
B-Complex Vitamins										
Biotin	ug	600	500	200	200	57.5	650	200	200	ND
Folic Acid	ug	600	400	300	400	600	900	300	400	1000 ug
Vitamin B_1	mg	75	50	37.5	55	42.5	25	55	50	ND
Vitamin B_2	mg	32.5	45	62.5	30	42.5	37.5	55	43	ND
Vitamin B_3	mg	107.5	130	62.5	75	62.5	52.5	75	75	35 mg (as niacin)
Vitamin B_5	mg	75	150	62.5	62.5	137.5	140	62.5	75	ND
Vitamin B_6	mg	75	50	75	62.5	55	37.5	62.5	63	100 mg
Vitamin B_{12}	ug	300	100	550	400	55	175	300	300	ND
Antioxidant Vitamins and Nutrients										
alpha-Carotene							650		insufficient data	ND
beta-Carotene	IU	15000	12500	12500	15000	11250	12500	15000	12,500	ND
Coenzyme Q_{10}	mg	65	30	60	100	15	25		45	ND
Lipoic Acid	mg		100		35		22.5		35	ND
Para-Aminobenzoic Acid	mg	30	35			52.5			35	ND
Vitamin C	mg	2000	3250	2000	1000	4750	1500	175	2,000	2000 mg
Vitamin E	IU	500	400	400	600	500	600	600	500	1467 IU (1000 mg)
Vitamin E (mixed tocopherols)	IU		200						insufficient data	ND
Bioflavonoid Complex										
Bioflavonoids (mixed)	mg	350	250		4000				555	! * * ND
Hesperidin	mg	75							insufficient data	ND
Lutein	mg		6				3.5		insufficient data	ND
Lycopene	mg		15				2		insufficient data	ND
Phenolic compounds ^ ^ ^	mg		900		350				25	^ ^ ^ ND
Pinus Epicatechins	mg		10						insufficient data	ND
Procyanidolic Oligomers	mg		285		50	50	100		75	ND
Quercetin	mg	105			900				insufficient data	ND
Rutin	mg	25							insufficient data	ND
Zeaxanthin	mg	90							insufficient data	ND
Glutathione Complex										
Cysteine (n-acetyl)	mg	375	50			50	62.5		56	ND
Glutathione	mg		100				15		insufficient data	ND
Lipid Metabolism										
Carnitine	mg	800		750		50			750	ND
Choline	mg	125		62.5	55	55	150	55	59	* 3500 mg
Inositol	mg	125	200	200	55	55	200	55	125	ND
Lecithin	mg	350	200			1500			350	^ ND
Linoleic Acid	mg		150						insufficient data	ND
Linolenic Acid (alpha)	mg		250						insufficient data	ND
Linolenic Acid (gamma)	mg		25						insufficient data	ND
Phosphatidylcholine	mg								insufficient data	^ ND
Phosphatidylserine	mg		180		300				insufficient data	ND
Minerals										
Boron	mg	4.5	3	3	3.5	1.5	2.5	1.5	3	
Calcium	mg	1750	800	900	750	250	1150	500	800	2500 mg
Chromium (trivalent)	ug	275	200	300	300	200	250	300	275	ND
Copper	mg	2.5	0.5	3	1.5	2	2	1.5	2	10 mg
Iodine	ug	162.5	100		100	75	150	100	100	1100 ug
Iron	mg	24	10		22.5	10		22.5	23	* * * 45 mg
Magnesium	mg	875	600	450	375	300	650	375	450	250 mg
Manganese	mg	6.5	6	10	12.5	3	4.5	12.5	7	11 mg
Molybdenum	ug	65	60		17.5	87.5	75	17.5	63	2000 ug
Potassium	mg	299.5	100		350	12.5		350	300	ND
Selenium	ug	150	300	37.5	150	137.5	200	150	150	400 ug
Silicon	mg				13	12.5	3	0.6	8	ND
Vanadium	ug	600		112.5	75		65	75	75	ND
Zinc	mg	40	15	12.5	30	20	25	22.5	23	40 mg
Other Nutritional Factors										
Dimethylglycine (DMG)	mg					50	350		insufficient data	^ ^ ND
Gingko biloba	mg		80						insufficient data	ND
Glucosamine	mg				1500				insufficient data	ND
Lysine	mg	75							insufficient data	ND
Melatonin	mg			1.5	3				insufficient data	ND
Methionine	mg	75							insufficient data	ND
Taurine	mg	300							insufficient data	ND
Tyrosine	mg	500							insufficient data	ND

Upper Limits (UL) - The upper level of intake considered safe for use by adults, incorporating a safety factor, Food and Nutrition Board of the Institute of Medicine
^^^ Recommended level of Phenolic Acids adapted from: Visioli F and Galli C. "Natural antioxidants and prevention of coronary heart disease: the potential role of olive oil and its minor constituents." *Nutr Metab Cardiovasc Dis* 1995, **5**: 306-314.

References by author

Balch, PA, *Prescription for Nutritional Healing*, Avery Books, New York, NY, 2002
Colgan, M, *Hormonal Health*, Apple Publishing, Vancouver, BC, 1996
Mindell, E, *What You Should Know about Creating Your Personal Vitamin Plan*, Keats Pub., New Canaan, CT, 1996.
Murray, M and Pizzorino J, *Encyclopedia of Natural Medicine*, Prima Publishing, Rocklin, CA, 1998
Murray, M, *Encyclopedia of Nutritional Supplements*, Prima Publishing, Rocklin, CA, 1996
Passwater, RA, *The New Supernutrition*, Simon and Schuster Inc. New York, NY, 1991
Strand, R, *What Your Doctor Doesn't Know about Nutritional Medicine May Be Killing You*, Thomas Nelson Inc. Nashville TN, 2002
Whitaker, J, *Dr. Whitaker's Guide to Natural Healing*, Prima Publishing, Rocklin CA, 1996

*	Colgan: lecitin specified in form of p-choline
* *	Strand: no amount specified
* * *	Balch: only if an iron deficiency exists
^	Passwater: 1-2 caps estimated at 1000 mg/cap as lecithin
^ ^	Strand: recommends trimethylglycine
^ ^ ^	See comment above
!	also includes values for hesperedin, quercetin and rutin
ND	Not Determined

**The fundamentals of our nutrition
may be at the heart of some of our greatest cures.**

— *J. Greenberg*

CHAPTER EIGHTEEN

Top Rated Products

Over 1,000 reviewed — over 500 Compared

We examined over 1,000 American and Canadian nutritional products in writing this *Comparative Guide*. From this, 508 qualifying products, representing the best in the line-up of 213 companies, were further evaluated and compared to the selected nutritional standards, according to nutrient content and daily intake. Graphical comparisons were completed on two hundred and thirty-two (232) finalists, representing the top-rated product(s) from each manufacturer. (Some companies have more than one product represented, if they market in both Canada and the United States.)

The table below is a list of the top-rated twenty-five nutritional supplements in the line-up of over 500 products assessed in this comparative guide. The *Final Product Score* is a percentage-based score with a maximum value of 100%. A score of 80 percent or above is exceptionally strong and is evidence of outstanding nutritional merit, based on the assessment criteria — a commendable feat, indeed. Fewer than 0.8 percent of the 1000+ products initially reviewed were able to surpass this benchmark.

All of the twenty-five finalists exhibit strong scores. However, only those products with scores exceeding 90% earn their appointment as our *Top Products Overall.* The following chapter provides detailed information on these six outstanding nutritional products and the four companies that manufacture or distribute them.

For a complete listing of all products and their *Final Product Scores*, please refer to Appendices A and B.

Brand Name	*Product Name*	*Country*	*Score*
USANA Health Sciences	Essentials *	U.S.	96.1
Douglas Laboratories	Ultra Preventive X	U.S.	95.4
Vitamin Research Products	Extend Plus	U.S.	93.1
Source Naturals	Life Force Multiple	U.S.	92.8
Source Naturals	Élan Vitàl	U.S.	91.8
USANA Health Sciences	Essentials *	CA	90.2
FreeLife	Basic Mindell Plus	U.S.	82.3
Life Extension Foundation	Life Extension Mix	U.S.	81.4
Karuna	Maxxum 4	U.S.	79.0
Ultimate Nutrition	Super Complete	U.S.	75.8
Douglas Laboratories	Ultra Preventive Beta	U.S.	75.1
SportPharma	Multiguard	U.S.	74.9
Dr. Julian Whitaker's	Forward Multi-Nutrient	U.S.	74.7
Douglas Laboratories	Ultra Preventive III	U.S.	70.0
amni	Added Protection III	U.S.	69.1
Purity Products	Perfect Multi Focus Formula	U.S.	68.9
DaVinci Laboratories	Spectra Woman	U.S.	66.8
Doctor's Nutrition	Mega Vites Woman	U.S.	66.8
Mountain Naturals of Vermont	Women's Superior	U.S.	66.8
Douglas Laboratories	Ultra Preventive IX	U.S.	66.6
Nutrition Dynamics	Optimum Health Essentials	U.S.	66.6
Karuna	Maxxum 2	U.S.	65.7
DaVinci Laboratories	Spectra	U.S.	64.7
FoodScience of Vermont	Superior Care	U.S.	64.7
Mountain Naturals of Vermont	Superior Care	U.S.	64.7

* Score differential due to Canadian regulations, which prohibit inclusion of vitamin K and boron in nutritional supplements

The way to gain a good reputation is
to endeavor to be what you desire to appear.
Socrates (469 BC - 399 BC)

CHAPTER NINETEEN

TOP PRODUCTS OVERALL

Leaders in the nutritional supplement marketplace

USANA Health Sciences

3838 West Parkway Blvd., Salt Lake City, Utah 84120
Phone: 801-954-7100
Order Line: 888-950-9595
Web Site (corporate): www.usanahealthsciences.com
Web Site (product): www.usana-nutritionals.com
Availability: Online, multi-level marketing
Ownership: Publicly traded on NASDAQ as USNA
General Information: Microbiologist and immunologist Dr. Myron Wentz established USANA Health Sciences in 1992 to create products that provide antioxidant protection and overall cellular nutrition for the body. The primary focus of the company is to develop and market scientifically advanced nutritional products to help prevent degenerative disease and promote optimal health. USANA products are sold directly to Preferred Customers and Associates in the United States, Canada, Australia, New Zealand, the United Kingdom, the Netherlands, Hong Kong, Japan and Taiwan. In 2001, net sales reached $114.3 million. The company was featured in a December 2002 CBS Marketwatch report as the #3 performing U.S. stock in that year.
Philosophy: The Company's Mission Statement is "to develop and provide the highest quality, science-based health products, distributed internationally through Network Marketing, creating a rewarding financial opportunity for our Independent Associates, shareholders and employees."
Quality: The Company voluntarily meets Good Manufacturing Practices (GMP) for pharmaceutical-grade products, eclipsing the standards followed by most nutritional product manufacturers. Raw ingredients are quarantined until tested and quality control tests are conducted on the product during manufacturing. Written quality assurance criteria track all testing and evaluation from raw materials to finished product. Products are laboratory tested and guaranteed to meet USP specifications for quality, potency and disintegration, where applicable. The company is registered with the FDA as a pharmaceutical manufacturer.

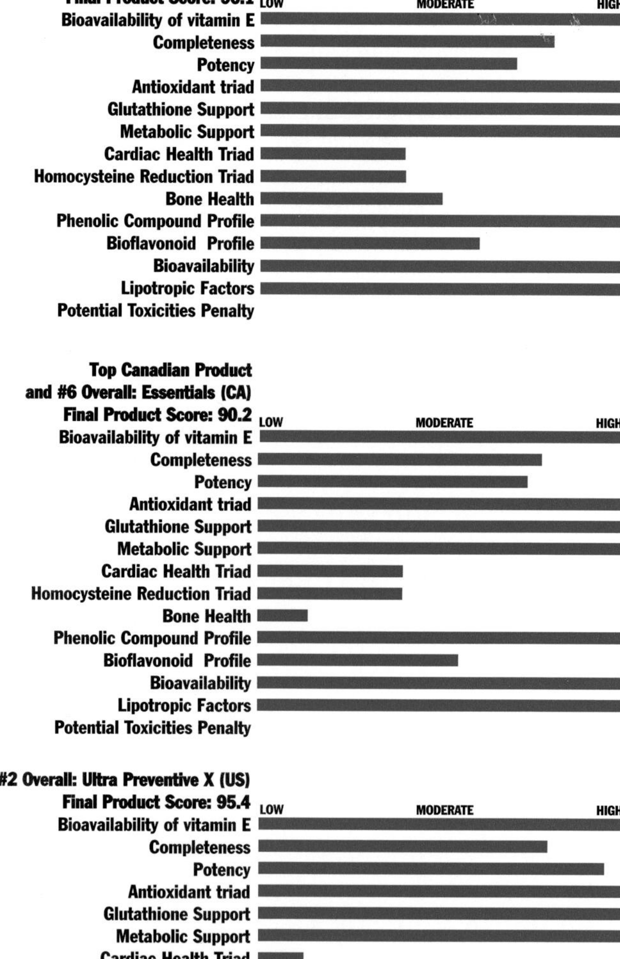

Douglas Laboratories

600 Boyce Road, Pittsburgh, PA 15205
Phone: 412-494-0122 Toll-free (US): 888-368-4522 (CA) 866-856-9954
Fax: 412-494-0155
Web Site: www.douglaslabs.com
Availability: Retail, online
Ownership: Private
General Information: Under the direction of President Jeffry Lioon and CEO Douglas Lioon, the company has a staff of over 250 laboratory employees. With three in-house laboratories, outfitted with the latest high-tech analytical equipment, and on-staff Ph.D.'s, the company produces nearly 1000 products that meet USP, GMP and other worldwide standards. The company also provides custom formulations, private labelling and packaging for those customers who wish to market their own brand of natural products.
Philosophy: The company is committed to raising the standard for nutrition and wellness.
Quality: Products meet, and often exceed, USP standards. Facility is routinely inspected by the FDA and international representatives. Products approved by Health Canada and the Commission of the European Communities. Written procedures for each aspect of production adhere to strict quality control standards. Testing and sampling of all raw materials is conducted and records kept of each component and the quantity used in every batch of product. Microbiological testing on all products ensures that they meet or exceed USP microbial limit requirements. Finished products tested to ensure USP standards for dissolution tests and pH. Product potency verified with High Pressure Liquid Chromatography.

Vitamin Research Products

3579 Highway 50 East, Carson City, NV 89701
Phone: 800-877-2447 Int'l: 775-884-8210
Order Line: 775-884-1300
Fax: 775-884-1331
Web Site: www.vrp.com
Availability: Online
Ownership: Private

General Information: Vitamin Research Products was born in 1979, when a small group of scientists, responding to the need for pharmaceutically pure high potency antioxidant formulations, decided to create their own company and develop their own special formulas. Today, Vitamin Research Products manufactures and distributes more than 450 supplements. Formulas are based on the latest clinical research and use pharmaceutical-quality ingredients. The company also provides online consultations with nutritional consultants.

Philosophy: The company is committed to making the world's finest nutritional formulas, underscored by the choice to provide most formulas in capsules, not tablets, which the company believes maximizes nutrient content, absorption and potency.

Quality: Vitamin Research Products uses USP grade ingredients in their formulations, with quality verification through high-pressure liquid chromatography (HPLC). Manufacturing standards are based on GMPs; however, there is no indication whether these GMPs are pharmaceutical-grade or food-grade.

#3 Overall: Extend Plus (US)
Final Product Score: 93.1 LOW MODERATE HIGH
Bioavailability of vitamin E
Completeness
Potency
Antioxidant triad
Glutathione Support
Metabolic Support
Cardiac Health Triad
Homocysteine Reduction Triad
Bone Health
Phenolic Compound Profile
Bioflavonoid Profile
Bioavailability
Lipotropic Factors
Potential Toxicities Penalty

Source Naturals

19 Janis Way, Scotts Valley, CA 95066
Phone: 831-438-1144 Toll-free: 800-815-2333
Fax: 831-438-7410
Web Site: www.sourcenaturals.com
Availability: Online, Retail
Ownership: Private, Threshold Enterprises Ltd.

General Information: Source Naturals was founded by CEO Ira Goldberg, in 1982. With the introduction of its Wellness Formula® for natural immune support, Source Naturals became an early pioneer in the use of integrated formulations, consisting of vitamins, minerals, herbs, amino acids, and nutraceuticals. Today, Source Naturals manufactures a line of comprehensive products using its proprietary Bio-Aligned Formulas,™ designed to help bring the power of "alignment" to the body by evaluating the root causes of body system imbalances, and then providing targeted nutrition. Source Naturals' line of more than 400 products reflects the latest advances in nutritional research, with a comprehensive selection of nutrients in their highest quality and most bioavailable forms. Products are sold through storefront retailers throughout the United States and through online retailers in the U.S. and Europe.

Philosophy: Corporate Mission Statement not available.

Quality: Raw materials are evaluated for certificate of analysis and finished products are "inspected to ensure that they meet a long list of Acceptable Quality Limits, based on industry standards and our own exacting requirements." The company seeks to minimize excipients in its products and to use the most natural sources available. There is no indication on the company's website or in its literature whether the company follows pharmaceutical GMPs or USP product quality standards.

#4 Overall: Life Force Multiple (US)
Final Product Score: 92.8 LOW MODERATE HIGH
Bioavailability of vitamin E
Completeness
Potency
Antioxidant triad
Glutathione Support
Metabolic Support
Cardiac Health Triad
Homocysteine Reduction Triad
Bone Health
Phenolic Compound Profile
Bioflavonoid Profile
Bioavailability
Lipotropic Factors
Potential Toxicities Penalty

#5 Overall: Élan Vitàl (US)
Final Product Score: 91.8 LOW MODERATE HIGH
Bioavailability of vitamin E
Completeness
Potency
Antioxidant triad
Glutathione Support
Metabolic Support
Cardiac Health Triad
Homocysteine Reduction Triad
Bone Health
Phenolic Compound Profile
Bioflavonoid Profile
Bioavailability
Lipotropic Factors
Potential Toxicities Penalty

Rating the Top Products

Scoring exceptionally well in all 14 criteria is rare; however, those companies profiled in this chapter have shown their commitment to nutritional science. There is a surprising eight percentage point difference between this leading group of products and the rest of the pack.

With new information about nutrients and their effects on cells coming out regularly, it's difficult for researchers to separate the wheat from the chaff.

Those companies listed here have avoided the buzzword of the week, opting instead for a comprehensive formulation that offers broad-spectrum protection to many critical functions of the body. Their high scores on a wide variety of criteria are ample evidence of this fact.

However, it's important to look at more than just the scores. Each company is free to follow either food or pharmaceutical standards in manufacturing and United States Pharmacopeia (USP) standards are entirely voluntary. Take the time to look beyond the ingredients to find a company whose practices are beyond reproach and whose philosophy agrees with yours.

The real benefits of nutritional supplementation are not necessarily immediate. The most important benefits come with time, as your body's resistance to aging and disease improves. Your supplement choice is an investment in your future health: make it wisely.

EXCERPT FROM THE RESEARCH NOTES

Hmmm . . . That's funny . . . .

What's on the menu?

The white tablecloths and candle centrepieces promised a wonderful meal. The waiter, dressed immaculately in black and white, looked friendly and competent as he quietly approached the table.

"Good afternoon," he said, softly. "What can I get for you today?" That should have been my first clue - I hadn't even had a chance to look at the menu yet.

I asked about the specials. The waiter beamed: he was obviously very proud of the restaurant's fare. "If you're going to be very active, perhaps going to the gym or participating in sports, I'd suggest our Active Combination," he said. "If you work at a desk job, perhaps the Ultra Plate would suit you better. We also have a Super Soup Bowl or Natural Veggie Delight if you are in a hurry."

You'd expect the companies quoted to be fly-by-night operations, hucksters trying to make a quick buck. On the contrary, they include well-known, national and international companies.

"They do sound appetizing," I said. "Can you tell me what's in each of them?"

"Ah," responded the waiter, "we use nothing but the finest ingredients, purchased directly from the growers daily!"

"That's really great," said I, beginning to wonder exactly what kind of restaurant this really was. "Does the Active Combo include pasta?"

"Absolutely," said the waiter.

"And what kind of pasta would that be, how much of it, and what kind of sauce?"

The waiter's smile faded, just a little, but he gushed enthusiasm as he replied: "It is very good pasta with a scrumptious sauce. You are sure to be satisfied."

"Terrific, but just exactly what is it? Is it linguine or macaroni? Tomato sauce or white wine sauce or pesto?"

"It's a carefully balanced recipe, which our Master Chef has perfected after years of painstaking experience in the best kitchens in the world," said the waiter.

I'd had enough guessing. As I stood up and put my coat over my arm, the waiter tried once more: "We really have your dining pleasure and satisfaction in mind. Are you sure you won't at least try one of our specials?"

I kept walking. How long could a restaurant stay in business if they wouldn't even tell you what was on the menu?

It sounds outrageous, but some nutritional supplement companies work in just this way. While most do offer product monographs or label information, either on their web sites or by email or fax, others offer absolutely no information about their products. Even when asked directly, many refuse to provide the ingredients contained in their products. While a level of trust is required in choosing any supplement, your health shouldn't require blind faith.

There are other strange things to be found in the supplement world. One company we examined claims to custom design a supplement program based on age, sex and health. Yet, no matter what profile we submitted - young or old, thin or fat, healthy or diabetic or stricken with cardiovascular disease, the same nutritional profile was recommended. It would appear the company actually has only one product, despite their claims of "customization."

When contacting companies, we specifically asked for ingredient lists, amounts, mineral forms and any other formulation information they could provide. Some of the responses we received from various companies when enquiring about their products included (names and other identifying details have been amended):

- ✔ "To order products from us, you will need to join first. Then you will have access to more detailed product information on the product labels and literature."
- ✔ "I am sorry but technical information on [our] products is only available to licensed health care providers."
- ✔ "Thank you for getting in touch with us. We appreciate your time. Please email us your contact numbers so we can call you and discuss the opportunities to work together."
- ✔ "Thank you for your interest. [We are] a natural pharmaceutical company dedicated to assisting health care practitioners help their patients through the use of clinical nutrition, homeopathics, botanicals, and other natural remedies. Please ask your practitioner for this info."
- ✔ "Information is available online for [our] members in the Reference Library."
- ✔ "Formulations are proprietary and therefore are not available."
- ✔ "This information is privileged."
- ✔ "There is no law stating that we must supply this information to you, so we are not going to do so."

Ask the tough questions

In summary, these companies either want you to join their sales program before telling you what is in their products, will not tell you at all, or they will only tell your doctor. What are they trying to hide?

You'd expect the companies quoted above to be fly-by-night operations, hucksters trying to make a quick buck by cashing in on the current raised awareness of disease prevention. On the contrary, they include well-known, national and international companies. Most of the smaller companies are only too happy to provide whatever information they can in the interest of promoting their products.

However, like the waiter in the restaurant, the customer service agents themselves may not know what they are selling. It's a scary concept, which emphasizes the need to purchase from a reputable company that can answer tough, technical questions — without demanding that you become a salesperson before they will release any product information.

Section IV

Graphical Comparisons

This section provides the reader with an in-depth look at:

- Graphical comparisons of products from 213 Canadian and U.S. companies
- Top-rated products from each company
- All products compared to *Blended Standard*
- All products rated by *Final Product Score*

Two hundred and thirty-two graphical comparisons of the top-performing multi-vitamin/mineral products from 213 U.S. and Canadian companies are presented. Relative scores, based on a five-star and percentage score are provided. Each product is graphically compared to the selected reference standard, based on the relative product scores.

Graphical Comparisons to the Blended Standard

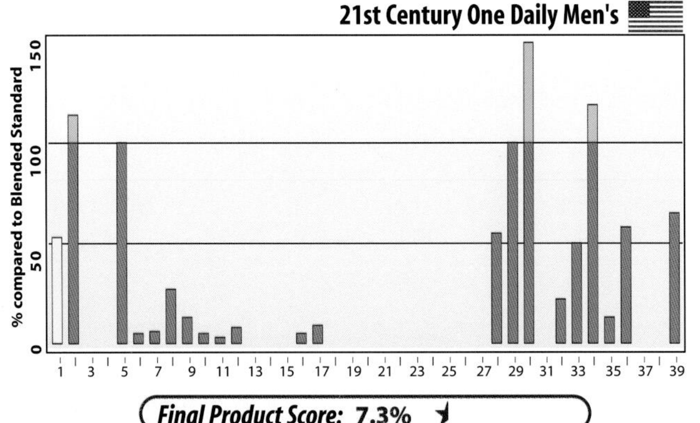

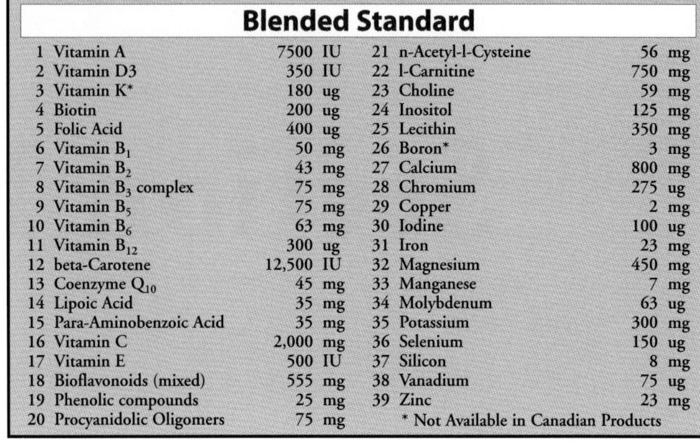

Blended Standard

	Nutrient	Amount	Unit		Nutrient	Amount	Unit
1	Vitamin A	7500	IU	21	n-Acetyl-l-Cysteine	56	mg
2	Vitamin D3	350	IU	22	l-Carnitine	750	mg
3	Vitamin K*	180	ug	23	Choline	59	mg
4	Biotin	200	ug	24	Inositol	125	mg
5	Folic Acid	400	ug	25	Lecithin	350	mg
6	Vitamin B_1	50	mg	26	Boron*	3	mg
7	Vitamin B_2	43	mg	27	Calcium	800	mg
8	Vitamin B_3 complex	75	mg	28	Chromium	275	ug
9	Vitamin B_5	75	mg	29	Copper	2	mg
10	Vitamin B_6	63	mg	30	Iodine	100	ug
11	Vitamin B_{12}	300	ug	31	Iron	23	mg
12	beta-Carotene	12,500	IU	32	Magnesium	450	mg
13	Coenzyme Q_{10}	45	mg	33	Manganese	7	mg
14	Lipoic Acid	35	mg	34	Molybdenum	63	ug
15	Para-Aminobenzoic Acid	35	mg	35	Potassium	300	mg
16	Vitamin C	2,000	mg	36	Selenium	150	ug
17	Vitamin E	500	IU	37	Silicon	8	mg
18	Bioflavonoids (mixed)	555	mg	38	Vanadium	75	ug
19	Phenolic compounds	25	mg	39	Zinc	23	mg
20	Procyanidolic Oligomers	75	mg				

* Not Available in Canadian Products

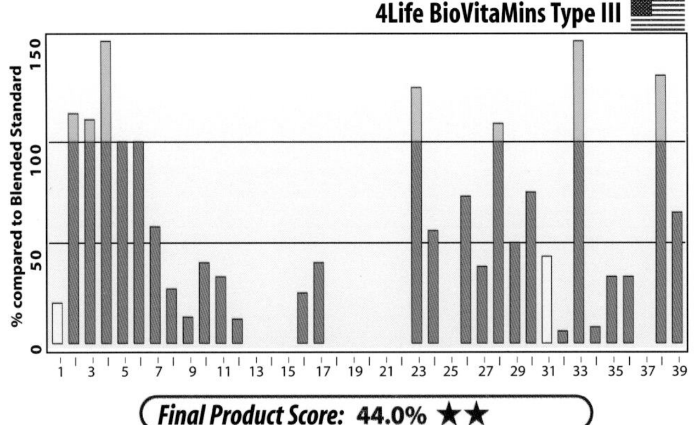

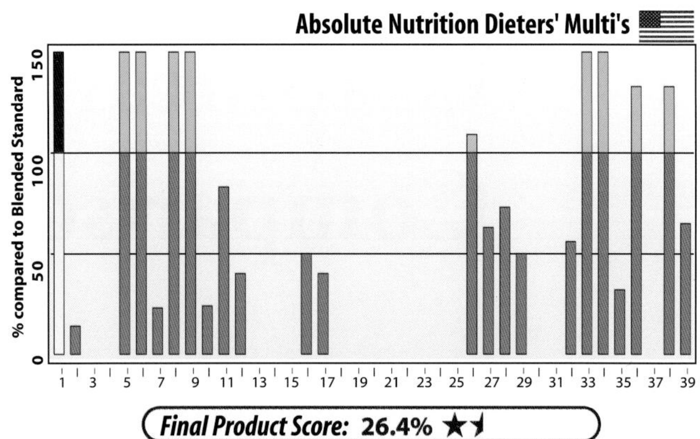

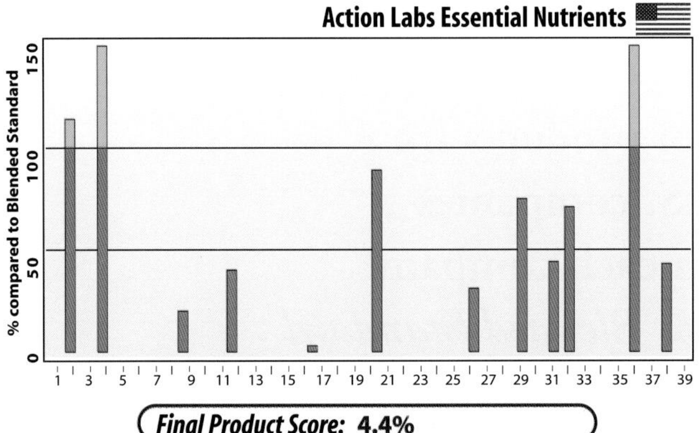

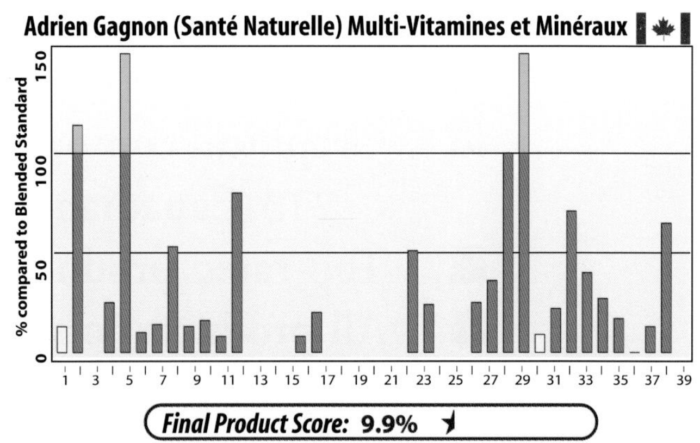

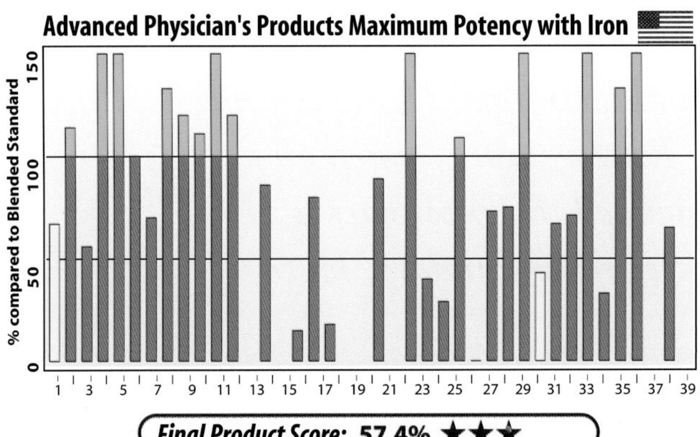

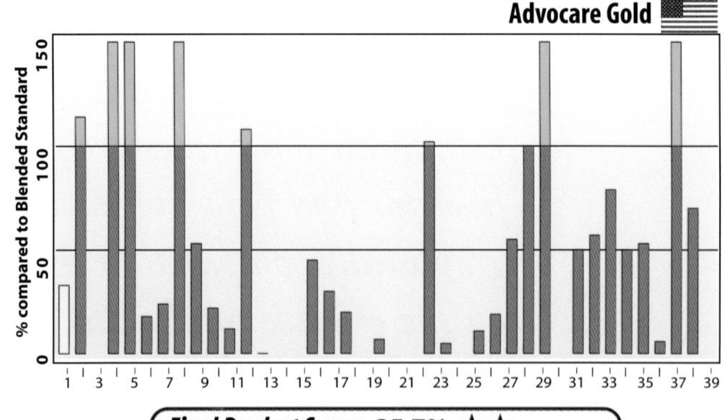

Graphical Comparisons to the Blended Standard

Albi Imports Rocky Mountain Multiple

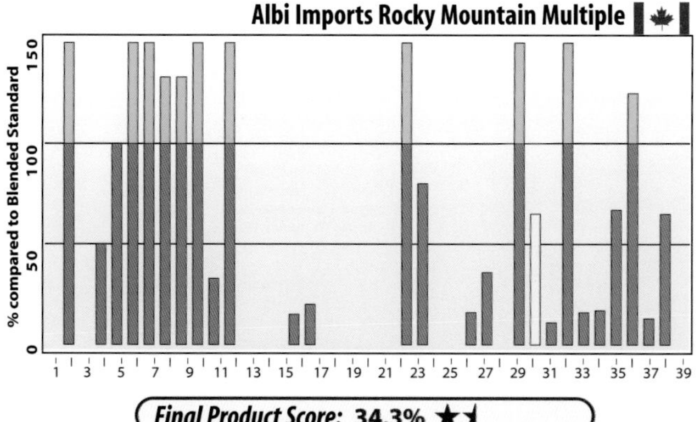

Final Product Score: **34.3%** ★½

Alive Vitamins Super One Plus

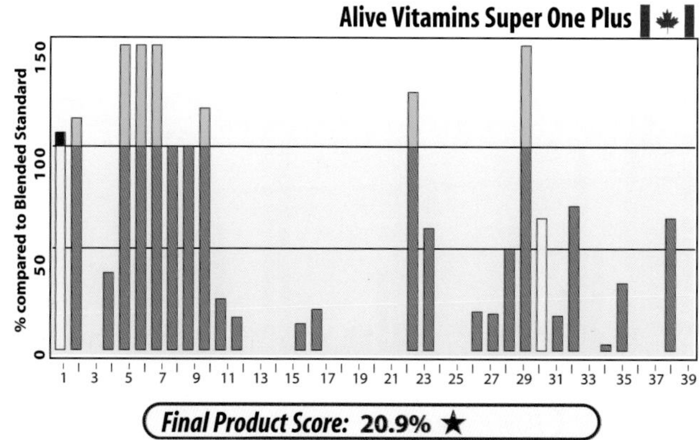

Final Product Score: **20.9%** ★

All One Powder Multiple Vitamins & Minerals

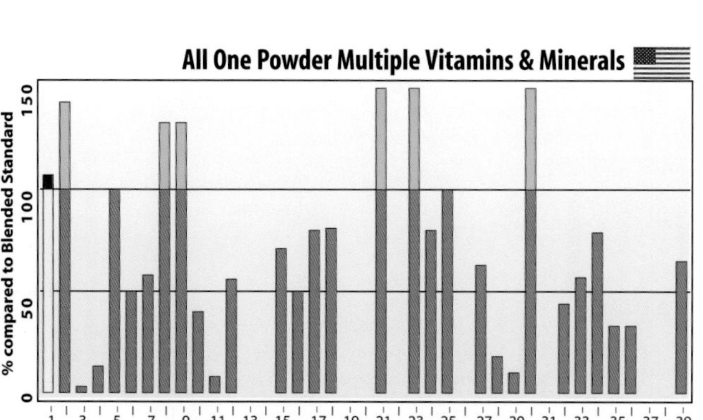

Final Product Score: **49.9%** ★★½

Allergy Research Group Multi-Vi-Min without Copper & Iron

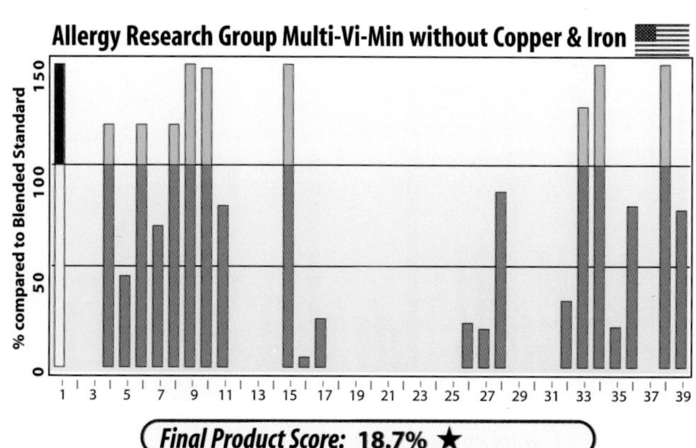

Final Product Score: **18.7%** ★

Alpha Nutrition Alpha ENF

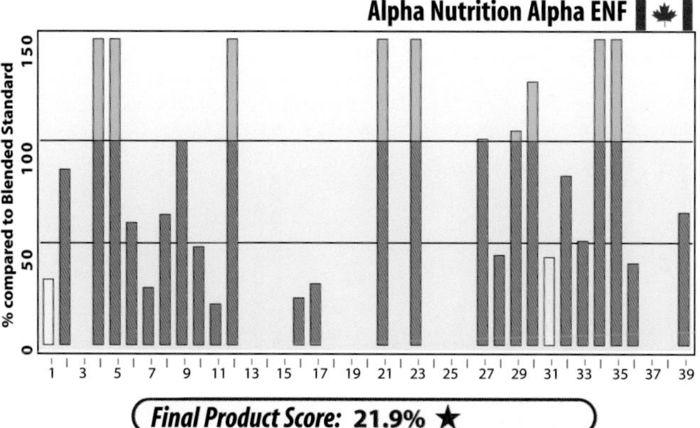

Final Product Score: **21.9%** ★

American Longevity Ultimate Daily

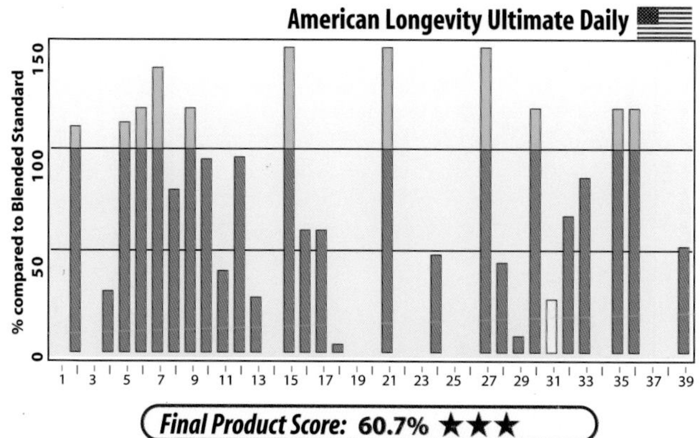

Final Product Score: **60.7%** ★★★

amni Added Protection III

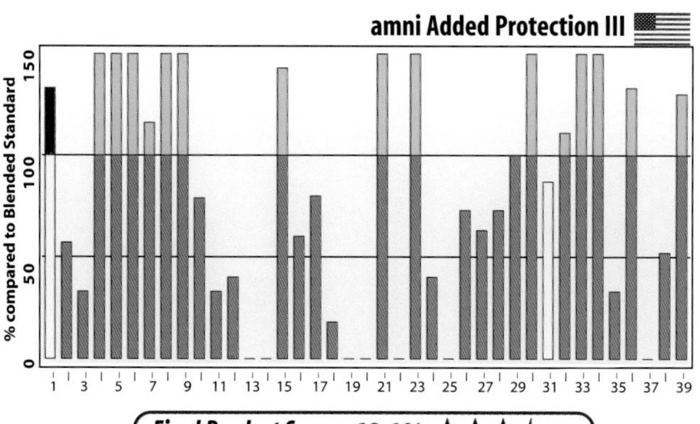

Final Product Score: **69.1%** ★★★½

Andrew Lessman's Maximum Complete for Women

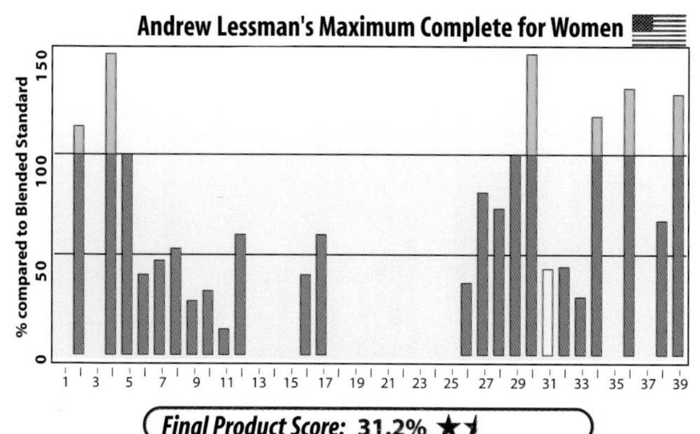

Final Product Score: **31.2%** ★½

Graphical Comparisons to the Blended Standard

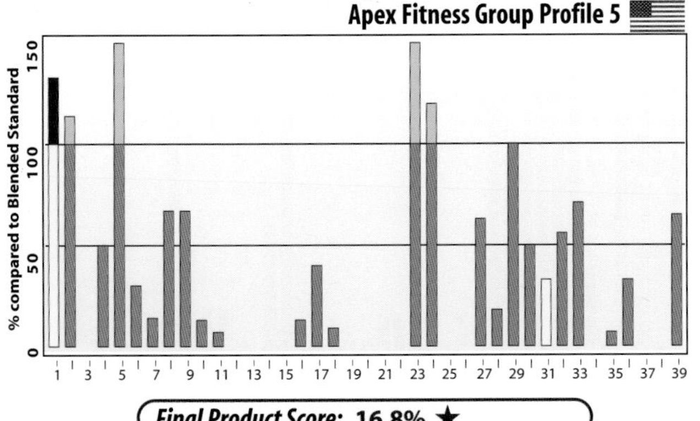

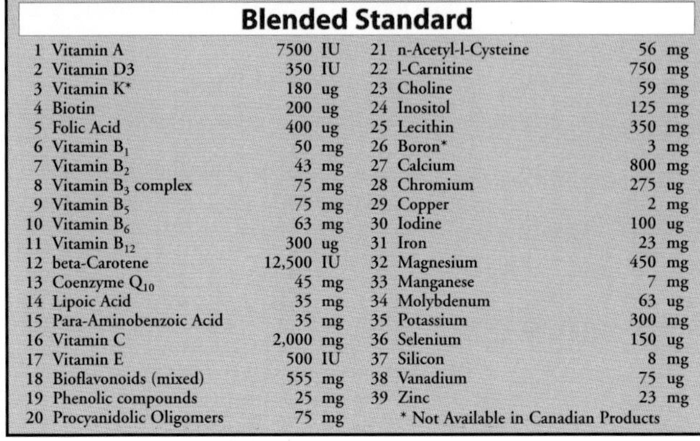

Blended Standard

1	Vitamin A	7500	IU	21	n-Acetyl-l-Cysteine	56	mg
2	Vitamin D3	350	IU	22	l-Carnitine	750	mg
3	Vitamin K*	180	ug	23	Choline	59	mg
4	Biotin	200	ug	24	Inositol	125	mg
5	Folic Acid	400	ug	25	Lecithin	350	mg
6	Vitamin B_1	50	mg	26	Boron*	3	mg
7	Vitamin B_2	43	mg	27	Calcium	800	mg
8	Vitamin B_3 complex	75	mg	28	Chromium	275	ug
9	Vitamin B_5	75	mg	29	Copper	2	mg
10	Vitamin B_6	63	mg	30	Iodine	100	ug
11	Vitamin B_{12}	300	ug	31	Iron	23	mg
12	beta-Carotene	12,500	IU	32	Magnesium	450	mg
13	Coenzyme Q_{10}	45	mg	33	Manganese	7	mg
14	Lipoic Acid	35	mg	34	Molybdenum	63	ug
15	Para-Aminobenzoic Acid	35	mg	35	Potassium	300	mg
16	Vitamin C	2,000	mg	36	Selenium	150	ug
17	Vitamin E	500	IU	37	Silicon	8	mg
18	Bioflavonoids (mixed)	555	mg	38	Vanadium	75	ug
19	Phenolic compounds	25	mg	39	Zinc	23	mg
20	Procyanidolic Oligomers	75	mg		* Not Available in Canadian Products		

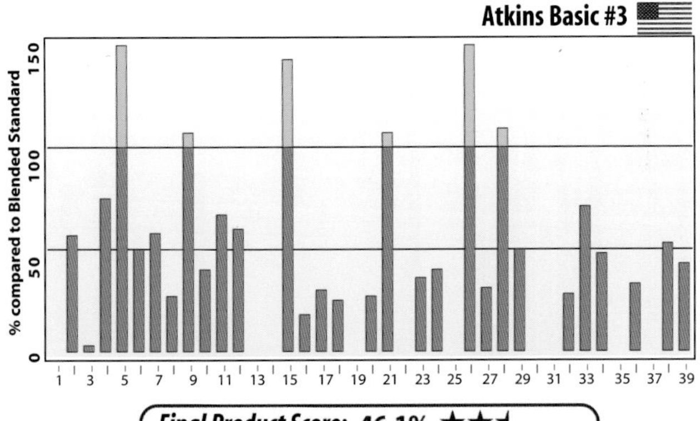

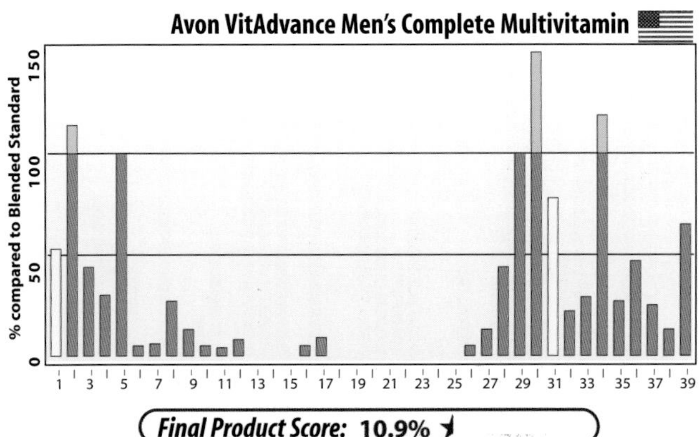

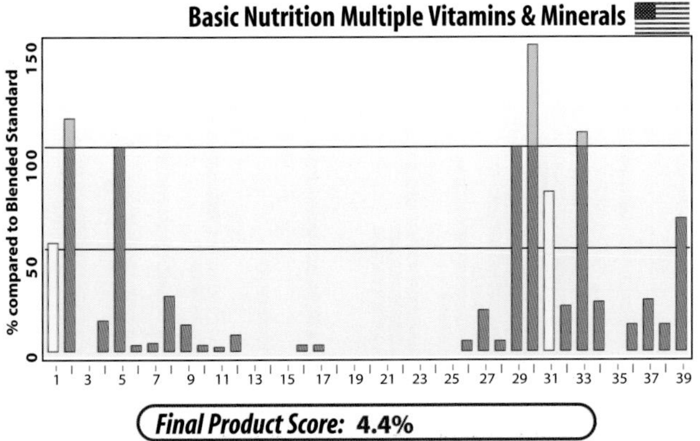

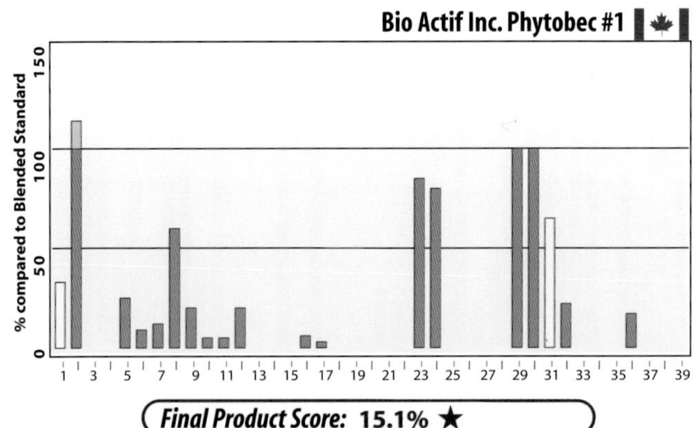

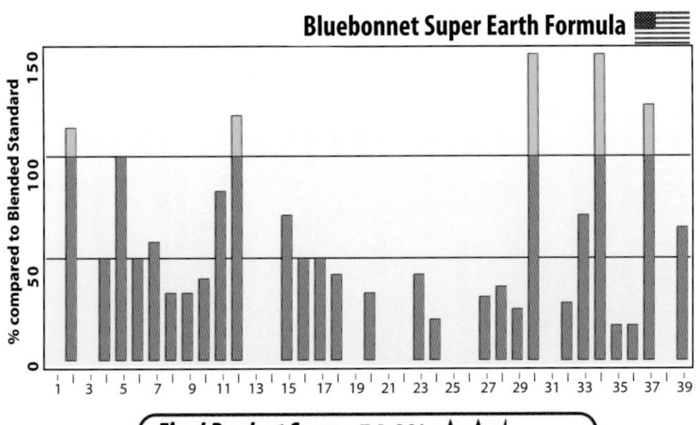

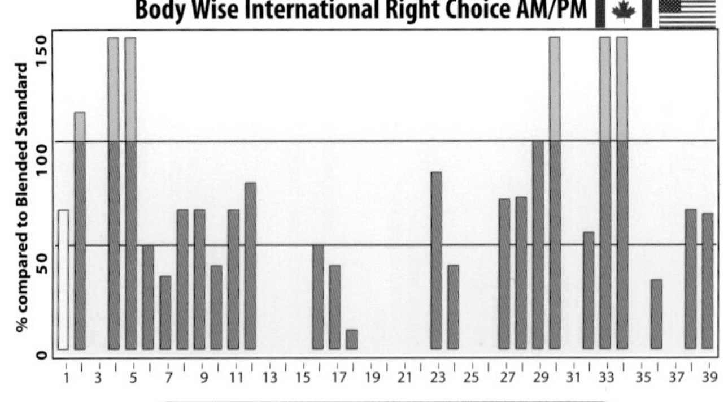

Graphical Comparisons to the Blended Standard

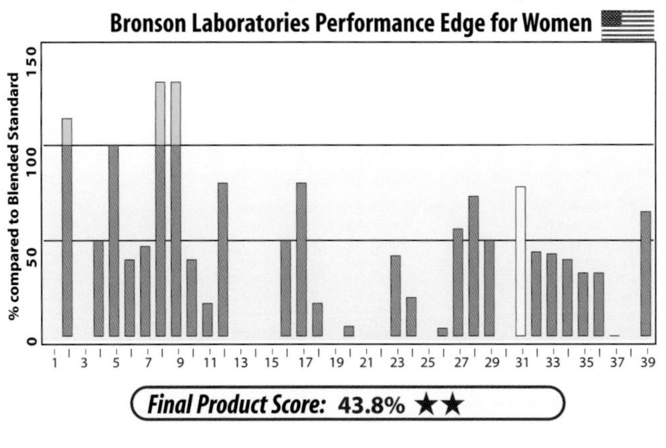

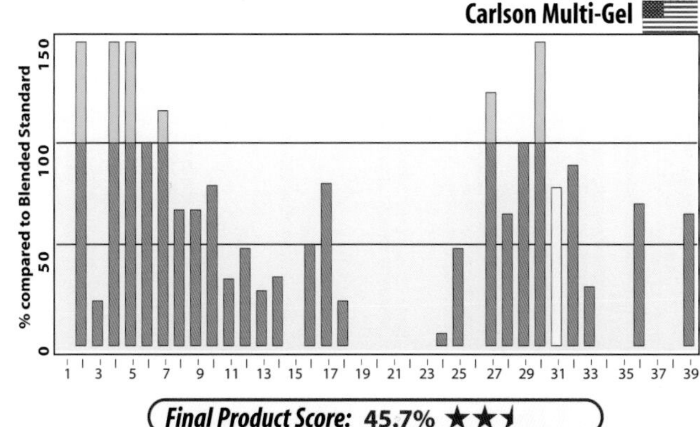

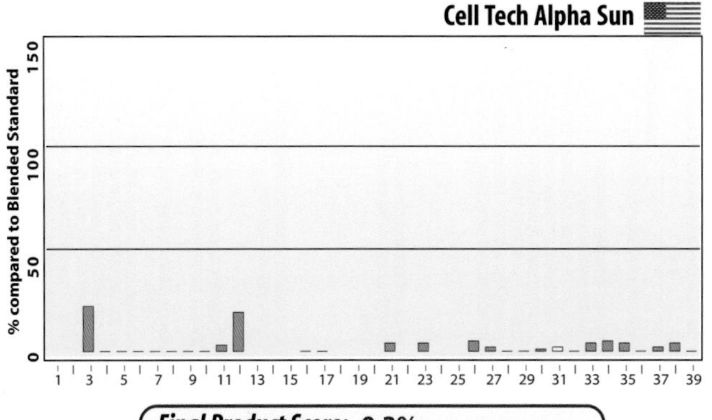

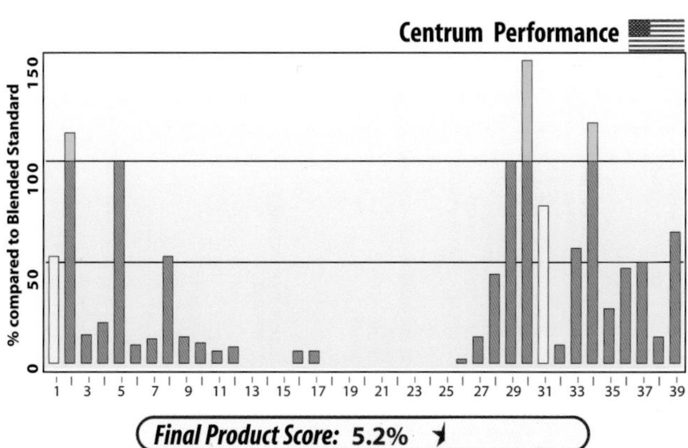

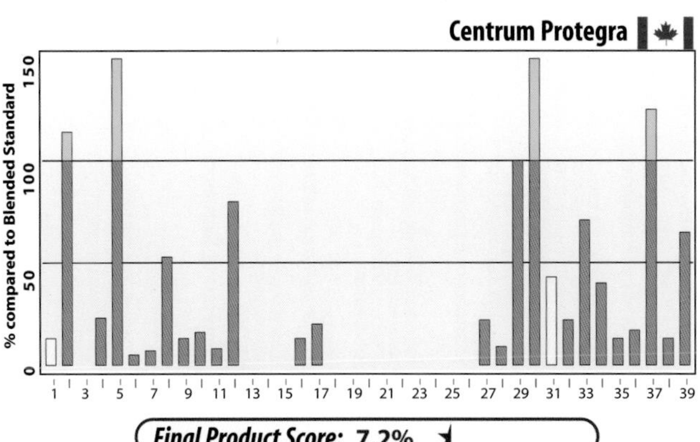

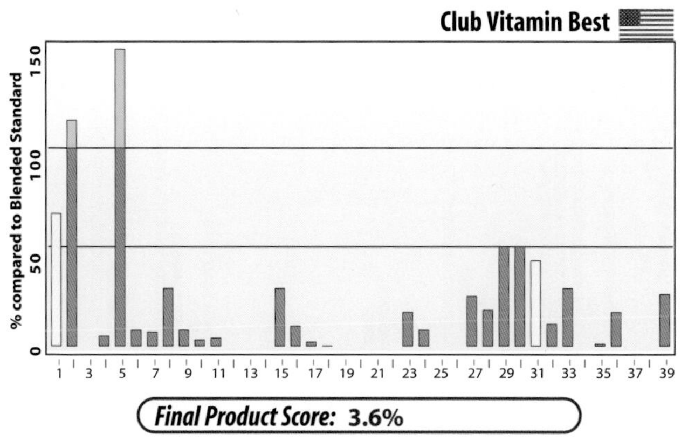

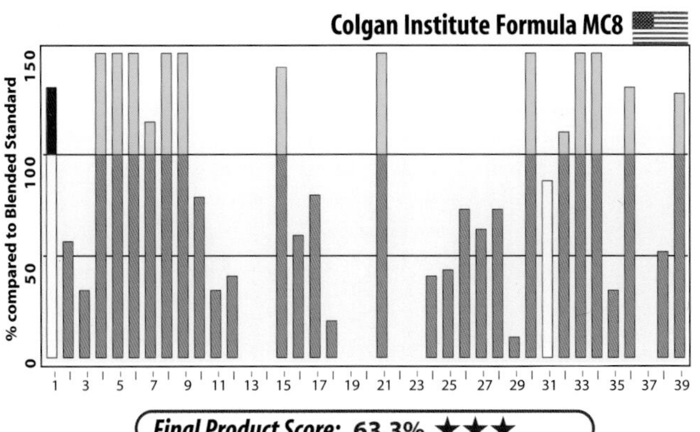

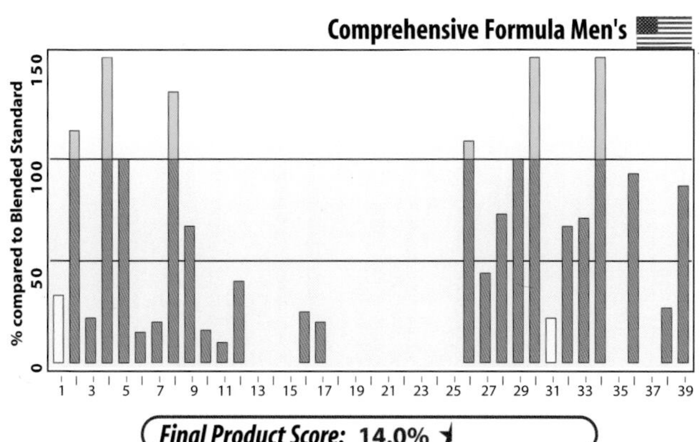

Graphical Comparisons to the Blended Standard

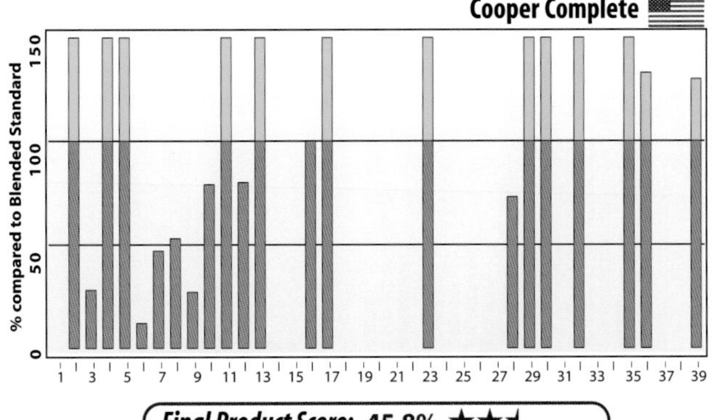

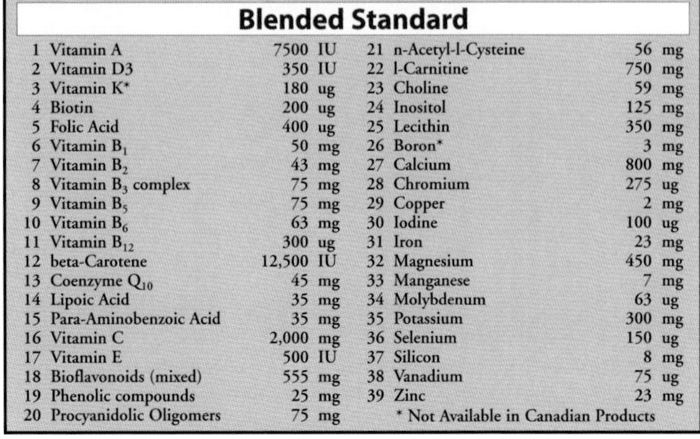

Blended Standard

#	Nutrient	Amount	Unit	#	Nutrient	Amount	Unit
1	Vitamin A	7500	IU	21	n-Acetyl-l-Cysteine	56	mg
2	Vitamin D3	350	IU	22	l-Carnitine	750	mg
3	Vitamin K*	180	ug	23	Choline	59	mg
4	Biotin	200	ug	24	Inositol	125	mg
5	Folic Acid	400	ug	25	Lecithin	350	mg
6	Vitamin B_1	50	mg	26	Boron*	3	mg
7	Vitamin B_2	43	mg	27	Calcium	800	mg
8	Vitamin B_3 complex	75	mg	28	Chromium	275	ug
9	Vitamin B_5	75	mg	29	Copper	2	mg
10	Vitamin B_6	63	mg	30	Iodine	100	ug
11	Vitamin B_{12}	300	ug	31	Iron	23	mg
12	beta-Carotene	12,500	IU	32	Magnesium	450	mg
13	Coenzyme Q_{10}	45	mg	33	Manganese	7	mg
14	Lipoic Acid	35	mg	34	Molybdenum	63	ug
15	Para-Aminobenzoic Acid	35	mg	35	Potassium	300	mg
16	Vitamin C	2,000	mg	36	Selenium	150	ug
17	Vitamin E	500	IU	37	Silicon	8	mg
18	Bioflavonoids (mixed)	555	mg	38	Vanadium	75	ug
19	Phenolic compounds	25	mg	39	Zinc	23	mg
20	Procyanidolic Oligomers	75	mg				

* Not Available in Canadian Products

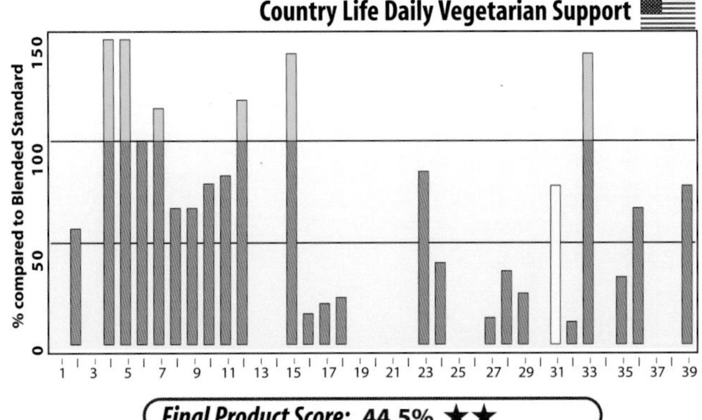

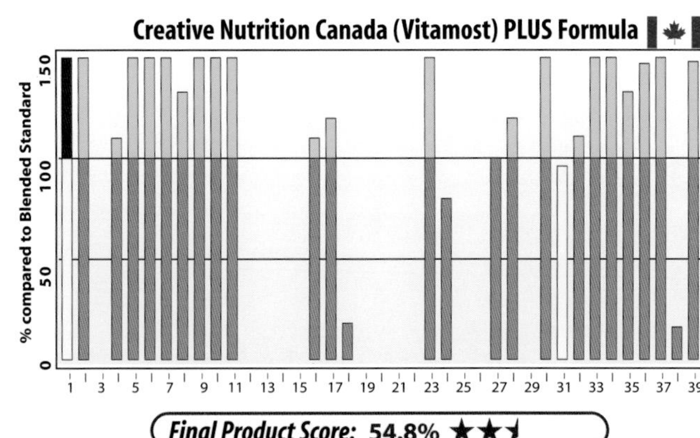

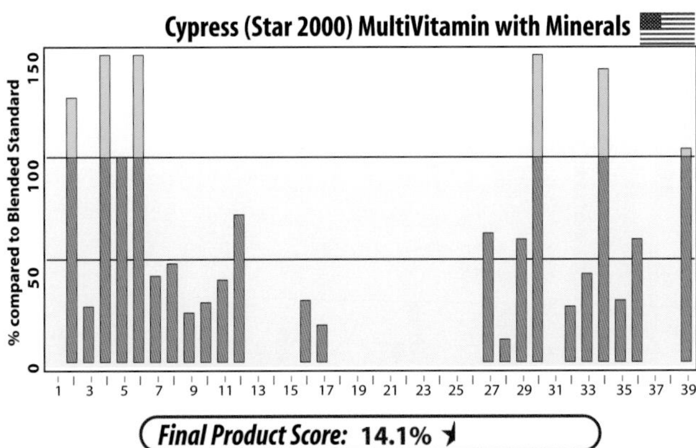

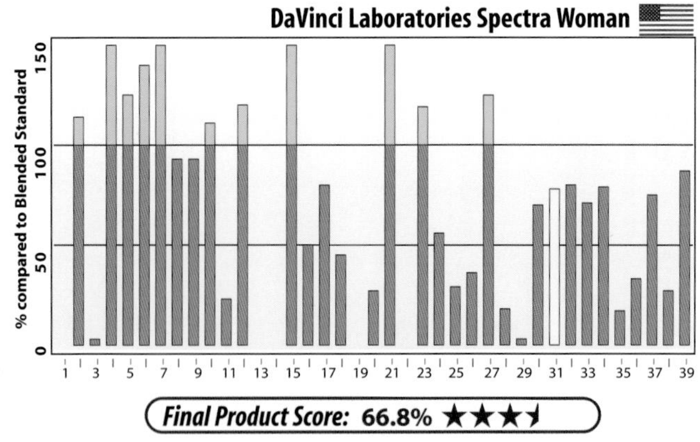

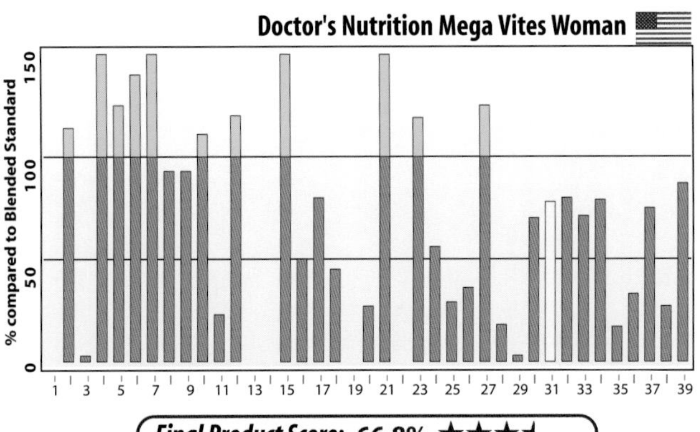

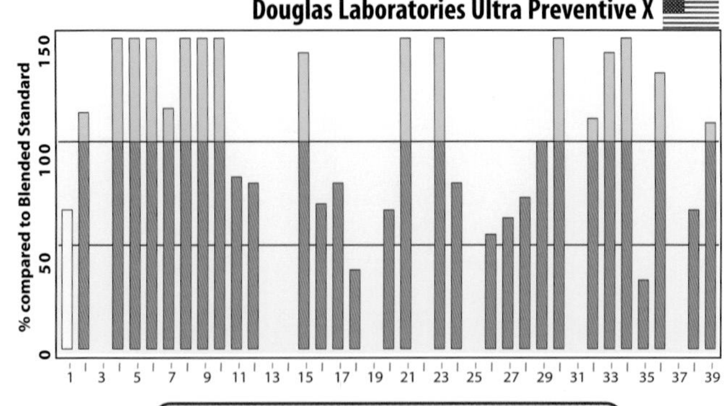

Graphical Comparisons to the Blended Standard

Dr. Julian Whitaker's Forward Multi-Nutrient

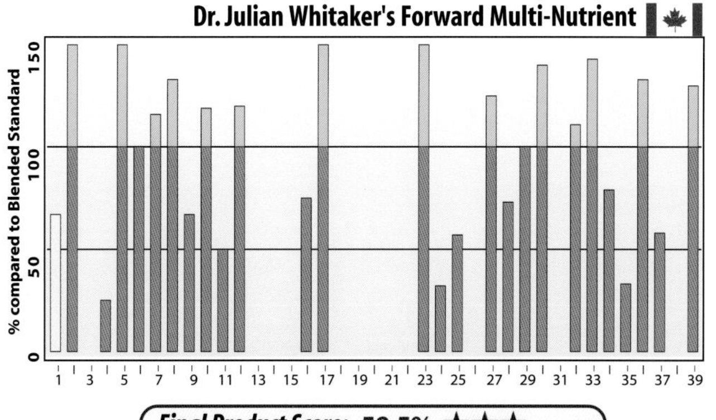

Final Product Score: **58.5% ★★★**

Dr. Julian Whitaker's Forward Multi-Nutrient

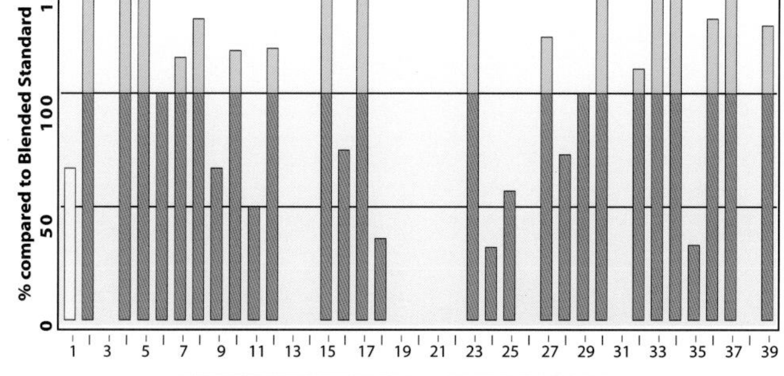

Final Product Score: **74.7% ★★★½**

EAS Multi-Blend

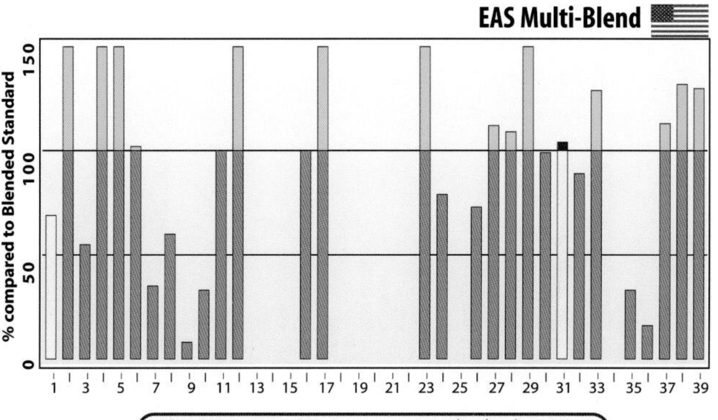

Final Product Score: **62.1% ★★★**

EcoNugenics Women's Longevity Rhythms Gold

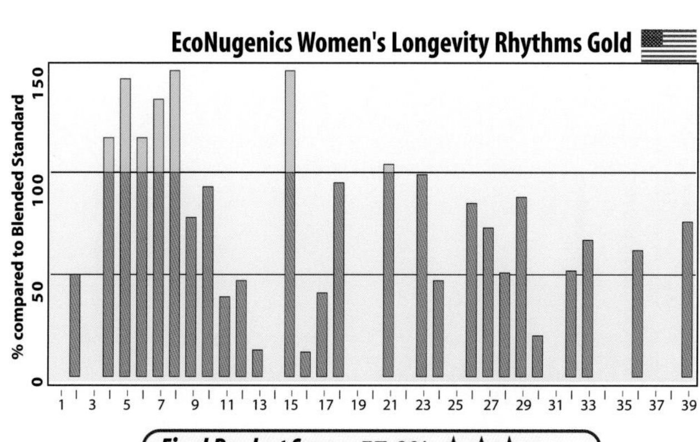

Final Product Score: **57.0% ★★★**

EHN Inc. protect+

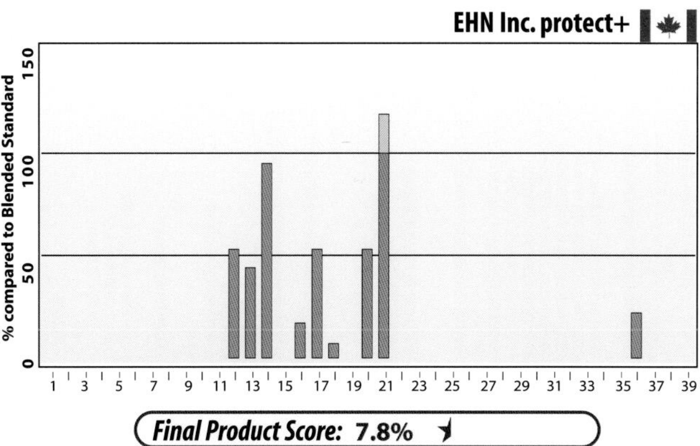

Final Product Score: **7.8% ½**

Enerex Sona

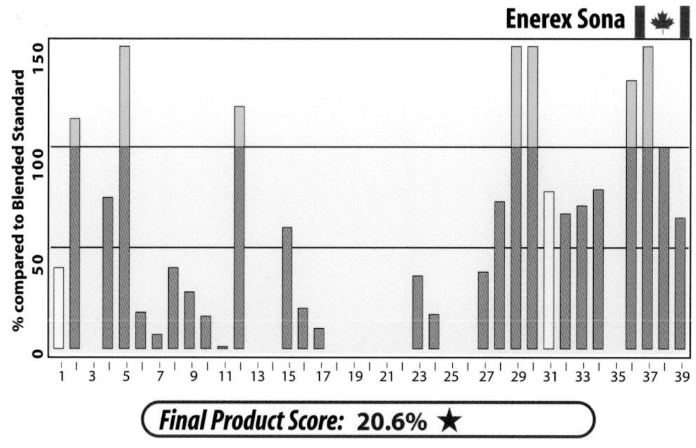

Final Product Score: **20.6% ★**

Enzymatic Therapy Doctor's Choice for Women

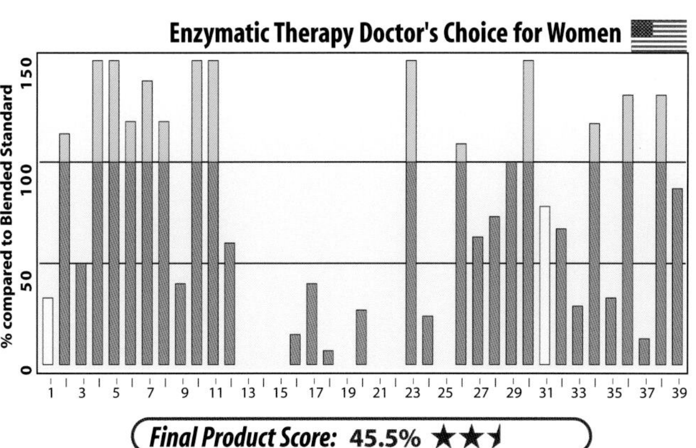

Final Product Score: **45.5% ★★½**

Epic4Health Physician's Multi Vitamin Formula

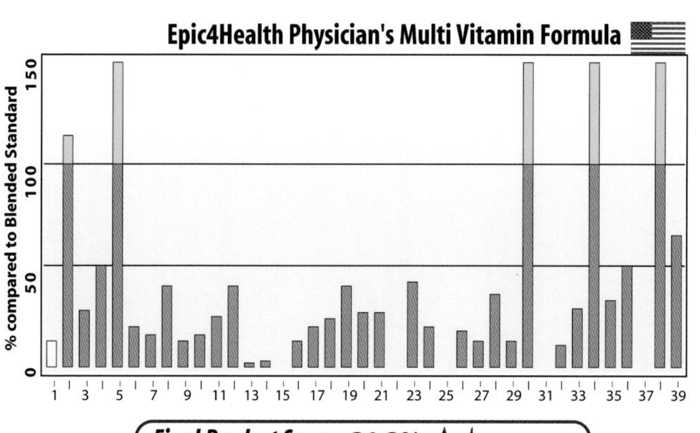

Final Product Score: **31.3% ★½**

Graphical Comparisons to the Blended Standard

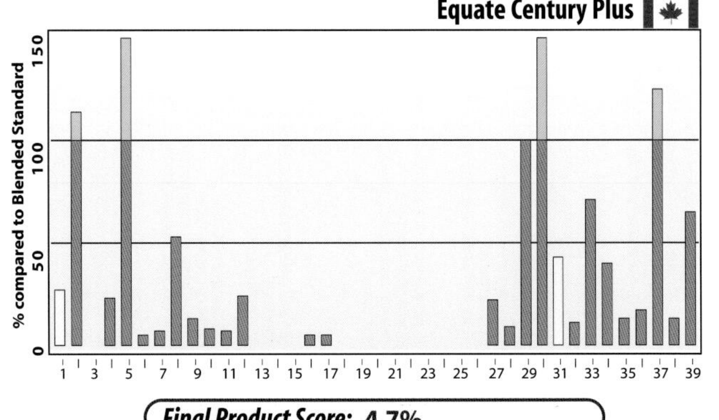

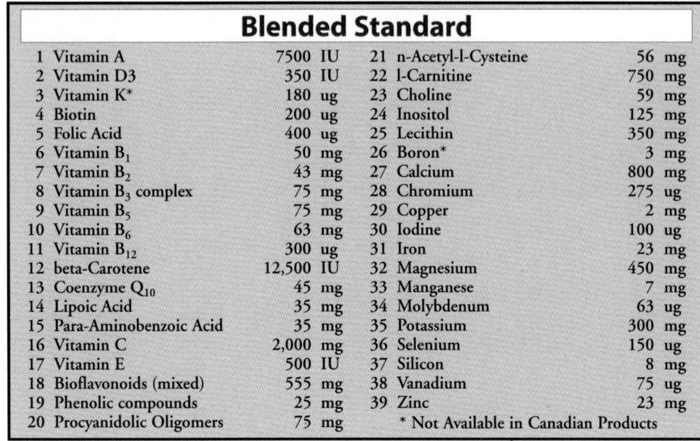

Blended Standard

#	Nutrient	Amount	Unit	#	Nutrient	Amount	Unit
1	Vitamin A	7500	IU	21	n-Acetyl-l-Cysteine	56	mg
2	Vitamin D3	350	IU	22	l-Carnitine	750	mg
3	Vitamin K*	180	ug	23	Choline	59	mg
4	Biotin	200	ug	24	Inositol	125	mg
5	Folic Acid	400	ug	25	Lecithin	350	mg
6	Vitamin B_1	50	mg	26	Boron*	3	mg
7	Vitamin B_2	43	mg	27	Calcium	800	mg
8	Vitamin B_3 complex	75	mg	28	Chromium	275	ug
9	Vitamin B_5	75	mg	29	Copper	2	mg
10	Vitamin B_6	63	mg	30	Iodine	100	ug
11	Vitamin B_{12}	300	ug	31	Iron	23	mg
12	beta-Carotene	12,500	IU	32	Magnesium	450	mg
13	Coenzyme Q_{10}	45	mg	33	Manganese	7	mg
14	Lipoic Acid	35	mg	34	Molybdenum	63	ug
15	Para-Aminobenzoic Acid	35	mg	35	Potassium	300	mg
16	Vitamin C	2,000	mg	36	Selenium	150	ug
17	Vitamin E	500	IU	37	Silicon	8	mg
18	Bioflavonoids (mixed)	555	mg	38	Vanadium	75	ug
19	Phenolic compounds	25	mg	39	Zinc	23	mg
20	Procyanidolic Oligomers	75	mg				

* Not Available in Canadian Products

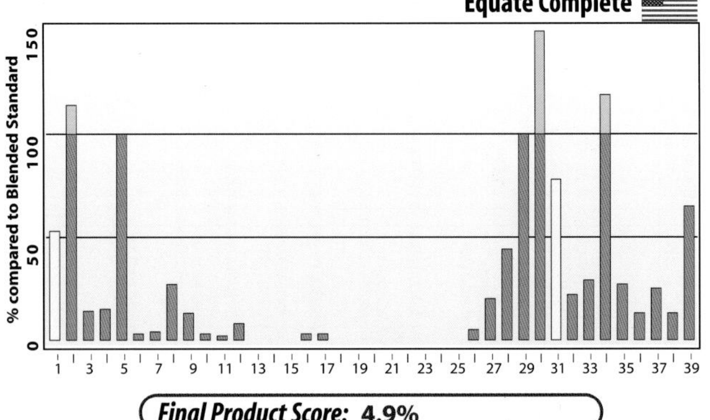

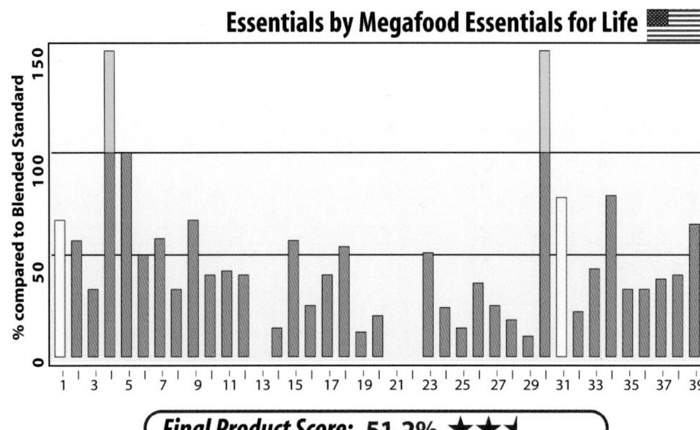

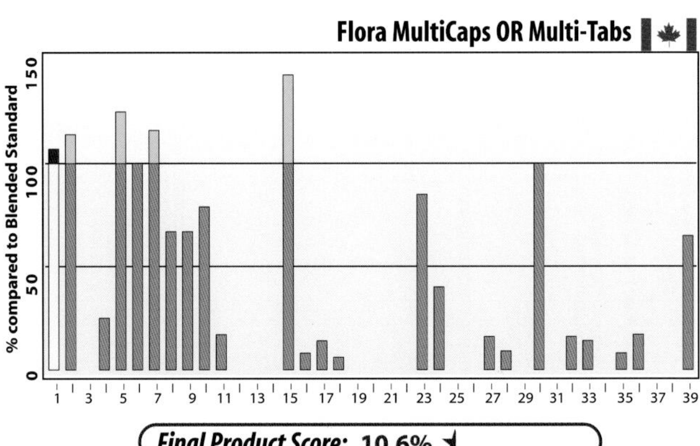

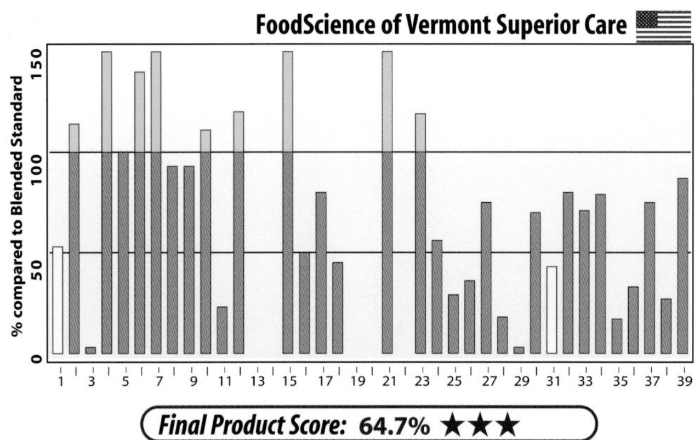

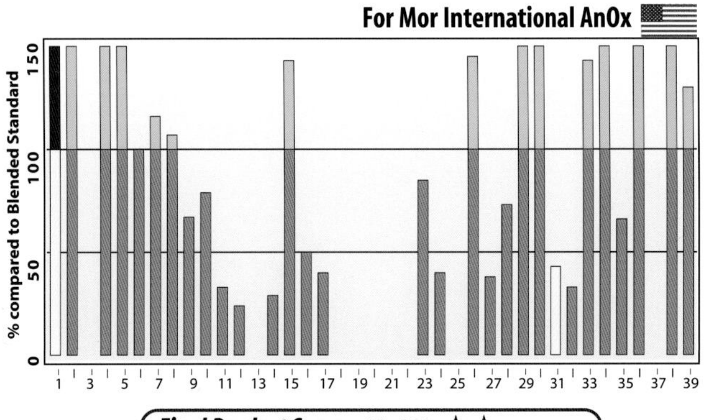

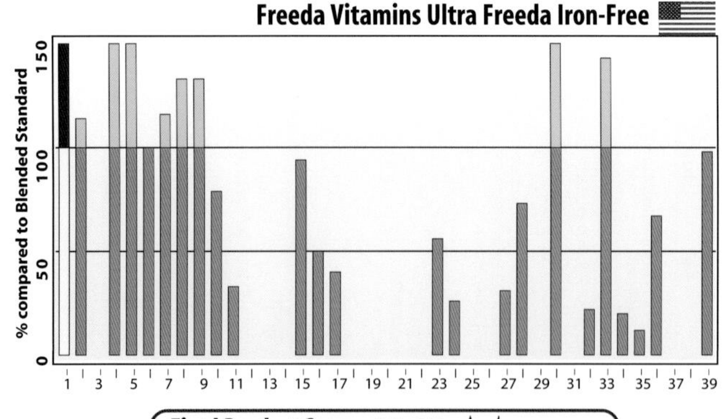

Graphical Comparisons to the Blended Standard

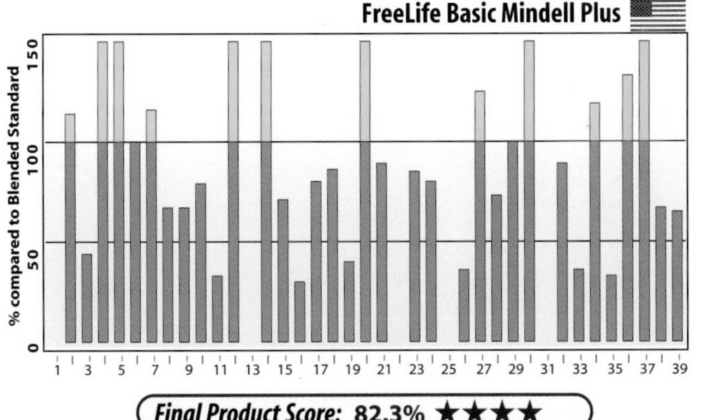

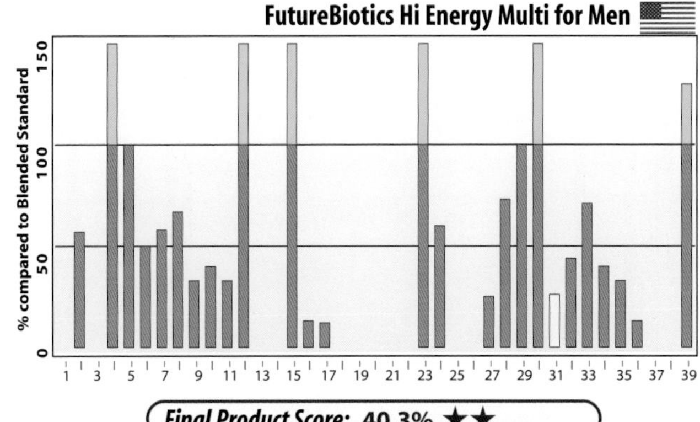

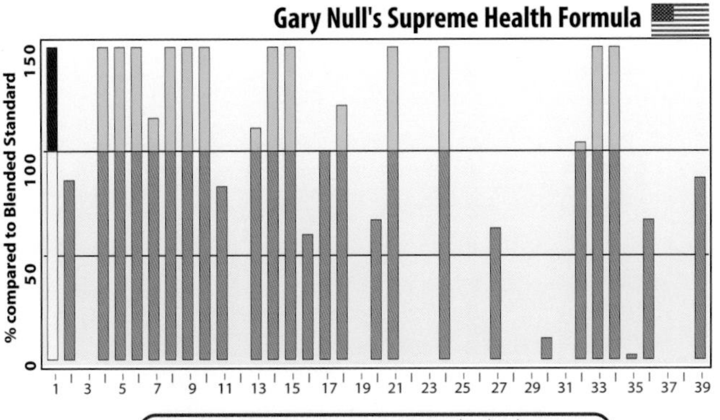

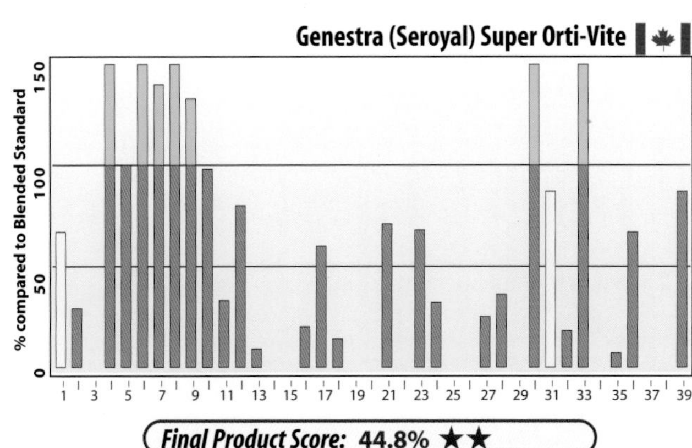

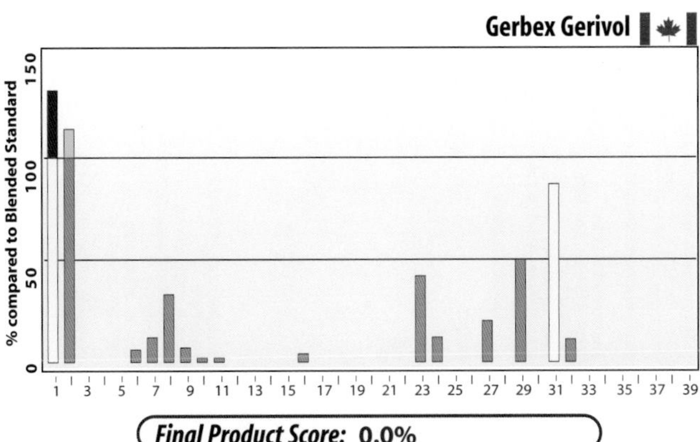

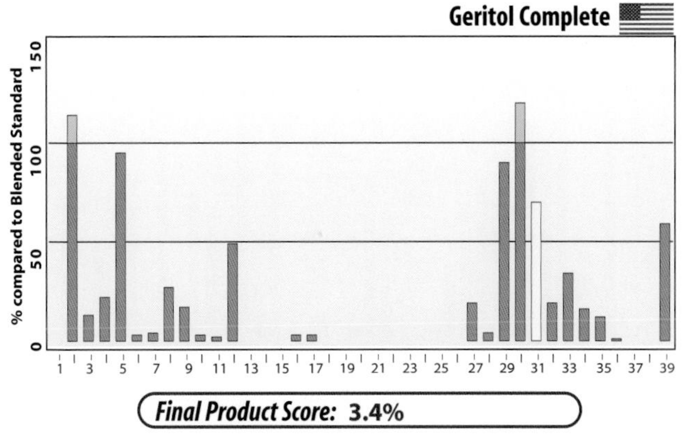

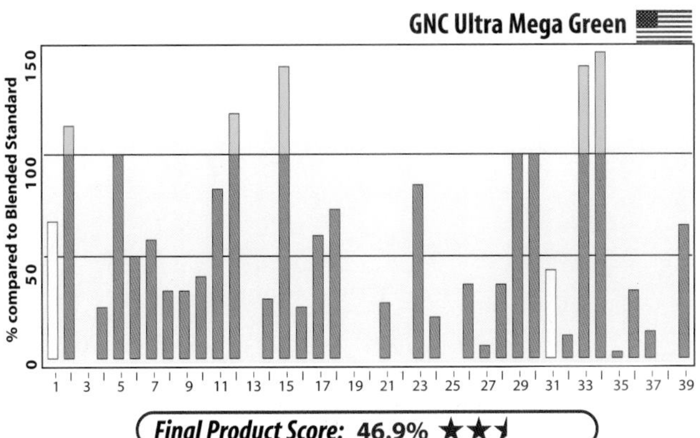

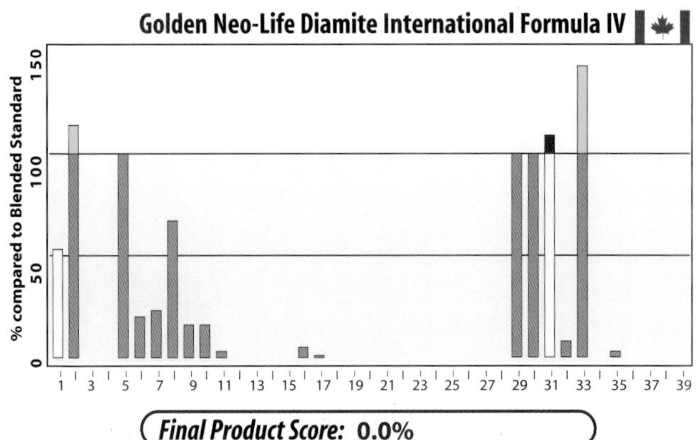

Graphical Comparisons to the Blended Standard

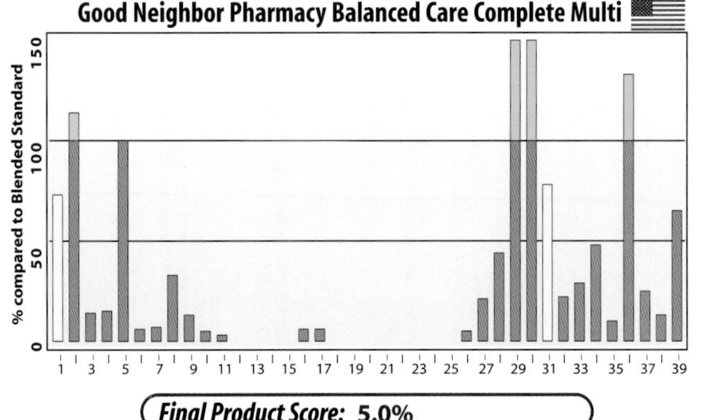

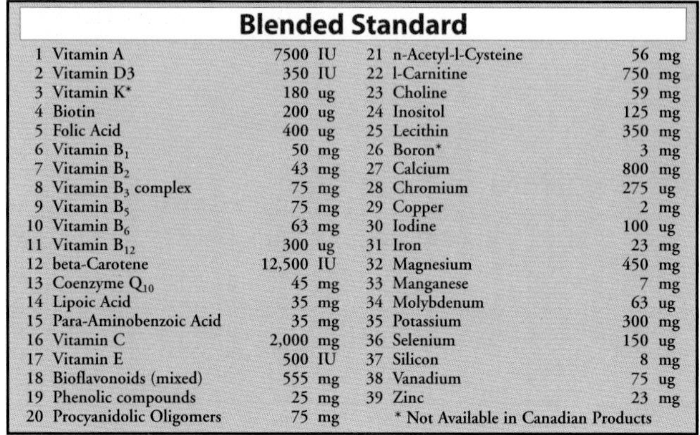

Blended Standard

#	Nutrient	Amount	Unit	#	Nutrient	Amount	Unit
1	Vitamin A	7500	IU	21	n-Acetyl-l-Cysteine	56	mg
2	Vitamin D3	350	IU	22	l-Carnitine	750	mg
3	Vitamin K*	180	ug	23	Choline	59	mg
4	Biotin	200	ug	24	Inositol	125	mg
5	Folic Acid	400	ug	25	Lecithin	350	mg
6	Vitamin B_1	50	mg	26	Boron*	3	mg
7	Vitamin B_2	43	mg	27	Calcium	800	mg
8	Vitamin B_3 complex	75	mg	28	Chromium	275	ug
9	Vitamin B_5	75	mg	29	Copper	2	mg
10	Vitamin B_6	63	mg	30	Iodine	100	ug
11	Vitamin B_{12}	300	ug	31	Iron	23	mg
12	beta-Carotene	12,500	IU	32	Magnesium	450	mg
13	Coenzyme Q_{10}	45	mg	33	Manganese	7	mg
14	Lipoic Acid	35	mg	34	Molybdenum	63	ug
15	Para-Aminobenzoic Acid	35	mg	35	Potassium	300	mg
16	Vitamin C	2,000	mg	36	Selenium	150	ug
17	Vitamin E	500	IU	37	Silicon	8	mg
18	Bioflavonoids (mixed)	555	mg	38	Vanadium	75	ug
19	Phenolic compounds	25	mg	39	Zinc	23	mg
20	Procyanidolic Oligomers	75	mg				

* Not Available in Canadian Products

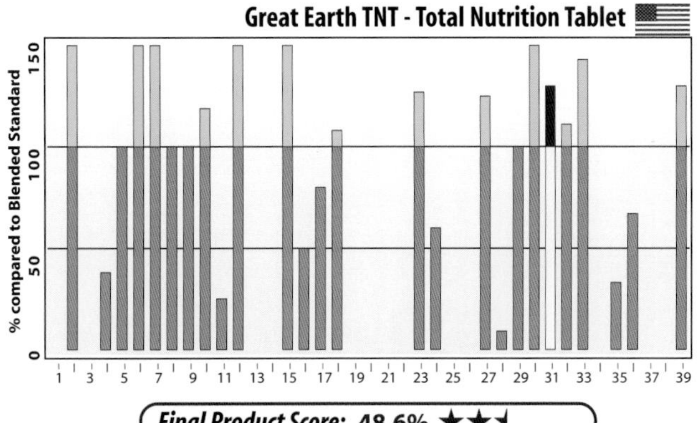

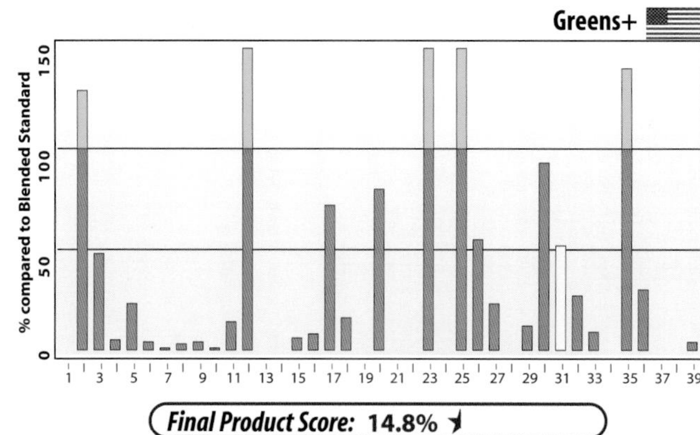

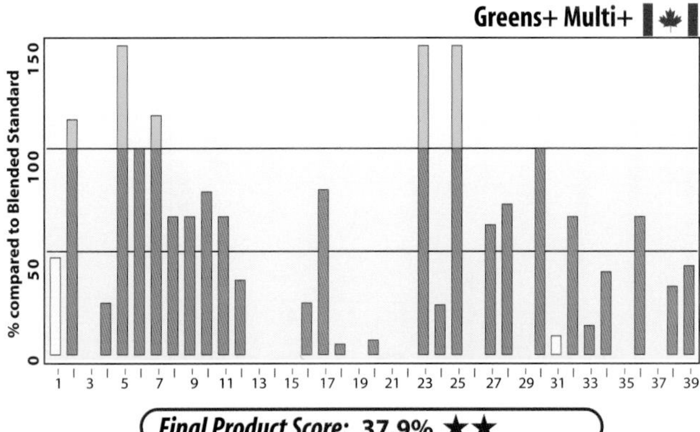

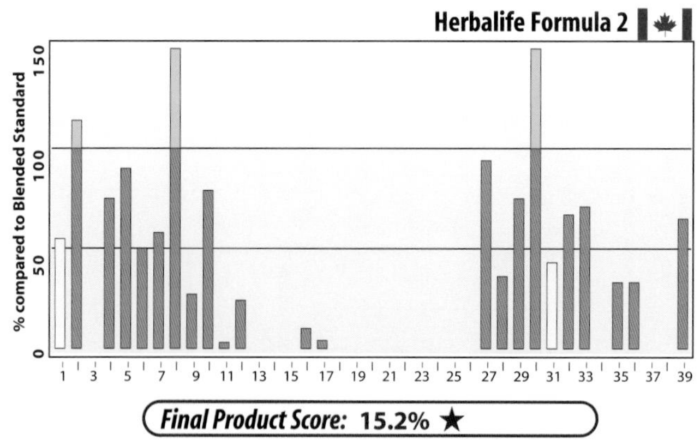

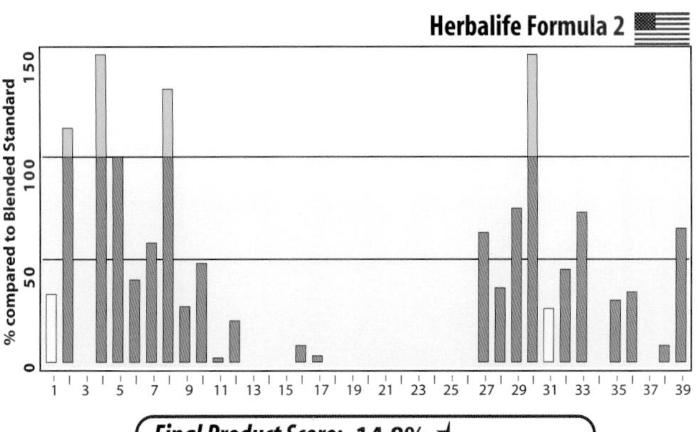

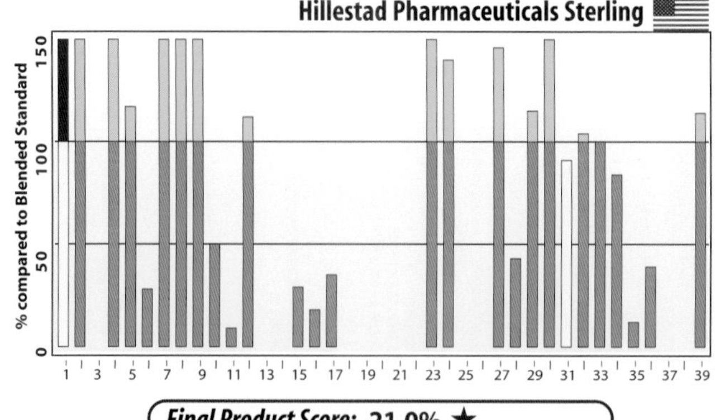

Graphical Comparisons to the Blended Standard

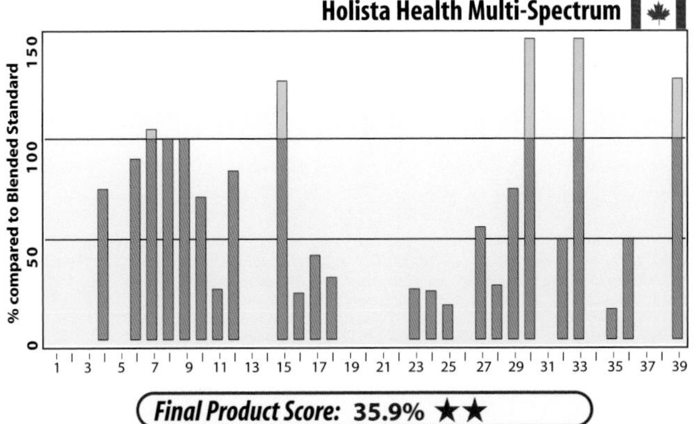

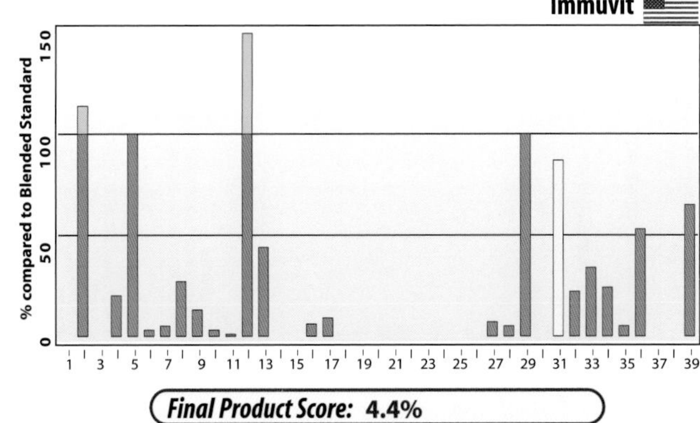

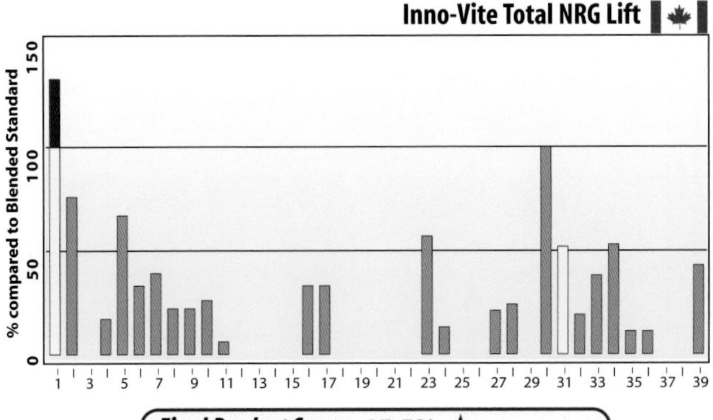

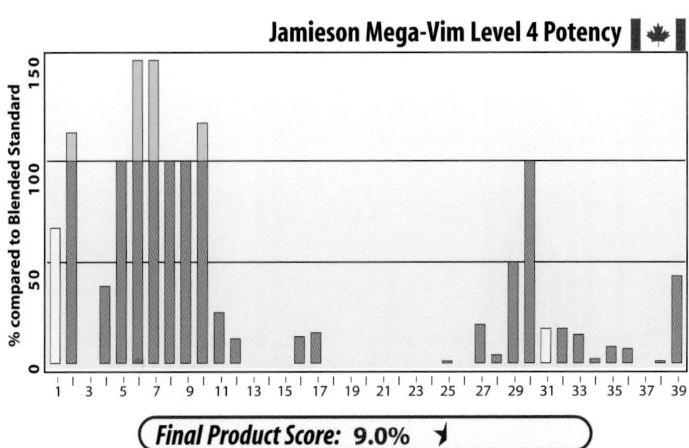

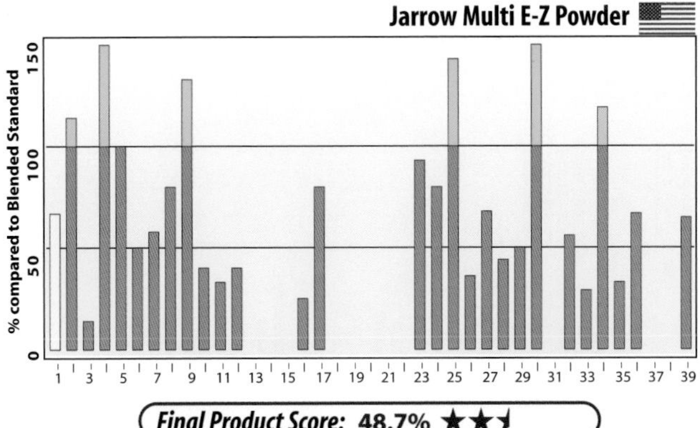

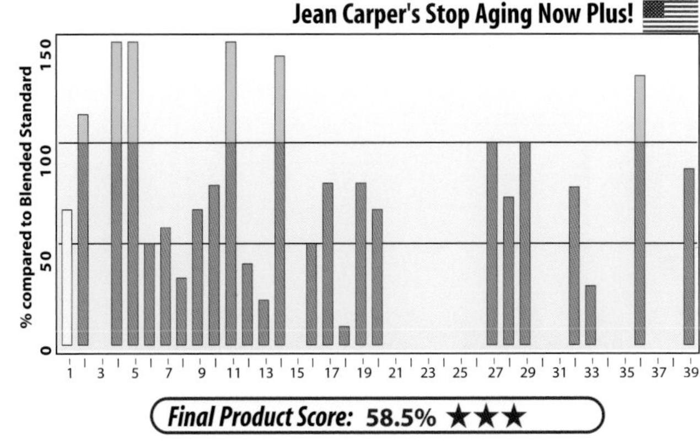

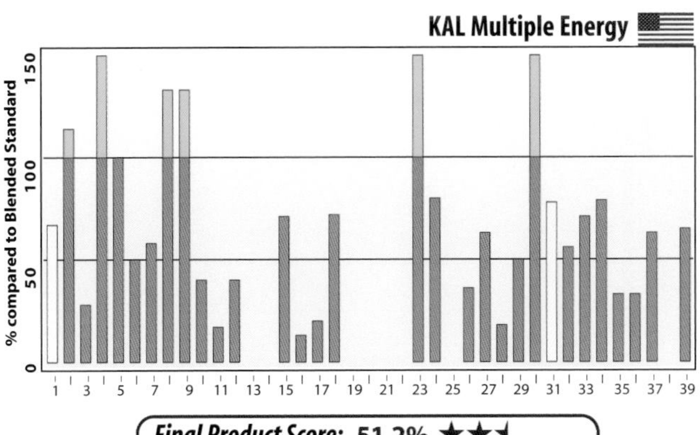

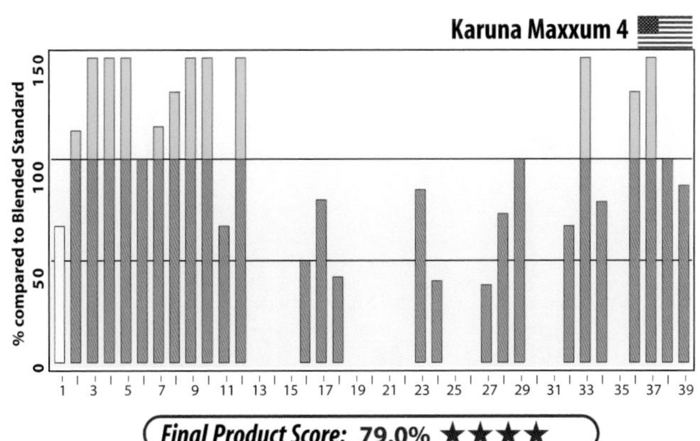

Graphical Comparisons to the Blended Standard

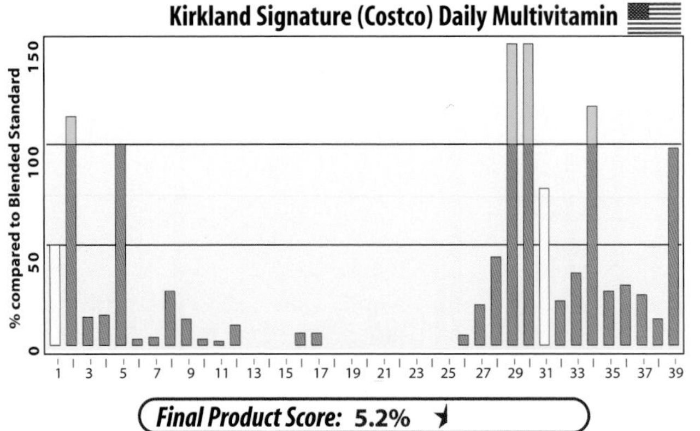

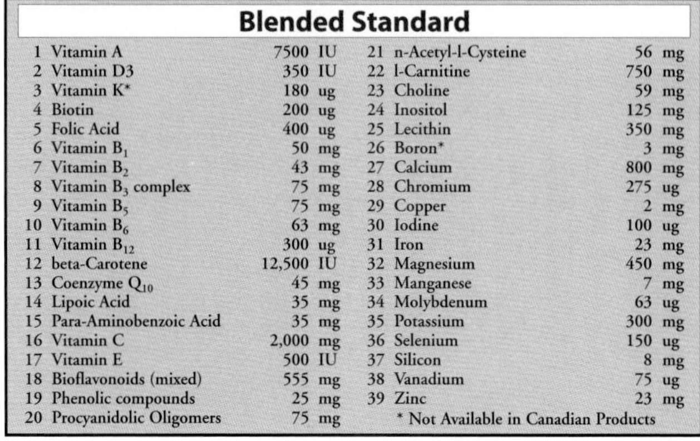

Blended Standard

1	Vitamin A	7500	IU	21	n-Acetyl-l-Cysteine	56	mg
2	Vitamin D3	350	IU	22	l-Carnitine	750	mg
3	Vitamin K*	180	ug	23	Choline	59	mg
4	Biotin	200	ug	24	Inositol	125	mg
5	Folic Acid	400	ug	25	Lecithin	350	mg
6	Vitamin B_1	50	mg	26	Boron*	3	mg
7	Vitamin B_2	43	mg	27	Calcium	800	mg
8	Vitamin B_3 complex	75	mg	28	Chromium	275	ug
9	Vitamin B_5	75	mg	29	Copper	2	mg
10	Vitamin B_6	63	mg	30	Iodine	100	ug
11	Vitamin B_{12}	300	ug	31	Iron	23	mg
12	beta-Carotene	12,500	IU	32	Magnesium	450	mg
13	Coenzyme Q_{10}	45	mg	33	Manganese	7	mg
14	Lipoic Acid	35	mg	34	Molybdenum	63	ug
15	Para-Aminobenzoic Acid	35	mg	35	Potassium	300	mg
16	Vitamin C	2,000	mg	36	Selenium	150	ug
17	Vitamin E	500	IU	37	Silicon	8	mg
18	Bioflavonoids (mixed)	555	mg	38	Vanadium	75	ug
19	Phenolic compounds	25	mg	39	Zinc	23	mg
20	Procyanidolic Oligomers	75	mg		* Not Available in Canadian Products		

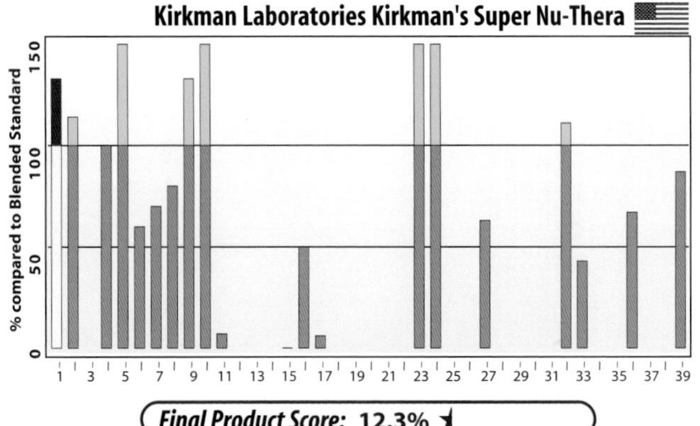

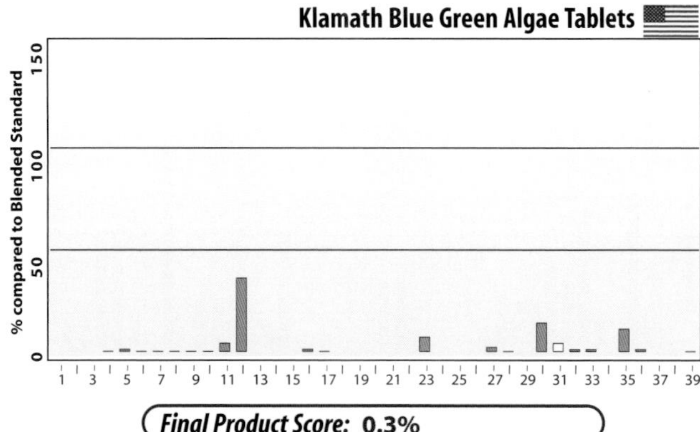

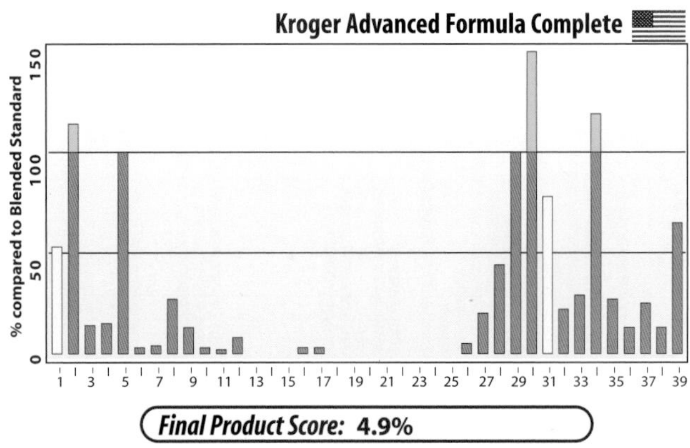

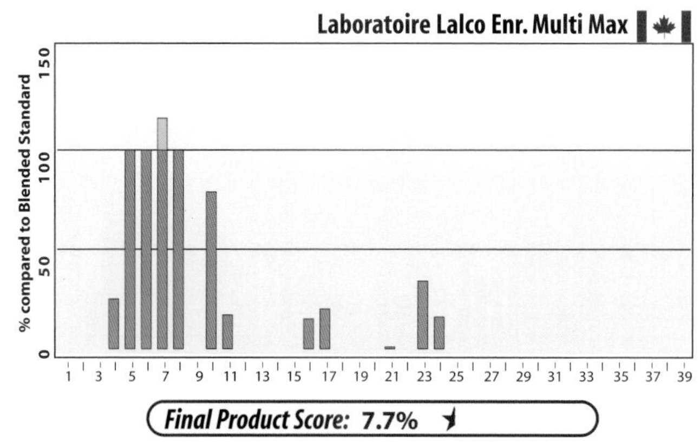

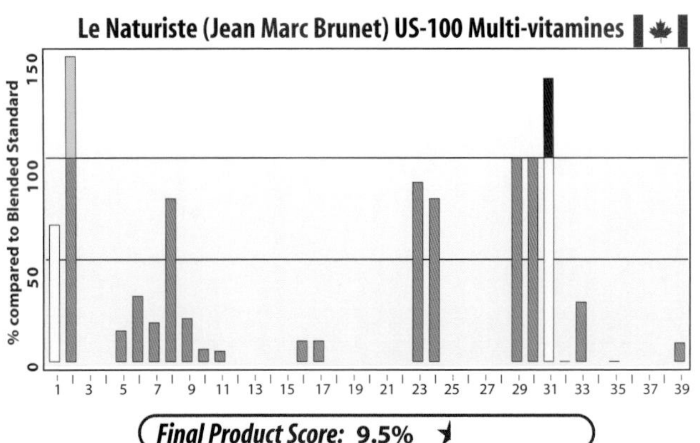

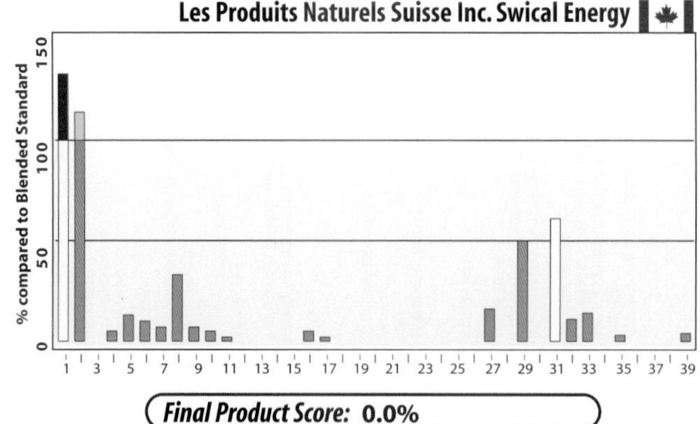

Graphical Comparisons to the Blended Standard

Life Brand Optimum

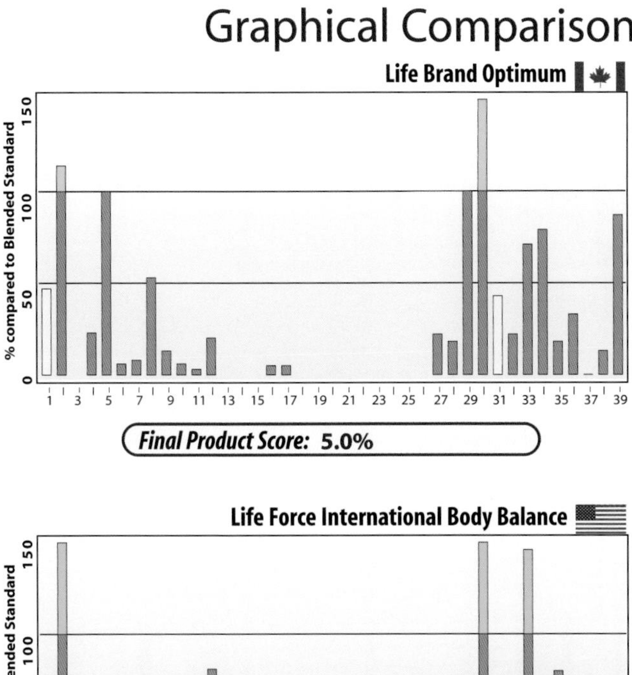

Final Product Score: 5.0%

Life Extension Foundation Life Extension Mix

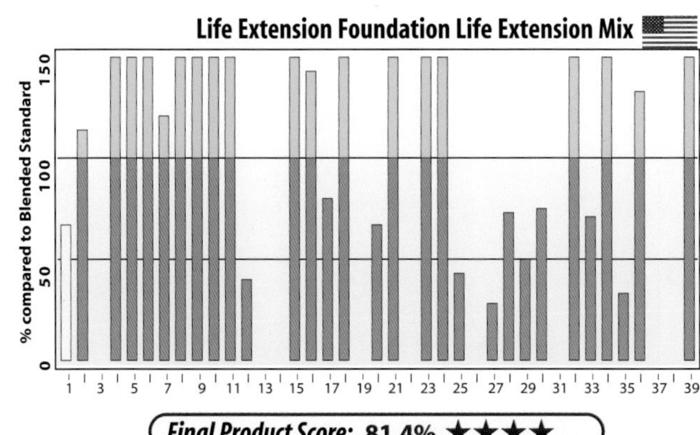

Final Product Score: 81.4% ★★★★

Life Force International Body Balance

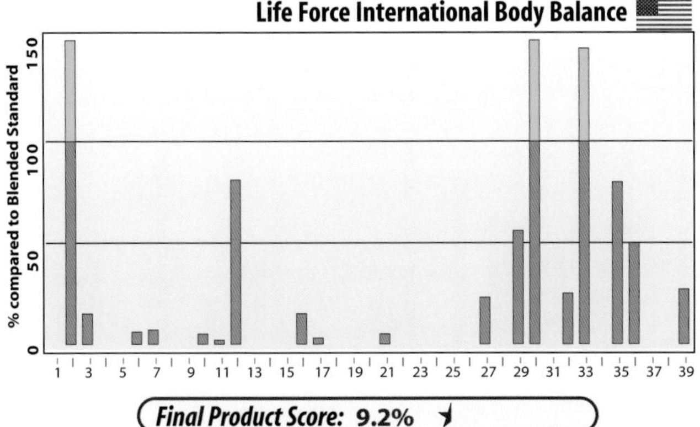

Final Product Score: 9.2% ½

Life Plus Daily Bio-Basics

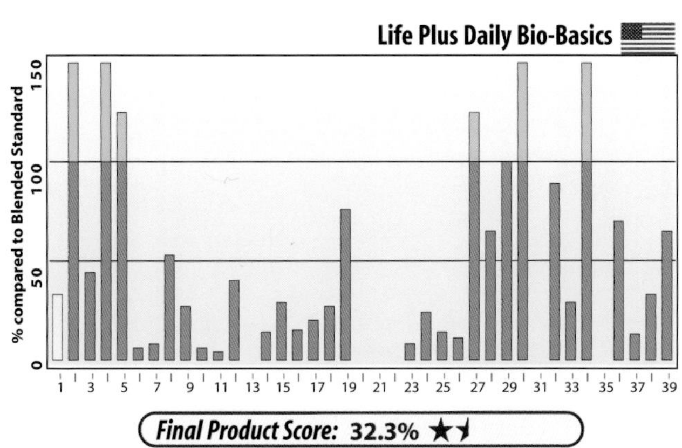

Final Product Score: 32.3% ★½

LifeScript Daily Essentials, plus Calcium Complete

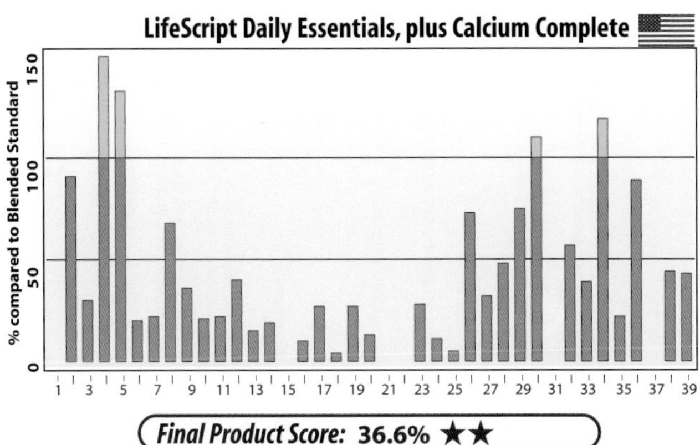

Final Product Score: 36.6% ★★

Lifestyles Lifecycles for Mature Men

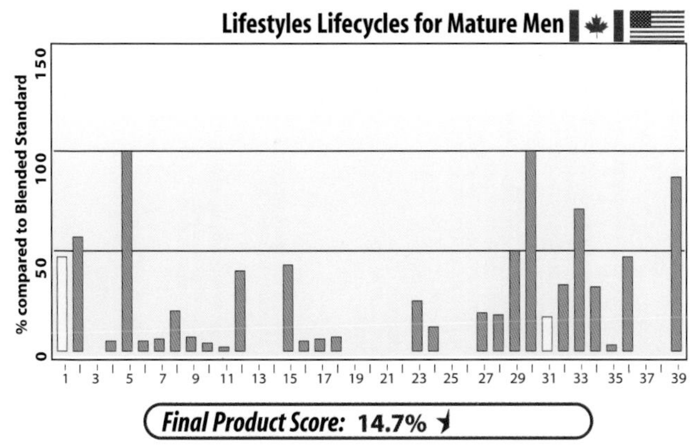

Final Product Score: 14.7% ½

LifeTime Nutrilife

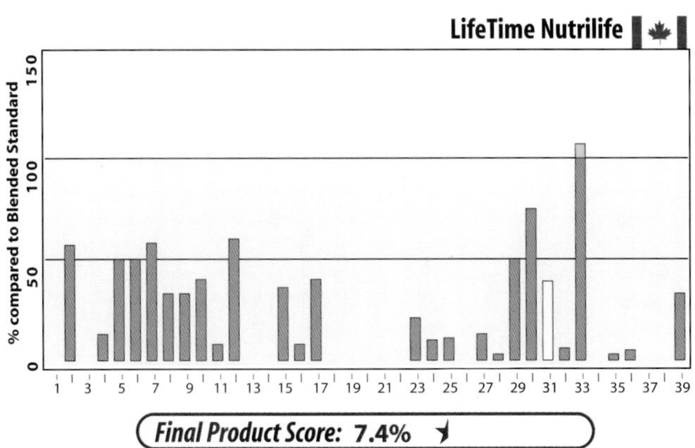

Final Product Score: 7.4% ½

LiFizz Multivitamin

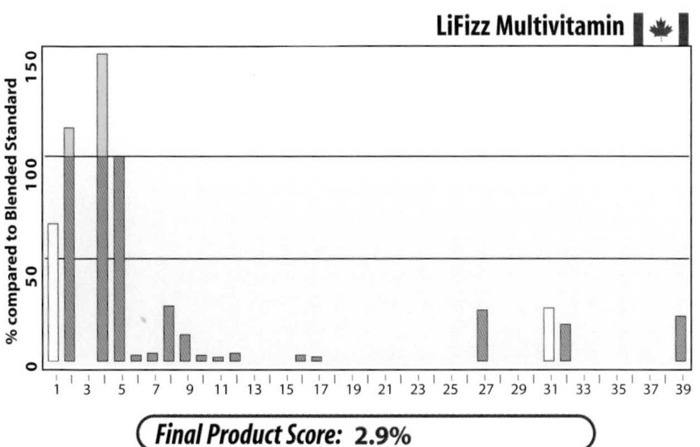

Final Product Score: 2.9%

Graphical Comparisons to the Blended Standard

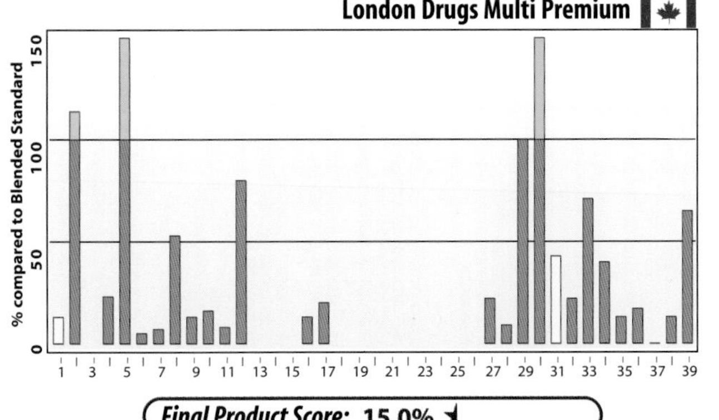

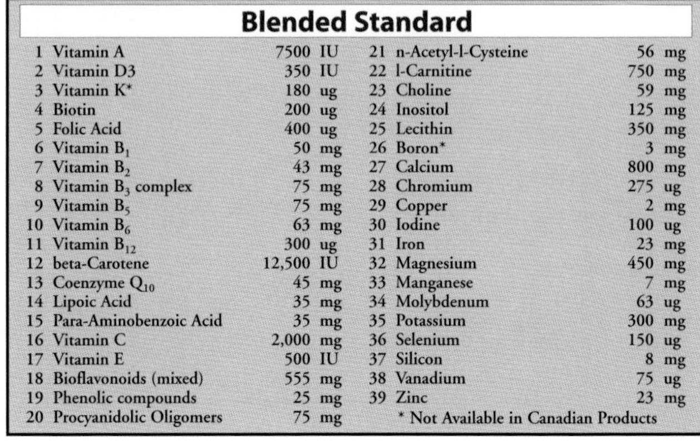

Blended Standard

#	Nutrient	Amount	#	Nutrient	Amount
1	Vitamin A	7500 IU	21	n-Acetyl-l-Cysteine	56 mg
2	Vitamin D3	350 IU	22	l-Carnitine	750 mg
3	Vitamin K*	180 ug	23	Choline	59 mg
4	Biotin	200 ug	24	Inositol	125 mg
5	Folic Acid	400 ug	25	Lecithin	350 mg
6	Vitamin B_1	50 mg	26	Boron*	3 mg
7	Vitamin B_2	43 mg	27	Calcium	800 mg
8	Vitamin B_3 complex	75 mg	28	Chromium	275 ug
9	Vitamin B_5	75 mg	29	Copper	2 mg
10	Vitamin B_6	63 mg	30	Iodine	100 ug
11	Vitamin B_{12}	300 ug	31	Iron	23 mg
12	beta-Carotene	12,500 IU	32	Magnesium	450 mg
13	Coenzyme Q_{10}	45 mg	33	Manganese	7 mg
14	Lipoic Acid	35 mg	34	Molybdenum	63 ug
15	Para-Aminobenzoic Acid	35 mg	35	Potassium	300 mg
16	Vitamin C	2,000 mg	36	Selenium	150 ug
17	Vitamin E	500 IU	37	Silicon	8 mg
18	Bioflavonoids (mixed)	555 mg	38	Vanadium	75 ug
19	Phenolic compounds	25 mg	39	Zinc	23 mg
20	Procyanidolic Oligomers	75 mg		* Not Available in Canadian Products	

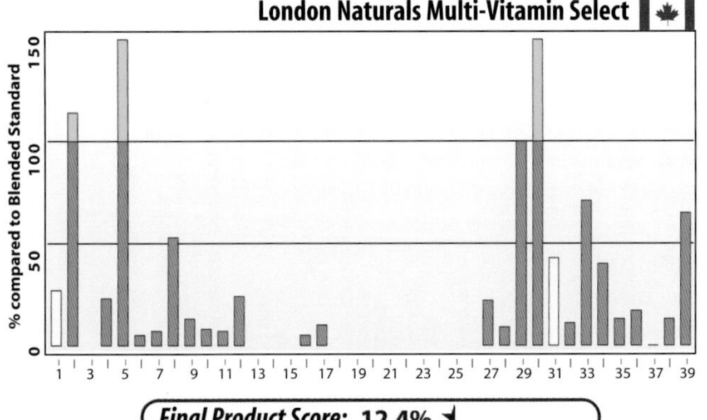

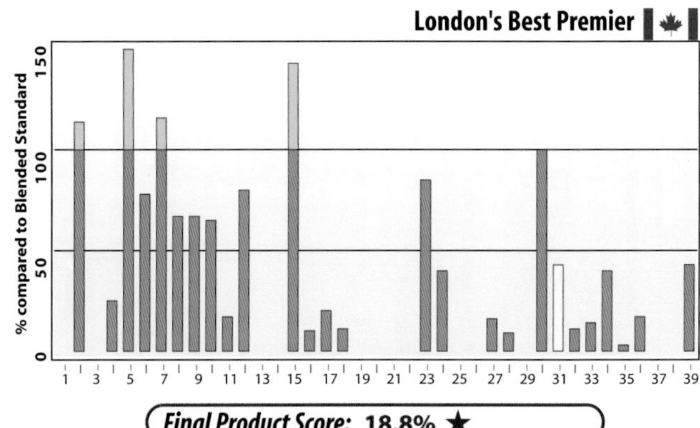

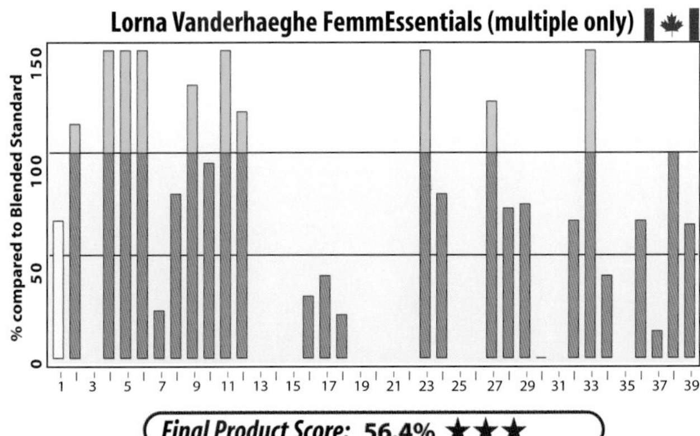

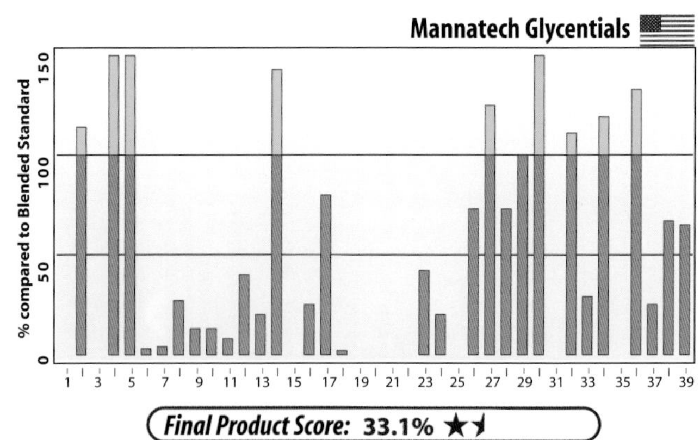

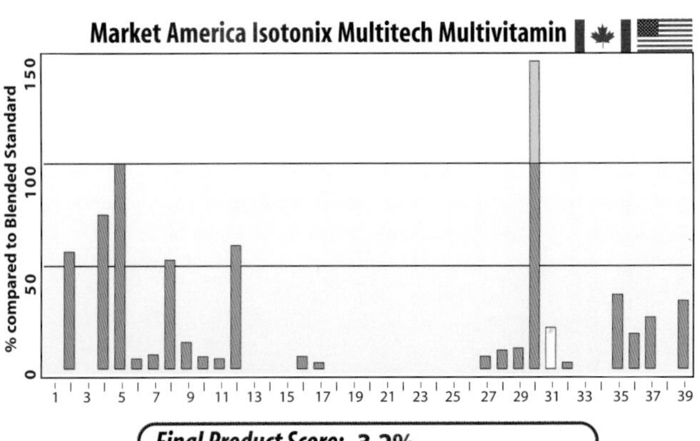

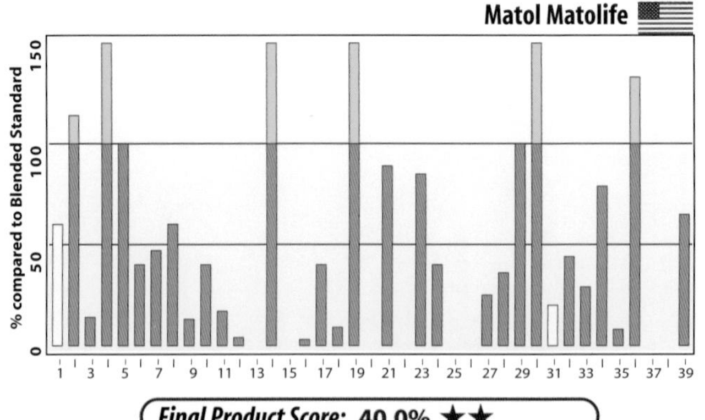

Graphical Comparisons to the Blended Standard

MD Healthline Advanced Green Multi

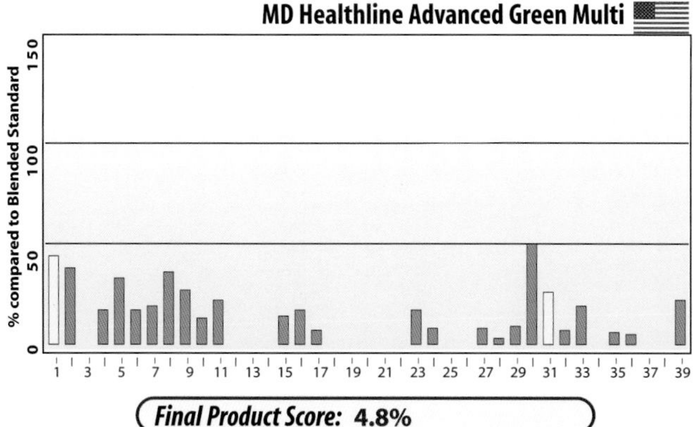

Final Product Score: 4.8%

Melaleuca Vitality Pak (Mel-Vita, Mela-Cal)

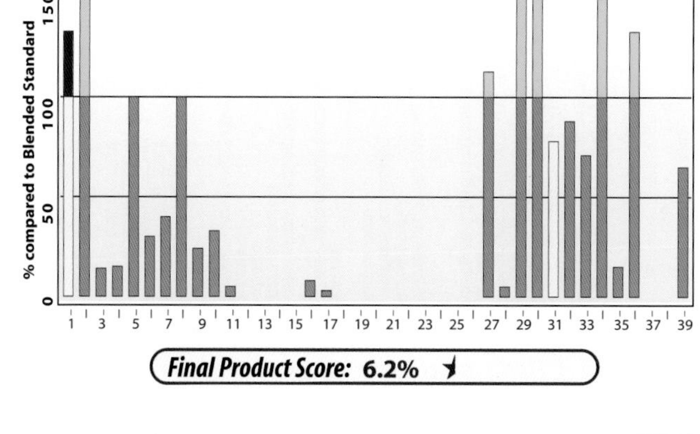

Final Product Score: 6.2%

Metagenics Multigenics Intensive Care Formula

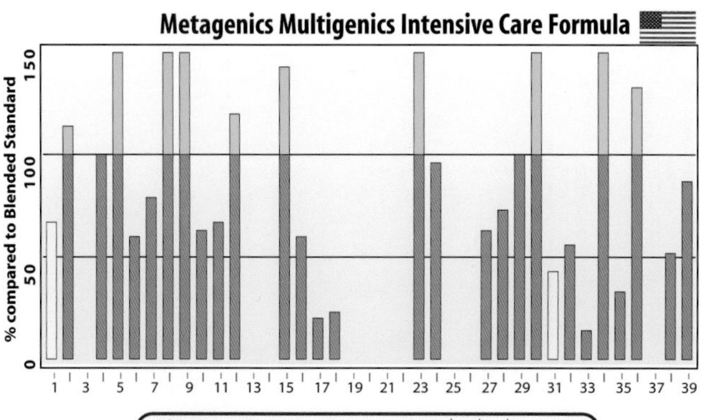

Final Product Score: 51.0%

Michael's Naturopathic Programs Active Senior Tabs

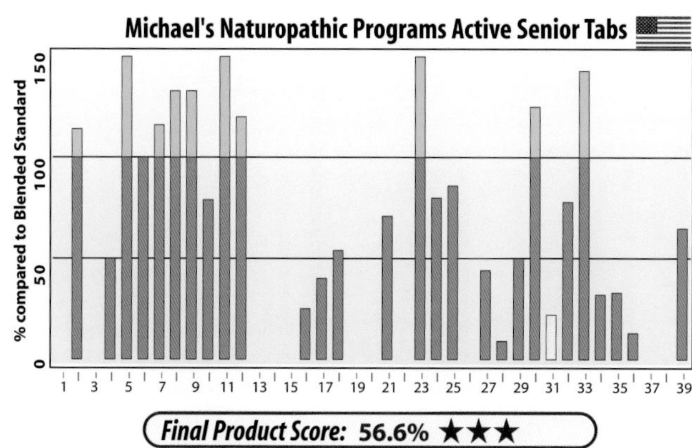

Final Product Score: 56.6%

MMS Pro Preventamins

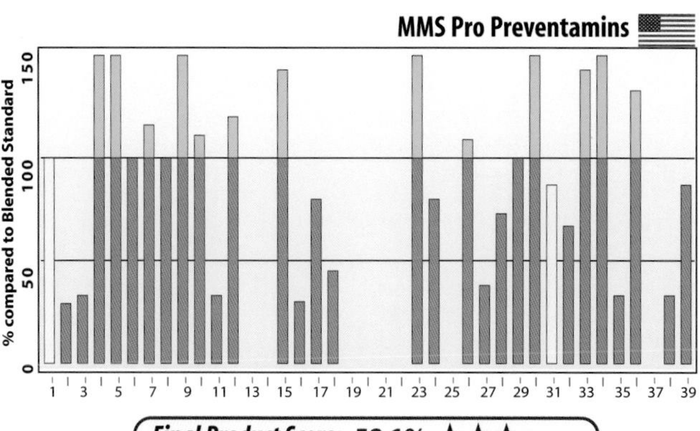

Final Product Score: 58.1%

Moducare Multi-mune

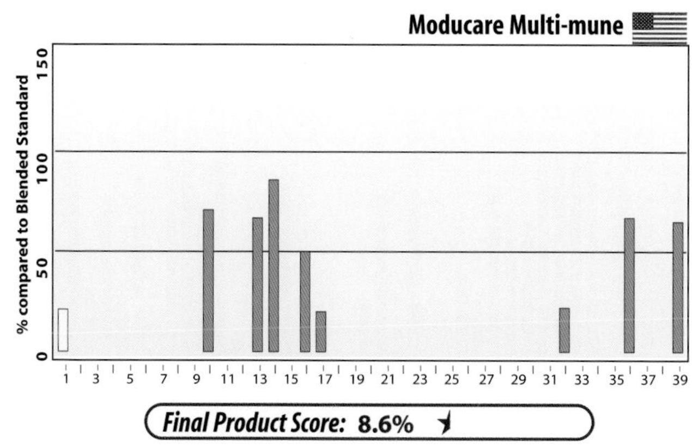

Final Product Score: 8.6%

Molecular Biologics Derma-Vites

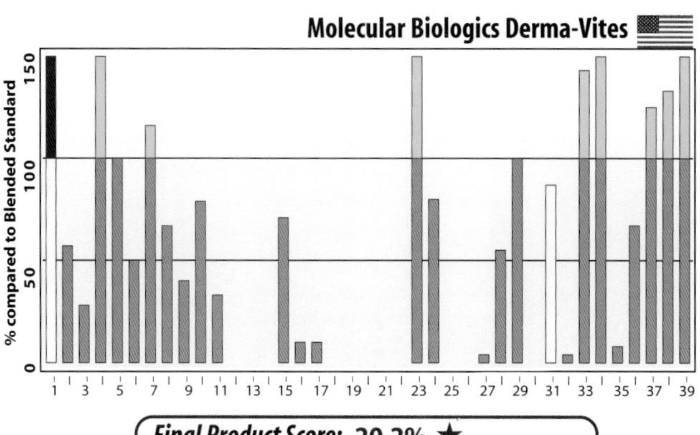

Final Product Score: 20.2%

More Than A Multiple

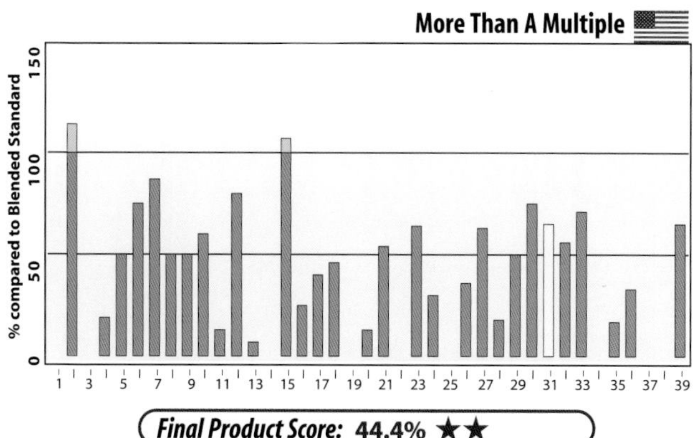

Final Product Score: 44.4%

Graphical Comparisons to the Blended Standard

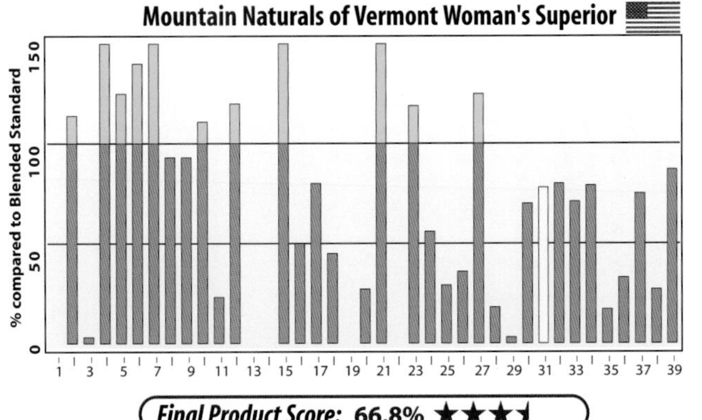

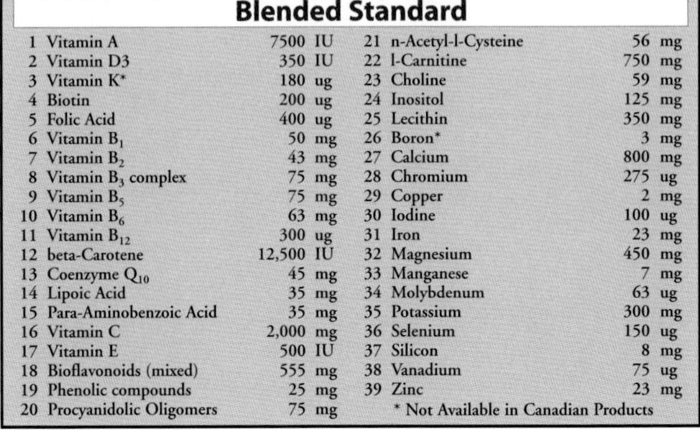

Blended Standard

#	Nutrient	Amount	Unit	#	Nutrient	Amount	Unit
1	Vitamin A	7500	IU	21	n-Acetyl-l-Cysteine	56	mg
2	Vitamin D3	350	IU	22	l-Carnitine	750	mg
3	Vitamin K*	180	ug	23	Choline	59	mg
4	Biotin	200	ug	24	Inositol	125	mg
5	Folic Acid	400	ug	25	Lecithin	350	mg
6	Vitamin B_1	50	mg	26	Boron*	3	mg
7	Vitamin B_2	43	mg	27	Calcium	800	mg
8	Vitamin B_3 complex	75	mg	28	Chromium	275	ug
9	Vitamin B_5	75	mg	29	Copper	2	mg
10	Vitamin B_6	63	mg	30	Iodine	100	ug
11	Vitamin B_{12}	300	ug	31	Iron	23	mg
12	beta-Carotene	12,500	IU	32	Magnesium	450	mg
13	Coenzyme Q_{10}	45	mg	33	Manganese	7	mg
14	Lipoic Acid	35	mg	34	Molybdenum	63	ug
15	Para-Aminobenzoic Acid	35	mg	35	Potassium	300	mg
16	Vitamin C	2,000	mg	36	Selenium	150	ug
17	Vitamin E	500	IU	37	Silicon	8	mg
18	Bioflavonoids (mixed)	555	mg	38	Vanadium	75	ug
19	Phenolic compounds	25	mg	39	Zinc	23	mg
20	Procyanidolic Oligomers	75	mg				

* Not Available in Canadian Products

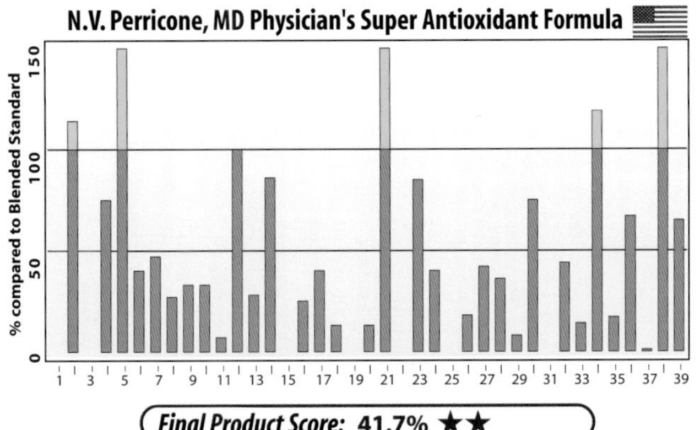

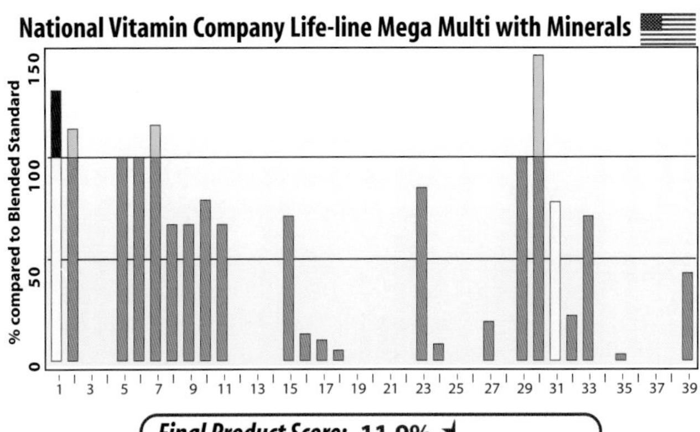

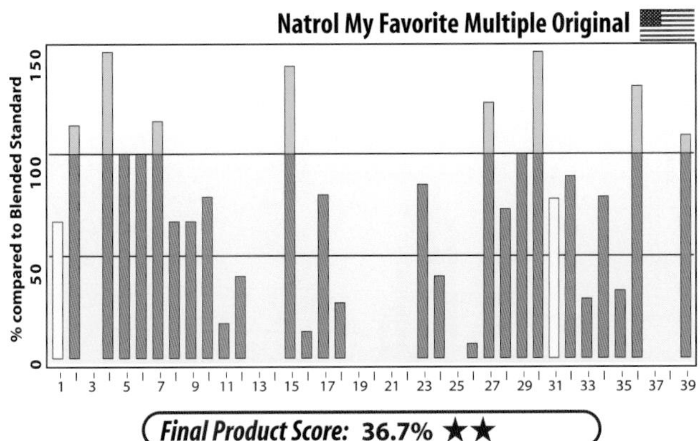

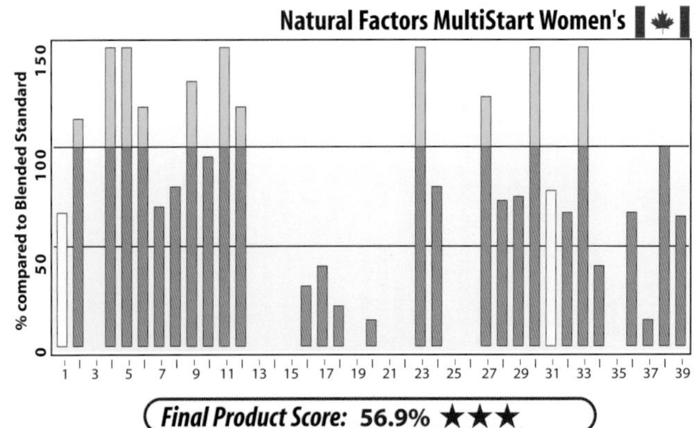

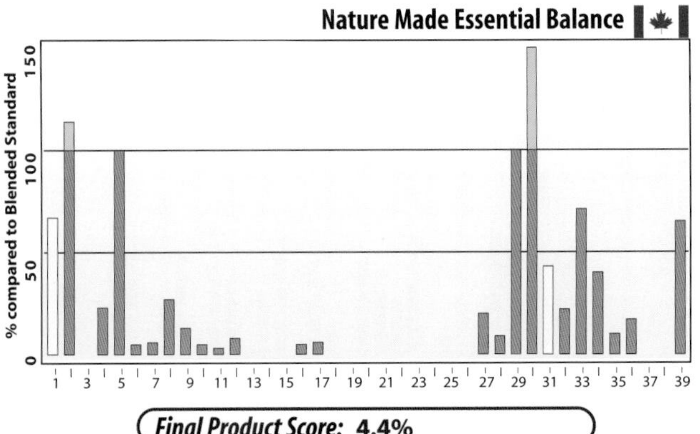

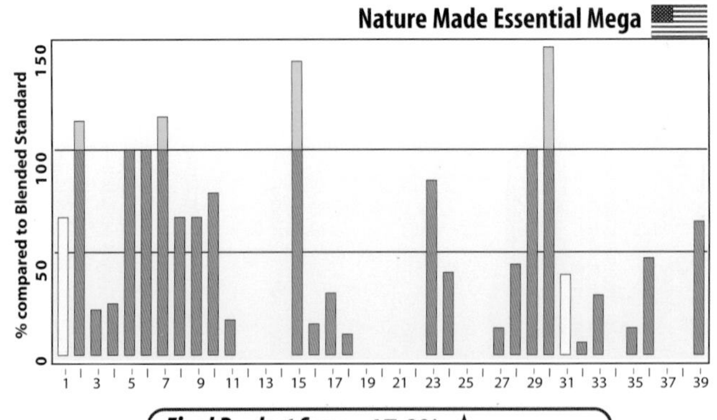

Graphical Comparisons to the Blended Standard

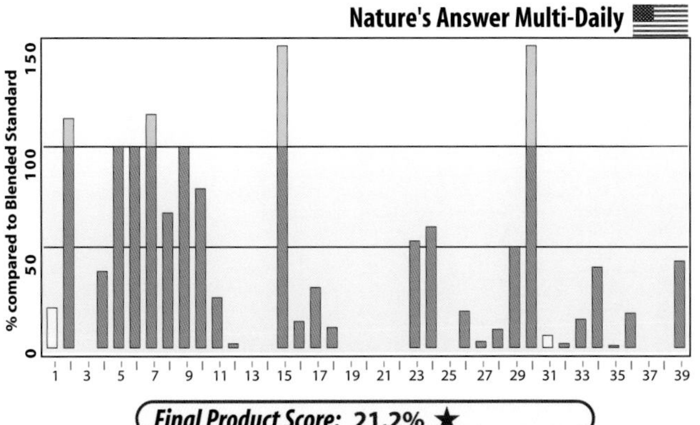

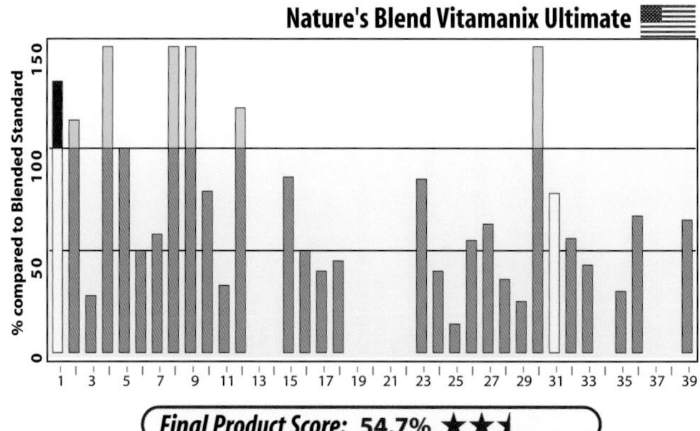

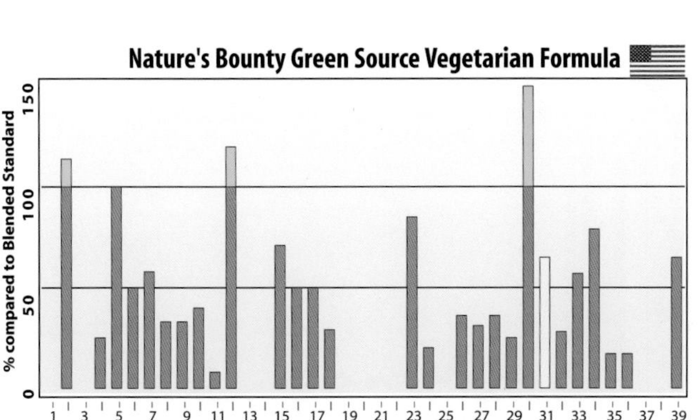

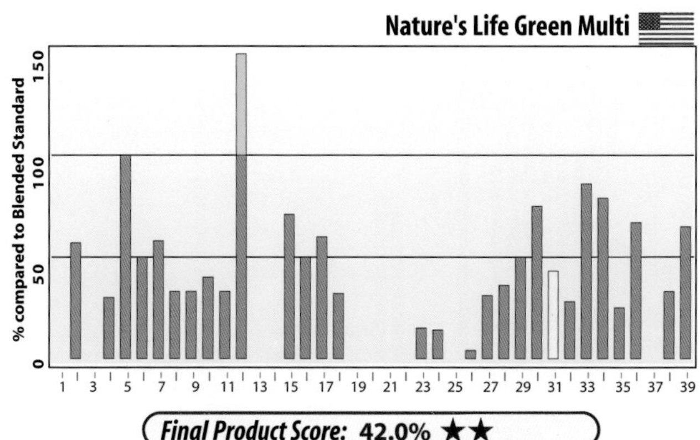

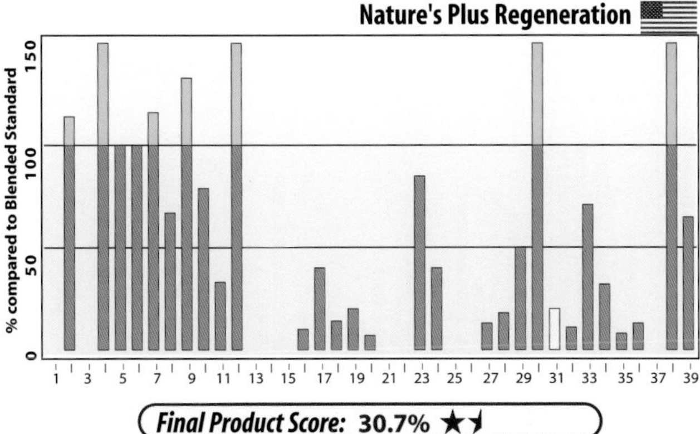

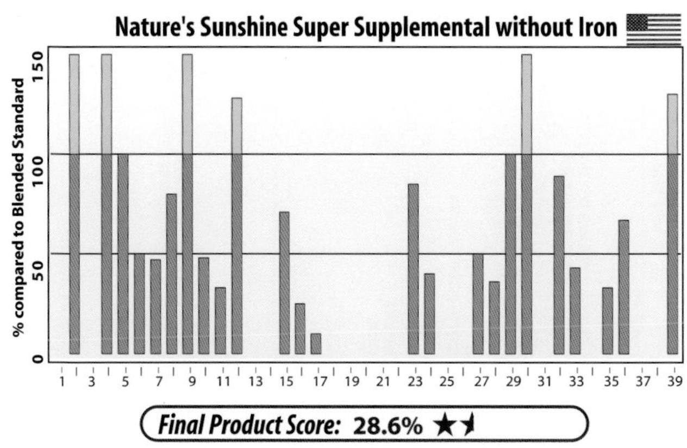

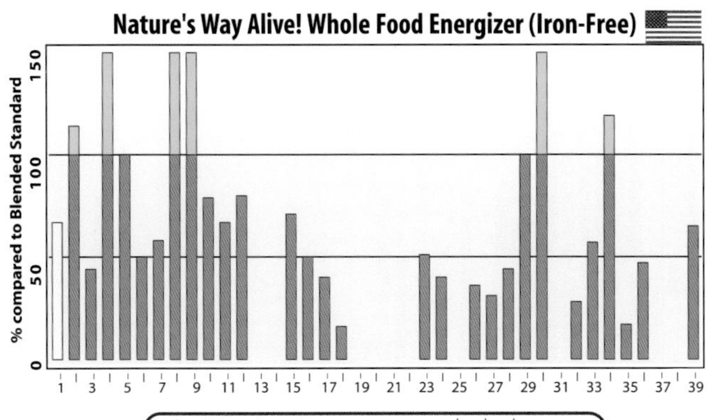

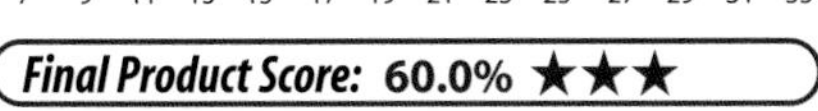

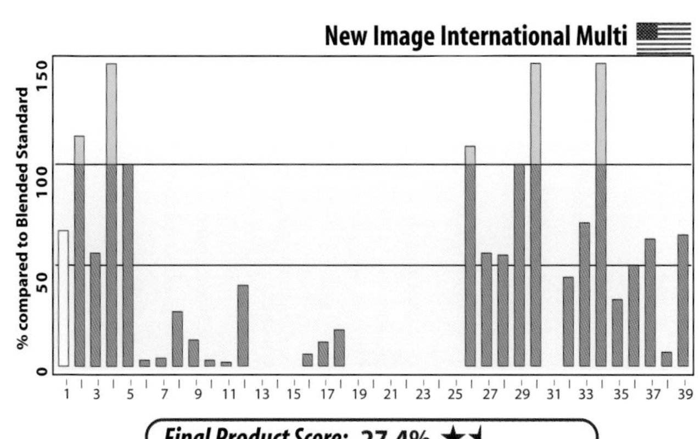

Graphical Comparisons to the Blended Standard

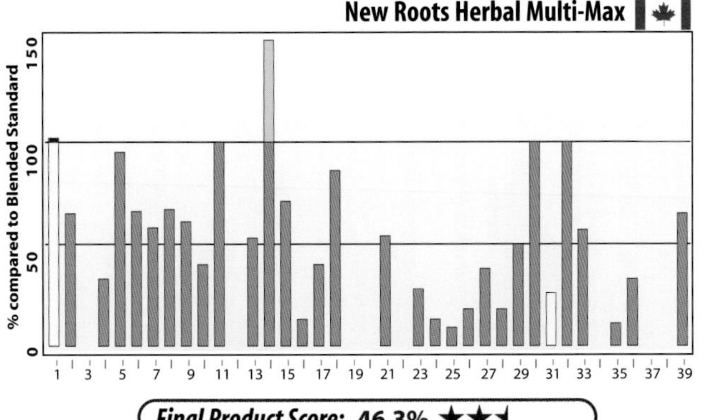

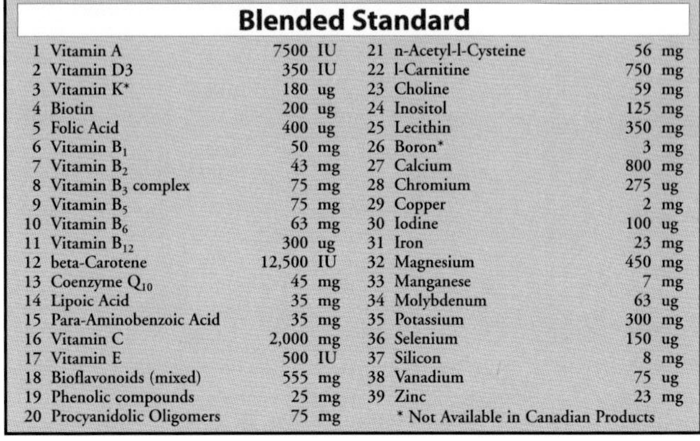

Blended Standard

#	Nutrient	Amount	Unit	#	Nutrient	Amount	Unit
1	Vitamin A	7500	IU	21	n-Acetyl-l-Cysteine	56	mg
2	Vitamin D3	350	IU	22	l-Carnitine	750	mg
3	Vitamin K*	180	ug	23	Choline	59	mg
4	Biotin	200	ug	24	Inositol	125	mg
5	Folic Acid	400	ug	25	Lecithin	350	mg
6	Vitamin B_1	50	mg	26	Boron*	3	mg
7	Vitamin B_2	43	mg	27	Calcium	800	mg
8	Vitamin B_3 complex	75	mg	28	Chromium	275	ug
9	Vitamin B_5	75	mg	29	Copper	2	mg
10	Vitamin B_6	63	mg	30	Iodine	100	ug
11	Vitamin B_{12}	300	ug	31	Iron	23	mg
12	beta-Carotene	12,500	IU	32	Magnesium	450	mg
13	Coenzyme Q_{10}	45	mg	33	Manganese	7	mg
14	Lipoic Acid	35	mg	34	Molybdenum	63	ug
15	Para-Aminobenzoic Acid	35	mg	35	Potassium	300	mg
16	Vitamin C	2,000	mg	36	Selenium	150	ug
17	Vitamin E	500	IU	37	Silicon	8	mg
18	Bioflavonoids (mixed)	555	mg	38	Vanadium	75	ug
19	Phenolic compounds	25	mg	39	Zinc	23	mg
20	Procyanidolic Oligomers	75	mg				

* Not Available in Canadian Products

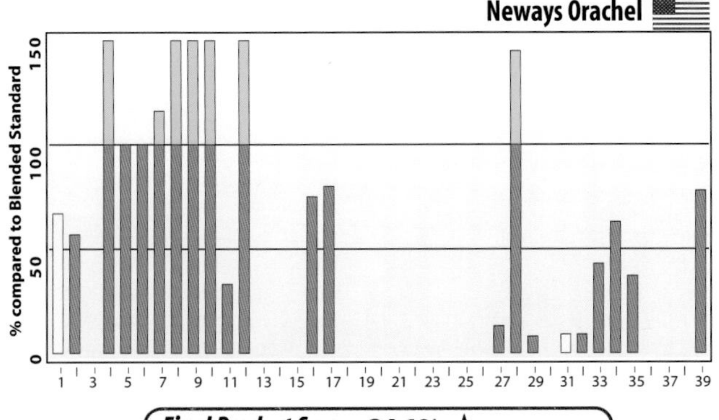

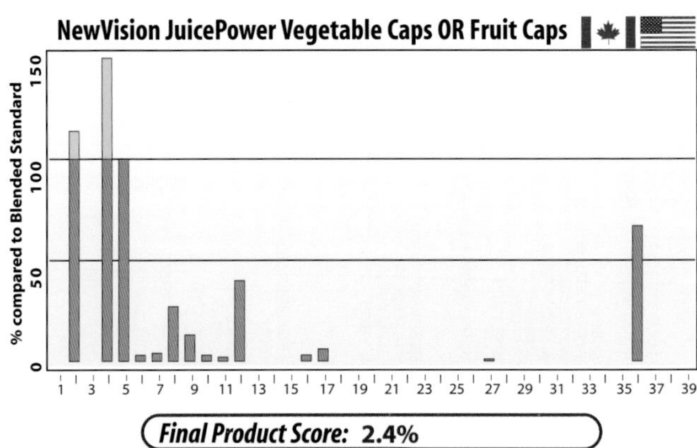

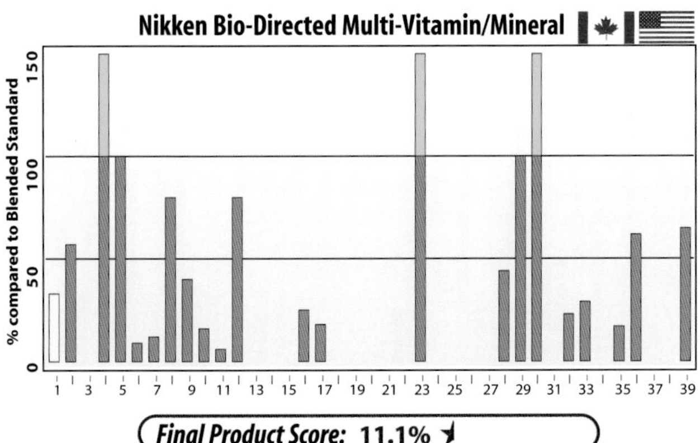

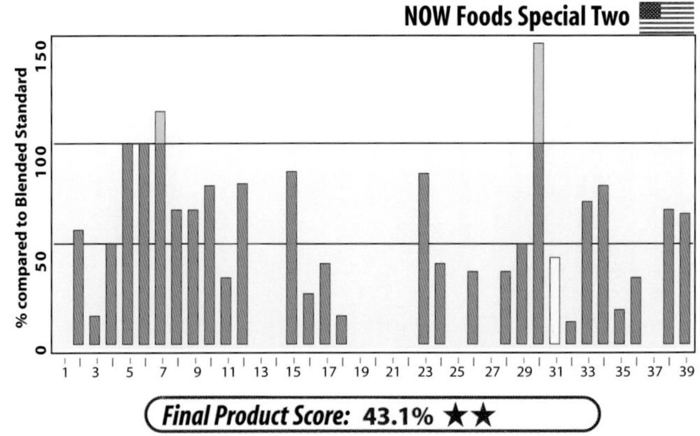

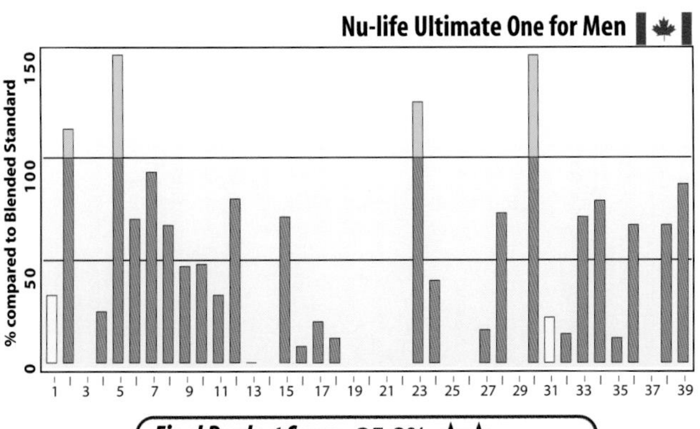

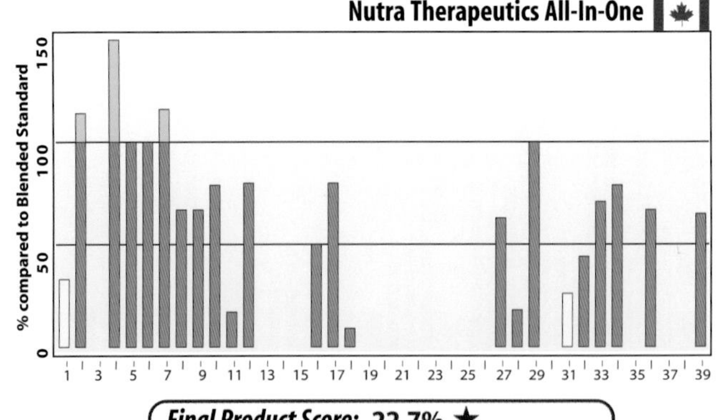

Graphical Comparisons to the Blended Standard

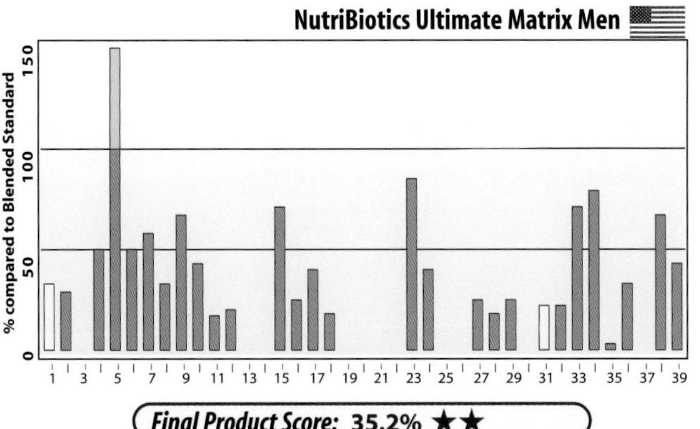

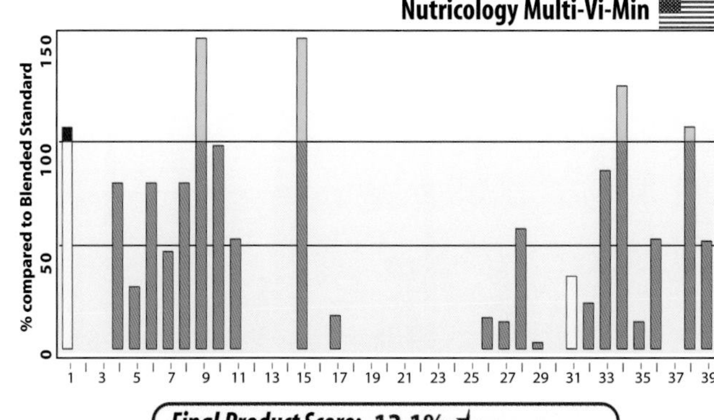

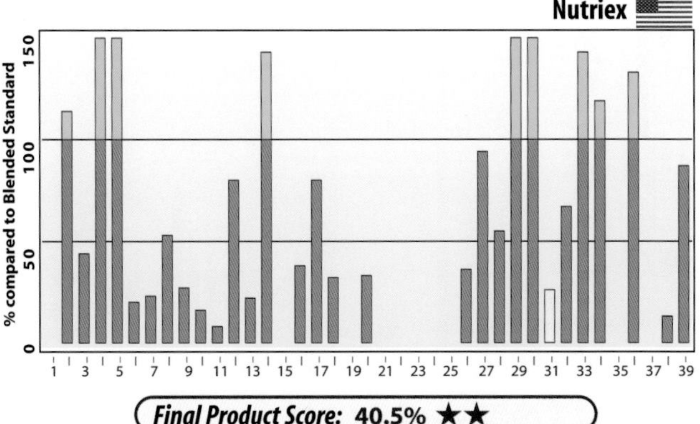

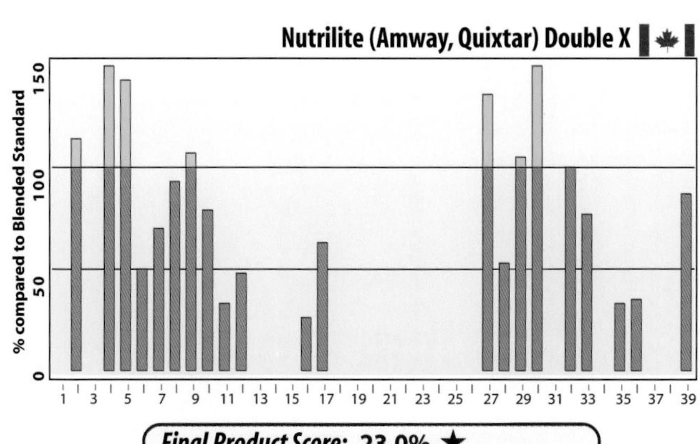

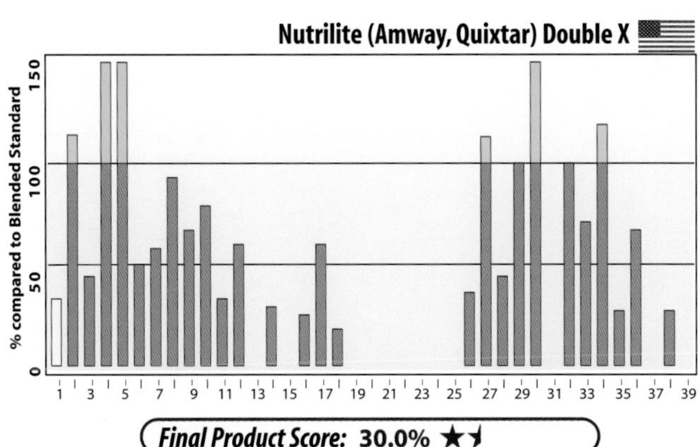

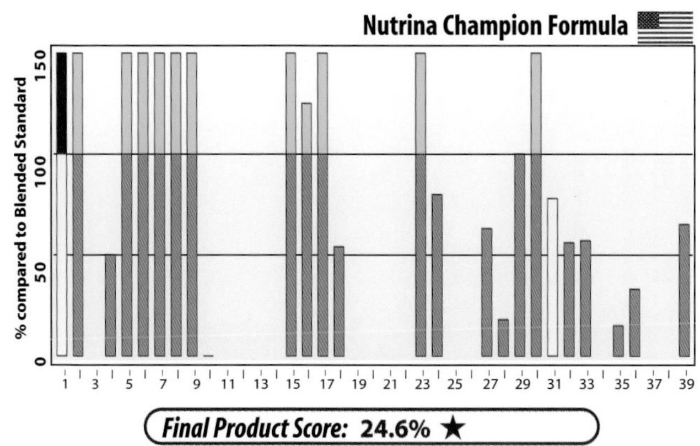

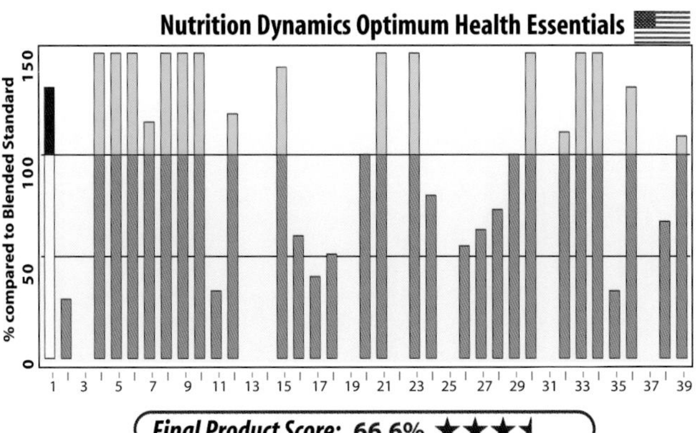

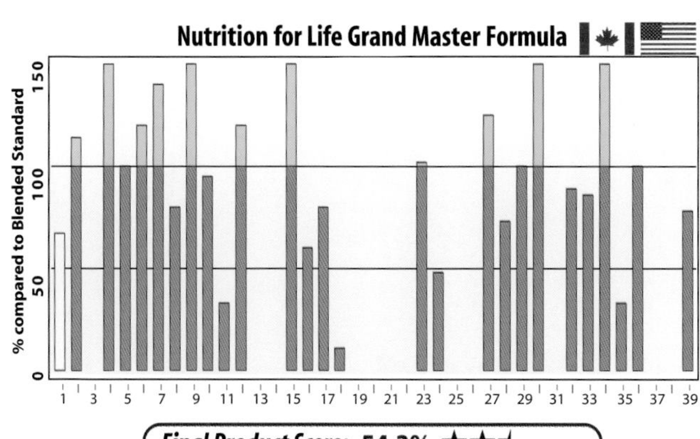

Graphical Comparisons to the Blended Standard

Nutri-West Whole System Health Maintenance

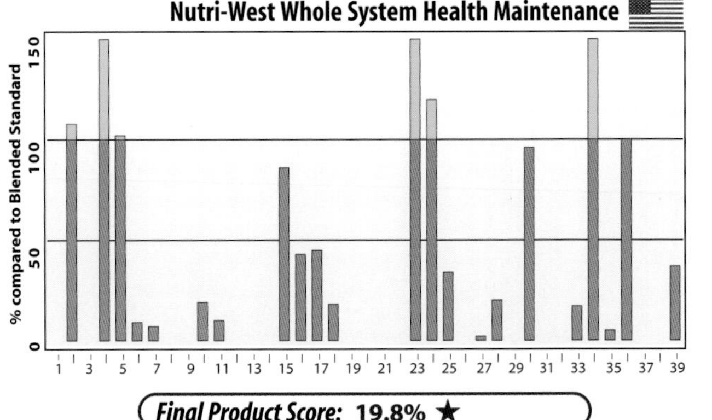

Final Product Score: 19.8% ★

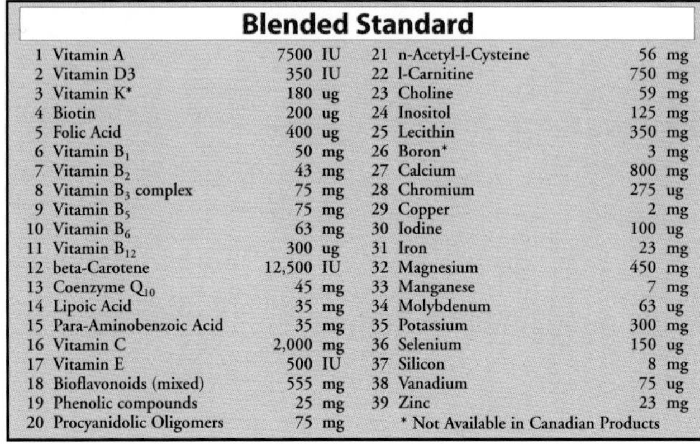

Blended Standard

1	Vitamin A	7500	IU	21	n-Acetyl-l-Cysteine	56	mg
2	Vitamin D3	350	IU	22	l-Carnitine	750	mg
3	Vitamin K*	180	ug	23	Choline	59	mg
4	Biotin	200	ug	24	Inositol	125	mg
5	Folic Acid	400	ug	25	Lecithin	350	mg
6	Vitamin B_1	50	mg	26	Boron*	3	mg
7	Vitamin B_2	43	mg	27	Calcium	800	mg
8	Vitamin B_3 complex	75	mg	28	Chromium	275	ug
9	Vitamin B_5	75	mg	29	Copper	2	mg
10	Vitamin B_6	63	mg	30	Iodine	100	ug
11	Vitamin B_{12}	300	ug	31	Iron	23	mg
12	beta-Carotene	12,500	IU	32	Magnesium	450	mg
13	Coenzyme Q_{10}	45	mg	33	Manganese	7	mg
14	Lipoic Acid	35	mg	34	Molybdenum	63	ug
15	Para-Aminobenzoic Acid	35	mg	35	Potassium	300	mg
16	Vitamin C	2,000	mg	36	Selenium	150	ug
17	Vitamin E	500	IU	37	Silicon	8	mg
18	Bioflavonoids (mixed)	555	mg	38	Vanadium	75	ug
19	Phenolic compounds	25	mg	39	Zinc	23	mg
20	Procyanidolic Oligomers	75	mg		* Not Available in Canadian Products		

Olympian Labs Vita-Vitamin

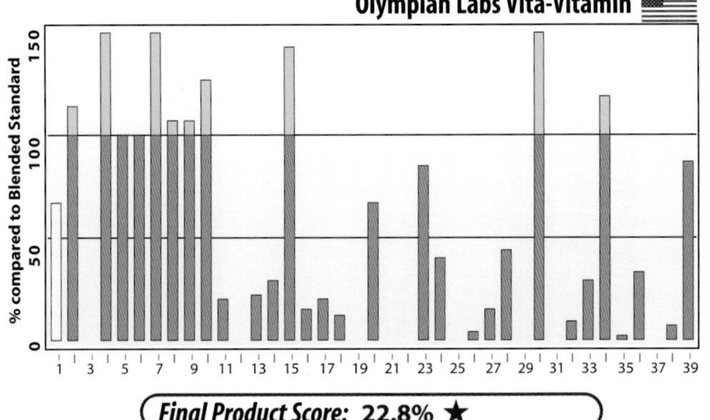

Final Product Score: 22.8% ★

Omnitrition Omni 4

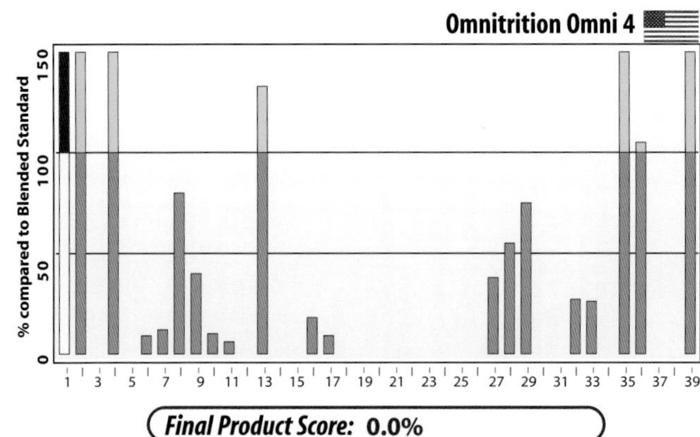

Final Product Score: 0.0%

One A Day Active

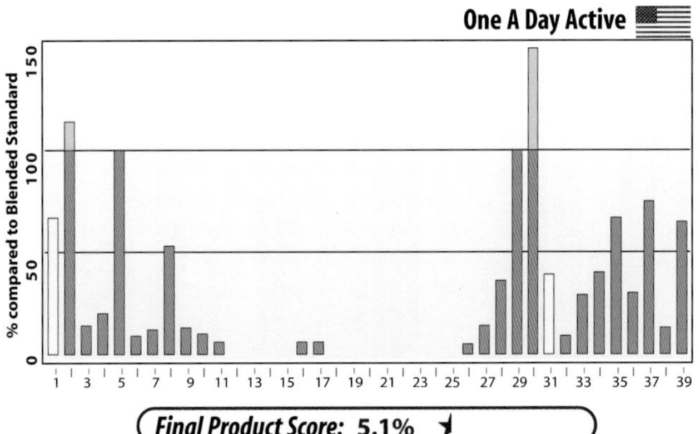

Final Product Score: 5.1%

One A Day Advance Men's Formula

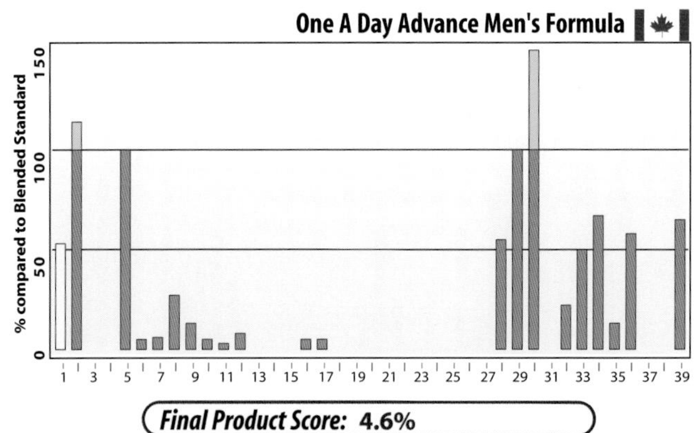

Final Product Score: 4.6%

OneSource Multivitamins and Minerals for Adults

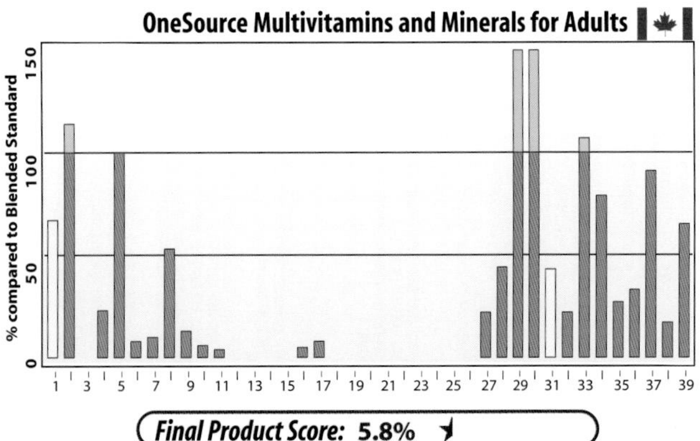

Final Product Score: 5.8%

Optimox Androvite for Men

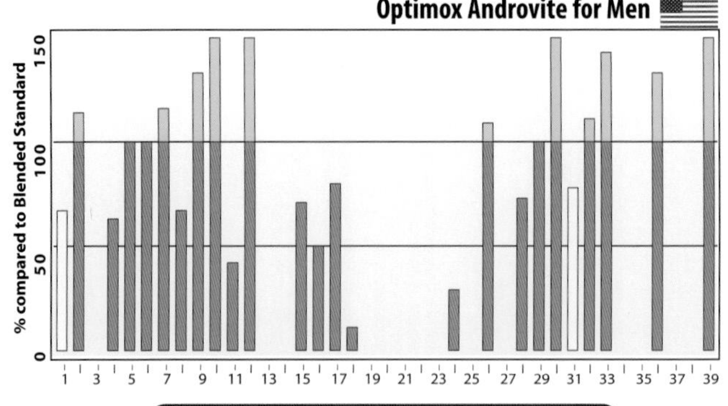

Final Product Score: 50.1% ★★

Graphical Comparisons to the Blended Standard

Oregon Health Multi-Guard with CoQ10

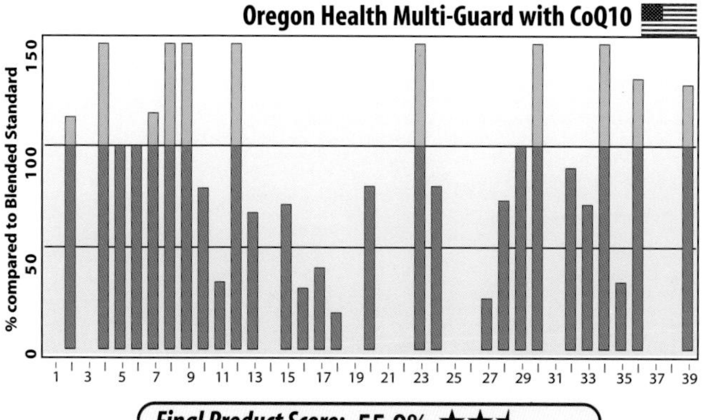

Final Product Score: **55.0%** ★★½

Paramettes Adults Complete

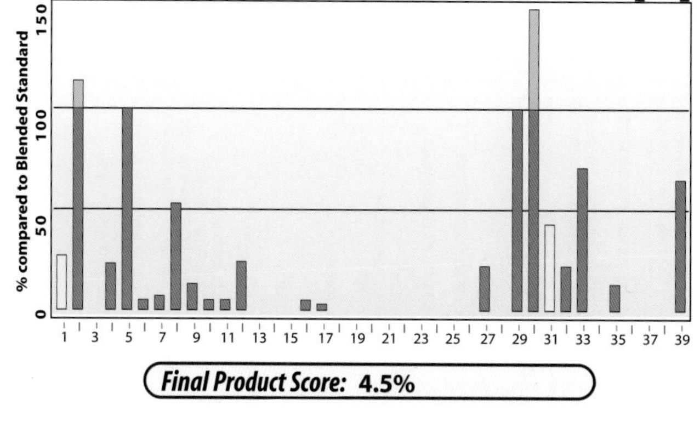

Final Product Score: **4.5%**

Pataki USA 2101 Formula

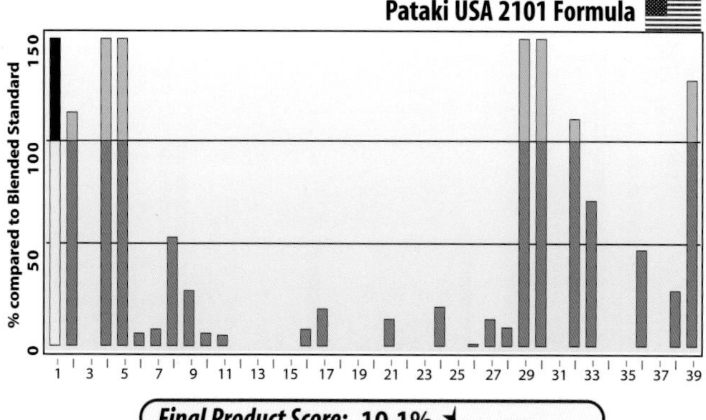

Final Product Score: **10.1%** ½

Perfect Choice Multivitamin Specially Formulated for Women

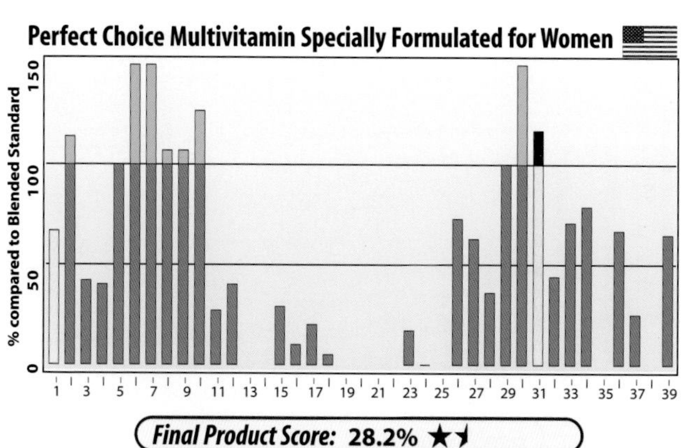

Final Product Score: **28.2%** ★½

Performance Labs Vitalert

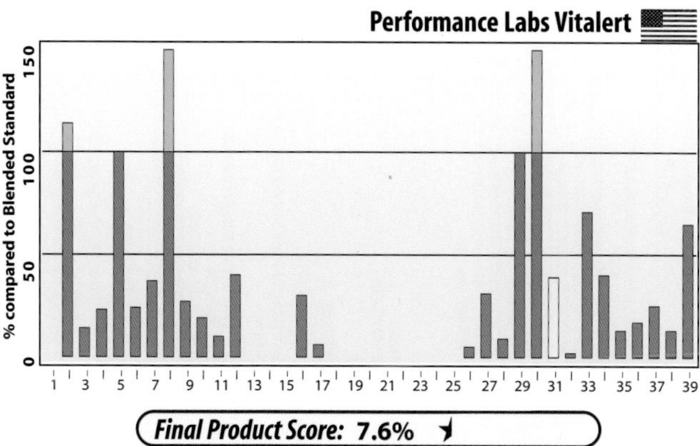

Final Product Score: **7.6%** ½

Personnelle (Pharmetics Inc.) Preventa-Tab

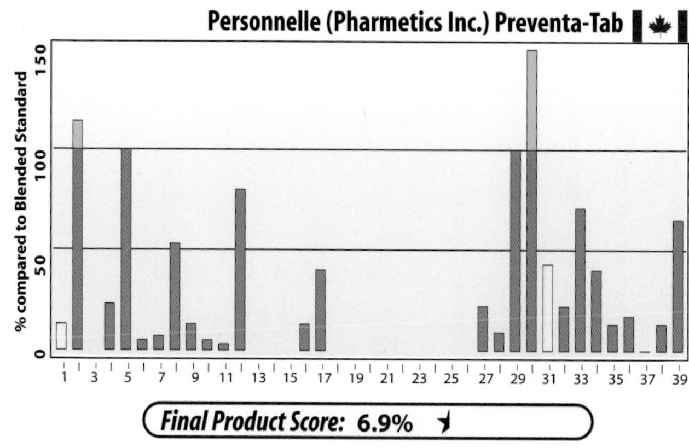

Final Product Score: **6.9%** ½

Pharmacist's Ultimate Health Woman's Ultimate Formula

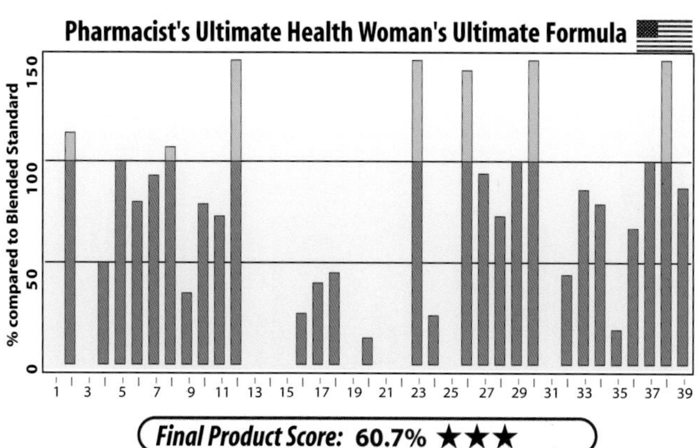

Final Product Score: **60.7%** ★★★

Pharmanex (Nu Skin) LifePak Prime

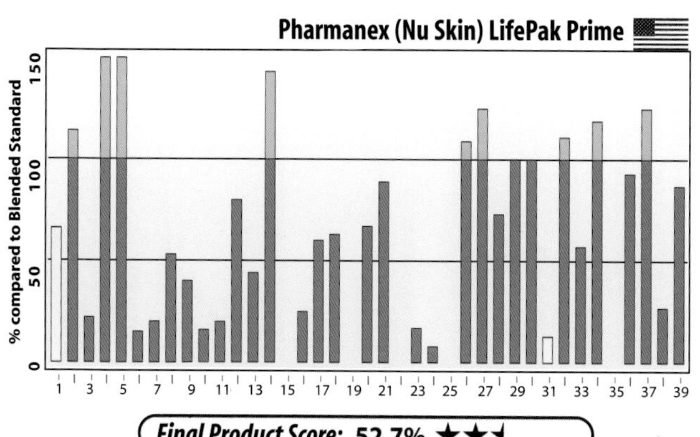

Final Product Score: **52.7%** ★★½

Graphical Comparisons to the Blended Standard

Pharmanex (Nu Skin) LifePak with Catechins

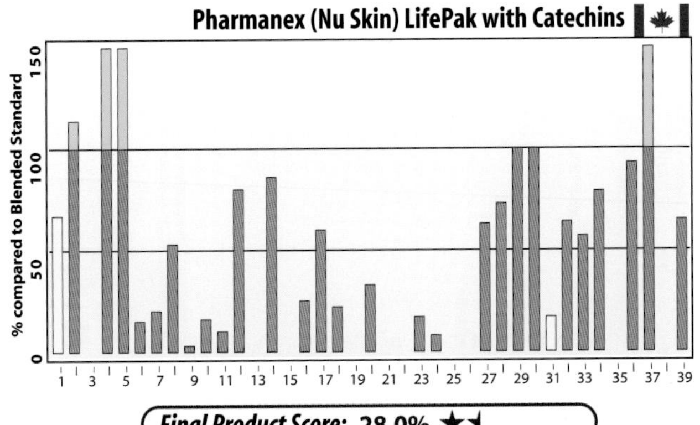

Final Product Score: 28.0% ★½

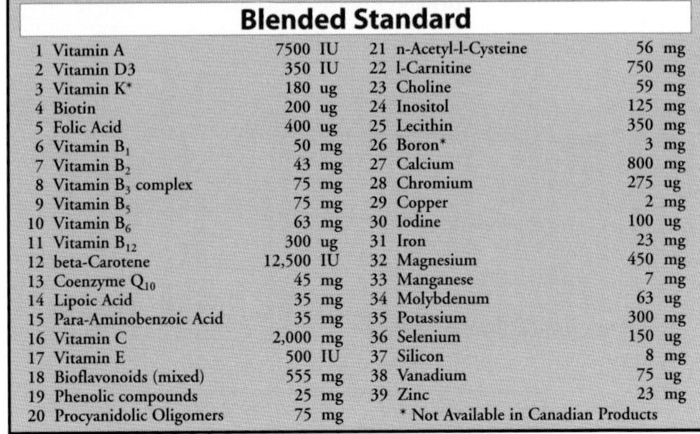

Blended Standard

1	Vitamin A	7500 IU		21	n-Acetyl-l-Cysteine	56 mg
2	Vitamin D3	350 IU		22	l-Carnitine	750 mg
3	Vitamin K*	180 ug		23	Choline	59 mg
4	Biotin	200 ug		24	Inositol	125 mg
5	Folic Acid	400 ug		25	Lecithin	350 mg
6	Vitamin B_1	50 mg		26	Boron*	3 mg
7	Vitamin B_2	43 mg		27	Calcium	800 mg
8	Vitamin B_3 complex	75 mg		28	Chromium	275 ug
9	Vitamin B_5	75 mg		29	Copper	2 mg
10	Vitamin B_6	63 mg		30	Iodine	100 ug
11	Vitamin B_{12}	300 ug		31	Iron	23 mg
12	beta-Carotene	12,500 IU		32	Magnesium	450 mg
13	Coenzyme Q_{10}	45 mg		33	Manganese	7 mg
14	Lipoic Acid	35 mg		34	Molybdenum	63 ug
15	Para-Aminobenzoic Acid	35 mg		35	Potassium	300 mg
16	Vitamin C	2,000 mg		36	Selenium	150 ug
17	Vitamin E	500 IU		37	Silicon	8 mg
18	Bioflavonoids (mixed)	555 mg		38	Vanadium	75 ug
19	Phenolic compounds	25 mg		39	Zinc	23 mg
20	Procyanidolic Oligomers	75 mg			* Not Available in Canadian Products	

Pharmasave MultiSelect 29

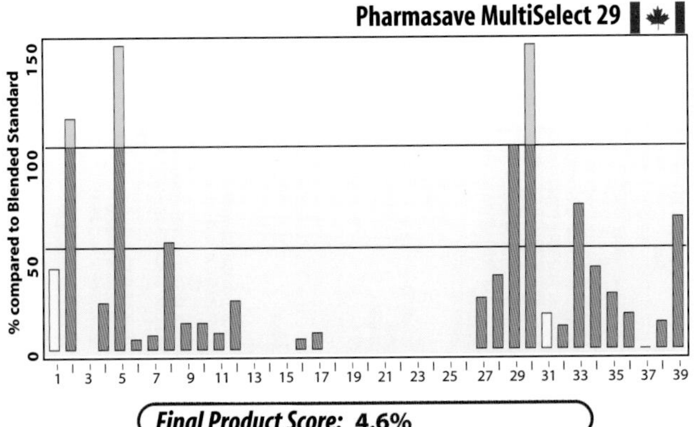

Final Product Score: 4.6%

PharmAssure Women's Biomultiple

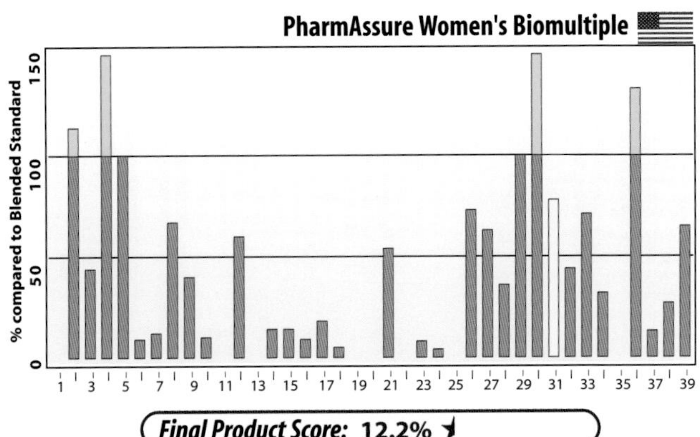

Final Product Score: 12.2% ½

Pharmetics Multivitamins and Minerals with beta-Carotene

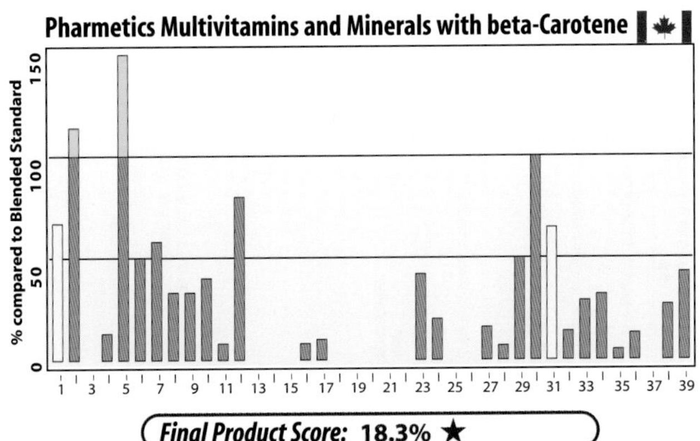

Final Product Score: 18.3% ★

PhytoPharmica Clinical Nutrients for Women

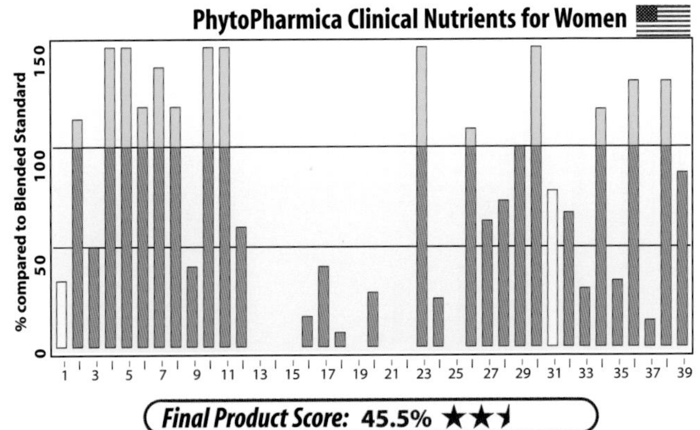

Final Product Score: 45.5% ★★½

Pilgrim's Sense of Energy

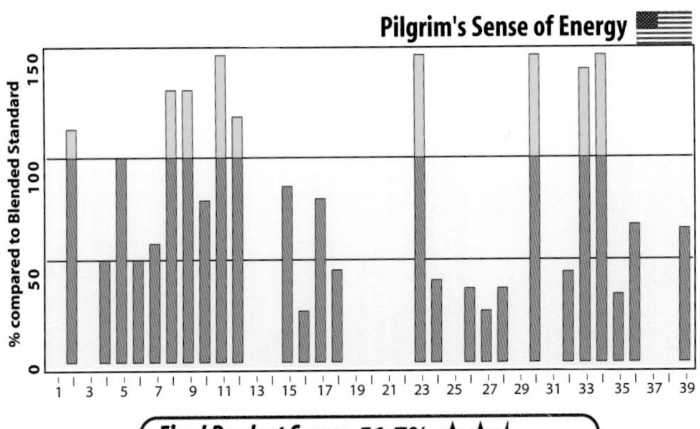

Final Product Score: 51.7% ★★½

Prairie Naturals Multi-Force

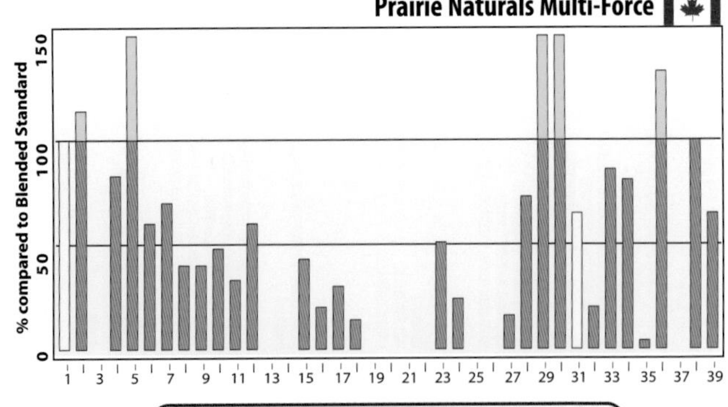

Final Product Score: 35.8% ★★

Graphical Comparisons to the Blended Standard

ProActive for Active Men

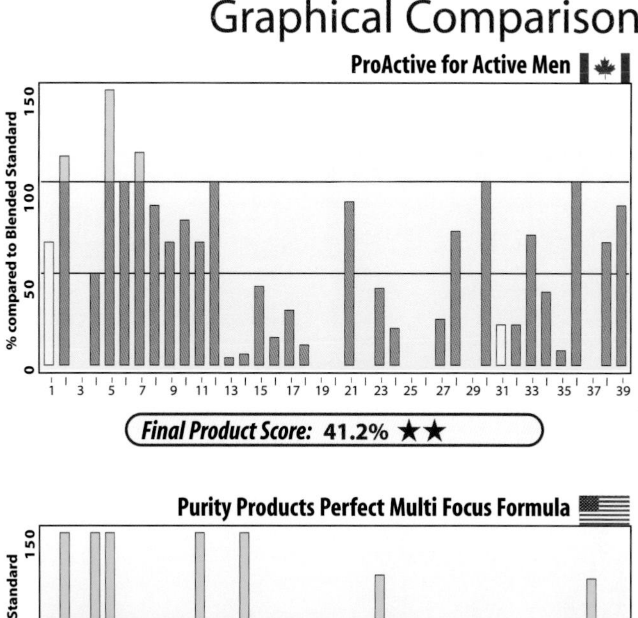

Final Product Score: **41.2% ★★**

Puritan's Pride Green Source Iron Free

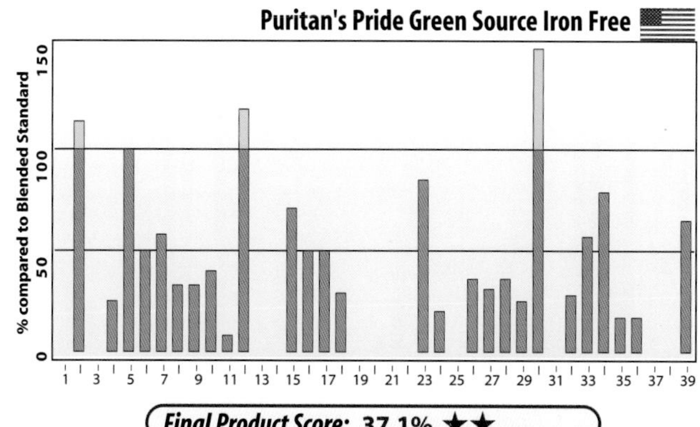

Final Product Score: **37.1% ★★**

Purity Products Perfect Multi Focus Formula

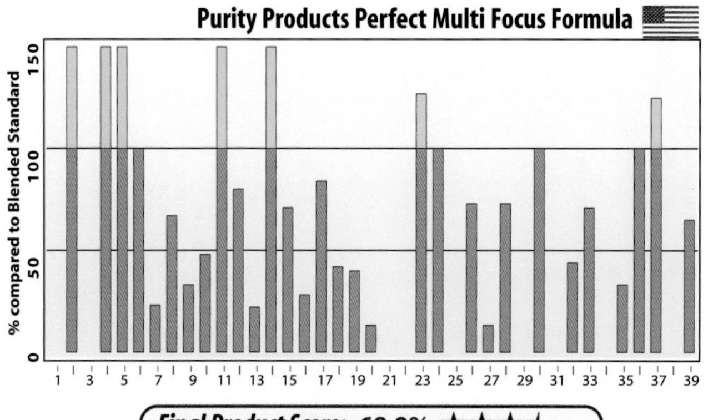

Final Product Score: **68.9% ★★★½**

QCI Nutritionals Ultra Vitality #2

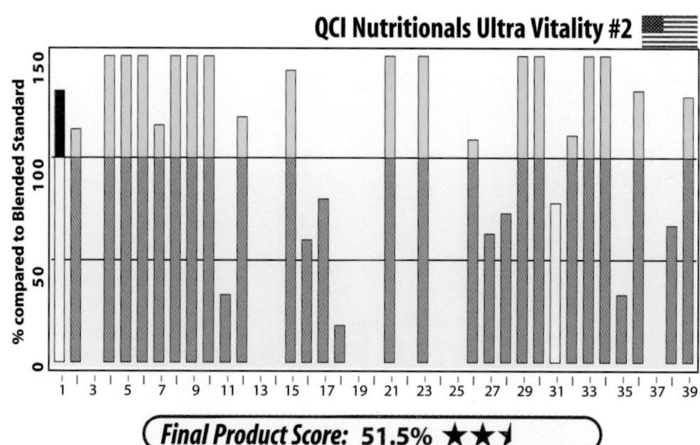

Final Product Score: **51.5% ★★½**

Quest Maximum Once A Day

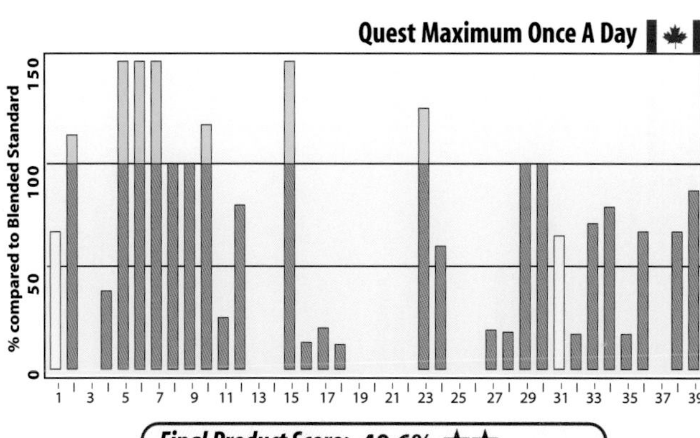

Final Product Score: **40.6% ★★**

R Garden Internationale Multiple Vitamin Mineral Formula

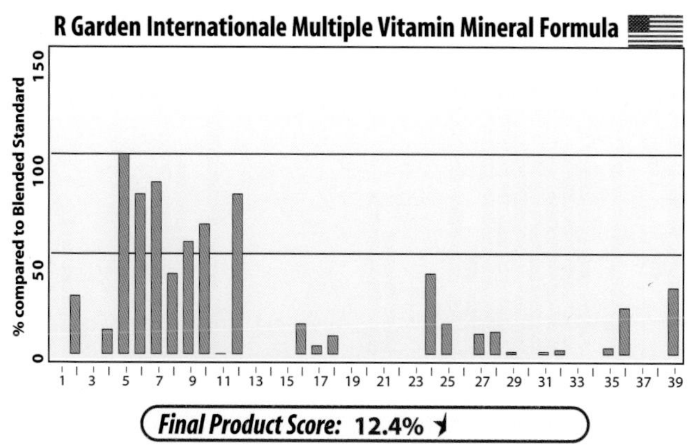

Final Product Score: **12.4% ½**

Rainbow Light Advanced Nutritional System

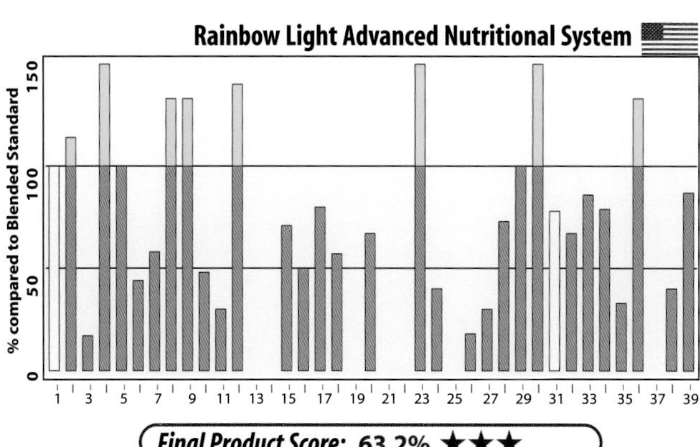

Final Product Score: **63.2% ★★★**

Reliv Classic

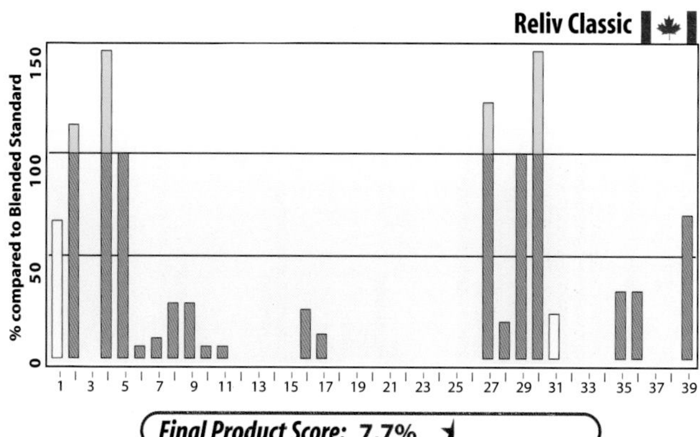

Final Product Score: **7.7% ½**

Graphical Comparisons to the Blended Standard

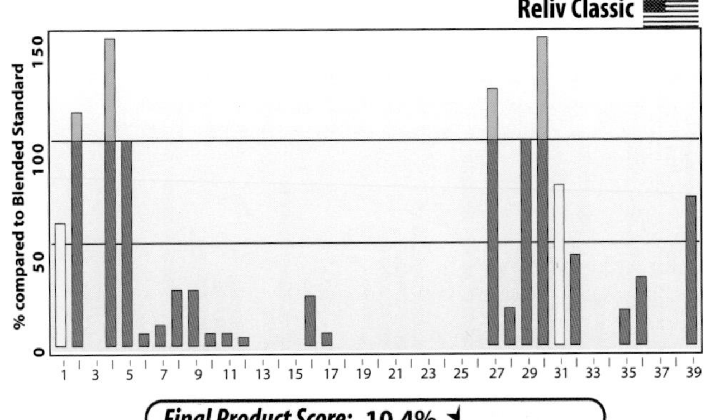

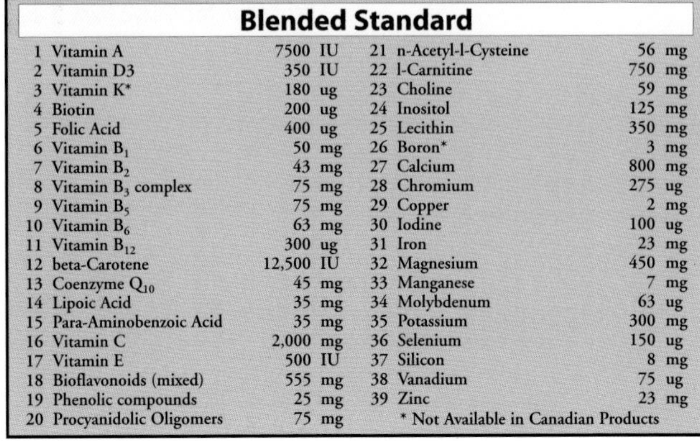

Blended Standard

#	Nutrient	Amount	Unit	#	Nutrient	Amount	Unit
1	Vitamin A	7500	IU	21	n-Acetyl-l-Cysteine	56	mg
2	Vitamin D3	350	IU	22	l-Carnitine	750	mg
3	Vitamin K*	180	ug	23	Choline	59	mg
4	Biotin	200	ug	24	Inositol	125	mg
5	Folic Acid	400	ug	25	Lecithin	350	mg
6	Vitamin B_1	50	mg	26	Boron*	3	mg
7	Vitamin B_2	43	mg	27	Calcium	800	mg
8	Vitamin B_3 complex	75	mg	28	Chromium	275	ug
9	Vitamin B_5	75	mg	29	Copper	2	mg
10	Vitamin B_6	63	mg	30	Iodine	100	ug
11	Vitamin B_{12}	300	ug	31	Iron	23	mg
12	beta-Carotene	12,500	IU	32	Magnesium	450	mg
13	Coenzyme Q_{10}	45	mg	33	Manganese	7	mg
14	Lipoic Acid	35	mg	34	Molybdenum	63	ug
15	Para-Aminobenzoic Acid	35	mg	35	Potassium	300	mg
16	Vitamin C	2,000	mg	36	Selenium	150	ug
17	Vitamin E	500	IU	37	Silicon	8	mg
18	Bioflavonoids (mixed)	555	mg	38	Vanadium	75	ug
19	Phenolic compounds	25	mg	39	Zinc	23	mg
20	Procyanidolic Oligomers	75	mg				

* Not Available in Canadian Products

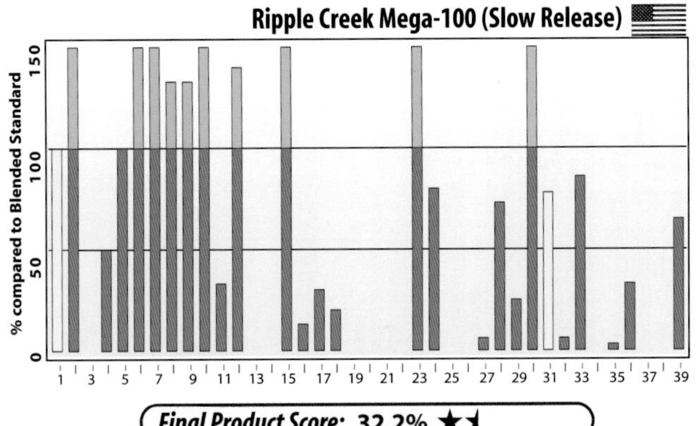

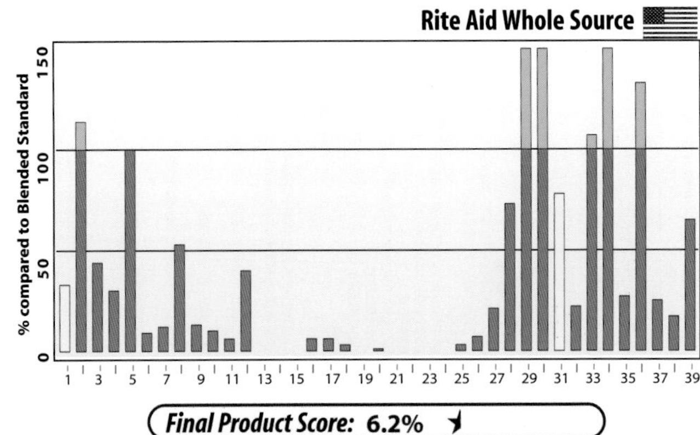

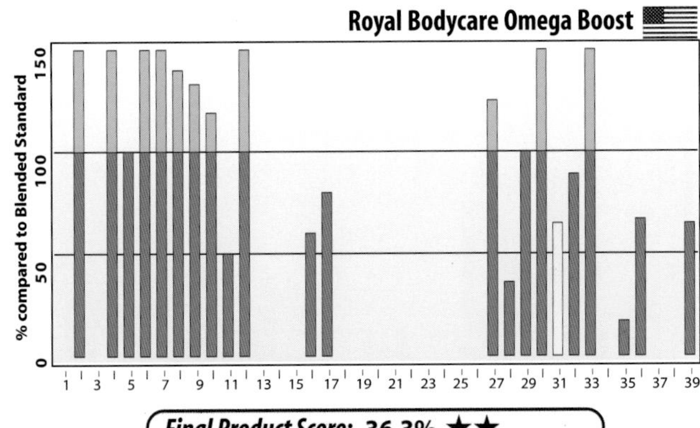

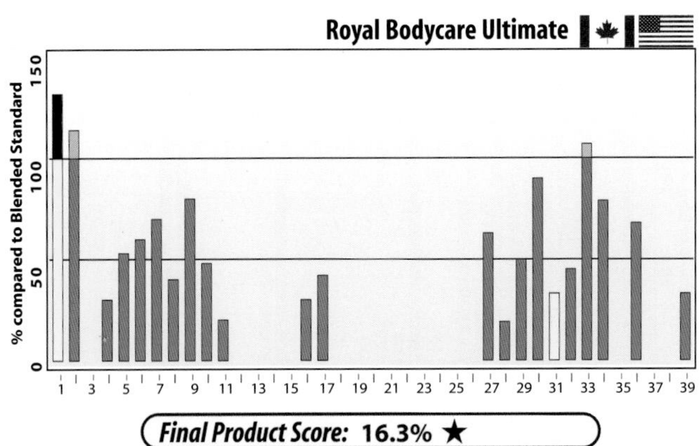

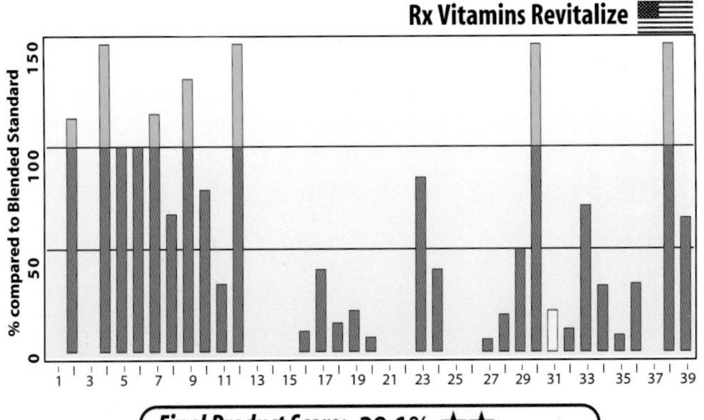

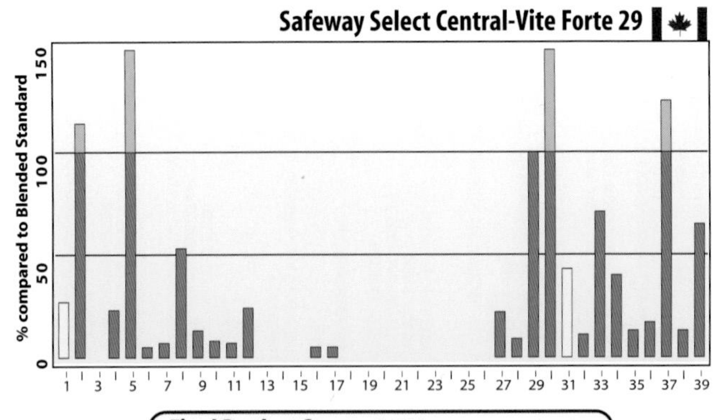

Graphical Comparisons to the Blended Standard

Safeway Select Super Women's Multivitamin

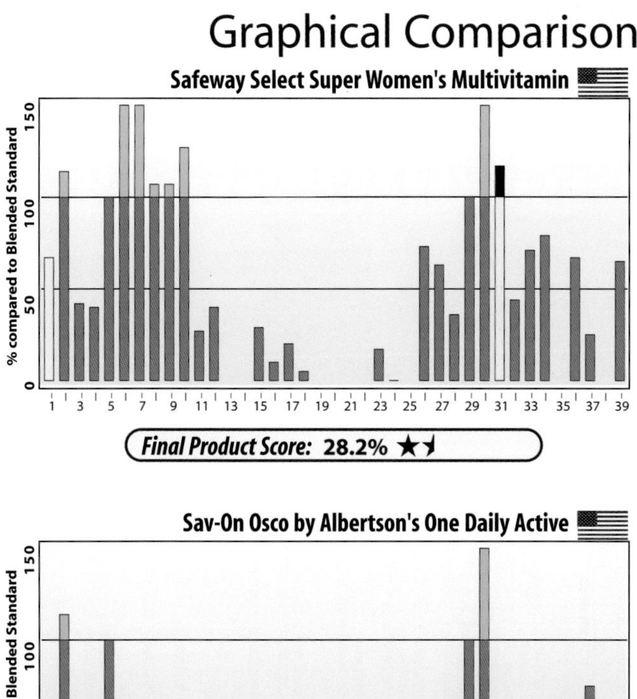

Final Product Score: 28.2% ★½

Santé Naturelle Feminex Multi

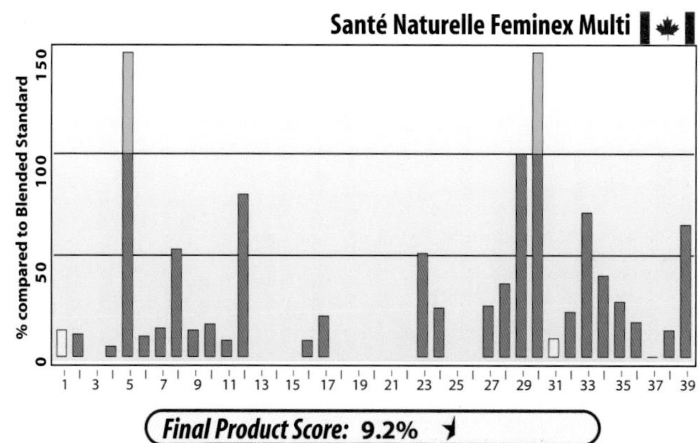

Final Product Score: 9.2% ½

Sav-On Osco by Albertson's One Daily Active

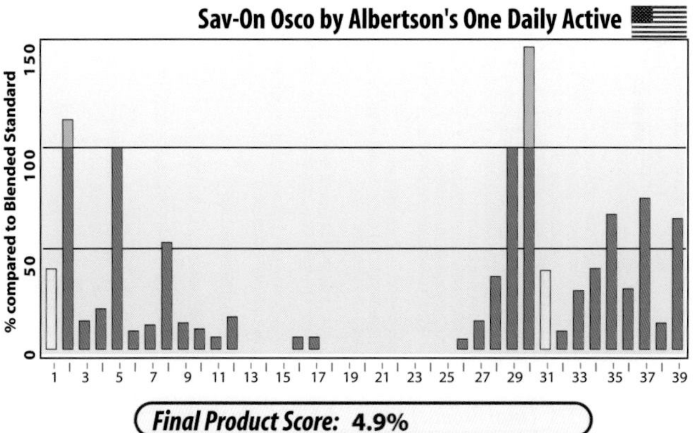

Final Product Score: 4.9%

Schiff Single Day

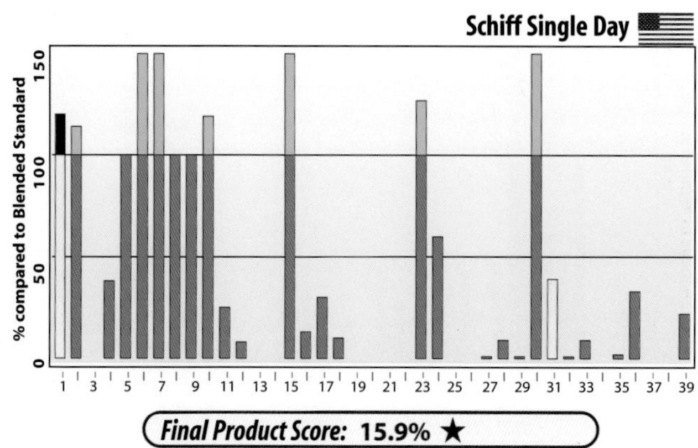

Final Product Score: 15.9% ★

Shaklee Vita-Lea Advanced Formula

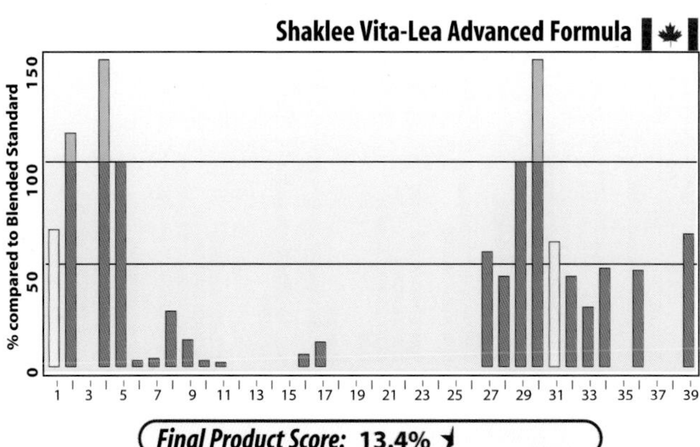

Final Product Score: 13.4% ½

Sisu Vegi-Mins

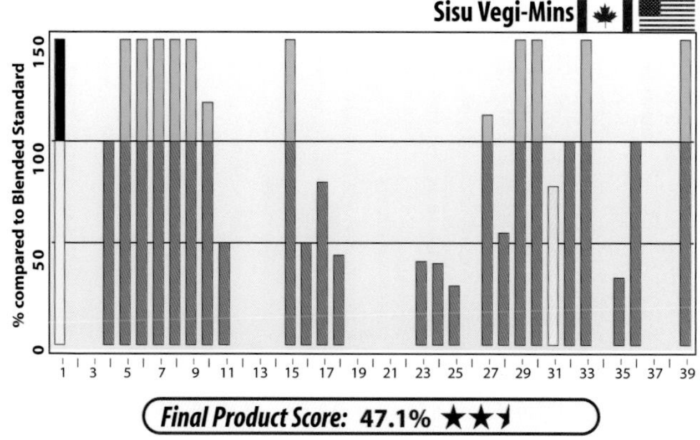

Final Product Score: 47.1% ★★½

Solaray Iron-Free Spectro Multi-Vita-Min

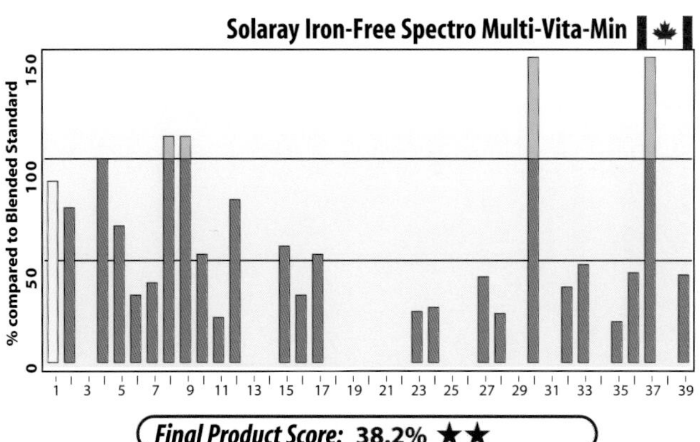

Final Product Score: 38.2% ★★

Solaray Spectro Multi-Vita-Min

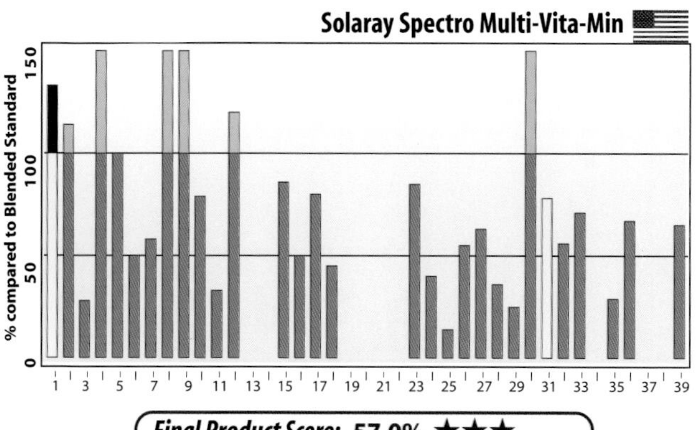

Final Product Score: 57.0% ★★★

Graphical Comparisons to the Blended Standard

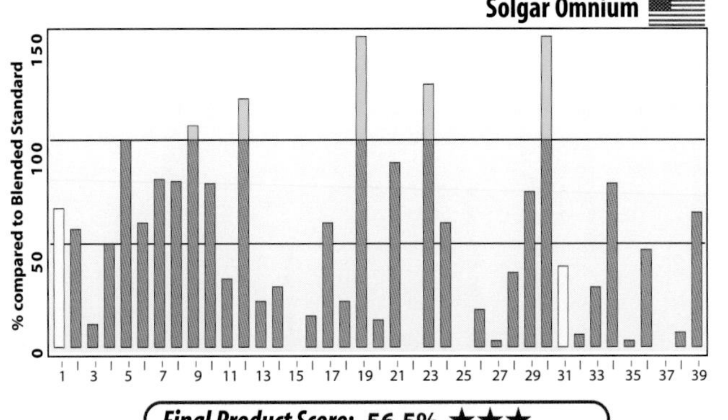

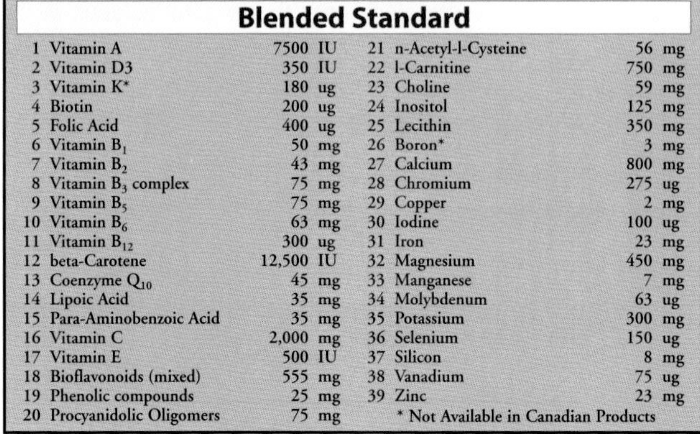

Blended Standard

#	Nutrient	Amount	#	Nutrient	Amount
1	Vitamin A	7500 IU	21	n-Acetyl-l-Cysteine	56 mg
2	Vitamin D3	350 IU	22	l-Carnitine	750 mg
3	Vitamin K*	180 ug	23	Choline	59 mg
4	Biotin	200 ug	24	Inositol	125 mg
5	Folic Acid	400 ug	25	Lecithin	350 mg
6	Vitamin B_1	50 mg	26	Boron*	3 mg
7	Vitamin B_2	43 mg	27	Calcium	800 mg
8	Vitamin B_3 complex	75 mg	28	Chromium	275 ug
9	Vitamin B_5	75 mg	29	Copper	2 mg
10	Vitamin B_6	63 mg	30	Iodine	100 ug
11	Vitamin B_{12}	300 ug	31	Iron	23 mg
12	beta-Carotene	12,500 IU	32	Magnesium	450 mg
13	Coenzyme Q_{10}	45 mg	33	Manganese	7 mg
14	Lipoic Acid	35 mg	34	Molybdenum	63 ug
15	Para-Aminobenzoic Acid	35 mg	35	Potassium	300 mg
16	Vitamin C	2,000 mg	36	Selenium	150 ug
17	Vitamin E	500 IU	37	Silicon	8 mg
18	Bioflavonoids (mixed)	555 mg	38	Vanadium	75 ug
19	Phenolic compounds	25 mg	39	Zinc	23 mg
20	Procyanidolic Oligomers	75 mg			

* Not Available in Canadian Products

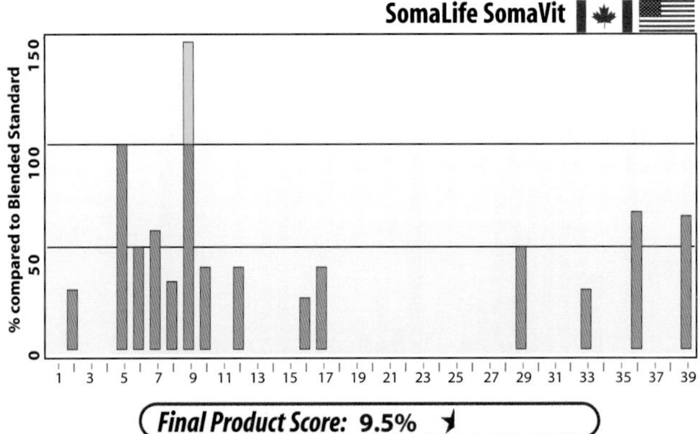

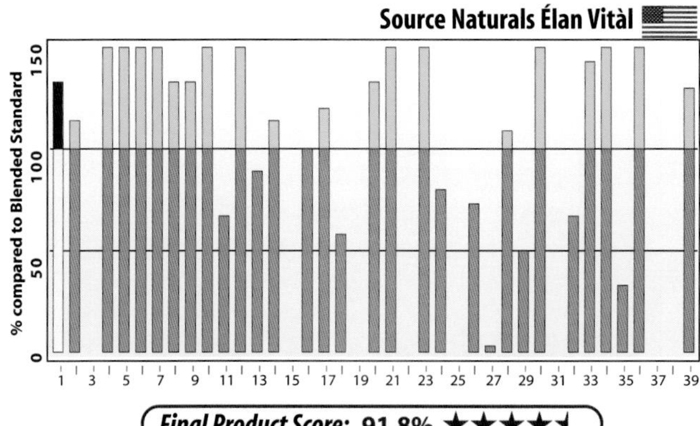

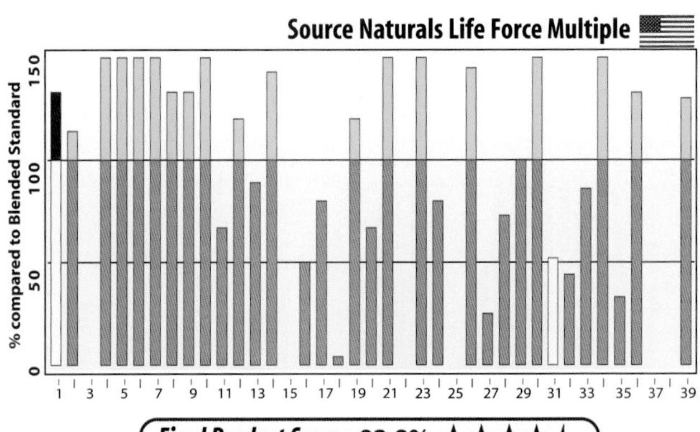

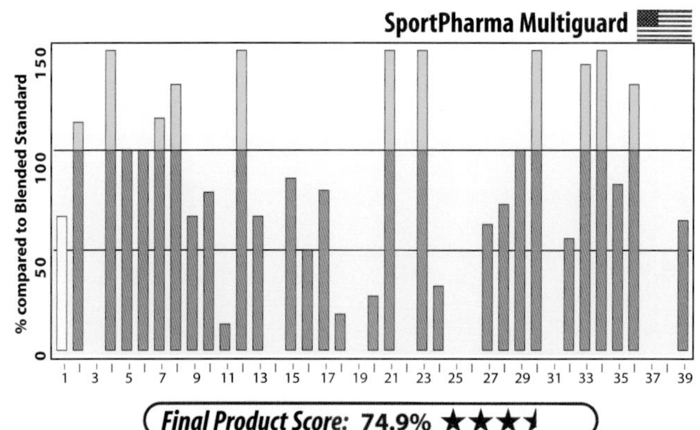

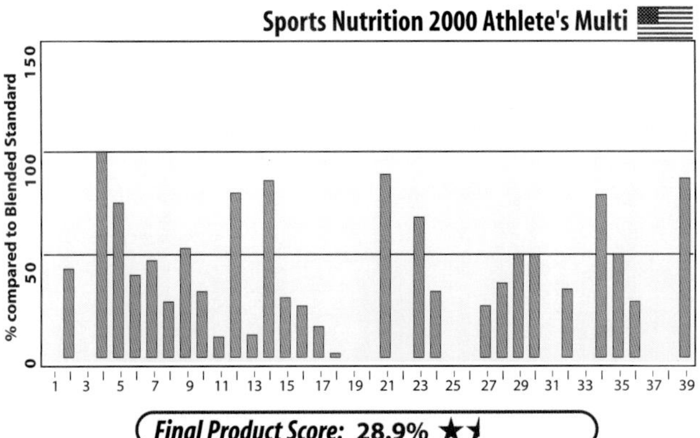

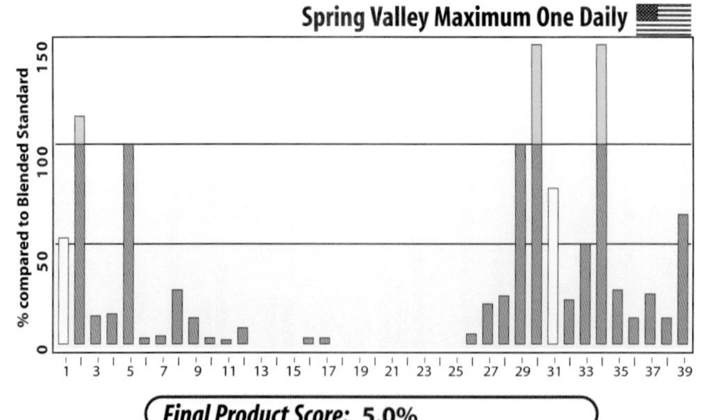

Graphical Comparisons to the Blended Standard

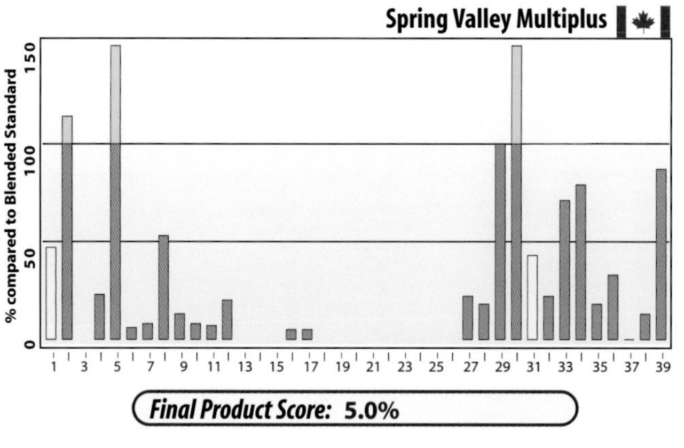

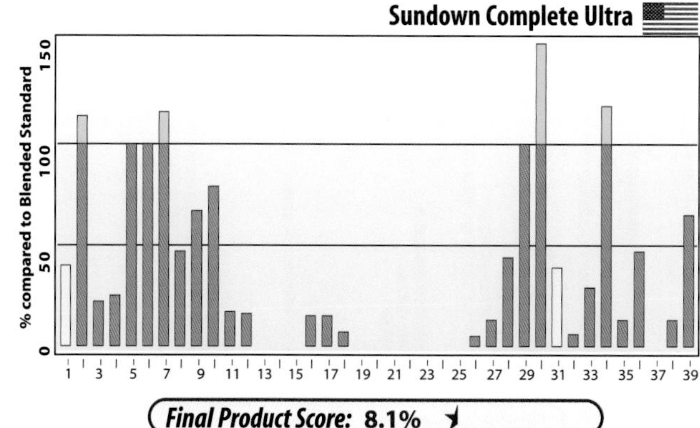

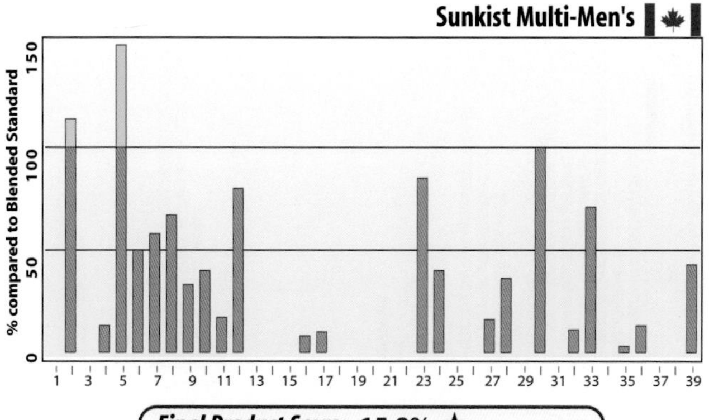

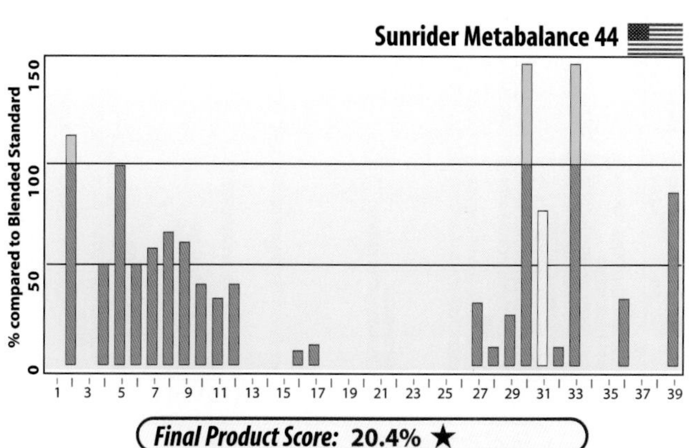

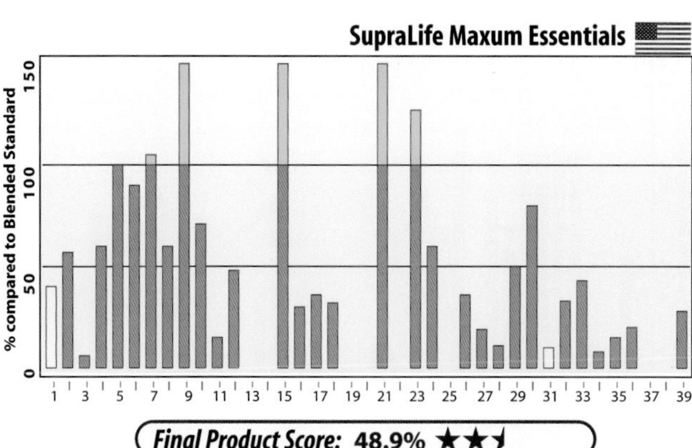

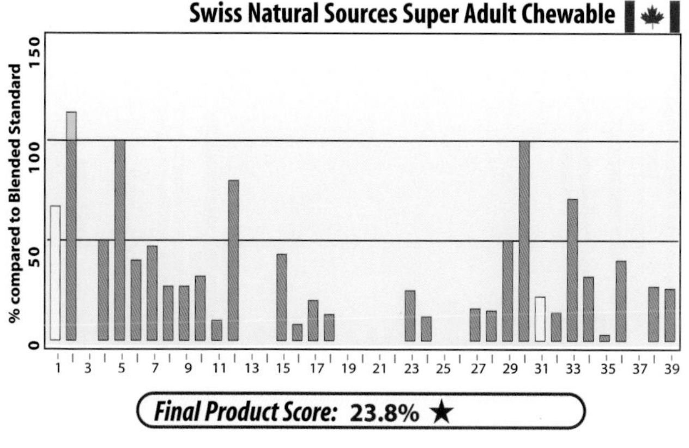

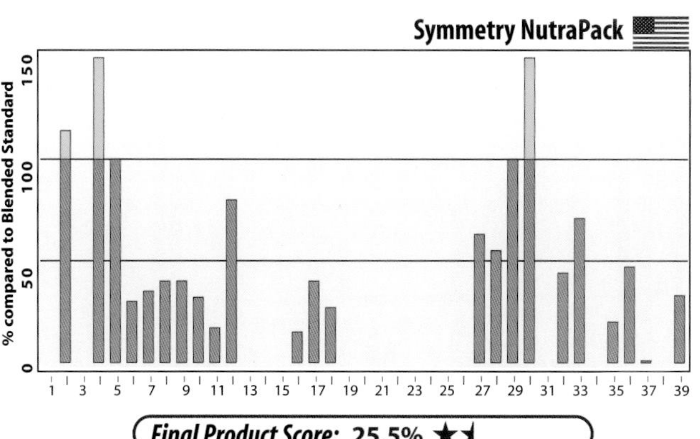

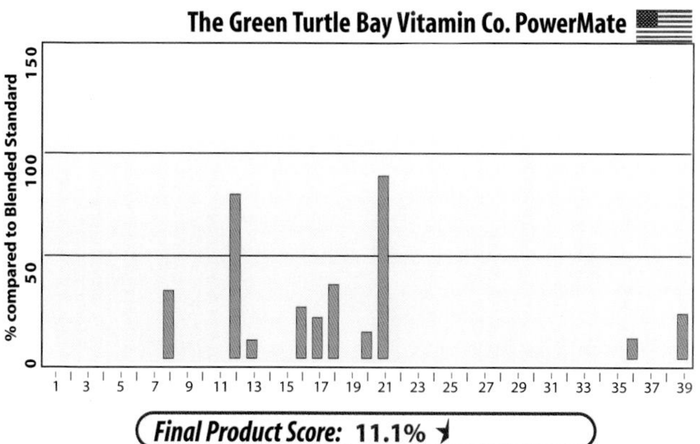

Graphical Comparisons to the Blended Standard

Thompson Human Nature Green Multi

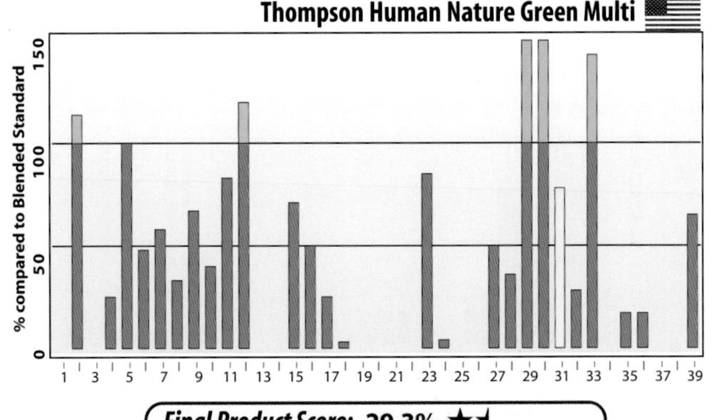

Final Product Score: **29.3%**

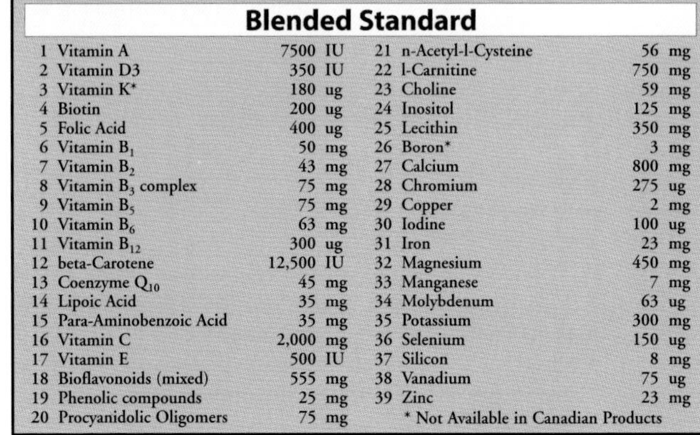

Blended Standard

1	Vitamin A	7500 IU		21	n-Acetyl-l-Cysteine	56 mg
2	Vitamin D3	350 IU		22	l-Carnitine	750 mg
3	Vitamin K*	180 ug		23	Choline	59 mg
4	Biotin	200 ug		24	Inositol	125 mg
5	Folic Acid	400 ug		25	Lecithin	350 mg
6	Vitamin B_1	50 mg		26	Boron*	3 mg
7	Vitamin B_2	43 mg		27	Calcium	800 mg
8	Vitamin B_3 complex	75 mg		28	Chromium	275 ug
9	Vitamin B_5	75 mg		29	Copper	2 mg
10	Vitamin B_6	63 mg		30	Iodine	100 ug
11	Vitamin B_{12}	300 ug		31	Iron	23 mg
12	beta-Carotene	12,500 IU		32	Magnesium	450 mg
13	Coenzyme Q_{10}	45 mg		33	Manganese	7 mg
14	Lipoic Acid	35 mg		34	Molybdenum	63 ug
15	Para-Aminobenzoic Acid	35 mg		35	Potassium	300 mg
16	Vitamin C	2,000 mg		36	Selenium	150 ug
17	Vitamin E	500 IU		37	Silicon	8 mg
18	Bioflavonoids (mixed)	555 mg		38	Vanadium	75 ug
19	Phenolic compounds	25 mg		39	Zinc	23 mg
20	Procyanidolic Oligomers	75 mg			* Not Available in Canadian Products	

Thorne Research Al's Formula

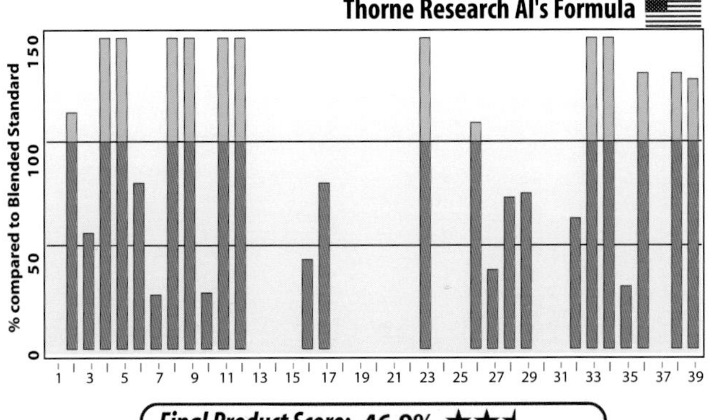

Final Product Score: **46.9%**

Total Health Solutions Vita Actives

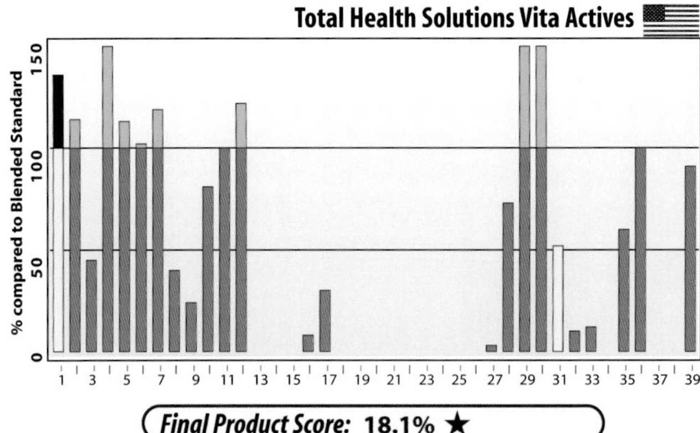

Final Product Score: **18.1%**

Trace Minerals Electro-Vita-Min

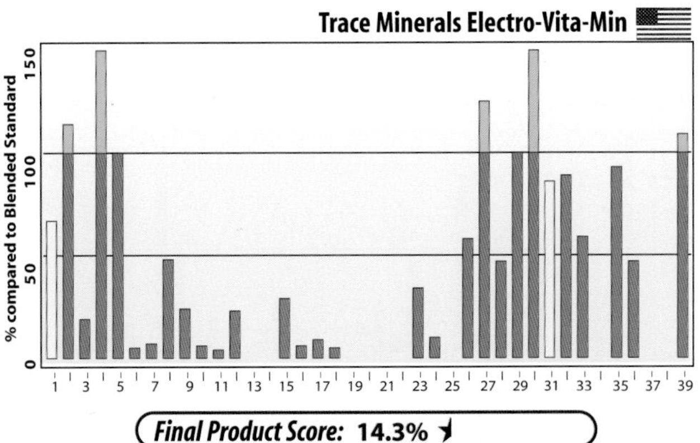

Final Product Score: **14.3%**

Trophic Select

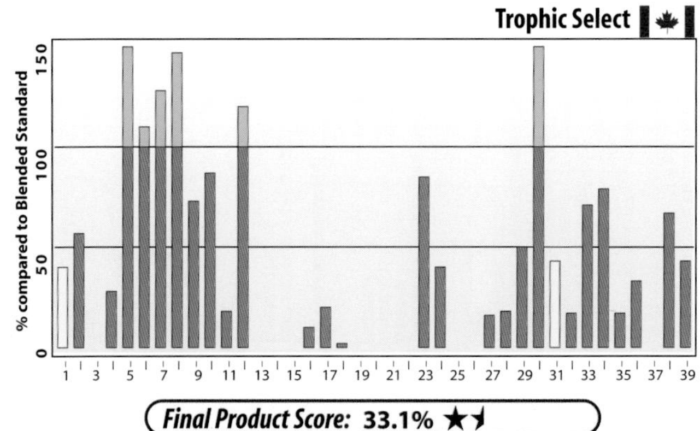

Final Product Score: **33.1%**

Truehope Empowerplus

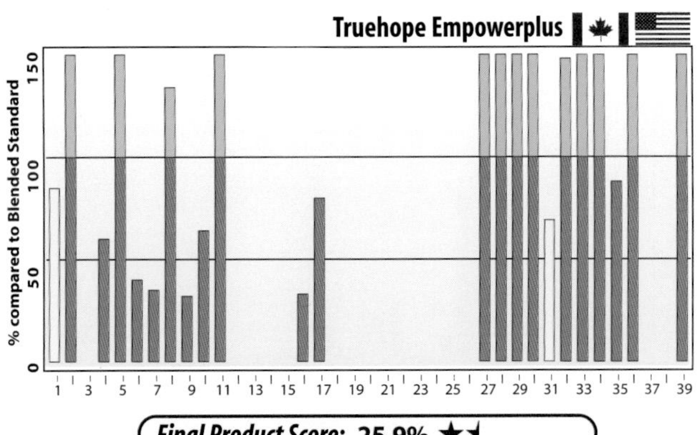

Final Product Score: **25.9%**

Truly Health Century Premium

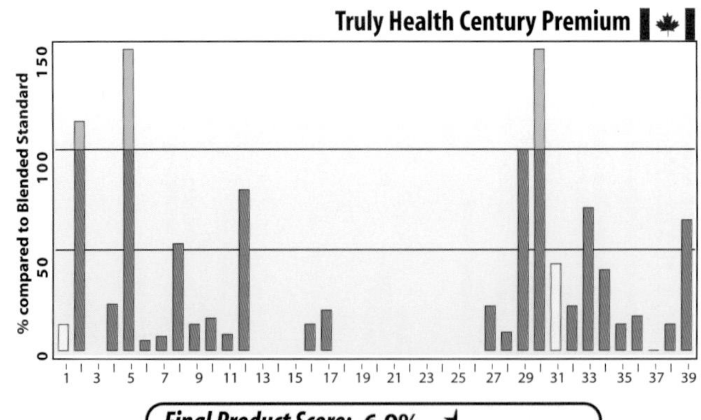

Final Product Score: **6.9%**

Graphical Comparisons to the Blended Standard

TwinLab Mega 6 Caps

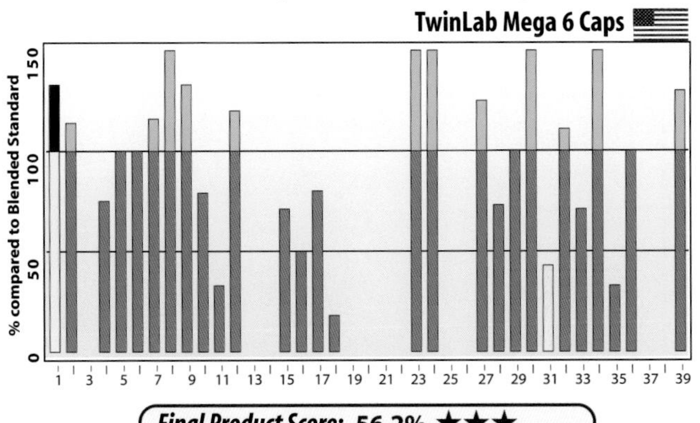

Final Product Score: **56.2% ★★★**

Tyler Multiplex-2 without Iron

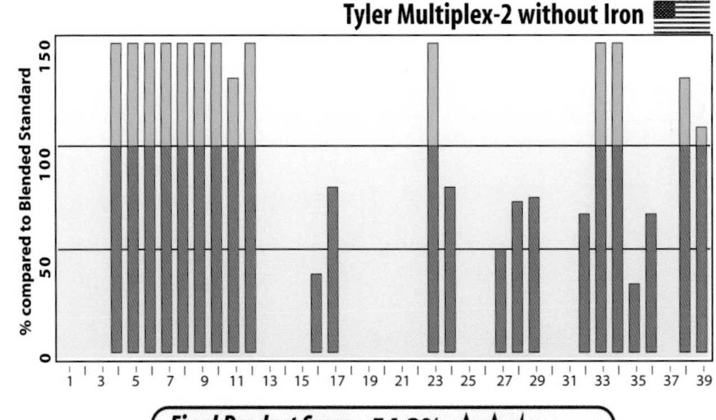

Final Product Score: **54.2% ★★½**

Ultimate Health 40+ Multiple

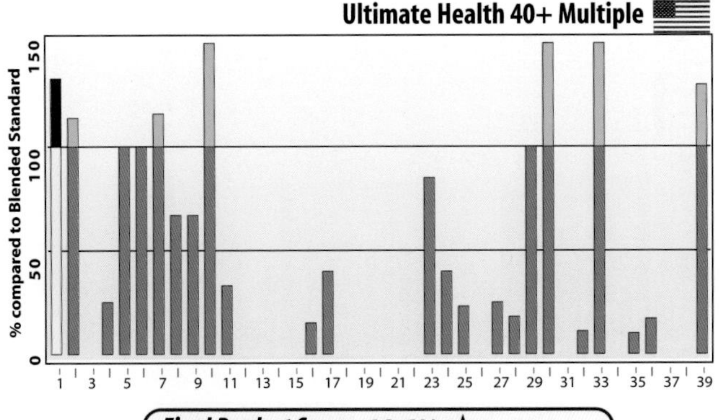

Final Product Score: **18.6% ★**

Ultimate Nutrition Super Complete

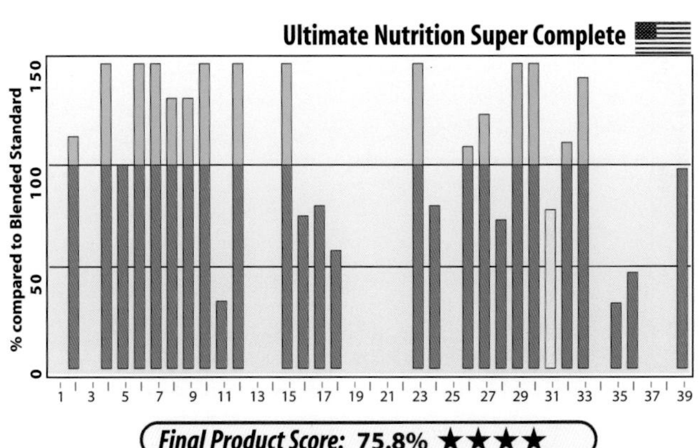

Final Product Score: **75.8% ★★★★**

Unicity Network (Rexall, Enrich International) Cardio-Basics

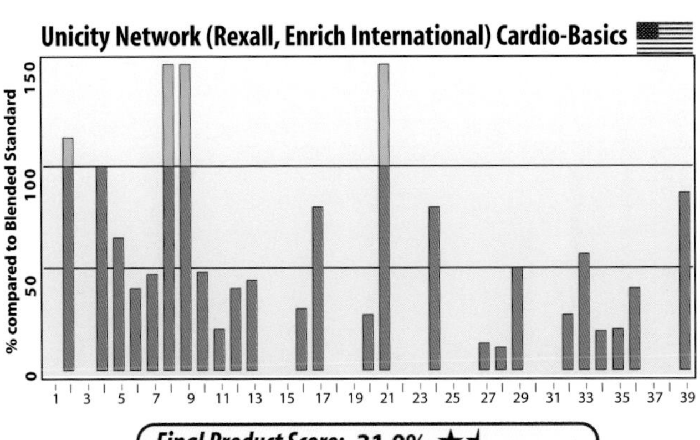

Final Product Score: **31.0% ★½**

USANA Health Sciences Essentials

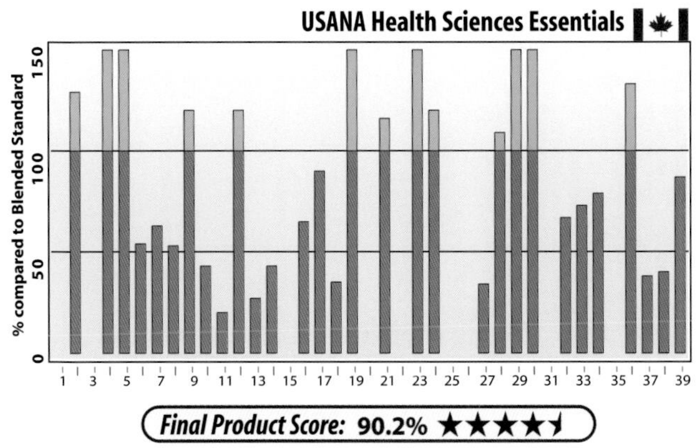

Final Product Score: **90.2% ★★★★½**

USANA Health Sciences Essentials

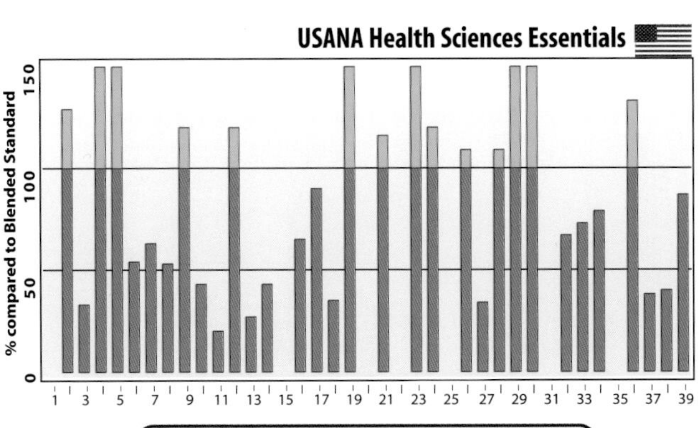

Final Product Score: **96.1% ★★★★★**

Valu-Rite Advanced Formula Complete Premium

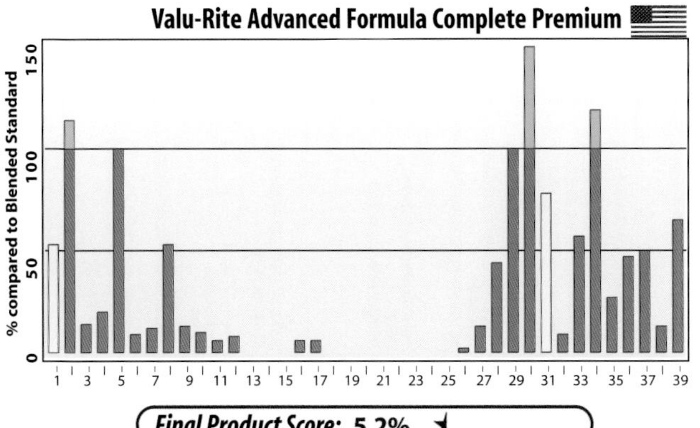

Final Product Score: **5.2% ½**

Graphical Comparisons to the Blended Standard

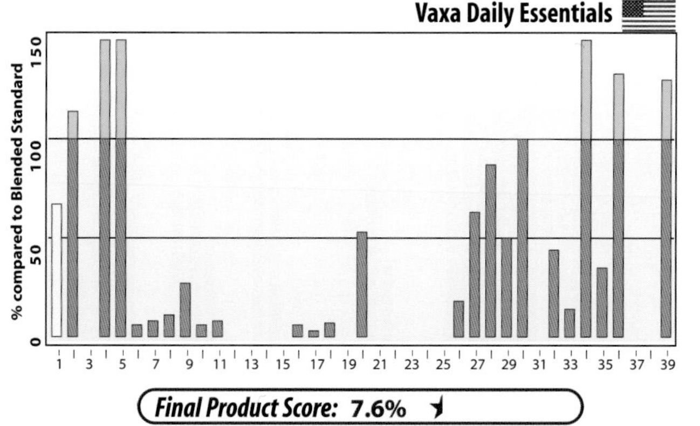

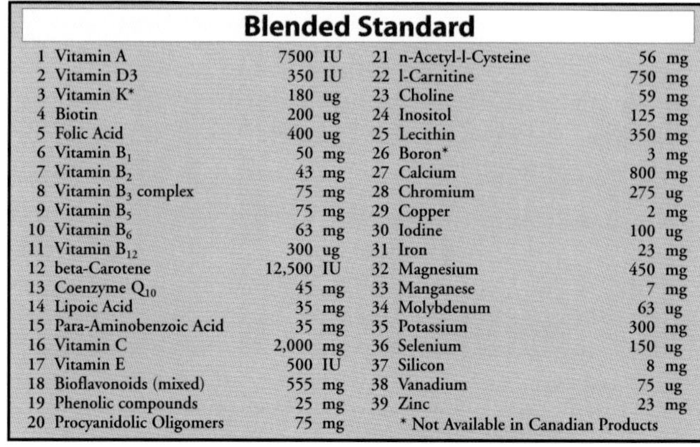

Blended Standard

#	Nutrient	Amount	Unit	#	Nutrient	Amount	Unit
1	Vitamin A	7500	IU	21	n-Acetyl-l-Cysteine	56	mg
2	Vitamin D3	350	IU	22	l-Carnitine	750	mg
3	Vitamin K*	180	ug	23	Choline	59	mg
4	Biotin	200	ug	24	Inositol	125	mg
5	Folic Acid	400	ug	25	Lecithin	350	mg
6	Vitamin B_1	50	mg	26	Boron*	3	mg
7	Vitamin B_2	43	mg	27	Calcium	800	mg
8	Vitamin B_3 complex	75	mg	28	Chromium	275	ug
9	Vitamin B_5	75	mg	29	Copper	2	mg
10	Vitamin B_6	63	mg	30	Iodine	100	ug
11	Vitamin B_{12}	300	ug	31	Iron	23	mg
12	beta-Carotene	12,500	IU	32	Magnesium	450	mg
13	Coenzyme Q_{10}	45	mg	33	Manganese	7	mg
14	Lipoic Acid	35	mg	34	Molybdenum	63	ug
15	Para-Aminobenzoic Acid	35	mg	35	Potassium	300	mg
16	Vitamin C	2,000	mg	36	Selenium	150	ug
17	Vitamin E	500	IU	37	Silicon	8	mg
18	Bioflavonoids (mixed)	555	mg	38	Vanadium	75	ug
19	Phenolic compounds	25	mg	39	Zinc	23	mg
20	Procyanidolic Oligomers	75	mg				

* Not Available in Canadian Products

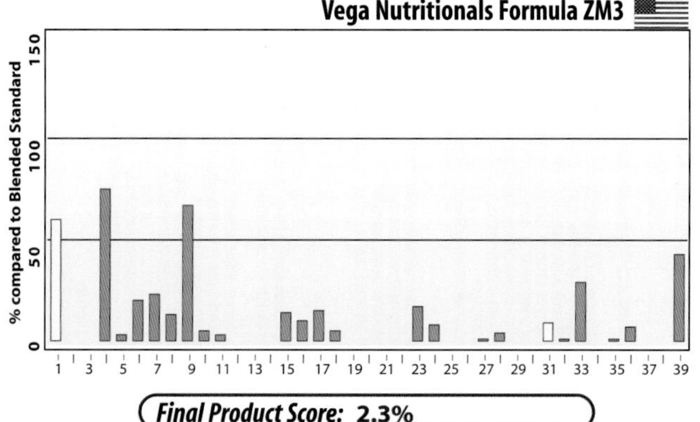

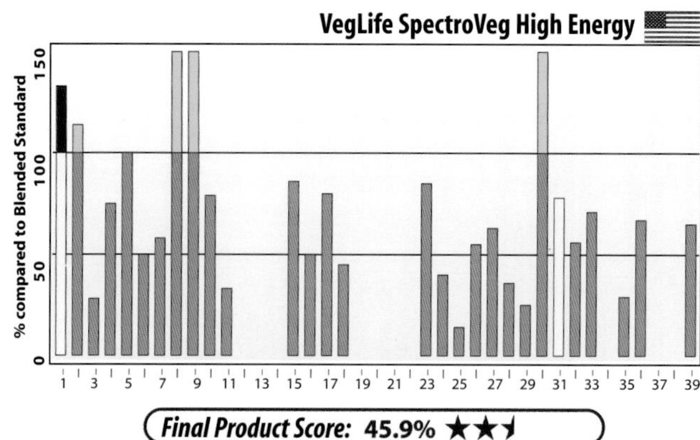

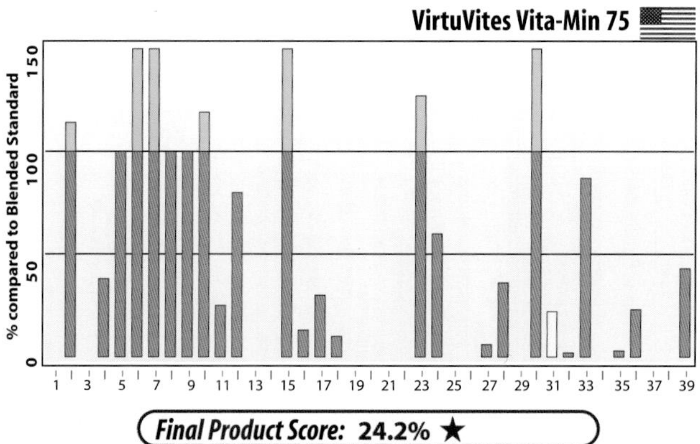

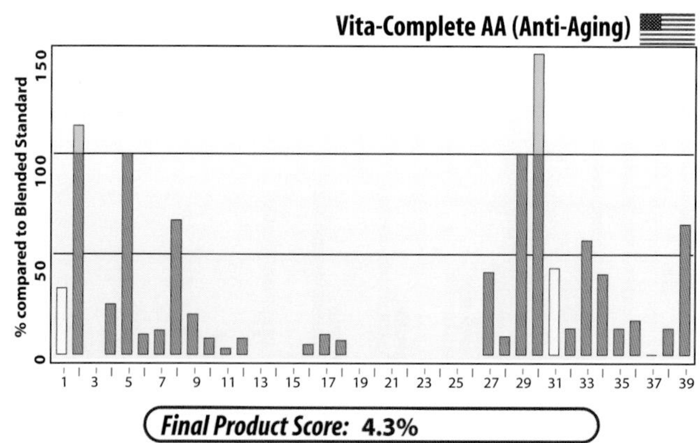

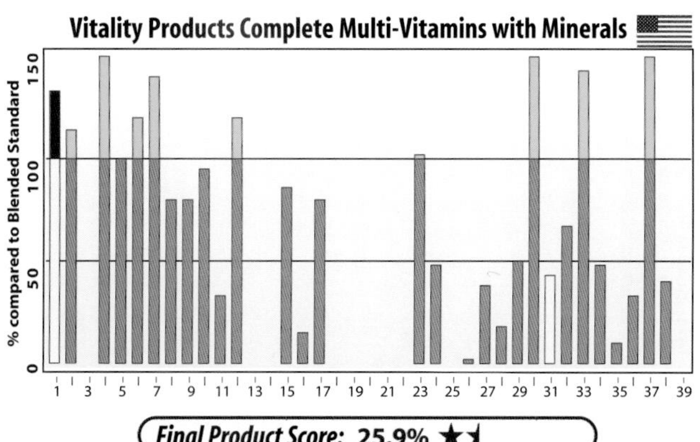

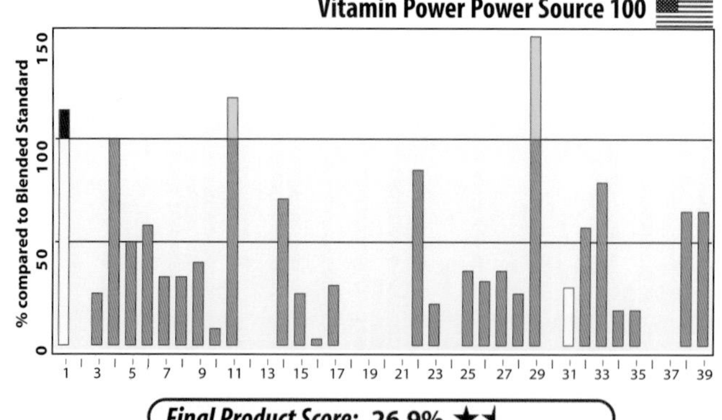

Graphical Comparisons to the Blended Standard

Vitamin Research Products Extend Plus

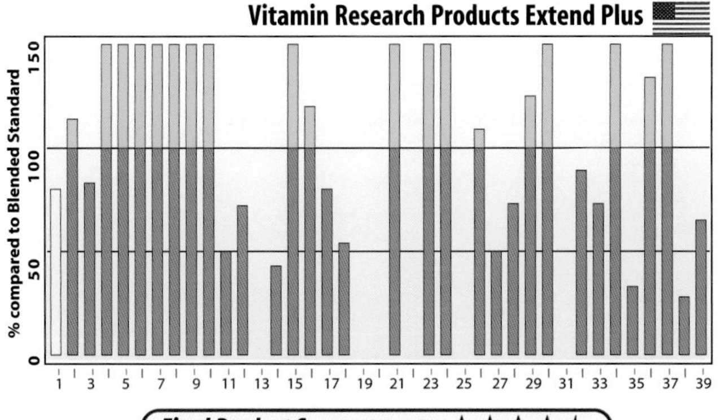

Final Product Score: **93.1% ★★★★½**

Vitamin World Daily 3 With Antioxidant Factors

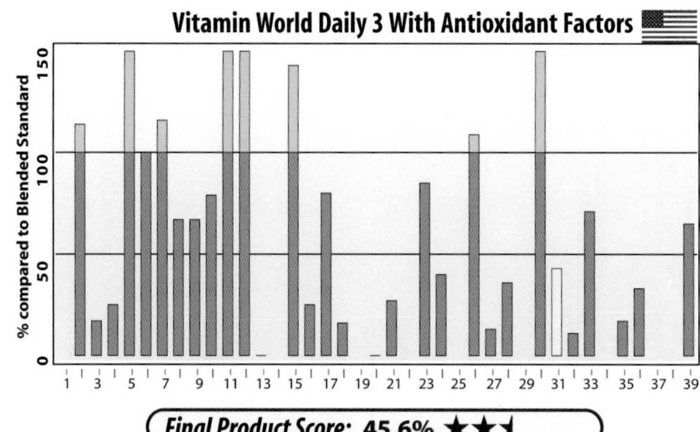

Final Product Score: **45.6% ★★½**

VitaSmart Century Advantage

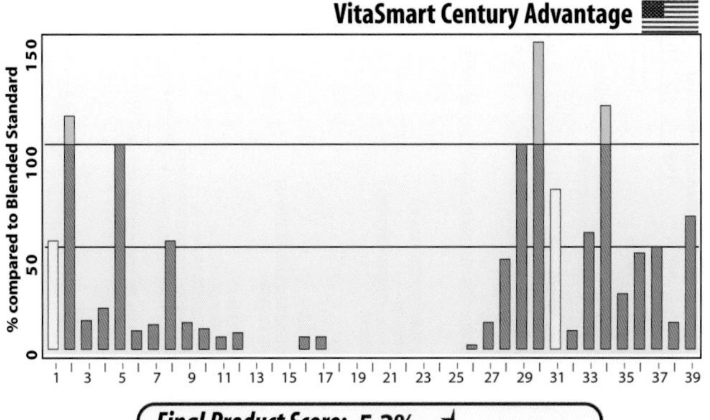

Final Product Score: **5.2% ½**

Vitazan Herbs and Vitamins ORO #1

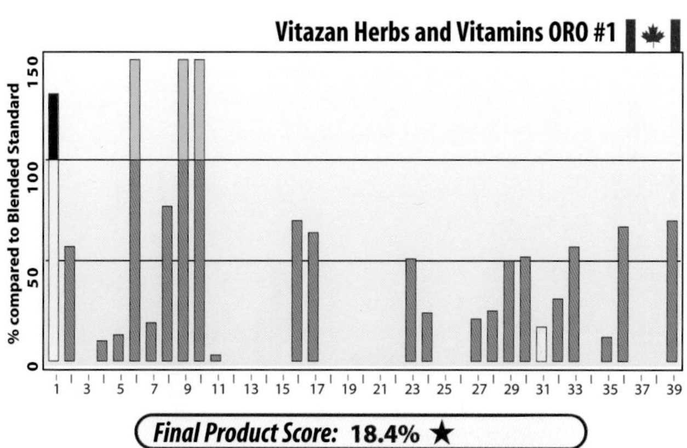

Final Product Score: **18.4% ★**

Viva Life Sciences DailyGuard

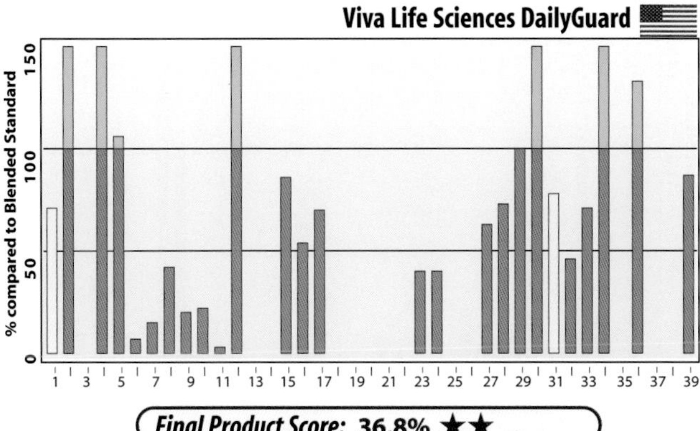

Final Product Score: **36.8% ★★**

Walgreens Ultra Choice Premium Women

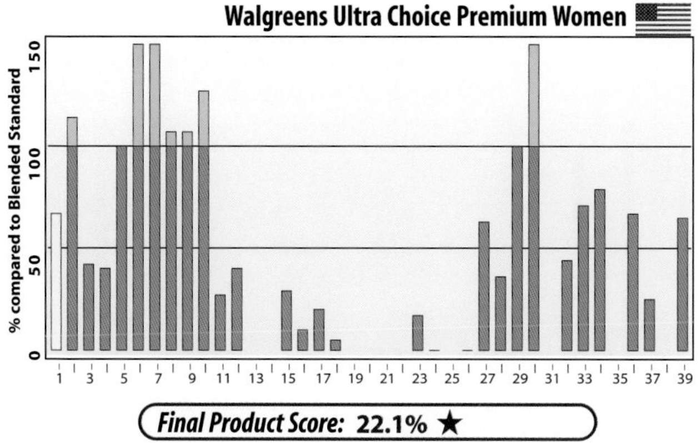

Final Product Score: **22.1% ★**

Wampole Complete Multi-Adult

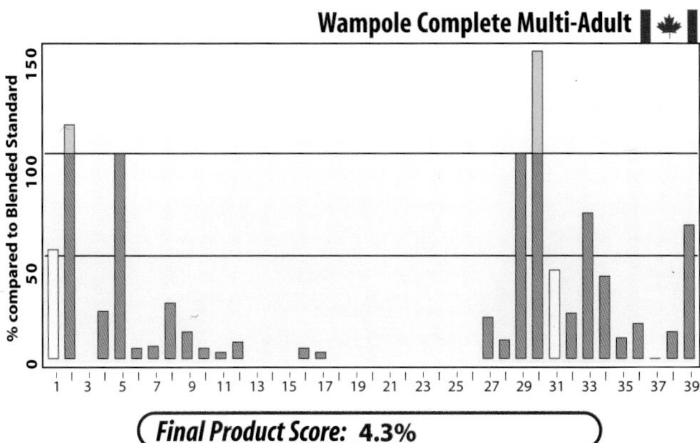

Final Product Score: **4.3%**

Watkins Super Multi

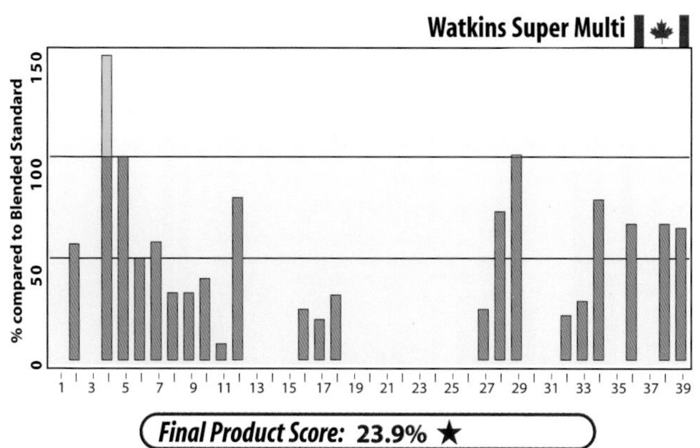

Final Product Score: **23.9% ★**

Graphical Comparisons to the Blended Standard

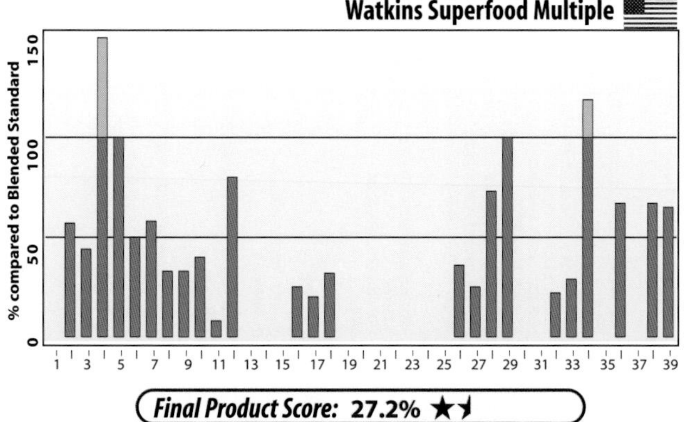

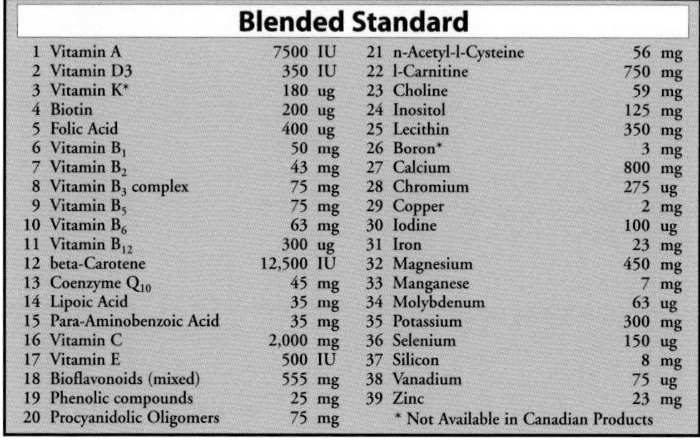

Blended Standard

No.	Nutrient	Amount	Unit	No.	Nutrient	Amount	Unit
1	Vitamin A	7500	IU	21	n-Acetyl-l-Cysteine	56	mg
2	Vitamin D3	350	IU	22	l-Carnitine	750	mg
3	Vitamin K*	180	ug	23	Choline	59	mg
4	Biotin	200	ug	24	Inositol	125	mg
5	Folic Acid	400	ug	25	Lecithin	350	mg
6	Vitamin B_1	50	mg	26	Boron*	3	mg
7	Vitamin B_2	43	mg	27	Calcium	800	mg
8	Vitamin B_3 complex	75	mg	28	Chromium	275	ug
9	Vitamin B_5	75	mg	29	Copper	2	mg
10	Vitamin B_6	63	mg	30	Iodine	100	ug
11	Vitamin B_{12}	300	ug	31	Iron	23	mg
12	beta-Carotene	12,500	IU	32	Magnesium	450	mg
13	Coenzyme Q_{10}	45	mg	33	Manganese	7	mg
14	Lipoic Acid	35	mg	34	Molybdenum	63	ug
15	Para-Aminobenzoic Acid	35	mg	35	Potassium	300	mg
16	Vitamin C	2,000	mg	36	Selenium	150	ug
17	Vitamin E	500	IU	37	Silicon	8	mg
18	Bioflavonoids (mixed)	555	mg	38	Vanadium	75	ug
19	Phenolic compounds	25	mg	39	Zinc	23	mg
20	Procyanidolic Oligomers	75	mg				

* Not Available in Canadian Products

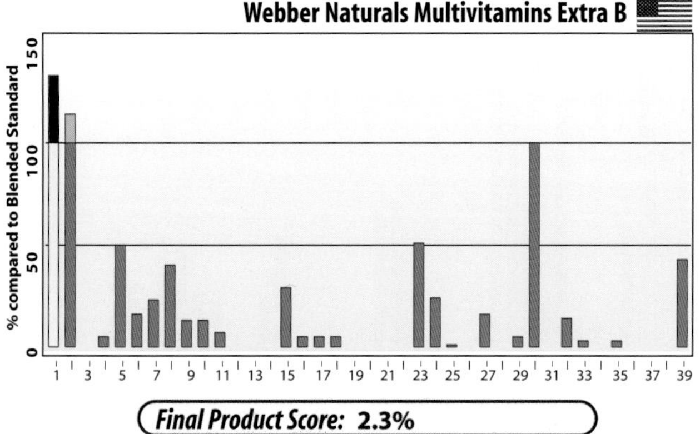

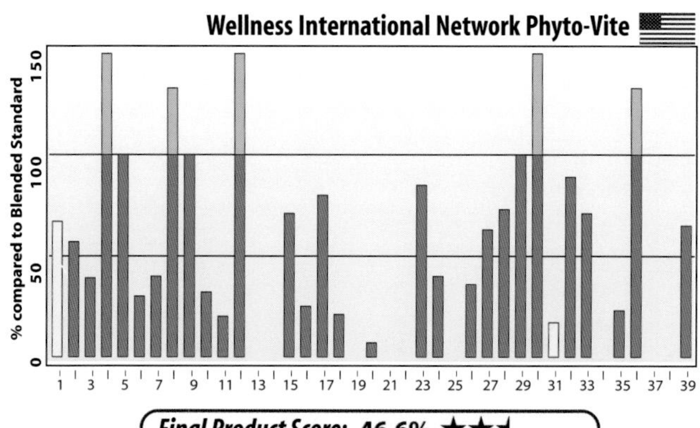

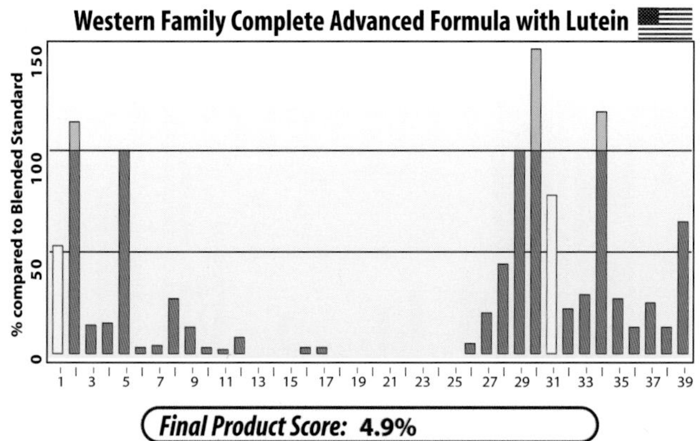

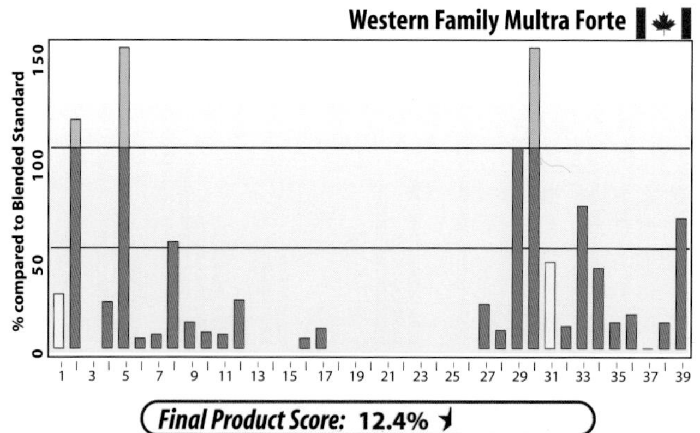

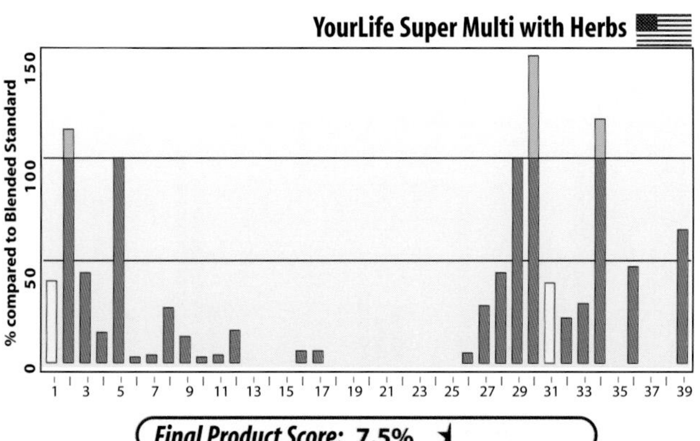

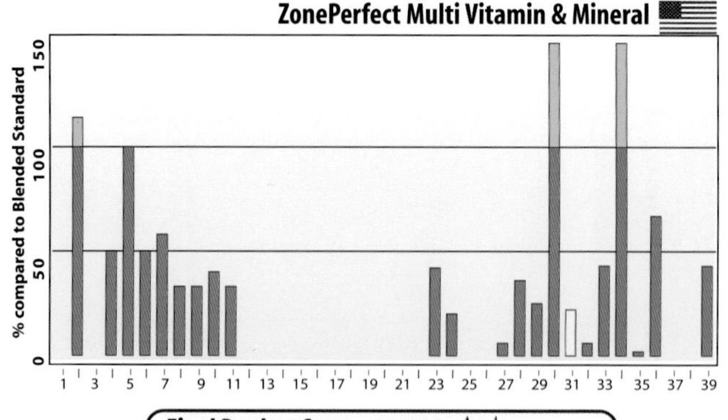

Section V

Appendices

- alphabetical listing of products reviewed
- product-score listing of products reviewed
- details of *Final Product Score*

Appendix A: Products sorted by Company Name

Company	Product	Country	Score	Dosages & Considerations
21st Century	Advanced 21 with Lutein	US	4.9	
21st Century	One Daily Maximum	US	5.3	
21st Century	One Daily Men's	US	7.3	
21st Century	Therapeutic-M With Lutein	US	4.6	
4Life	BioVitaMins Type I	US	21.6	
4Life	BioVitaMins Type II	US	33.2	
4Life	BioVitamins Type III	US	44.0	
4Life	MultiPlex Stress Formula	US	5.9	
Absolute Nutrition	Dieters' Multi's	US	26.4	
Action Labs	Action-Tabs Made for Men	US	1.3	
Action Labs	Action-Tabs Made for Women	US	0.0	
Action Labs	Essential Nutrients	US	4.4	
Adrien Gagnon (Santé Naturelle)	Multi-Vitamines et Minéraux	CA	9.9	
Advanced Physician's Products	Complete MultiVitamin/Mineral with Iron	US	49.1	
Advanced Physician's Products	Complete MultiVitamin/Mineral without Iron	US	49.1	
Advanced Physician's Products	Maximum MultiVitamin/Mineral without Iron	US	57.2	
Advanced Physician's Products	Maximum Potency MultiVitamin/Mineral with Iron	US	57.4	
Advocare	Gold	US	35.7	
Albi Imports	Rocky Mountain Multiple	CA	34.3	DPD data only - dosage derived
Albi Imports	Super One a Day	CA	10.9	DPD data only - dosage derived
Alive Vitamins	Super One Plus	CA	20.9	DPD data only - dosage derived
All One Powder	Multiple Vitamins and Minerals	US	49.9	
Allergy Research Group	EDP Basic	US	18.3	
Allergy Research Group	Multi-Vi-Min	US	16.6	
Allergy Research Group	Multi-Vi-Min without Copper and Iron	US	18.7	
Alpha Nutrition	Alpha ENF	CA	21.9	
American Longevity	Ultimate Daily	US	60.7	
amni	Added Protection III	US	69.1	
amni	Basic Preventive 1	US	60.2	
amni	Basic Preventive 2	US	59.6	
amni	Basic Preventive 3	US	60.2	
amni	Basic Preventive 4	US	59.6	
amni	Basic Preventive 5	US	59.9	
amni	Basic Preventive with Extra D	US	60.0	
amni	Essential Basics	US	51.5	
Andrew Lessman's	Maximum Complete for Men	US	30.8	dosage derived
Andrew Lessman's	Maximum Complete for Women	US	31.2	dosage derived
Apex Fitness Group	Profile 5	US	16.8	dosage derived
Atkins	Basic #1	US	38.2	
Atkins	Basic #3	US	46.1	
Atkins	Immune	US	14.6	
Avon	VitAdvance Men's Complete Multivitamin	US	10.9	
Avon	VitAdvance Women's Complete I Balanced Multi	US	10.5	
Avon	VitAdvance Women's Complete II Balanced Multi	US	10.5	
Basic Nutrition	Multiple Vitamins & Minerals	US	4.4	
Bio Actif Inc.	Phytobec #1	CA	15.1	
Bluebonnet	Super Earth Formula	US	54.0	
Body Wise International	Right Choice AM/PM	CA/US	52.2	
Bronson Laboratories	Advanced Mature Gold	US	18.0	
Bronson Laboratories	Fortified Vitamin & Mineral Insurance Formula	US	33.2	
Bronson Laboratories	Mature Formula	US	8.6	
Bronson Laboratories	Men's Complete Formula with 7-Keto	US	21.5	
Bronson Laboratories	Performance Edge for Men	US	43.6	
Bronson Laboratories	Performance Edge for Women	US	43.8	
Carlson	Multi-Gel	US	45.7	
Cell Tech	Alpha Sun	US	0.3	
Cell Tech	Omega Sun	US	0.3	
Centrum	Centrum	US	3.2	
Centrum	Forte	CA/US	4.7	
Centrum	Performance	US	5.2	
Centrum	Protegra	CA	7.2	
Centrum	Select	CA	4.6	
Centrum	Select Chewables	CA	4.0	
Centrum	Select Chewables for Adults over 50	CA	4.7	
Centrum	Select for Adults over 50	CA	5.0	
Centrum	Silver	US	4.7	
Club Vitamin	Best	US	3.6	dosage derived
Colgan Institute	Formula MC8	US	63.3	dosage derived from Vit A, folate
Comprehensive Formula	Men's	US	14.0	
Comprehensive Formula	Women's	US	11.8	
Cooper	Complete	US	45.8	
Cooper	Complete with Iron	US	38.0	
Country Life	Adult's Multi	US	9.8	
Country Life	Daily Vegetarian Support	US	44.5	
Country Life	Hi Potency Action 75	US	24.0	
Country Life	Max for Men	US	32.8	

Country Life	Maxine	US	43.1	
Country Life	VegiCaps	US	19.2	
Creative Nutrition Canada	PLUS Formula	CA/US	54.8	dosage derived
Creative Nutrition Canada	PRIME Formula	CA	52.4	dosage derived
Cypress (Star 2000)	MultiVitamin with Minerals	US	14.1	dosage derived
DaVinci Laboratories	Daily Best	US	21.9	
DaVinci Laboratories	Omni	US	63.6	
DaVinci Laboratories	Spectra	US	64.7	
DaVinci Laboratories	Spectra Man	US	62.5	
DaVinci Laboratories	Spectra Vegetarian	US	48.6	
DaVinci Laboratories	Spectra without Copper and Iron	US	64.5	
DaVinci Laboratories	Spectra Woman	US	66.8	
Doctor's Nutrition	Mega Veggie Vites	US	43.3	
Doctor's Nutrition	Mega Vites Senior	US	54.7	
Doctor's Nutrition	Mega Vites without Copper & Iron	US	64.2	
Doctor's Nutrition	Mega Vites Woman	US	66.8	
Doctor's Nutrition	UltraNutrient	US	55.9	
Douglas Laboratories	Ultra Preventive Beta	US	75.1	
Douglas Laboratories	Ultra Preventive III	US	70.0	
Douglas Laboratories	Ultra Preventive IX	US	66.6	
Douglas Laboratories	Ultra Preventive X	US	95.4	
Douglas Laboratories	Ultra Vita 75 II	US	16.2	
Dr. Julian Whitaker's	Forward Multi-Nutrient	CA	58.5	
Dr. Julian Whitaker's	Forward Multi-Nutrient	US	74.7	
EAS	Multi-Blend	US	62.1	
EcoNugenics	Men's Longevity Essentials Plus	US	20.3	
EcoNugenics	Women's Longevity Rhythms Gold	US	57.0	
EHN Inc.	protect+	CA	7.8	
Enerex	Sona	CA	20.6	
Enzymatic Therapy	Doctor's Choice for Men	US	42.5	
Enzymatic Therapy	Doctor's Choice for Women	US	45.5	
Epic4Health	Physician's Multi Vitamin Formula	US	31.3	
Equate	Century Complete	CA	3.5	
Equate	Century Plus	CA	4.7	
Equate	Complete	US	4.9	
Equate	Complete Mature	US	4.7	
Equate	Multi-Vitamin & Minerals	CA	2.8	
Essentials by Megafood	Essentials for Life	US	51.2	
Essentials by Megafood	Essentials for Women	US	34.8	
Essentials by Megafood	One Daily for Men	US	20.6	
Flora	MultiCaps	CA	10.6	
Flora	MultiTabs	CA	10.6	
FoodScience of Vermont	Daily Best	US	21.9	
FoodScience of Vermont	Men's Superior	US	62.5	
FoodScience of Vermont	Superior Care	US	64.7	
FoodScience of Vermont	Total Care	US	13.3	
FoodScience of Vermont	Women's Superior	US	63.8	
For Mor International	AnOx	US	42.1	
For Mor International	Oral Chelate	US	13.7	
Freeda Vitamins	Quintabs-M	US	1.5	
Freeda Vitamins	Ultra Freeda Iron-Free	US	25.8	
Freeda Vitamins	Ultra Freeda with Iron	US	23.4	
FreeLife	Basic Mindell Plus	US	82.3	
Futurebiotics	Hi Energy Multi for Men	US	40.3	dosage derived
Futurebiotics	Multi-Vitamin Energy Plus for Women	US	18.7	dosage derived
Futurebiotics	Vegetarian Super Multi	US	40.3	
Garry Null's	Super AM Formula	US	17.7	
Garry Null's	Supreme Health Formula	US	47.2	
Genestra (Seroyal)	Super Orti-Vite	CA	44.8	
Gerbex	Gerivol	CA	0.0	
Geritol	Complete	US	3.4	
GNC	Mega Men's	US	21.1	
GNC	Preventron	US	9.9	
GNC	SoloCaps	US	10.6	
GNC	Solotron without Iron	US	7.7	
GNC	Ultra Mega Gold without Iron	US	37.1	
GNC	Ultra Mega Green	US	46.9	
GNC	Ultra Mega Two without Iron	US	24.5	
GNC	Women's Ultra Mega	US	28.2	
Golden Neo-Life Diamite International	Formula IV	CA	0.0	DPD data only - dosage derived
Good Neighbor Pharmacy	Balanced Care Complete Multi	US	5.0	
Good Neighbor Pharmacy	Century Senior	US	4.7	
Great Earth	Super Hy-Vites-Ultra Strength/Timed Release	US	29.4	
Great Earth	TNT - Total Nutrition Tablet	US	48.6	
Greens+	Greens+	US	14.8	
Greens+	Multi+	CA	37.9	
Herbalife	Formula 2	CA	15.2	
Herbalife	Formula 2	US	14.8	
Hillestad Pharmaceuticals	Sterling	US	21.0	
Hillestad Pharmaceuticals	Summit Gold	US	19.1	

Holista Health	Multi-Spectrum	CA	35.9	
Immuvit	Immuvit	US	4.4	
Inno-Vite	Total NRG Lift	CA	15.5	
Jamieson	Adult's 50+ Vita-Vim	CA	4.4	
Jamieson	Mega-Vim Level 4 Potency	CA	9.0	
Jamieson	Power Vitamins for Men	CA	3.5	
Jamieson	Super Vita-Vim	CA	8.3	
Jarrow	Multi E-Z Powder	US	48.7	
Jarrow	Multi 1-to-3	US	37.7	
Jarrow	Women's Multi	US	31.5	
Jean Carper's	Stop Aging Now!	US	58.5	
Jean Carper's	Stop Aging Now! Plus	US	58.5	
KAL	Enhanced Energy with Lutein, Iron-Free	US	49.2	
KAL	High Potency Soft Multiple, Iron-Free	US	19.1	
KAL	Multi-Four	US	33.0	
KAL	Multiple Energy	US	51.2	
KAL	Vegetarian Multiple	US	31.7	
KAL	Vitality for Women	US	35.0	
Karuna	HIM	US	41.2	
Karuna	Maxxum 2	US	65.7	
Karuna	Maxxum 4	US	79.0	
Kirkland Signature (Costco)	Daily Multivitamin	US	5.2	
Kirkman Laboratories	Kirkman's Everyday	US	3.1	
Kirkman Laboratories	Kirkman's Super Nu-Thera	US	12.3	
Klamath Blue Green Algae	Tablets	US	0.3	
Klamath Blue Green Algae	Vegicaps	US	0.3	
Kroger	Advanced Formula Complete	US	4.9	
Laboratoire Lalco Enr.	Multi Max	CA	7.7	
Le Naturiste (Jean Marc Brunet)	US-100 Multi-vitamines	CA	9.5	
Les Produits Naturels Suisse Inc.	Swical Energy	CA	0.0	dosage derived
Life Brand	Optimum	CA	5.0	
Life Brand	Optimum 50+	CA	5.0	
Life Brand	Spectrum Forte	CA	4.3	
Life Extension Foundation	Life Extension Mix	US	81.4	
Life Force International	Body Balance	US	9.2	based on av. body wt. of 150 lbs.
Life Plus	Daily Bio-Basics	US	32.3	
Life Plus	TVM-Plus	US	22.7	
LifeScript	Daily Essentials, plus Calcium Complete	US	36.6	
Lifestyles	Lifecycles for Mature Men	CA/US	14.7	
Lifestyles	Lifecycles for Mature Women	CA/US	14.7	
Lifestyles	Lifecycles for Men	CA/US	5.8	
Lifestyles	Lifecycles for Women	CA/US	14.5	
LifeTime	Nutrilife	CA	7.4	
LiFizz	Multivitamin	CA	2.9	
London Drugs	Multi Premium	CA	15.0	
London Naturals	Multi-Vitamin Select	CA	12.4	
London's Best	Premier	CA	18.8	dosage derived
Lorna Vanderhaeghe	FemmEssentials (multiple only)	CA	56.5	
Mannatech	Glycentials	US	33.1	
Mannatech	GlycoLEAN Catalyst	US	26.2	
Market America	Isotonix Multitech Multivitamin	CA/US	3.2	
Matol	Matolife	US	40.0	
MD Healthline	Advanced Green Multi	US	4.8	
Melaleuca	Vitality Pak (Mel-Vita, Mela-Cal)	US	6.2	
Metagenics	Multigenics Intensive Care Formula	US	51.0	
Metagenics	Multigenics Intensive Care Formula without Iron	US	50.5	
Michael's Naturopathic Programs	Active Senior Tabs	US	56.6	
Michael's Naturopathic Programs	for Men	US	36.9	
Michael's Naturopathic Programs	for Women	US	36.9	
Michael's Naturopathic Programs	Just One	US	23.6	
MMS Pro	Preventamins	US	58.1	
Moducare	Multi-mune	US	8.6	
Molecular Biologics	Allervimin	US	8.3	dosage derived
Molecular Biologics	Bio-Naturalvite	US	9.7	dosage derived
Molecular Biologics	Derma-Vites	US	20.2	dosage derived
More Than A Multiple	More Than A Multiple	US	44.4	
Mountain Naturals of Vermont	Men's Superior	US	62.5	
Mountain Naturals of Vermont	Superior Care	US	64.7	
Mountain Naturals of Vermont	Women's Superior	US	66.8	
N.V. Perricone, MD	Physician's Super Antioxidant Vitamin, Mineral & Phyto-Nutrient Formula	US	41.7	
National Vitamin Company	Life-line Mega Multi with Minerals	US	11.9	
Natrol	My Favorite Multiple Complete Care	US	27.3	
Natrol	My Favorite Multiple Original	US	36.7	
Natrol	My Favorite Multiple Take One	US	27.2	
Natural Factors	MultiStart	CA	13.3	
Natural Factors	MultiStart Men's	CA	47.7	
Natural Factors	MultiStart Women's	CA	56.9	
Nature Made	Essential Balance	CA	4.4	
Nature Made	Essential Mega	US	17.9	
Nature's Answer	Multi-Daily	US	21.2	

Nature's Blend	Maximum Daily Green	US	37.5	
Nature's Blend	Vitaminix Ultimate	US	54.7	
Nature's Bounty	Green Source Vegetarian Formula	US	40.1	
Nature's Bounty	Mega Vita Min for Women Time Release	US	19.4	
Nature's Bounty	Ultra Man Time Release	US	12.5	
Nature's Bounty	Ultra Vita-Time Iron Free	US	4.7	
Nature's Life	Green Multi	US	42.0	
Nature's Plus	Regeneration	US	30.7	
Nature's Plus	Source of Life No Iron	US	29.2	
Nature's Plus	Ultra II	US	18.6	
Nature's Plus	Ultra-One	US	18.6	
Nature's Plus	Ultra-One Iron-Free Sustained Release	US	23.7	
Nature's Sunshine	Super Supplemental Vitamins and Minerals	US	26.2	
Nature's Sunshine	Super Supplemental without Iron	US	28.6	
Nature's Sunshine	SynerPro	US	4.9	
Nature's Way	Age Right Formula	US	38.0	
Nature's Way	Alive! Whole Food Energizer (Iron-Free)	US	60.0	
Nature's Way	Completia Ultra Energy Multi (Iron-Free)	US	17.6	
Nature's Way	Daily Two Multi Iron-Free	US	34.8	
Nature's Way	Multivitamin Iron-Free	US	33.2	
New Image International	Multi	US	27.4	
New Roots Herbal	Multi-Max	CA	46.3	
New Roots Herbal	Phytomax	CA	2.5	
Neways	Orachel	US	24.1	
NewVision	JuicePower Vegetable Caps	CA/US	2.4	
Nikken	Bio-Directed Multi-Vitamin/Mineral	CA/US	11.1	
NOW Foods	Iron-Free Vit-Min 75+	US	32.6	
NOW Foods	Special Two	US	43.1	
NOW Foods	Vit-Min 100 (Timed Release High Potency)	US	32.8	
NOW Foods	Vit-Min Caps High Potency Multiple	US	26.2	
Nu-life	Gourmet Multiple	CA	23.8	
Nu-life	The Legend for Women	CA	33.8	
Nu-life	Ultimate One for Men	CA	35.8	
Nu-life	Ultimate One for Women	CA	21.4	
Nutra Therapeutics	All-In-One	CA	22.7	
NutriBiotics	Ultimate Matrix Men	US	35.2	
NutriBiotics	Ultimate Matrix Women	US	35.2	
Nutricology	Multi-Vi-Min	US	13.1	
Nutricology	Multi-Vi-Min without Copper & Iron	US	13.0	
Nutriex	Nutriex	US	40.5	
Nutrilite (Amway, Quixtar)	Daily	US	3.4	
Nutrilite (Amway, Quixtar)	Double X	CA	23.0	
Nutrilite (Amway, Quixtar)	Double X	US	30.0	
Nutrina	Athlete Formula	US	18.1	
Nutrina	Champion Formula	US	24.6	
Nutrina	Fitness Formula	US	19.9	
Nutrition Dynamics	Basic Formula	US	37.0	dosage derived
Nutrition Dynamics	Day Start/Day End Essentials	US	63.0	
Nutrition Dynamics	Iodine Free "Vegi" Formula	US	16.5	
Nutrition Dynamics	Multi-vitasorb	US	0.7	
Nutrition Dynamics	Optimum Health Essentials	US	66.6	
Nutrition for Life	Essentials	CA/US	15.1	
Nutrition for Life	Grand Master Formula	CA/US	54.3	
Nutri-West	Multi Complex	US	10.5	
Nutri-West	Multibalance for Men	US	16.6	
Nutri-West	Multibalance for Women	US	16.6	
Nutri-West	Whole System Health Maintenance	US	19.8	
Olympian Labs	Vita-Vitamin	US	22.8	dosage derived
Omnitrition	Omni 4	US	0.0	
One A Day	Active	US	5.1	
One A Day	Advance Men's Formula	CA	4.6	
One A Day	Advance Women's Formula	CA	1.9	
OneSource	Multivitamins and Minerals for Adults	CA	5.8	
Optimox	Androvite for Men	US	50.1	
Optimox	Gynovite Plus	US	30.5	
Optimox	Optivite PMT for Women	US	42.5	
Oregon Health	Multi-Guard with CoQ10	US	55.0	
Paramettes	Adults Complete	CA	4.5	
Pataki USA	2101 Formula	US	10.1	
Perfect Choice	Complete Extra	US	6.0	
Perfect Choice	Multivitamin Specially Formulated for Men	US	21.1	
Perfect Choice	Multivitamin Specially Formulated for Women	US	28.2	
Performance Labs	Vitalert	US	7.6	
Personnelle (Pharmetics Inc.)	Multivitamines et Minéraux Forte	CA	4.3	
Personnelle (Pharmetics Inc.)	Multivitamines et Minéraux Natura Senior	CA	4.9	
Personnelle (Pharmetics Inc.)	Multivitamines et Minéraux Preventa-Tab	CA	6.9	
Pharmacist's Ultimate Health	Man's Ultimate Formula	US	37.8	
Pharmacist's Ultimate Health	Woman's Ultimate Formula	US	60.7	
Pharmanex (Nu Skin)	Life Essentials	US	13.8	
Pharmanex (Nu Skin)	LifePak Prime	US	52.7	

Pharmanex (Nu Skin)	LifePak with Catechins	CA	28.0	
Pharmasave	MultiForte 29	CA	4.3	
Pharmasave	MultiSelect 29	CA	4.6	
PharmAssure	Men's Biomultiple	US	11.5	
PharmAssure	Women's Biomultiple	US	12.2	
Pharmetics	Formula Forte	CA	4.3	DPD data only - dosage derived
Pharmetics	Multivitamins and Minerals with beta-Carotene	CA	18.3	DPD data only - dosage derived
PhytoPharmica	Clinical Nutrients for 45-Plus Women	US	45.3	
PhytoPharmica	Clinical Nutrients for 50-Plus Men	US	45.4	
PhytoPharmica	Clinical Nutrients for Men	US	42.5	
PhytoPharmica	Clinical Nutrients for Women	US	45.5	
Pilgrim's	Sense of Energy	US	51.7	
Pilgrim's	Silver Stars Multi	US	26.4	
Prairie Naturals	Multi-Force	CA	35.8	
ProActive	for Active Men	CA	41.2	
ProActive	for Adult Men	CA	30.5	
Puritan's Pride	Green Source Iron Free	US	37.1	
Puritan's Pride	High Potency Puritron	US	0.0	
Puritan's Pride	Mega Vita Min for Women	US	19.4	
Puritan's Pride	Solovites	US	12.2	
Puritan's Pride	Super All Day Nutricom	US	5.7	
Puritan's Pride	Time Release Mega Vita-Min	US	15.3	
Puritan's Pride	Ultra-Vita-Min	US	5.1	
Puritan's Pride	Ultra-Vita-Min Iron-Free	US	4.3	
Puritan's Pride	Vita-Min	US	0.0	
Purity Products	Perfect Multi Focus Formula	US	68.9	
Purity Products	Purity's Perfect Multi	US	62.2	
QCI Nutritionals	Daily Preventive #1	US	48.4	
QCI Nutritionals	Daily Preventive #3	US	48.1	
QCI Nutritionals	Ultra Vitality #1	US	51.2	
QCI Nutritionals	Ultra Vitality #2	US	51.5	
QCI Nutritionals	Ultra Vitality #3	US	50.9	
Quest	Extra Once A Day	CA	18.6	
Quest	Maximum Once A Day	CA	40.6	
Quest	Once A Day	CA	0.3	
Quest	Premium Multi-One with Niacinamide	CA	23.2	
Quest	Super Once a Day	CA	11.4	
R Garden Internationale	Multiple Vitamin Mineral Formula	US	12.4	
Rainbow Light	Advanced Nutritional System	US	63.2	
Rainbow Light	Complete Nutritional System	US	36.0	
Rainbow Light	Iron-Free Advanced Nutritional System	US	62.2	
Rainbow Light	Just Once Iron Free	US	9.9	
Rainbow Light	Performance Energy Multivitamin for Men	US	41.9	
Reliv	Classic	CA	7.7	
Reliv	Classic	US	10.4	
Reliv	Now	CA	6.0	
Reliv	Now	US	9.0	
Re-Vita	Liqua Health	US	5.8	
Ripple Creek	Mega-100 (Slow Release)	US	32.2	
Ripple Creek	Mega-Caps 2 (Quick Release)	US	23.0	
Ripple Creek	Mega-One 75 (Slow Release)	US	16.4	
Rite Aid	Central-Vite	US	4.9	
Rite Aid	Central-Vite Select	US	4.8	
Rite Aid	Whole Source	US	6.2	
Rite Aid	Whole Source Complete Formula for Men	US	5.6	
Rite Aid	Whole Source Complete Formula for Women	US	4.8	
Royal Bodycare	Omega Boost	US	36.3	
Royal Bodycare	Ultimate	CA/US	16.3	dosage derived
Rx Vitamins	Revitalize	US	39.1	
Rx Vitamins	Revitalize No Iron	US	39.1	
Safeway Select	Central-Vite Forte 29	CA	4.7	
Safeway Select	One Tablet Daily	CA	3.7	
Safeway Select	One Tablet Daily Advanced Formula for Women	CA	0.0	
Safeway Select	Super Men's Multivitamin	US	18.0	
Safeway Select	Super Women's Multivitamin	US	28.2	
Santé Naturelle	Feminex Multi	CA	9.2	
Sav-On Osco by Albertson's	One Daily Active	US	4.9	
Sav-On Osco by Albertson's	Therapeutic-M	US	4.3	
Schiff	Double Day	US	4.9	
Schiff	Prime Years	US	7.0	
Schiff	Single Day	US	15.9	
Shaklee	Vita-Lea Advanced Formula	CA	13.4	DPD data only - dosage derived
Sisu	Man Only One, Iron Free	CA/US	16.4	
Sisu	Nutricology Multi-Vi-Min	CA	10.1	
Sisu	Only One	CA/US	16.4	
Sisu	Vegi-Mins	CA/US	47.1	
Solaray	Iron-Free Spectro Multi-Vita-Min	CA	38.2	
Solaray	Iron-Free Spectro Multi-Vita-Min	US	56.7	
Solaray	Spectro 3 Iron Free	US	56.7	
Solaray	Spectro Multi-Vita-Min	US	57.0	

Solaray	Vegetarian Spectro Multi-Vita-Min	US	57.0	
Solgar	Earth Source Multi-Nutrient	US	51.4	
Solgar	Female Multiple	US	50.1	
Solgar	Formula VM-2000	US	32.5	
Solgar	Iron-Free Omnium	US	45.1	
Solgar	Multi II Vegicaps	US	15.5	dosage derived
Solgar	Naturvite	US	14.5	dosage derived
Solgar	Omnium	US	56.5	
Solgar	Solovite Iron-Free	US	5.6	
Solgar	Vegicaps Vegetarian Multiple	US	25.9	
Solgar	VM-75 Iron-Free	US	18.5	
SomaLife	SomaVit	CA/US	9.5	
Source Naturals	Élan Vitàl	US	91.8	
Source Naturals	Life Force Multiple	US	92.8	
Source Naturals	Mega-One Multiple	US	30.6	
Source Naturals	Ultra Multiple	US	7.5	
SportPharma	Multiguard	US	74.9	
Sports Nutrition 2000	Athlete's Multi	US	28.9	
Spring Valley	Maximum One Daily	US	5.0	
Spring Valley	Multiplus	CA	5.0	
Sundown	Complete Energy	US	5.1	
Sundown	Complete Multi 50+	US	5.3	
Sundown	Complete Multi Daily	US	5.1	
Sundown	Complete Ultra	US	8.1	
Sunkist	Multi-Active	CA	12.4	dosage derived
Sunkist	Multi-Men's	CA	15.8	dosage derived
Sunrider	Metabalance 44	US	20.4	
SupraLife	Formula Plus	US	43.3	
SupraLife	Maxum Essentials	US	48.9	
SupraLife	Ultra Body Toddy	US	38.1	based on av. body wt. of 150 lbs.
Swiss Natural Sources	Hi Potency Swiss One "80"	CA	20.9	
Swiss Natural Sources	Super Adult Chewable	CA	23.8	
Swiss Natural Sources	Super Swiss One "50"	CA	19.6	
Symmetry	NutraPack	US	25.5	
Symmetry	Ultra Vitality	US	7.8	
The Green Turtle Bay Vitamin Co.	PowerMate	US	11.1	
The Green Turtle Bay Vitamin Co.	PowerVites	US	7.4	
The Green Turtle Bay Vitamin Co.	Sunnie	US	10.9	
Thompson	Human Nature Green Multi	US	29.3	
Thompson	Mega 80	US	4.9	
Thompson	Multi-Formula for Women	US	6.3	
Thompson	Multiple Choice	US	4.5	
Thompson	Super Maxicaps	US	19.0	
Thorne Research	Al's Formula	US	46.9	dosage derived
Thorne Research	Basic Nutrients III	US	38.7	dosage derived
Thorne Research	Basic Nutrients V	US	44.4	dosage derived
Total Health Solutions	Bone Plants	US	6.7	
Total Health Solutions	Vita Actives	US	18.1	
Trace Minerals	Electro-Vita-Min	US	14.3	
Trace Minerals	ImmunoMax	US	1.7	
Trace Minerals	Maxi Multi	US	13.9	
Trophic	Select	CA	33.1	
Truehope	Empowerplus	CA/US	25.9	
Truly Health	Century Premium	CA	6.9	
Truly Health	Century Silver	CA	4.6	dosage derived
TwinLab	Daily One without Iron	US	26.4	
TwinLab	Daily Two Caps without Iron	US	33.8	
TwinLab	DualTabs	US	40.1	
TwinLab	Mega 6 Caps	US	56.2	
TwinLab	SuperTwin	US	33.6	
Tyler	Multiplex-2 without Iron	US	54.2	
Ultimate Health	40+ Multiple	US	18.6	
Ultimate Health	P.M. Formula	US	14.1	
Ultimate Nutrition	Super Complete	US	75.8	
Unicity Network (Rexall, Enrich)	Cardio-Basics	US	31.0	
USANA Health Sciences	Essentials (U.S.)	US	96.1	
USANA Health Sciences	Essentials (Canadian)	CA	90.2	
Valu-Rite	Advanced Formula Complete Premium	US	5.2	
Valu-Rite	Iron-Free Multivitamin & Mineral Supplement	US	0.0	
Vaxa	Daily Essentials	US	7.6	dosage derived
Vega Nutritionals	Formula ZM3	US	2.3	
Vega Nutritionals	Spectrum	US	2.3	
VegLife	SpectroVeg High Energy	US	45.9	
VirtuVites	Vita-Min 75	US	24.2	
Vita-Complete	AA (Anti-Aging)	CA	4.3	
Vitality Products	Complete Multi-Vitamins with Minerals	US	25.9	
Vitality Products	Two-A-Day	US	21.1	
Vitamin Power	Power Source 100	US	26.9	
Vitamin Power	Super-Vite	US	15.3	
Vitamin Power	Ultra Multi 90 Plus	US	11.5	

Vitamin Power	Vita-Max 1	US	6.8	
Vitamin Research Products	Extend Plus	US	93.1	
Vitamin World	Daily 3 With Antioxidant Factors	US	45.6	
Vitamin World	Green Source Iron Free	US	39.8	
Vitamin World	Mega Vita Min for Women	US	19.4	
Vitamin World	Mega Vita Min for Women Iron Free	US	16.4	
Vitamin World	More Than A Multiple	US	44.4	dosage derived
Vitamin World	Nutri 100	US	25.6	
Vitamin World	Time Release Mega Vita-Min Iron-Free	US	15.3	
Vitamin World	Ultra Vita MAN	US	12.5	
Vitamin World	Ultra Vita-Min Iron Free	US	4.7	
VitaSmart	Century Advantage	US	5.2	
VitaSmart	Century Senior Iron Free	US	4.7	
Vitazan Herbs and Vitamins	Multi #2	CA	12.5	DPD data only - dosage derived
Vitazan Herbs and Vitamins	ORO #1	CA	18.4	DPD data only - dosage derived
Viva Life Sciences	DailyGuard	US	36.8	
Viva Life Sciences	VIVA for Life	US	17.9	
Walgreens	Ultra Choice Premium Men	US	21.1	
Walgreens	Ultra Choice Premium Women	US	22.1	
Wampole	Complete Multi-Adult	CA	4.3	
Watkins	Super Multi	CA	23.9	
Watkins	Superfood Multiple	US	27.2	
Webber Naturals	Multivitamins Extra B	US	2.3	
Wellness International Network	Phyto-Vite	US	46.6	
Western Family	Complete Advanced Formula with Lutein	US	4.9	
Western Family	Multra Forte	CA	12.4	
Western Family	Multra Plex	CA	11.6	
Western Family	Therapeutic-M	US	4.3	
YourLife	Natural Iron-Free	US	3.9	
YourLife	One Daily 50+	US	4.7	
YourLife	Super Multi with Herbs	US	7.5	
ZonePerfect	Multi Vitamin & Mineral	US	25.1	

Appendix B: Products sorted by Final Product Score

Company	Product	Country	Score	Dosages & Considerations
USANA Health Sciences	Essentials (U.S.)	US	96.1	
Douglas Laboratories	Ultra Preventive X	US	95.4	
Vitamin Research Products	Extended Plus	US	93.1	
Source Naturals	Life Force Multiple	US	92.8	
Source Naturals	Élan Vitàl	US	91.8	
USANA Health Sciences	Essentials (Canadian)	CA	90.2	
FreeLife	Basic Mindell Plus	US	82.3	
Life Extension Foundation	Life Extension Mix	US	81.4	
Karuna	Maxxum 4	US	79.0	
Ultimate Nutrition	Super Complete	US	75.8	
Douglas Laboratories	Ultra Preventive Beta	US	75.1	
SportPharma	Multiguard	US	74.9	
Dr. Julian Whitaker's	Forward Multi-Nutrient	US	74.7	
Douglas Laboratories	Ultra Preventive III	US	70.0	
amni	Added Protection III	US	69.1	
Purity Products	Perfect Multi Focus Formula	US	68.9	
DaVinci Laboratories	Spectra Woman	US	66.8	
Doctor's Nutrition	Mega Vites Woman	US	66.8	
Mountain Naturals of Vermont	Women's Superior	US	66.8	
Douglas Laboratories	Ultra Preventive IX	US	66.6	
Nutrition Dynamics	Optimum Health Essentials	US	66.6	
Karuna	Maxxum 2	US	65.7	
DaVinci Laboratories	Spectra	US	64.7	
FoodScience of Vermont	Superior Care	US	64.7	
Mountain Naturals of Vermont	Superior Care	US	64.7	
DaVinci Laboratories	Spectra without Copper and Iron	US	64.5	
Doctor's Nutrition	Mega Vites without Copper & Iron	US	64.2	
FoodScience of Vermont	Women's Superior	US	63.8	
DaVinci Laboratories	Omni	US	63.6	
Colgan Institute	Formula MC8	US	63.3	dosage derived from Vit A, folate
Rainbow Light	Advanced Nutritional System	US	63.2	
Nutrition Dynamics	Day Start/Day End Essentials	US	63.0	
DaVinci Laboratories	Spectra Man	US	62.5	
FoodScience of Vermont	Men's Superior	US	62.5	
Mountain Naturals of Vermont	Men's Superior	US	62.5	
Purity Products	Purity's Perfect Multi	US	62.2	
Rainbow Light	Iron-Free Advanced Nutritional System	US	62.2	
EAS	Multi-Blend	US	62.1	
American Longevity	Ultimate Daily	US	60.7	
Pharmacist's Ultimate Health	Woman's Ultimate Formula	US	60.7	
amni	Basic Preventive 1	US	60.2	
amni	Basic Preventive 3	US	60.2	
amni	Basic Preventive with Extra D	US	60.0	
Nature's Way	Alive! Whole Food Energizer (Iron-Free)	US	60.0	
amni	Basic Preventive 5	US	59.9	
amni	Basic Preventive 2	US	59.6	
amni	Basic Preventive 4	US	59.6	
Dr. Julian Whitaker's	Forward Multi-Nutrient	CA	58.5	
Jean Carper's	Stop Aging Now!	US	58.5	
Jean Carper's	Stop Aging Now! Plus	US	58.5	
MMS Pro	Preventamins	US	58.1	
Advanced Physician's Products	Maximum Potency MultiVitamin/Mineral with Iron	US	57.4	
Advanced Physician's Products	Maximum MultiVitamin/Mineral without Iron	US	57.2	
EcoNugenics	Women's Longevity Rhythms Gold	US	57.0	
Solaray	Spectro Multi-Vita-Min	US	57.0	
Solaray	Vegetarian Spectro Multi-Vita-Min	US	57.0	
Natural Factors	MultiStart Women's	CA	56.9	
Solaray	Iron-Free Spectro Multi-Vita-Min	US	56.7	
Solaray	Spectro 3 Iron Free	US	56.7	
Michael's Naturopathic Programs	Active Senior Tabs	US	56.6	
Lorna Vanderhaeghe	FemmEssentials (multiple only)	CA	56.5	
Solgar	Omnium	US	56.5	
TwinLab	Mega 6 Caps	US	56.2	
Doctor's Nutrition	UltraNutrient	US	55.9	
Oregon Health	Multi-Guard with CoQ10	US	55.0	
Creative Nutrition Canada	PLUS Formula	CA/US	54.8	dosage derived
Doctor's Nutrition	Mega Vites Senior	US	54.7	
Nature's Blend	Vitaminix Ultimate	US	54.7	
Nutrition for Life	Grand Master Formula	CA/US	54.3	
Tyler	Multiplex-2 without Iron	US	54.2	
Bluebonnet	Super Earth Formula	US	54.0	
Pharmanex (Nu Skin)	LifePak Prime	US	52.7	
Creative Nutrition Canada	PRIME Formula	CA	52.4	dosage derived
Body Wise International	Right Choice AM/PM	CA/US	52.2	
Pilgrim's	Sense of Energy	US	51.7	
amni	Essential Basics	US	51.5	
QCI Nutritionals	Ultra Vitality #2	US	51.5	

Solgar	Earth Source Multi-Nutrient	US	51.4	
Essentials by Megafood	Essentials for Life	US	51.2	
KAL	Multiple Energy	US	51.2	
QCI Nutritionals	Ultra Vitality #1	US	51.2	
Metagenics	Multigenics Intensive Care Formula	US	51.0	
QCI Nutritionals	Ultra Vitality #3	US	50.9	
Metagenics	Multigenics Intensive Care Formula without Iron	US	50.5	
Optimox	Androvite for Men	US	50.1	
Solgar	Female Multiple	US	50.1	
All One Powder	Multiple Vitamins and Minerals	US	49.9	
KAL	Enhanced Energy with Lutein, Iron-Free	US	49.2	
Advanced Physician's Products	Complete MultiVitamin/Mineral with Iron	US	49.1	
Advanced Physician's Products	Complete MultiVitamin/Mineral without Iron	US	49.1	
SupraLife	Maxum Essentials	US	48.9	
Jarrow	Multi E-Z Powder	US	48.7	
DaVinci Laboratories	Spectra Vegetarian	US	48.6	
Great Earth	TNT - Total Nutrition Tablet	US	48.6	
QCI Nutritionals	Daily Preventive #1	US	48.4	
QCI Nutritionals	Daily Preventive #3	US	48.1	
Natural Factors	MultiStart Men's	CA	47.7	
Garry Null's	Supreme Health Formula	US	47.2	
Sisu	Vegi-Mins	CA/US	47.1	
GNC	Ultra Mega Green	US	46.9	
Thorne Research	Al's Formula	US	46.9	dosage derived
Wellness International Network	Phyto-Vite	US	46.6	
New Roots Herbal	Multi-Max	CA	46.3	
Atkins	Basic #3	US	46.1	
VegLife	SpectroVeg High Energy	US	45.9	
Cooper	Complete	US	45.8	
Carlson	Multi-Gel	US	45.7	
Vitamin World	Daily 3 With Antioxidant Factors	US	45.6	
Enzymatic Therapy	Doctor's Choice for Women	US	45.5	
PhytoPharmica	Clinical Nutrients for Women	US	45.5	
PhytoPharmica	Clinical Nutrients for 50-Plus Men	US	45.4	
PhytoPharmica	Clinical Nutrients for 45-Plus Women	US	45.3	
Solgar	Iron-Free Omnium	US	45.1	
Genestra (Seroyal)	Super Orti-Vite	CA	44.8	
Country Life	Daily Vegetarian Support	US	44.5	
More Than A Multiple	More Than A Multiple	US	44.4	
Thorne Research	Basic Nutrients V	US	44.4	dosage derived
Vitamin World	More Than A Multiple	US	44.4	dosage derived
4Life	BioVitamins Type III	US	44.0	
Bronson Laboratories	Performance Edge for Women	US	43.8	
Bronson Laboratories	Performance Edge for Men	US	43.6	
Doctor's Nutrition	Mega Veggie Vites	US	43.3	
SupraLife	Formula Plus	US	43.3	
Country Life	Maxine	US	43.1	
NOW Foods	Special Two	US	43.1	
Enzymatic Therapy	Doctor's Choice for Men	US	42.5	
Optimox	Optivite PMT for Women	US	42.5	
PhytoPharmica	Clinical Nutrients for Men	US	42.5	
For Mor International	AnOx	US	42.1	
Nature's Life	Green Multi	US	42.0	
Rainbow Light	Performance Energy Multivitamin for Men	US	41.9	
N.V. Perricone, MD	Physician's Super Antioxidant Vitamin, Mineral & Phyto-Nutrient Formula	US	41.7	
Karuna	HIM	US	41.2	
ProActive	for Active Men	CA	41.2	
Quest	Maximum Once A Day	CA	40.6	
Nutriex	Nutriex	US	40.5	
Futurebiotics	Hi Energy Multi for Men	US	40.3	dosage derived
Futurebiotics	Vegetarian Super Multi	US	40.3	
Nature's Bounty	Green Source Vegetarian Formula	US	40.1	
TwinLab	DualTabs	US	40.1	
Matol	Matolife	US	40.0	
Vitamin World	Green Source Iron Free	US	39.8	
Rx Vitamins	Revitalize	US	39.1	
Rx Vitamins	Revitalize No Iron	US	39.1	
Thorne Research	Basic Nutrients III	US	38.7	dosage derived
Atkins	Basic #1	US	38.2	
Solaray	Iron-Free Spectro Multi-Vita-Min	CA	38.2	
SupraLife	Ultra Body Toddy	US	38.1	based on av. body wt. of 150 lbs.
Cooper	Complete with Iron	US	38.0	
Nature's Way	Age Right Formula	US	38.0	
Greens+	Multi+	CA	37.9	
Pharmacist's Ultimate Health	Man's Ultimate Formula	US	37.8	
Jarrow	Multi 1-to-3	US	37.7	
Nature's Blend	Maximum Daily Green	US	37.5	
GNC	Ultra Mega Gold without Iron	US	37.1	
Puritan's Pride	Green Source Iron Free	US	37.1	
Nutrition Dynamics	Basic Formula	US	37.0	dosage derived

Michael's Naturopathic Programs	for Men	US	36.9	
Michael's Naturopathic Programs	for Women	US	36.9	
Viva Life Sciences	DailyGuard	US	36.8	
Natrol	My Favorite Multiple Original	US	36.7	
LifeScript	Daily Essentials, plus Calcium Complete	US	36.6	
Royal Bodycare	Omega Boost	US	36.3	
Rainbow Light	Complete Nutritional System	US	36.0	
Holista Health	Multi-Spectrum	CA	35.9	
Nu-life	Ultimate One for Men	CA	35.8	
Prairie Naturals	Multi-Force	CA	35.8	
Advocare	Gold	US	35.7	
NutriBiotics	Ultimate Matrix Men	US	35.2	
NutriBiotics	Ultimate Matrix Women	US	35.2	
KAL	Vitality for Women	US	35.0	
Essentials by Megafood	Essentials for Women	US	34.8	
Nature's Way	Daily Two Multi Iron-Free	US	34.8	
Albi Imports	Rocky Mountain Multiple	CA	34.3	DPD data only - dosage derived
Nu-life	The Legend for Women	CA	33.8	
TwinLab	Daily Two Caps without Iron	US	33.8	
TwinLab	SuperTwin	US	33.6	
4Life	BioVitaMins Type II	US	33.2	
Bronson Laboratories	Fortified Vitamin & Mineral Insurance Formula	US	33.2	
Nature's Way	Multivitamin Iron-Free	US	33.2	
Mannatech	Glycentials	US	33.1	
Trophic	Select	CA	33.1	
KAL	Multi-Four	US	33.0	
Country Life	Max for Men	US	32.8	
NOW Foods	Vit-Min 100 (Timed Release High Potency)	US	32.8	
NOW Foods	Iron-Free Vit-Min 75+	US	32.6	
Solgar	Formula VM-2000	US	32.5	
Life Plus	Daily Bio-Basics	US	32.3	
Ripple Creek	Mega-100 (Slow Release)	US	32.2	
KAL	Vegetarian Multiple	US	31.7	
Jarrow	Women's Multi	US	31.5	
Epic4Health	Physician's Multi Vitamin Formula	US	31.3	
Andrew Lessman's	Maximum Complete for Women	US	31.2	dosage derived
Unicity Network (Rexall, Enrich)	Cardio-Basics	US	31.0	
Andrew Lessman's	Maximum Complete for Men	US	30.8	dosage derived
Nature's Plus	Regeneration	US	30.7	
Source Naturals	Mega-One Multiple	US	30.6	
Optimox	Gynovite Plus	US	30.5	
ProActive	for Adult Men	CA	30.5	
Nutrilite (Amway, Quixtar)	Double X	US	30.0	
Great Earth	Super Hy-Vites-Ultra Strength/Timed Release	US	29.4	
Thompson	Human Nature Green Multi	US	29.3	
Nature's Plus	Source of Life No Iron	US	29.2	
Sports Nutrition 2000	Athlete's Multi	US	28.9	
Nature's Sunshine	Super Supplemental without Iron	US	28.6	
GNC	Women's Ultra Mega	US	28.2	
Perfect Choice	Multivitamin Specially Formulated for Women	US	28.2	
Safeway Select	Super Women's Multivitamin	US	28.2	
Pharmanex (Nu Skin)	LifePak with Catechins	CA	28.0	
New Image International	Multi	US	27.4	
Natrol	My Favorite Multiple Complete Care	US	27.3	
Natrol	My Favorite Multiple Take One	US	27.2	
Watkins	Superfood Multiple	US	27.2	
Vitamin Power	Power Source 100	US	26.9	
Absolute Nutrition	Dieters' Multi's	US	26.4	
Pilgrim's	Silver Stars Multi	US	26.4	
TwinLab	Daily One without Iron	US	26.4	
Mannatech	GlycoLEAN Catalyst	US	26.2	
Nature's Sunshine	Super Supplemental Vitamins and Minerals	US	26.2	
NOW Foods	Vit-Min Caps High Potency Multiple	US	26.2	
Solgar	Vegicaps Vegetarian Multiple	US	25.9	
Truehope	Empowerplus	CA/US	25.9	
Vitality Products	Complete Multi-Vitamins with Minerals	US	25.9	
Freeda Vitamins	Ultra Freeda Iron-Free	US	25.8	
Vitamin World	Nutri 100	US	25.6	
Symmetry	NutraPack	US	25.5	
ZonePerfect	Multi Vitamin & Mineral	US	25.1	
Nutrina	Champion Formula	US	24.6	
GNC	Ultra Mega Two without Iron	US	24.5	
VirtuVites	Vita-Min 75	US	24.2	
Neways	Orachel	US	24.1	
Country Life	Hi Potency Action 75	US	24.0	
Watkins	Super Multi	CA	23.9	
Nu-life	Gourmet Multiple	CA	23.8	
Swiss Natural Sources	Super Adult Chewable	CA	23.8	
Nature's Plus	Ultra-One Iron-Free Sustained Release	US	23.7	
Michael's Naturopathic Programs	Just One	US	23.6	

Freeda Vitamins	Ultra Freeda with Iron	US	23.4	
Quest	Premium Multi-One with Niacinamide	CA	23.2	
Nutrilite (Amway, Quixtar)	Double X	CA	23.0	
Ripple Creek	Mega-Caps 2 (Quick Release)	US	23.0	
Olympian Labs	Vita-Vitamin	US	22.8	dosage derived
Life Plus	TVM-Plus	US	22.7	
Nutra Therapeutics	All-In-One	CA	22.7	
Walgreens	Ultra Choice Premium Women	US	22.1	
Alpha Nutrition	Alpha ENF	CA	21.9	
DaVinci Laboratories	Daily Best	US	21.9	
FoodScience of Vermont	Daily Best	US	21.9	
4Life	BioVitaMins Type I	US	21.6	
Bronson Laboratories	Men's Complete Formula with 7-Keto	US	21.5	
Nu-life	Ultimate One for Women	CA	21.4	
Nature's Answer	Multi-Daily	US	21.2	
GNC	Mega Men's	US	21.1	
Perfect Choice	Multivitamin Specially Formulated for Men	US	21.1	
Vitality Products	Two-A-Day	US	21.1	
Walgreens	Ultra Choice Premium Men	US	21.1	
Hillestad Pharmaceuticals	Sterling	US	21.0	
Alive Vitamins	Super One Plus	CA	20.9	DPD data only - dosage derived
Swiss Natural Sources	Hi Potency Swiss One "80"	CA	20.9	
Enerex	Sona	CA	20.6	
Essentials by Megafood	One Daily for Men	US	20.6	
Sunrider	Metabalance 44	US	20.4	
EcoNugenics	Men's Longevity Essentials Plus	US	20.3	
Molecular Biologics	Derma-Vites	US	20.2	dosage derived
Nutrina	Fitness Formula	US	19.9	
Nutri-West	Whole System Health Maintenance	US	19.8	
Swiss Natural Sources	Super Swiss One "50"	CA	19.6	
Nature's Bounty	Mega Vita Min for Women Time Release	US	19.4	
Puritan's Pride	Mega Vita Min for Women	US	19.4	
Vitamin World	Mega Vita Min for Women	US	19.4	
Country Life	VegiCaps	US	19.2	
Hillestad Pharmaceuticals	Summit Gold	US	19.1	
KAL	High Potency Soft Multiple, Iron-Free	US	19.1	
Thompson	Super Maxicaps	US	19.0	
London's Best	Premier	CA	18.8	dosage derived
Allergy Research Group	Multi-Vi-Min without Copper and Iron	US	18.7	
Futurebiotics	Multi-Vitamin Energy Plus for Women	US	18.7	dosage derived
Nature's Plus	Ultra II	US	18.6	
Nature's Plus	Ultra-One	US	18.6	
Quest	Extra Once A Day	CA	18.6	
Ultimate Health	40+ Multiple	US	18.6	
Solgar	VM-75 Iron-Free	US	18.5	
Vitazan Herbs and Vitamins	ORO #1	CA	18.4	DPD data only - dosage derived
Allergy Research Group	EDP Basic	US	18.3	
Pharmetics	Multivitamins and Minerals with beta-Carotene	CA	18.3	DPD data only - dosage derived
Nutrina	Athlete Formula	US	18.1	
Total Health Solutions	Vita Actives	US	18.1	
Bronson Laboratories	Advanced Mature Gold	US	18.0	
Safeway Select	Super Men's Multivitamin	US	18.0	
Nature Made	Essential Mega	US	17.9	
Viva Life Sciences	VIVA for Life	US	17.9	
Garry Null's	Super AM Formula	US	17.7	
Nature's Way	Completia Ultra Energy Multi (Iron-Free)	US	17.6	
Apex Fitness Group	Profile 5	US	16.8	dosage derived
Allergy Research Group	Multi-Vi-Min	US	16.6	
Nutri-West	Multibalance for Men	US	16.6	
Nutri-West	Multibalance for Women	US	16.6	
Nutrition Dynamics	Iodine Free "Vegi" Formula	US	16.5	
Ripple Creek	Mega-One 75 (Slow Release)	US	16.4	
Sisu	Man Only One, Iron Free	CA/US	16.4	
Sisu	Only One	CA/US	16.4	
Vitamin World	Mega Vita Min for Women Iron Free	US	16.4	
Royal Bodycare	Ultimate	CA/US	16.3	dosage derived
Douglas Laboratories	Ultra Vita 75 II	US	16.2	
Schiff	Single Day	US	15.9	
Sunkist	Multi-Men's	CA	15.8	dosage derived
Inno-Vite	Total NRG Lift	CA	15.5	
Solgar	Multi II Vegicaps	US	15.5	dosage derived
Puritan's Pride	Time Release Mega Vita-Min	US	15.3	
Vitamin Power	Super-Vite	US	15.3	
Vitamin World	Time Release Mega Vita-Min Iron-Free	US	15.3	
Herbalife	Formula 2	CA	15.2	
Bio Actif Inc.	Phytobec #1	CA	15.1	
Nutrition for Life	Essentials	CA/US	15.1	
London Drugs	Multi Premium	CA	15.0	
Greens+	Greens+	US	14.8	
Herbalife	Formula 2	US	14.8	

Lifestyles	Lifecycles for Mature Men	CA/US	14.7	
Lifestyles	Lifecycles for Mature Women	CA/US	14.7	
Atkins	Immune	US	14.6	
Lifestyles	Lifecycles for Women	CA/US	14.5	
Solgar	Naturvite	US	14.5	dosage derived
Trace Minerals	Electro-Vita-Min	US	14.3	
Cypress (Star 2000)	MultiVitamin with Minerals	US	14.1	dosage derived
Ultimate Health	P.M. Formula	US	14.1	
Comprehensive Formula	Men's	US	14.0	
Trace Minerals	Maxi Multi	US	13.9	
Pharmanex (Nu Skin)	Life Essentials	US	13.8	
For Mor International	Oral Chelate	US	13.7	
Shaklee	Vita-Lea Advanced Formula	CA	13.4	DPD data only - dosage derived
FoodScience of Vermont	Total Care	US	13.3	
Natural Factors	MultiStart	CA	13.3	
Nutricology	Multi-Vi-Min	US	13.1	
Nutricology	Multi-Vi-Min without Copper & Iron	US	13.0	
Nature's Bounty	Ultra Man Time Release	US	12.5	
Vitamin World	Ultra Vita MAN	US	12.5	
Vitazan Herbs and Vitamins	Multi #2	CA	12.5	DPD data only - dosage derived
London Naturals	Multi-Vitamin Select	CA	12.4	
R Garden Internationale	Multiple Vitamin Mineral Formula	US	12.4	
Sunkist	Multi-Active	CA	12.4	dosage derived
Western Family	Multra Forte	CA	12.4	
Kirkman Laboratories	Kirkman's Super Nu-Thera	US	12.3	
PharmAssure	Women's Biomultiple	US	12.2	
Puritan's Pride	Solovites	US	12.2	
National Vitamin Company	Life-line Mega Multi with Minerals	US	11.9	
Comprehensive Formula	Women's	US	11.8	
Western Family	Multra Plex	CA	11.6	
PharmAssure	Men's Biomultiple	US	11.5	
Vitamin Power	Ultra Multi 90 Plus	US	11.5	
Quest	Super Once a Day	CA	11.4	
Nikken	Bio-Directed Multi-Vitamin/Mineral	CA/US	11.1	
The Green Turtle Bay Vitamin Co.	PowerMate	US	11.1	
Albi Imports	Super One a Day	CA	10.9	DPD data only - dosage derived
Avon	VitAdvance Men's Complete Multivitamin	US	10.9	
The Green Turtle Bay Vitamin Co.	Sunnie	US	10.9	
Flora	MultiCaps	CA	10.6	
Flora	MultiTabs	CA	10.6	
GNC	SoloCaps	US	10.6	
Avon	VitAdvance Women's Complete I Balanced Multi	US	10.5	
Avon	VitAdvance Women's Complete II Balanced Multi	US	10.5	
Nutri-West	Multi Complex	US	10.5	
Reliv	Classic	US	10.4	
Pataki USA	2101 Formula	US	10.1	
Sisu	Nutricology Multi-Vi-Min	CA	10.1	
Adrien Gagnon (Santé Naturelle)	Multi-Vitamines et Minéraux	CA	9.9	
GNC	Preventron	US	9.9	
Rainbow Light	Just Once Iron Free	US	9.9	
Country Life	Adult's Multi	US	9.8	
Molecular Biologics	Bio-Naturalvite	US	9.7	dosage derived
Le Naturiste (Jean Marc Brunet)	US-100 Multi-vitamines	CA	9.5	
SomaLife	SomaVit	CA/US	9.5	
Life Force International	Body Balance	US	9.2	based on av. body wt. of 150 lbs.
Santé Naturelle	Feminex Multi	CA	9.2	
Jamieson	Mega-Vim Level 4 Potency	CA	9.0	
Reliv	Now	US	9.0	
Bronson Laboratories	Mature Formula	US	8.6	
Moducare	Multi-mune	US	8.6	
Jamieson	Super Vita-Vim	CA	8.3	
Molecular Biologics	Allervimin	US	8.3	dosage derived
Sundown	Complete Ultra	US	8.1	
EHN Inc.	protect+	CA	7.8	
Symmetry	Ultra Vitality	US	7.8	
GNC	Solotron without Iron	US	7.7	
Laboratoire Lalco Enr.	Multi Max	CA	7.7	
Reliv	Classic	CA	7.7	
Performance Labs	Vitalert	US	7.6	
Vaxa	Daily Essentials	US	7.6	dosage derived
Source Naturals	Ultra Multiple	US	7.5	
YourLife	Super Multi with Herbs	US	7.5	
LifeTime	Nutrilife	CA	7.4	
The Green Turtle Bay Vitamin Co.	PowerVites	US	7.4	
21st Century	One Daily Men's	US	7.3	
Centrum	Protegra	CA	7.2	
Schiff	Prime Years	US	7.0	
Personnelle (Pharmetics Inc.)	Multivitamines et Minéraux Preventa-Tab	CA	6.9	
Truly Health	Century Premium	CA	6.9	
Vitamin Power	Vita-Max 1	US	6.8	

Total Health Solutions	Bone Plants	US	6.7	
Thompson	Multi-Formula for Women	US	6.3	
Melaleuca	Vitality Pak (Mel-Vita, Mela-Cal)	US	6.2	
Rite Aid	Whole Source	US	6.2	
Perfect Choice	Complete Extra	US	6.0	
Reliv	Now	CA	6.0	
4Life	MultiPlex Stress Formula	US	5.9	
Lifestyles	Lifecycles for Men	CA/US	5.8	
OneSource	Multivitamins and Minerals for Adults	CA	5.8	
Re-Vita	Liqua Health	US	5.8	
Puritan's Pride	Super All Day Nutricom	US	5.7	
Rite Aid	Whole Source Complete Formula for Men	US	5.6	
Solgar	Solovite Iron-Free	US	5.6	
21st Century	One Daily Maximum	US	5.3	
Sundown	Complete Multi 50+	US	5.3	
Centrum	Performance	US	5.2	
Kirkland Signature (Costco)	Daily Multivitamin	US	5.2	
Valu-Rite	Advanced Formula Complete Premium	US	5.2	
VitaSmart	Century Advantage	US	5.2	
One A Day	Active	US	5.1	
Puritan's Pride	Ultra-Vita-Min	US	5.1	
Sundown	Complete Energy	US	5.1	
Sundown	Complete Multi Daily	US	5.1	
Centrum	Select for Adults over 50	CA	5.0	
Good Neighbor Pharmacy	Balanced Care Complete Multi	US	5.0	
Life Brand	Optimum	CA	5.0	
Life Brand	Optimum 50+	CA	5.0	
Spring Valley	Maximum One Daily	US	5.0	
Spring Valley	Multiplus	CA	5.0	
21st Century	Advanced 21 with Lutein	US	4.9	
Equate	Complete	US	4.9	
Kroger	Advanced Formula Complete	US	4.9	
Nature's Sunshine	SynerPro	US	4.9	
Personnelle (Pharmetics Inc.)	Multivitamines et Minéraux Natura Senior	CA	4.9	
Rite Aid	Central-Vite	US	4.9	
Sav-On Osco by Albertson's	One Daily Active	US	4.9	
Schiff	Double Day	US	4.9	
Thompson	Mega 80	US	4.9	
Western Family	Complete Advanced Formula with Lutein	US	4.9	
MD Healthline	Advanced Green Multi	US	4.8	
Rite Aid	Central-Vite Select	US	4.8	
Rite Aid	Whole Source Complete Formula for Women	US	4.8	
Centrum	Forte	CA/US	4.7	
Centrum	Select Chewables for Adults over 50	CA	4.7	
Centrum	Silver	US	4.7	
Equate	Century Plus	CA	4.7	
Equate	Complete Mature	US	4.7	
Good Neighbor Pharmacy	Century Senior	US	4.7	
Nature's Bounty	Ultra Vita-Time Iron Free	US	4.7	
Safeway Select	Central-Vite Forte 29	CA	4.7	
Vitamin World	Ultra Vita-Min Iron Free	US	4.7	
VitaSmart	Century Senior Iron Free	US	4.7	
YourLife	One Daily 50+	US	4.7	
21st Century	Therapeutic-M With Lutein	US	4.6	
Centrum	Select	CA	4.6	
One A Day	Advance Men's Formula	CA	4.6	
Pharmasave	MultiSelect 29	CA	4.6	
Truly Health	Century Silver	CA	4.6	dosage derived
Paramettes	Adults Complete	CA	4.5	
Thompson	Multiple Choice	US	4.5	
Action Labs	Essential Nutrients	US	4.4	
Basic Nutrition	Multiple Vitamins & Minerals	US	4.4	
Immuvit	Immuvit	US	4.4	
Jamieson	Adult's 50+ Vita-Vim	CA	4.4	
Nature Made	Essential Balance	CA	4.4	
Life Brand	Spectrum Forte	CA	4.3	
Personnelle (Pharmetics Inc.)	Multivitamines et Minéraux Forte	CA	4.3	
Pharmasave	MultiForte 29	CA	4.3	
Pharmetics	Formula Forte	CA	4.3	DPD data only - dosage derived
Puritan's Pride	Ultra-Vita-Min Iron-Free	US	4.3	
Sav-On Osco by Albertson's	Therapeutic-M	US	4.3	
Vita-Complete	AA (Anti-Aging)	CA	4.3	
Wampole	Complete Multi-Adult	CA	4.3	
Western Family	Therapeutic-M	US	4.3	
Centrum	Select Chewables	CA	4.0	
YourLife	Natural Iron-Free	US	3.9	
Safeway Select	One Tablet Daily	CA	3.7	
Club Vitamin	Best	US	3.6	dosage derived
Equate	Century Complete	CA	3.5	
Jamieson	Power Vitamins for Men	CA	3.5	

Geritol	Complete	US	3.4	
Nutrilite (Amway, Quixtar)	Daily	US	3.4	
Centrum	Centrum	US	3.2	
Market America	Isotonix Multitech Multivitamin	CA/US	3.2	
Kirkman Laboratories	Kirkman's Everyday	US	3.1	
LiFizz	Multivitamin	CA	2.9	
Equate	Multi-Vitamin & Minerals	CA	2.8	
New Roots Herbal	Phytomax	CA	2.5	
NewVision	JuicePower Vegetable Caps	CA/US	2.4	
Vega Nutritionals	Formula ZM3	US	2.3	
Vega Nutritionals	Spectrum	US	2.3	
Webber Naturals	Multivitamins Extra B	US	2.3	
One A Day	Advance Women's Formula	CA	1.9	
Trace Minerals	ImmunoMax	US	1.7	
Freeda Vitamins	Quintabs-M	US	1.5	
Action Labs	Action-Tabs Made for Men	US	1.3	
Nutrition Dynamics	Multi-vitasorb	US	0.7	
Cell Tech	Alpha Sun	US	0.3	
Cell Tech	Omega Sun	US	0.3	
Klamath Blue Green Algae	Tablets	US	0.3	
Klamath Blue Green Algae	Vegicaps	US	0.3	
Quest	Once A Day	CA	0.3	
Action Labs	Action-Tabs Made for Women	US	0.0	
Gerbex	Gerivol	CA	0.0	
Golden Neo-Life Diamite International	Formula IV	CA	0.0	DPD data only - dosage derived
Les Produits Naturels Suisse Inc.	Swical Energy	CA	0.0	dosage derived
Omnitrition	Omni 4	US	0.0	
Puritan's Pride	High Potency Puritron	US	0.0	
Puritan's Pride	Vita-Min	US	0.0	
Safeway Select	One Tablet Daily Advanced Formula for Women	CA	0.0	
Valu-Rite	Iron-Free Multivitamin & Mineral Supplement	US	0.0